FOR THE KID I SAW IN MY Dreams

KEI SANBE

TRANSLATION: SHELDON DRZKA ✦ LETTERING: ABIGAIL BLACKMAN

YUME DE MITA ANO KO NO TAME NI Volume 2
© Kei SANBE 2018.
First published in Japan in 2018 by KADOKAWA CORPORATION, Tokyo.
English translation rights arranged with KADOKAWA CORPORATION, Tokyo through TUTTLE-MORI AGENCY INC., Tokyo.

English translation © 2019 by Yen Press, LLC

Yen Press
1290 Avenue of the Americas
New York, NY 10104

Visit us at yenpress.com
facebook.com/yenpress
twitter.com/yenpress
yenpress.tumblr.com
instagram.com/yenpress

First Yen Press Edition: June 2019

Yen Press is an imprint of Yen Press, LLC.
The Yen Press name and logo are trademarks of Yen Press, LLC.

Library of Congress Control Number: 2018958636

ISBNs: 978-1-9753-0353-2 (hardcover)
       978-1-9753-5792-4 (ebook)

10 9 8 7 6 5 4 3 2 1

WOR

Printed in the United States of America

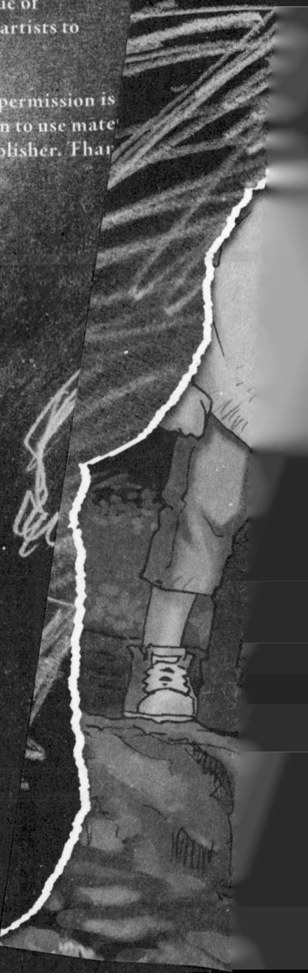

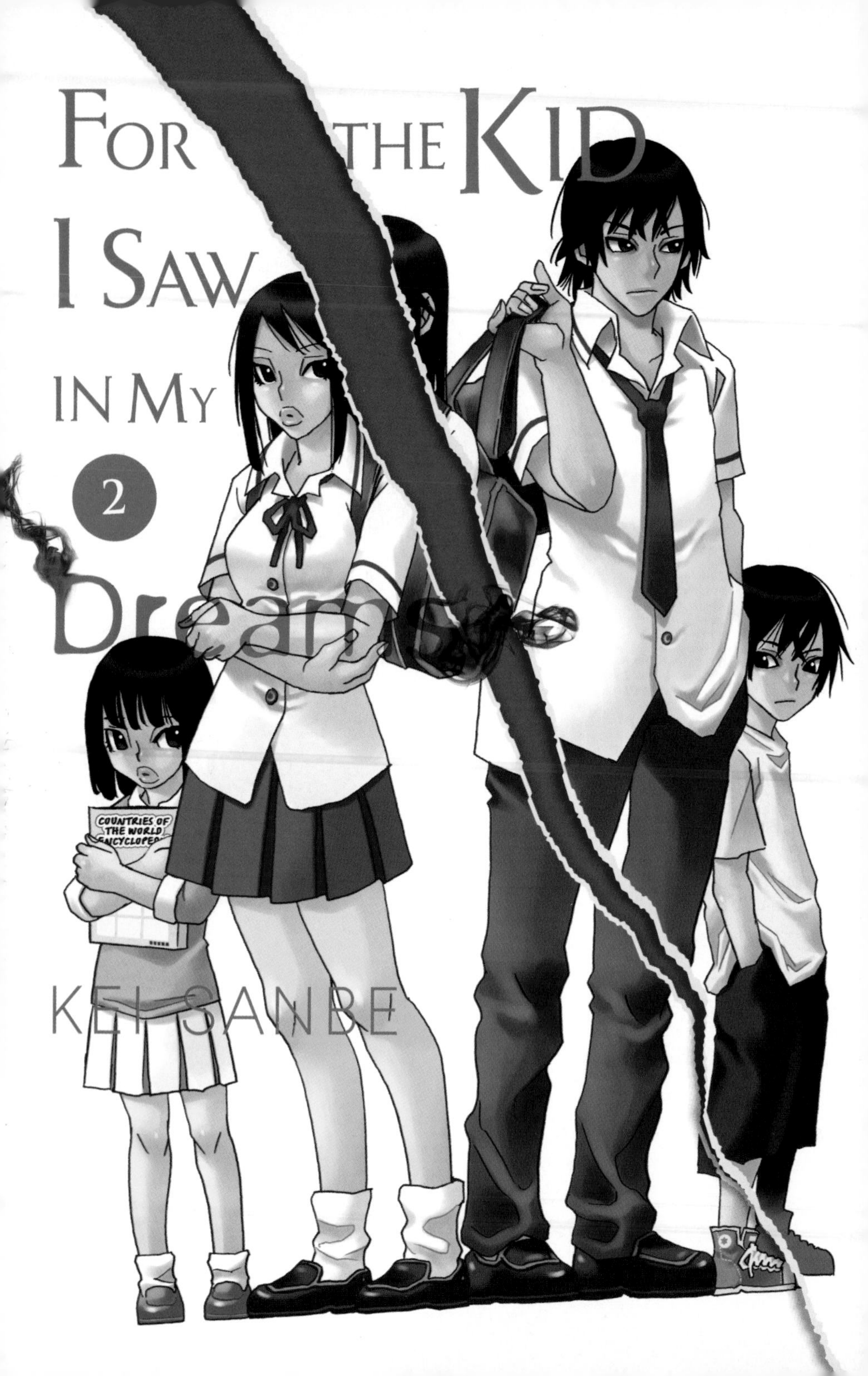
For the Kid
I Saw
in My
2
Dreams
COUNTRIES OF
THE WORLD
ENCYCLOPED
KEI SANBE

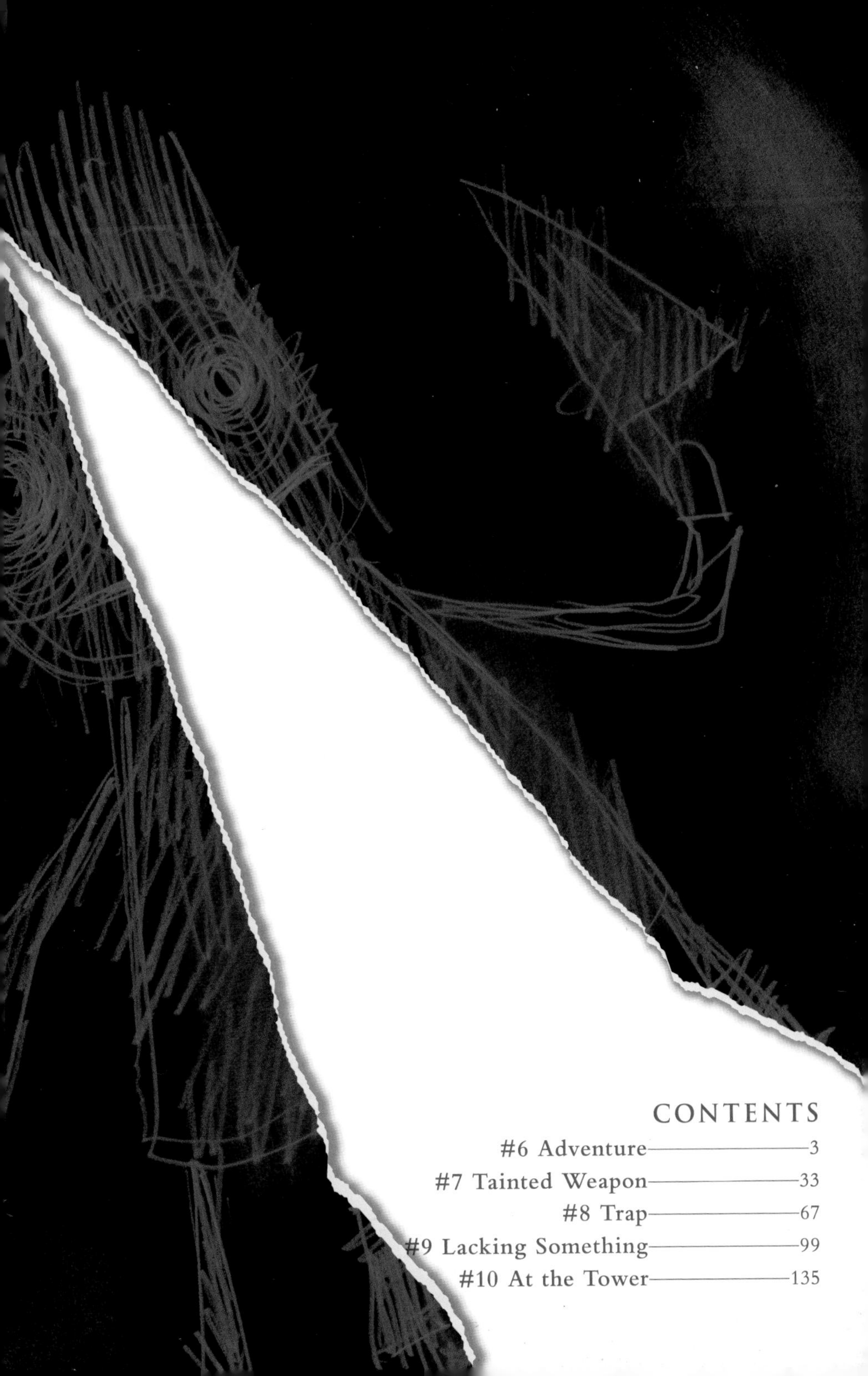

CONTENTS

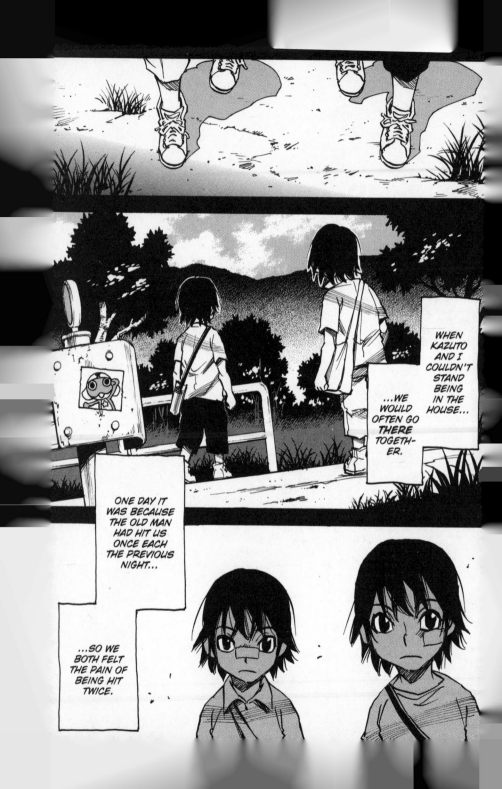

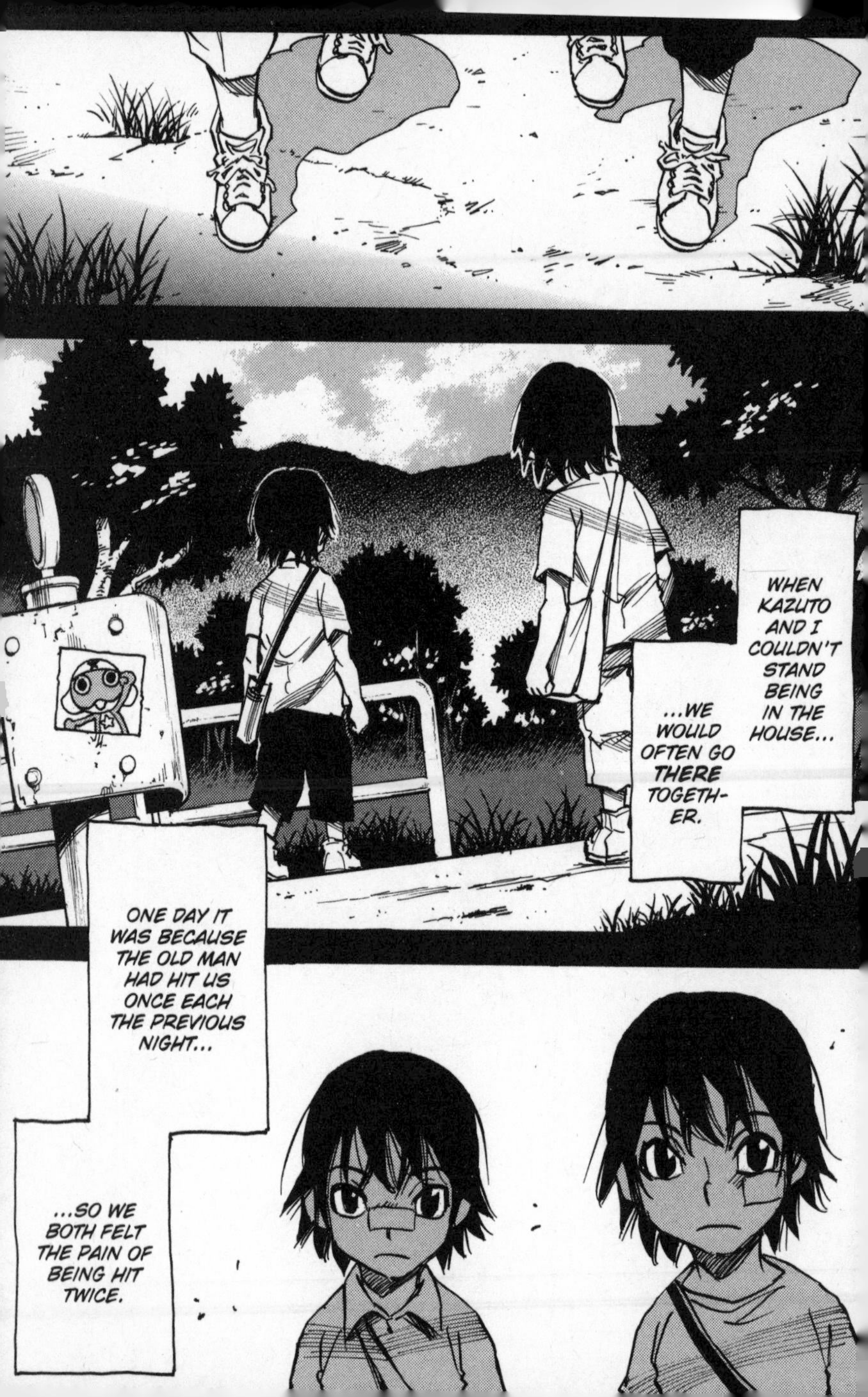
WHEN KAZUTO AND I COULDN'T STAND BEING IN THE HOUSE...
...WE WOULD OFTEN GO THERE TOGETHER.
ONE DAY IT WAS BECAUSE THE OLD MAN HAD HIT US ONCE EACH THE PREVIOUS NIGHT...
...SO WE BOTH FELT THE PAIN OF BEING HIT TWICE.

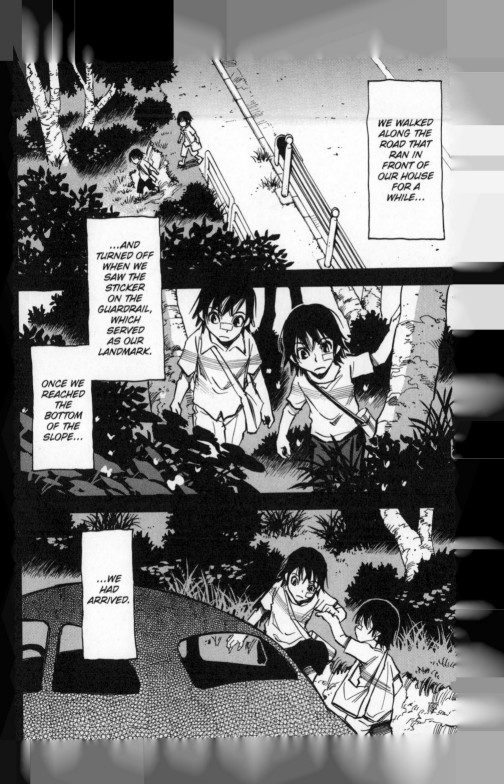

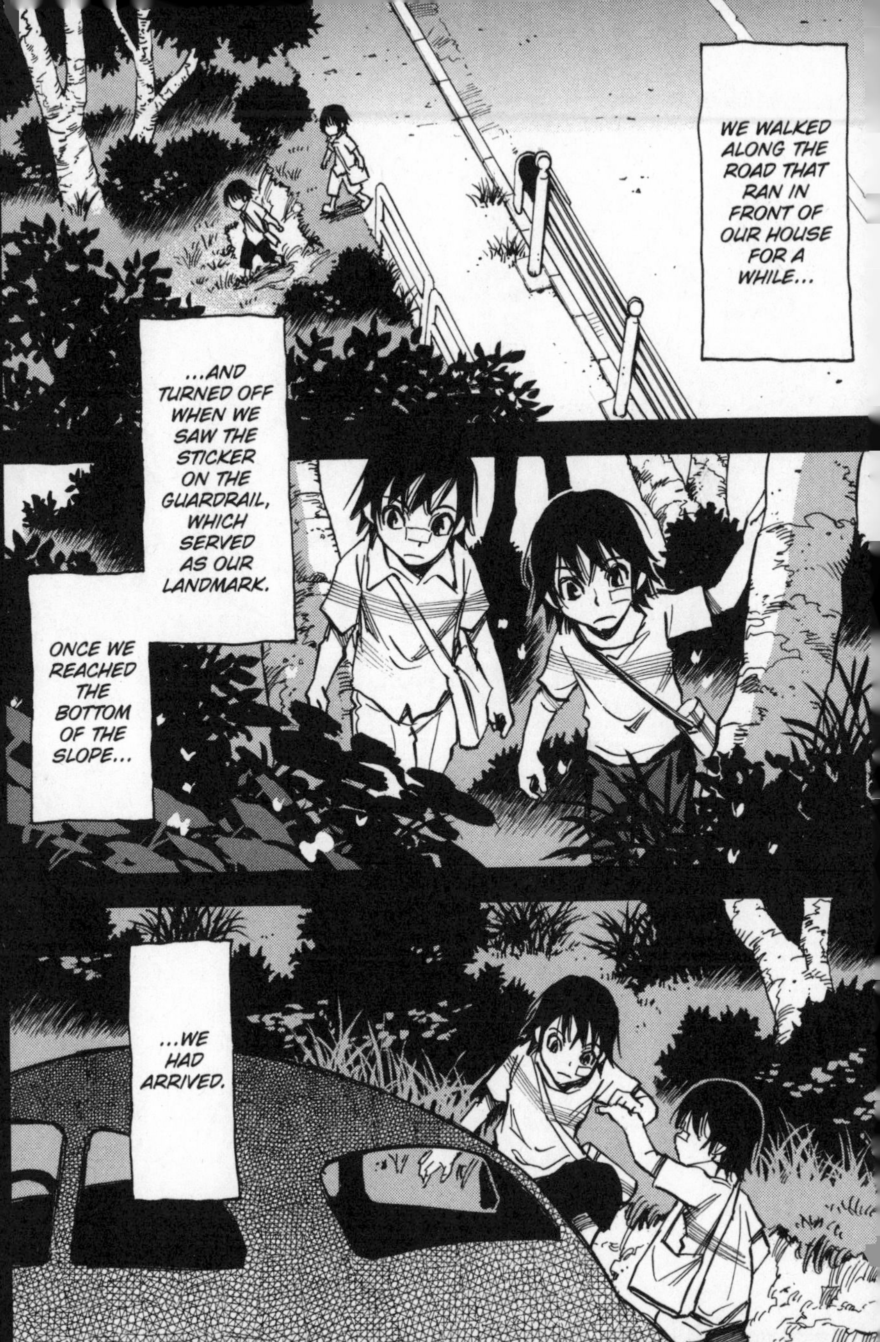
WE WALKED ALONG THE ROAD THAT RAN IN FRONT OF OUR HOUSE FOR A WHILE…
…AND TURNED OFF WHEN WE SAW THE STICKER ON THE GUARDRAIL, WHICH SERVED AS OUR LANDMARK.
ONCE WE REACHED THE BOTTOM OF THE SLOPE…
…WE HAD ARRIVED.

#6 Adventure

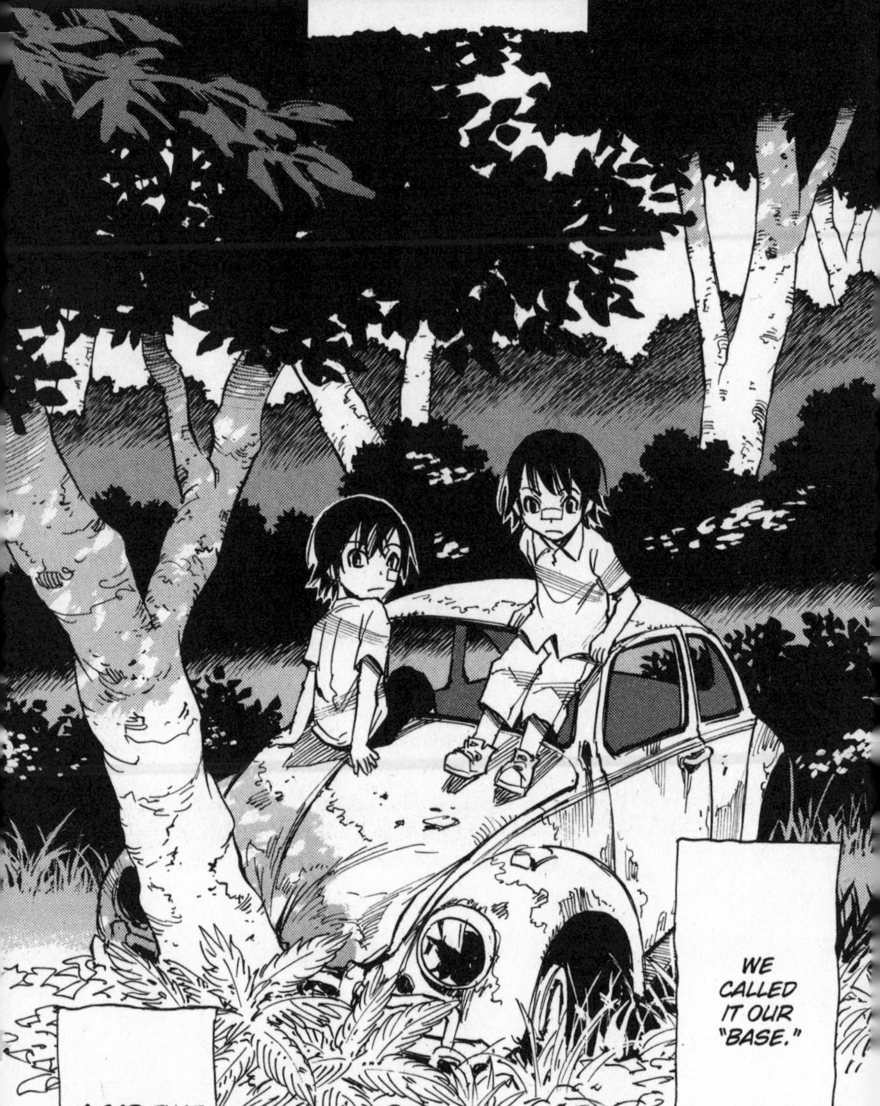
WE CALLED IT OUR "BASE."
A CAR THAT SOMEONE HAD ABANDONED LONG AGO...

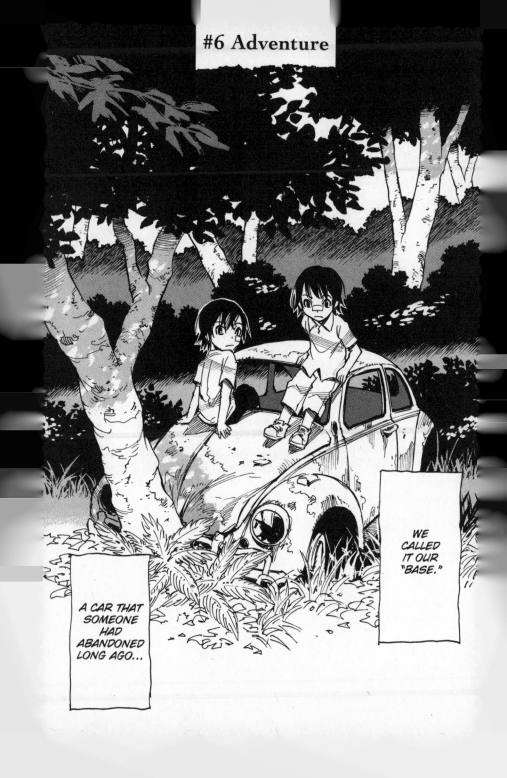

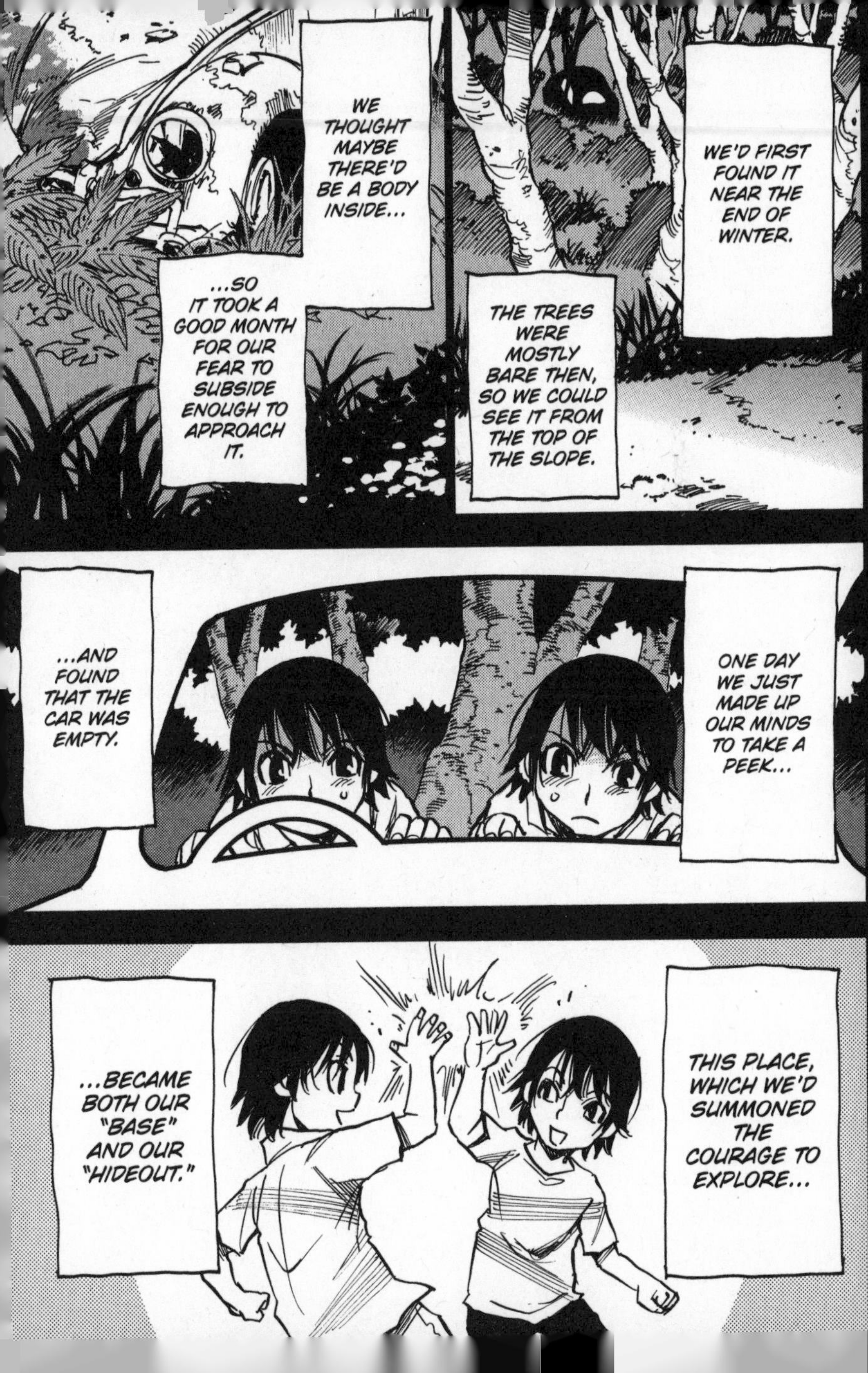
WE'D FIRST FOUND IT NEAR THE END OF WINTER.
THE TREES WERE MOSTLY BARE THEN, SO WE COULD SEE IT FROM THE TOP OF THE SLOPE.
WE THOUGHT MAYBE THERE'D BE A BODY INSIDE...
...SO IT TOOK A GOOD MONTH FOR OUR FEAR TO SUBSIDE ENOUGH TO APPROACH IT.
ONE DAY WE JUST MADE UP OUR MINDS TO TAKE A PEEK...
...AND FOUND THAT THE CAR WAS EMPTY.
THIS PLACE, WHICH WE'D SUMMONED THE COURAGE TO EXPLORE...
...BECAME BOTH OUR "BASE" AND OUR "HIDEOUT."

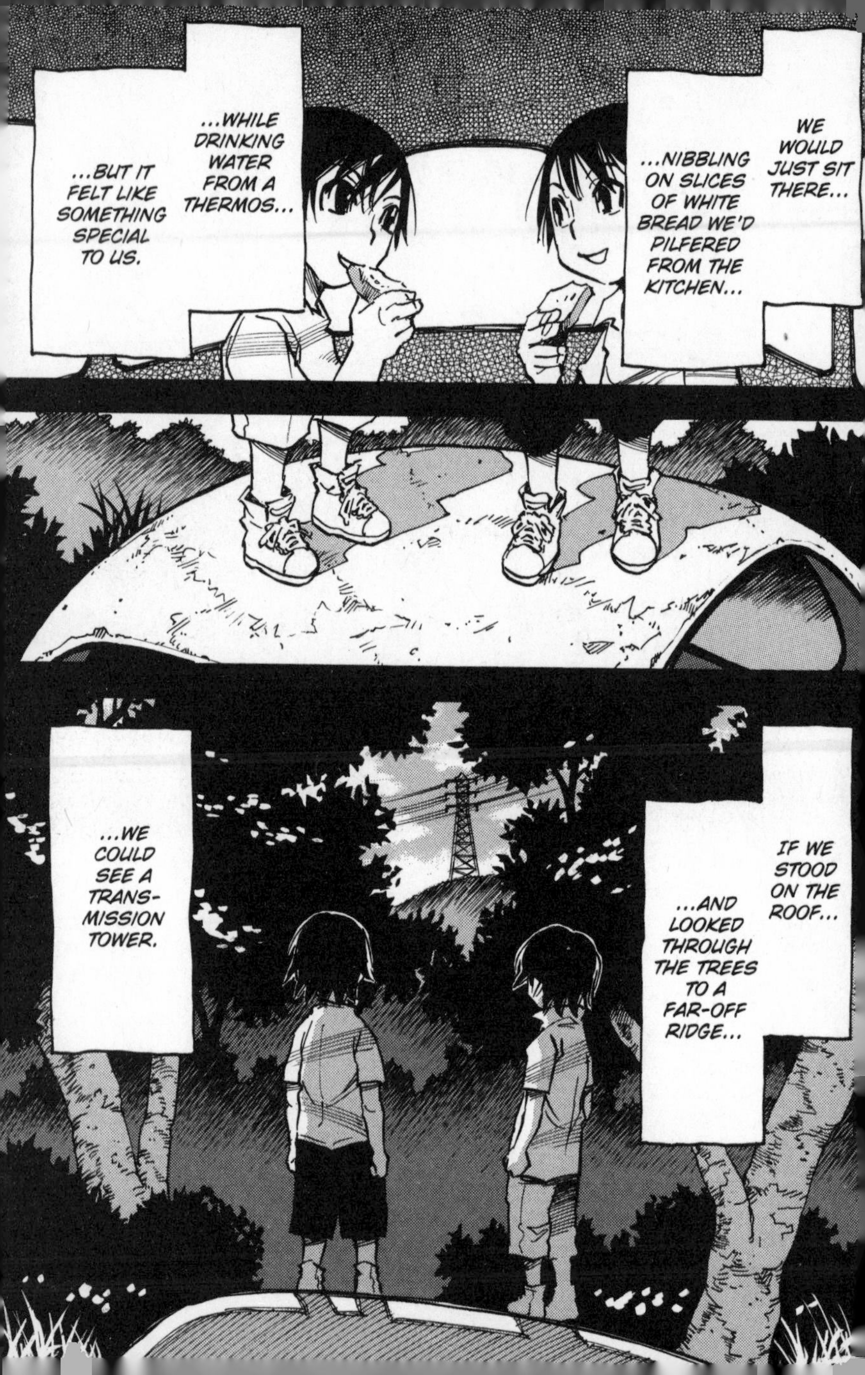
WE WOULD JUST SIT THERE...
...NIBBLING ON SLICES OF WHITE BREAD WE'D PILFERED FROM THE KITCHEN...
...WHILE DRINKING WATER FROM A THERMOS...
...BUT IT FELT LIKE SOMETHING SPECIAL TO US.
IF WE STOOD ON THE ROOF...
...AND LOOKED THROUGH THE TREES TO A FAR-OFF RIDGE...
...WE COULD SEE A TRANS-MISSION TOWER.

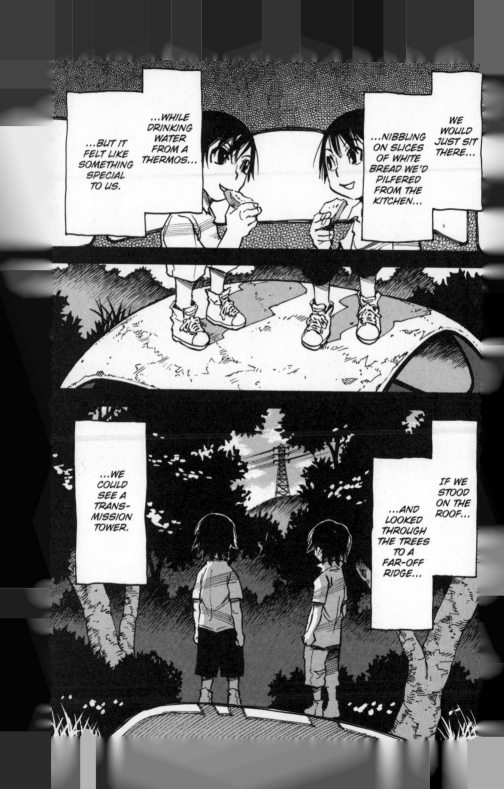

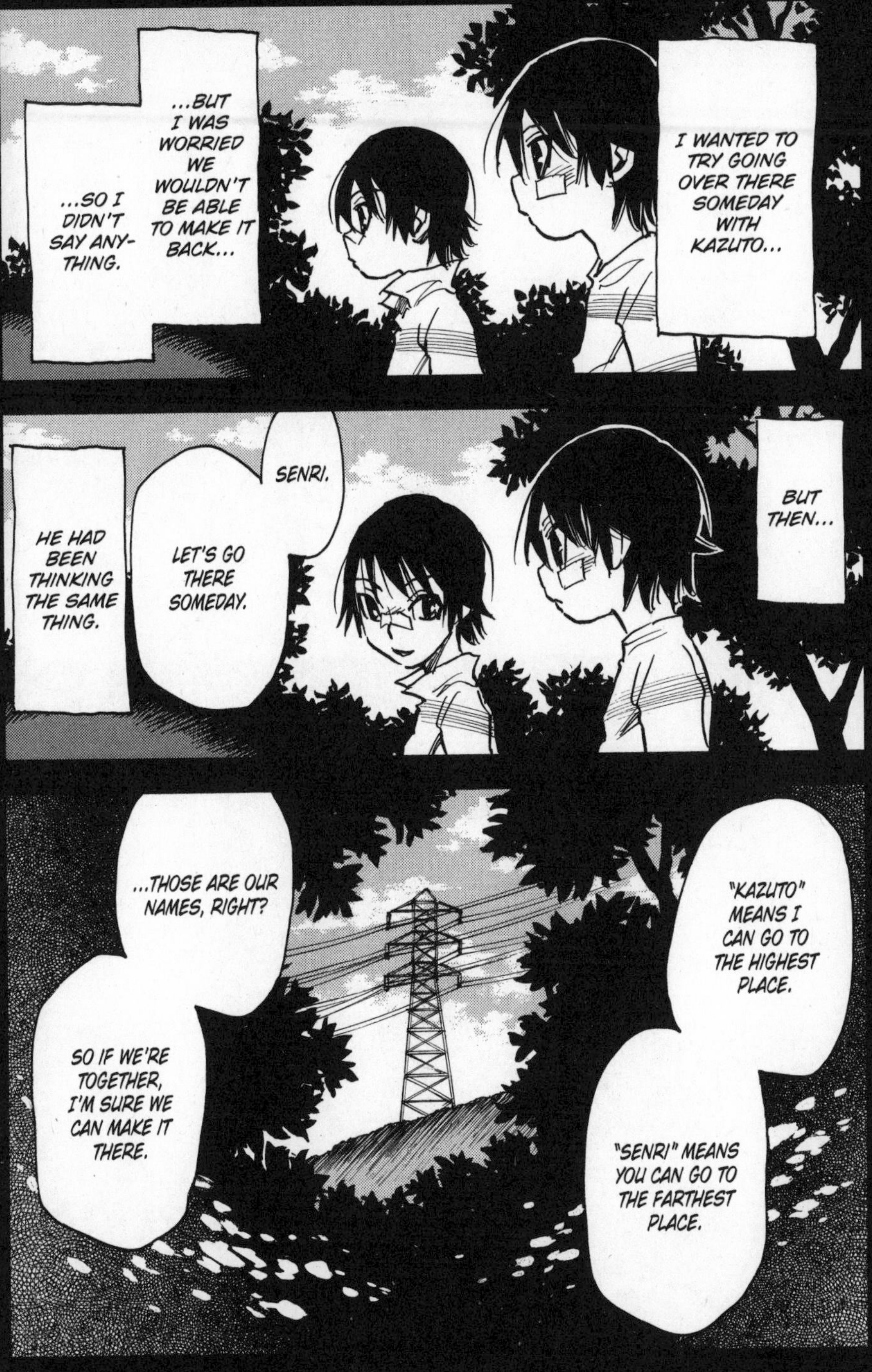
I WANTED TO TRY GOING OVER THERE SOMEDAY WITH KAZUTO...
...BUT I WAS WORRIED WE WOULDN'T BE ABLE TO MAKE IT BACK...
...SO I DIDN'T SAY ANY-THING.
BUT THEN...
SENRI.
LET'S GO THERE SOMEDAY.
HE HAD BEEN THINKING THE SAME THING.
"KAZUTO" MEANS I CAN GO TO THE HIGHEST PLACE.
"SENRI" MEANS YOU CAN GO TO THE FARTHEST PLACE.
...THOSE ARE OUR NAMES, RIGHT?
SO IF WE'RE TOGETHER, I'M SURE WE CAN MAKE IT THERE.

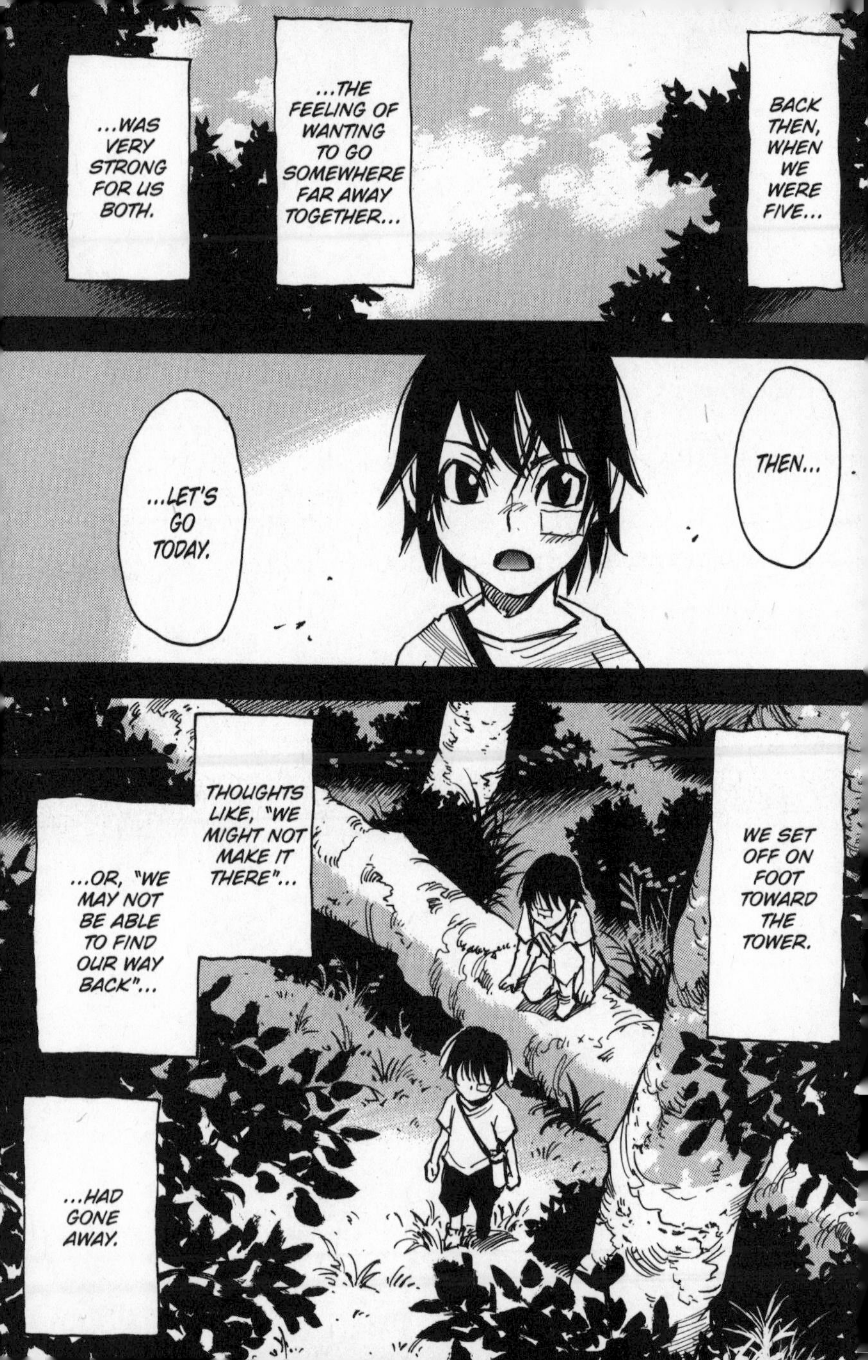
BACK THEN, WHEN WE WERE FIVE...
...THE FEELING OF WANTING TO GO SOMEWHERE FAR AWAY TOGETHER...
...WAS VERY STRONG FOR US BOTH.
THEN...
...LET'S GO TODAY.
WE SET OFF ON FOOT TOWARD THE TOWER.
THOUGHTS LIKE, "WE MIGHT NOT MAKE IT THERE"...
...OR, "WE MAY NOT BE ABLE TO FIND OUR WAY BACK"...
...HAD GONE AWAY.

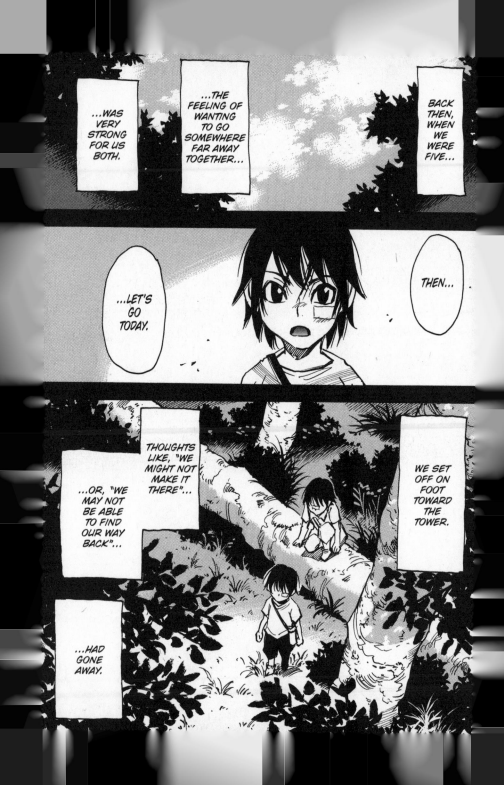

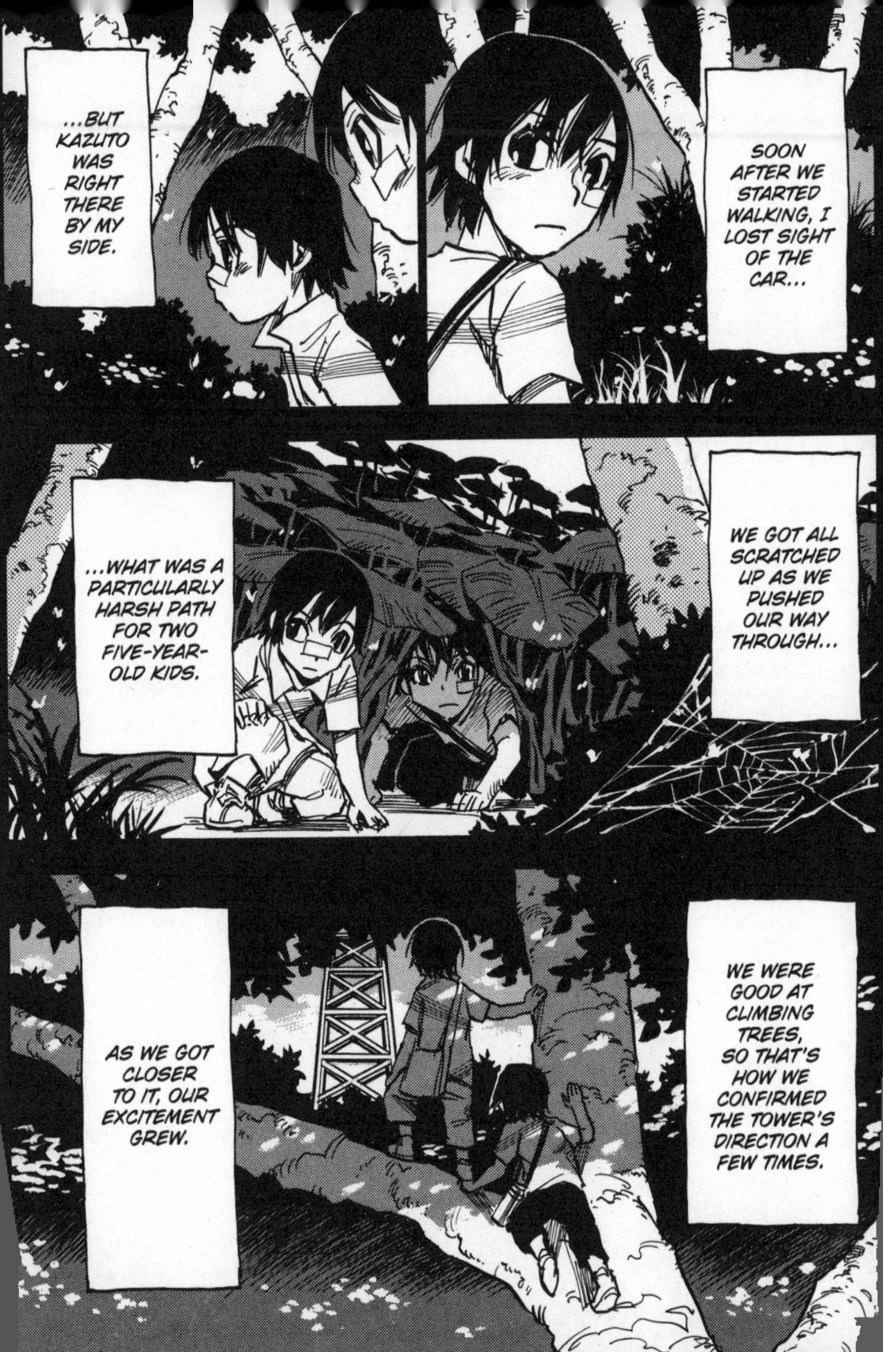
SOON AFTER WE STARTED WALKING, I LOST SIGHT OF THE CAR...
...BUT KAZUTO WAS RIGHT THERE BY MY SIDE.
WE GOT ALL SCRATCHED UP AS WE PUSHED OUR WAY THROUGH...
...WHAT WAS A PARTICULARLY HARSH PATH FOR TWO FIVE-YEAR-OLD KIDS.
WE WERE GOOD AT CLIMBING TREES, SO THAT'S HOW WE CONFIRMED THE TOWER'S DIRECTION A FEW TIMES.
AS WE GOT CLOSER TO IT, OUR EXCITEMENT GREW.

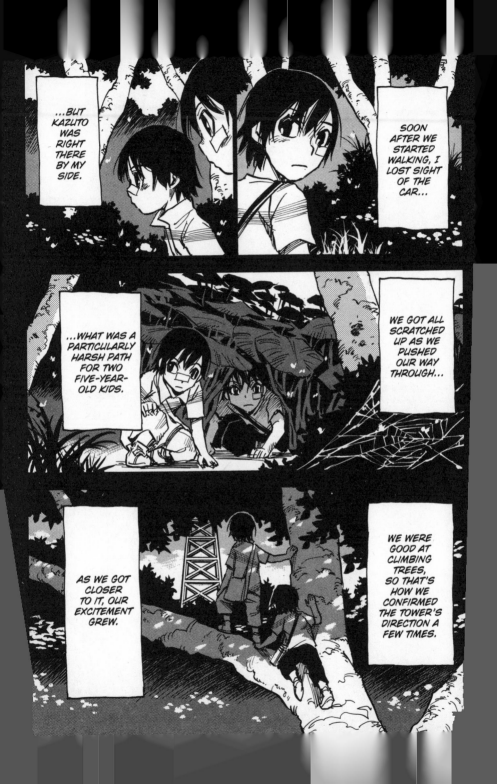

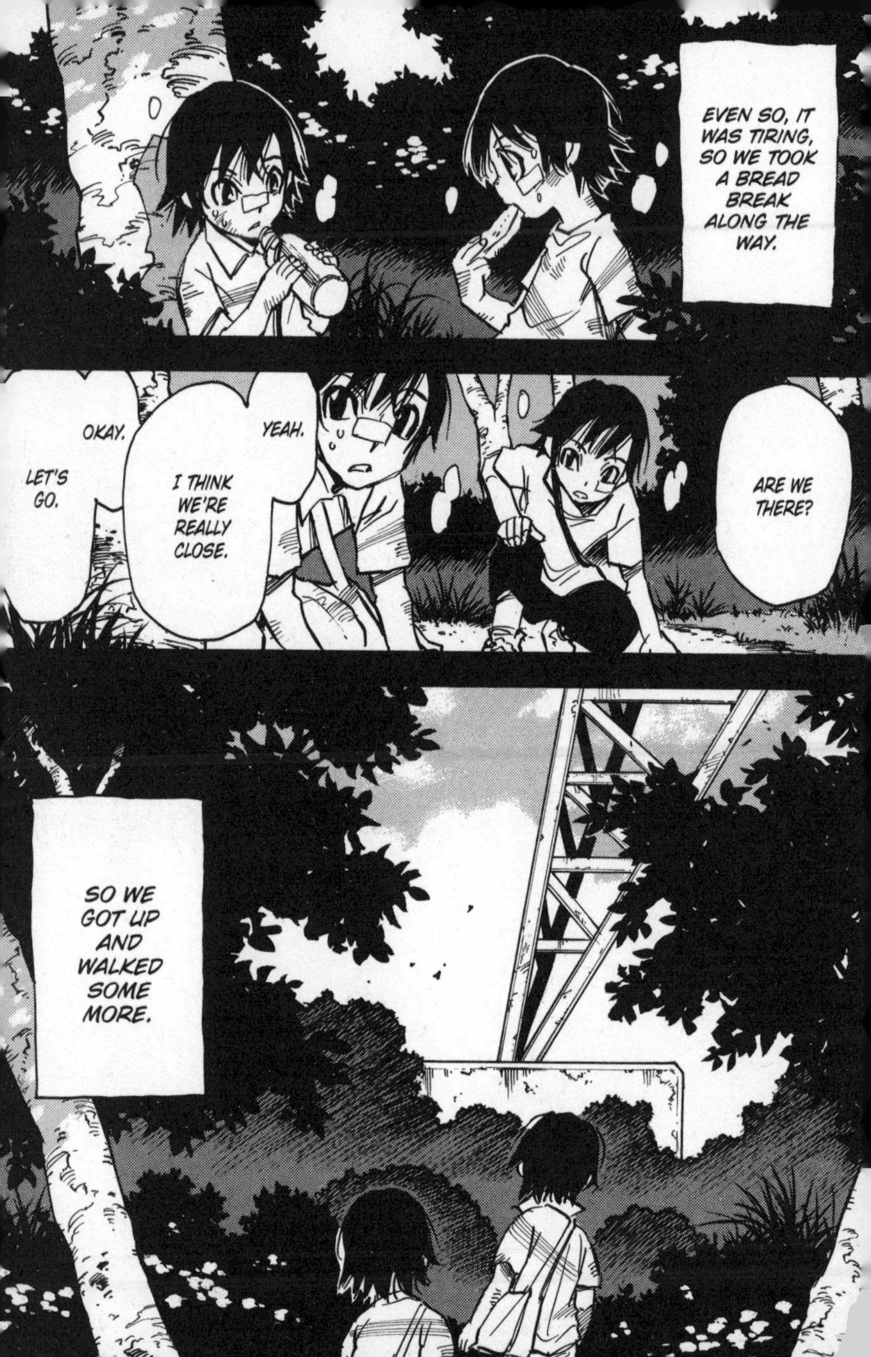
EVEN SO, IT WAS TIRING, SO WE TOOK A BREAD BREAK ALONG THE WAY.
ARE WE THERE?
YEAH.
I THINK WE'RE REALLY CLOSE.
OKAY.
LET'S GO.
SO WE GOT UP AND WALKED SOME MORE.

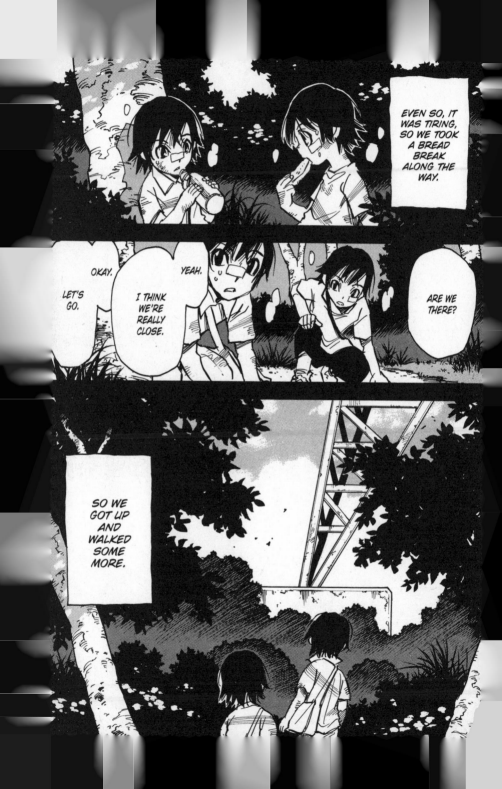

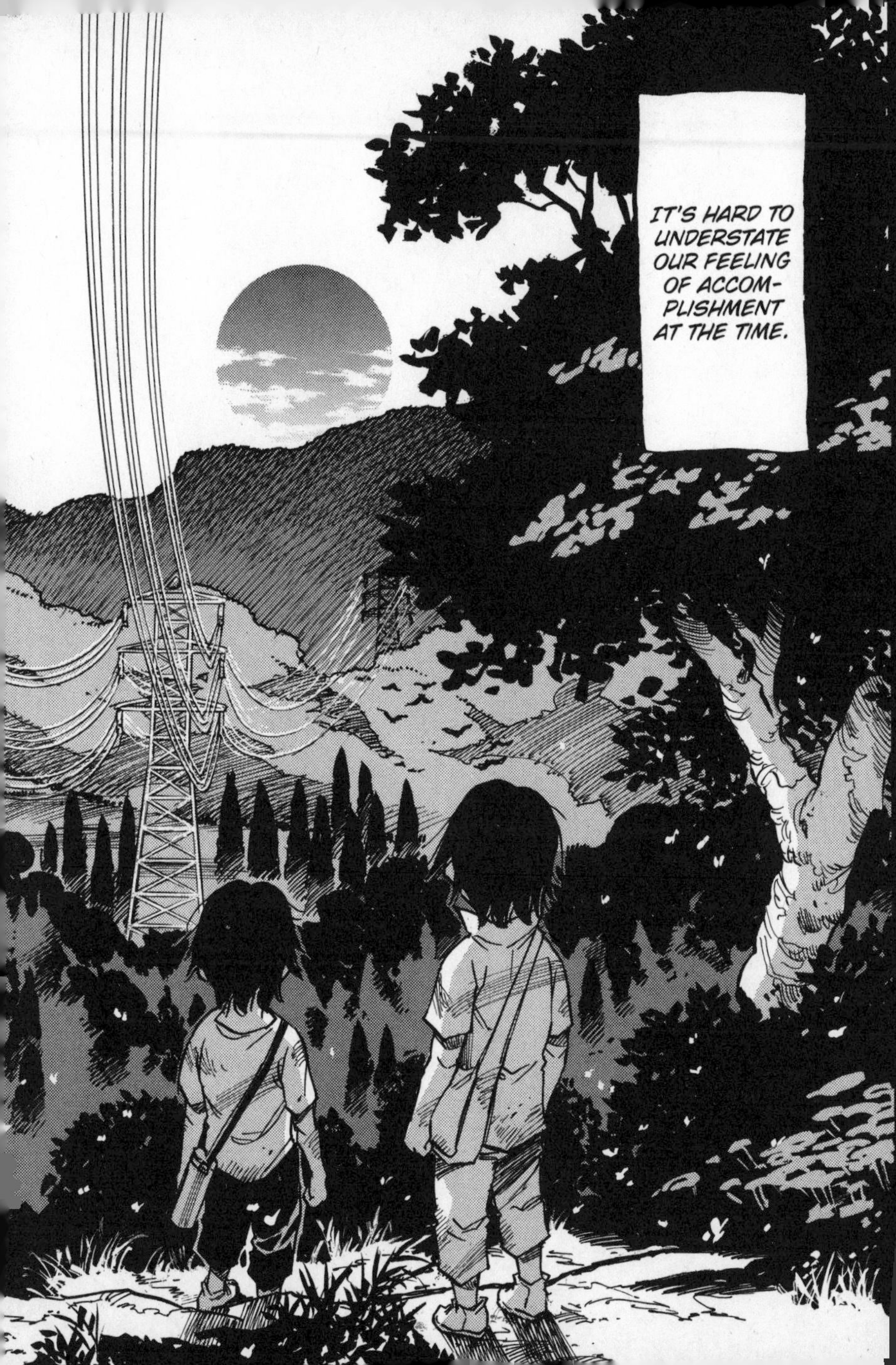
IT'S HARD TO UNDERSTATE OUR FEELING OF ACCOM-PLISHMENT AT THE TIME.

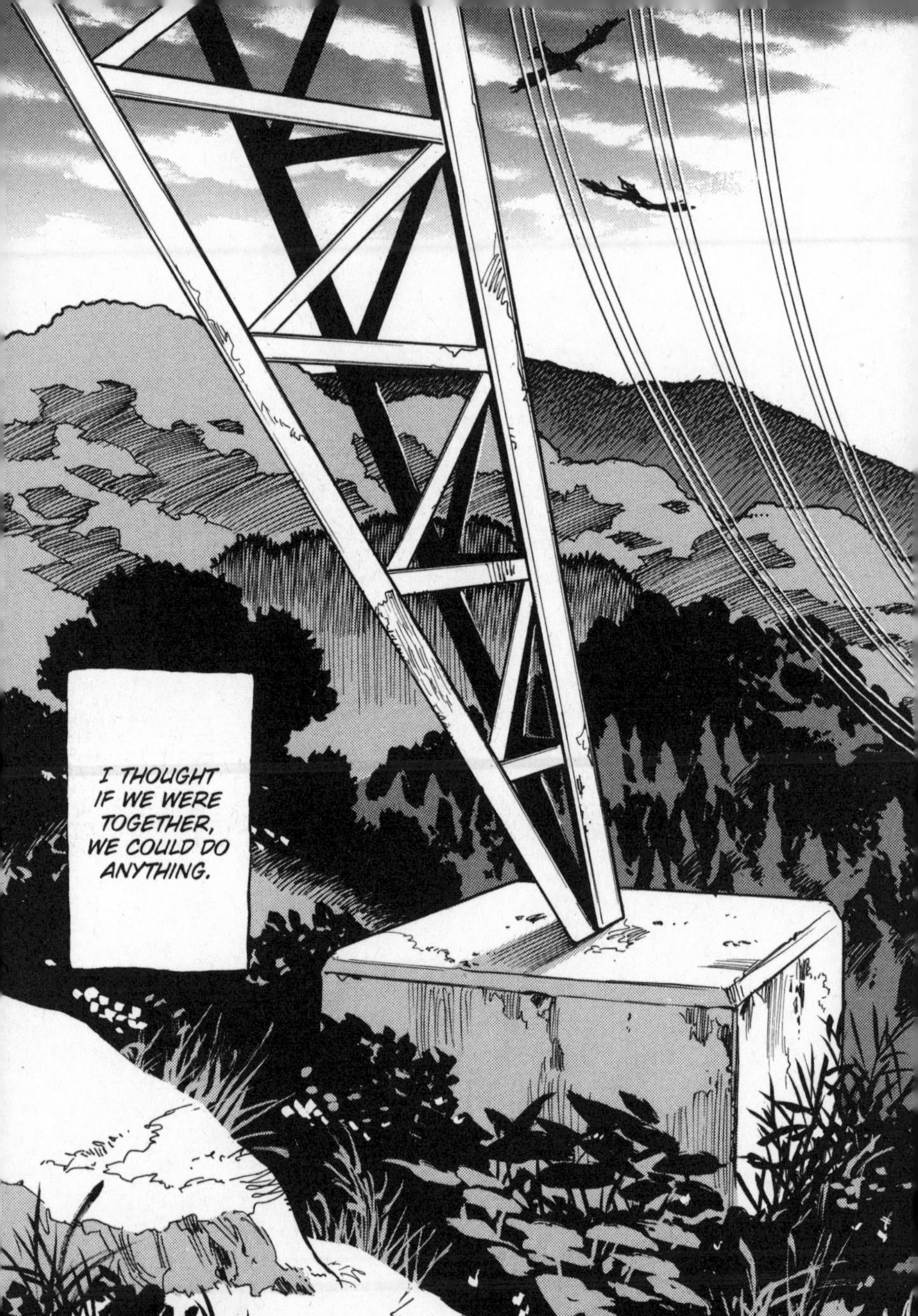
I THOUGHT IF WE WERE TOGETHER, WE COULD DO ANYTHING.

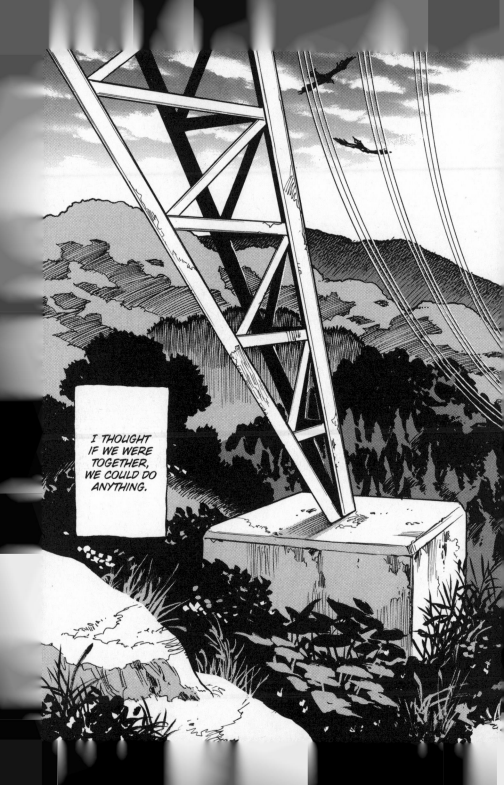

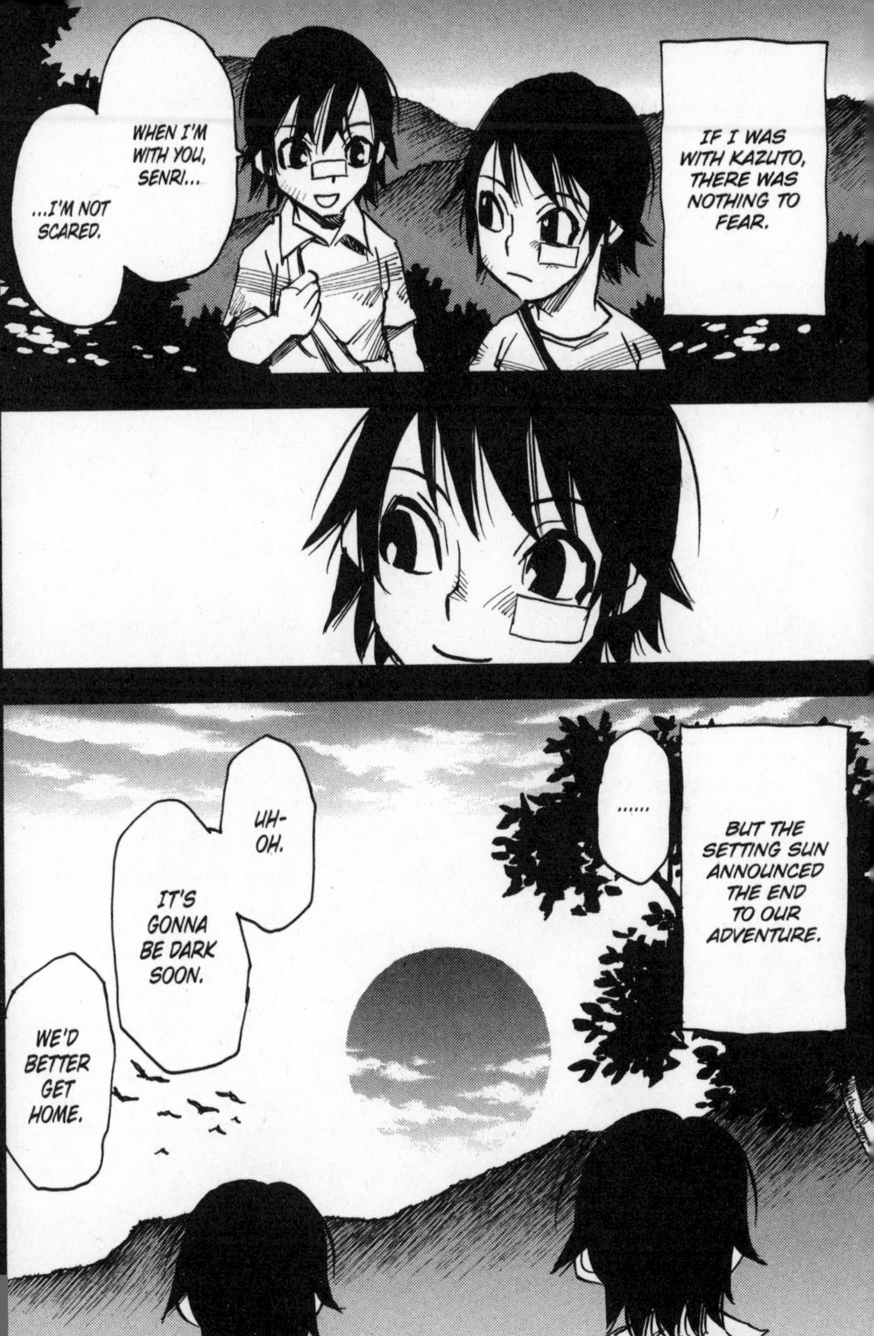
IF I WAS WITH KAZUTO, THERE WAS NOTHING TO FEAR.
WHEN I'M WITH YOU, SENRI...
...I'M NOT SCARED.
BUT THE SETTING SUN ANNOUNCED THE END TO OUR ADVENTURE.
......
UH-OH.
IT'S GONNA BE DARK SOON.
WE'D BETTER GET HOME.

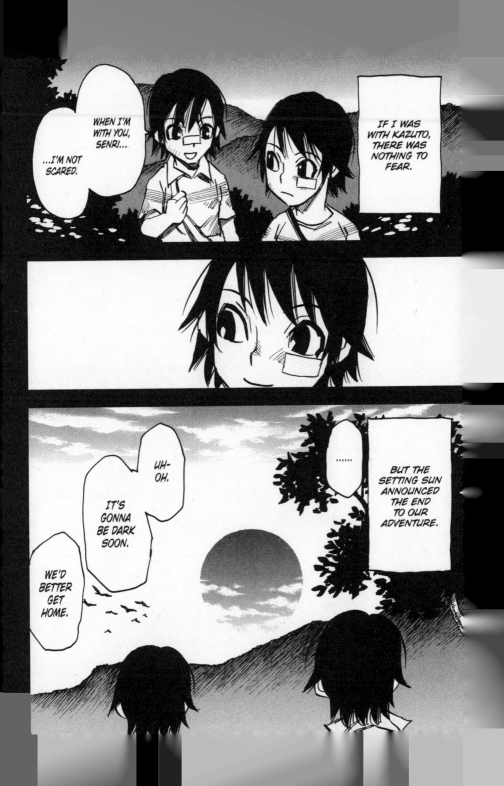

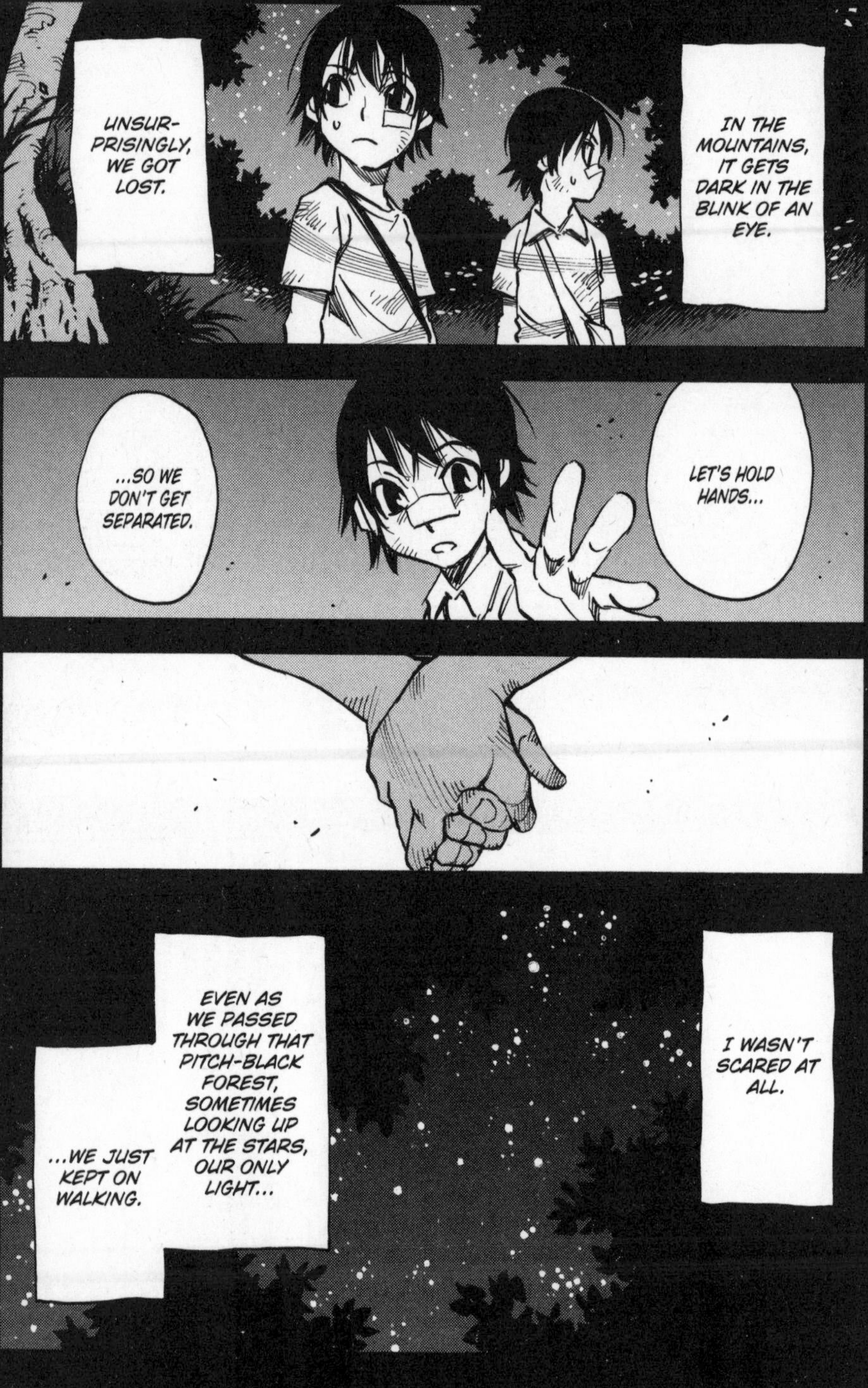
IN THE MOUNTAINS, IT GETS DARK IN THE BLINK OF AN EYE.
UNSURPRISINGLY, WE GOT LOST.
LET'S HOLD HANDS...
...SO WE DON'T GET SEPARATED.
I WASN'T SCARED AT ALL.
EVEN AS WE PASSED THROUGH THAT PITCH-BLACK FOREST, SOMETIMES LOOKING UP AT THE STARS, OUR ONLY LIGHT...
...WE JUST KEPT ON WALKING.

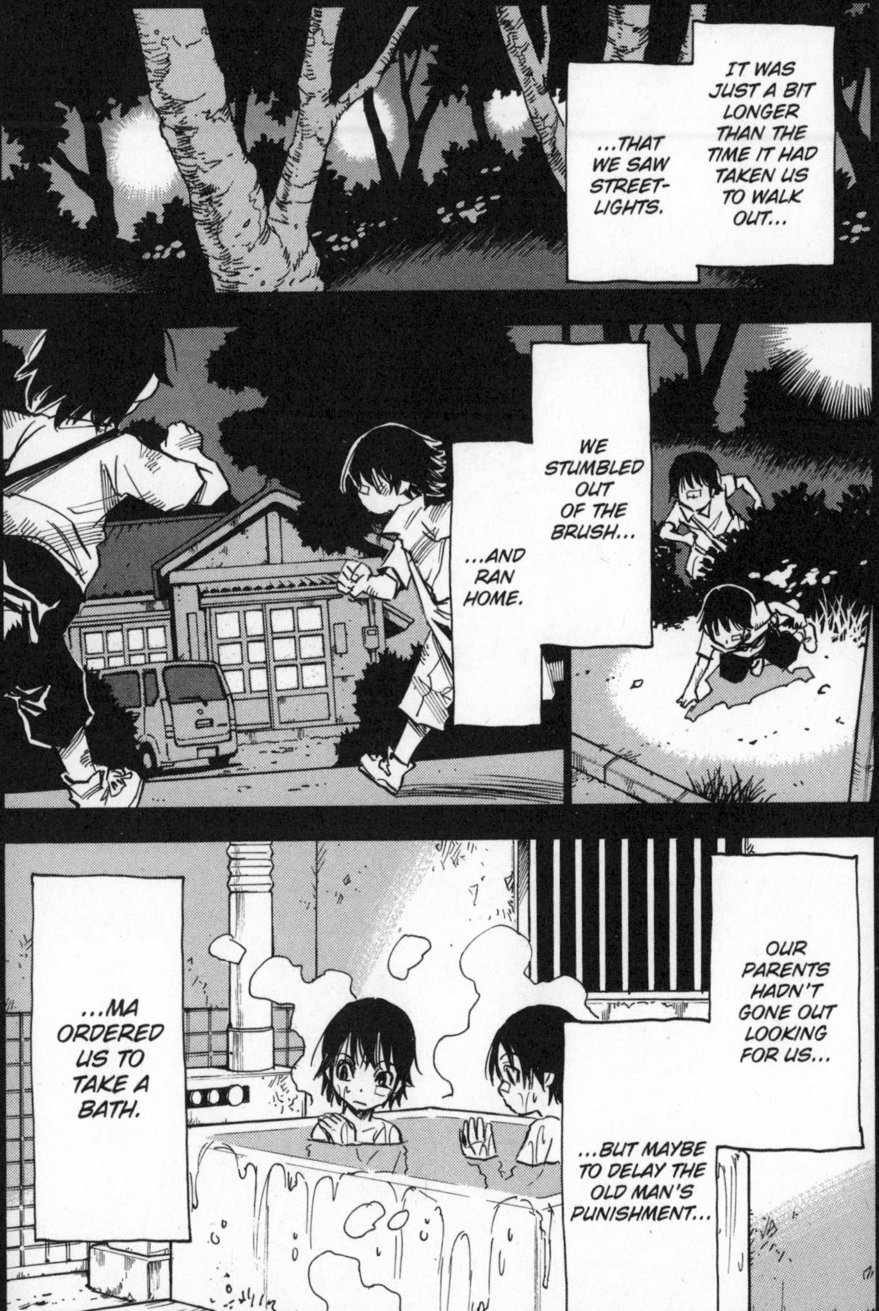
IT WAS JUST A BIT LONGER THAN THE TIME IT HAD TAKEN US TO WALK OUT...
...THAT WE SAW STREET-LIGHTS.
WE STUMBLED OUT OF THE BRUSH...
...AND RAN HOME.
OUR PARENTS HADN'T GONE OUT LOOKING FOR US...
...BUT MAYBE TO DELAY THE OLD MAN'S PUNISHMENT...
...MA ORDERED US TO TAKE A BATH.

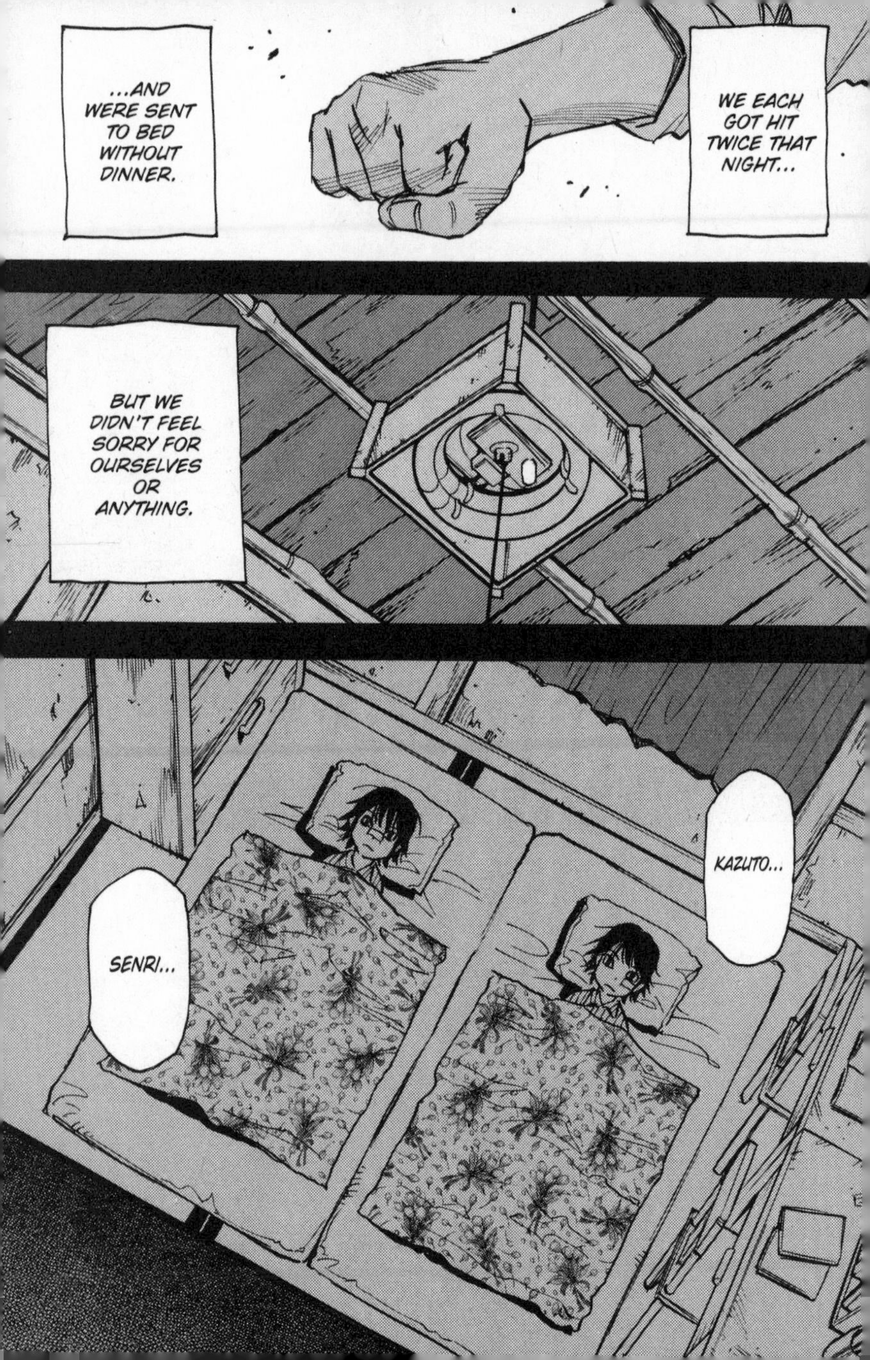
WE EACH GOT HIT TWICE THAT NIGHT...
...AND WERE SENT TO BED WITHOUT DINNER.
BUT WE DIDN'T FEEL SORRY FOR OURSELVES OR ANYTHING.
KAZUTO...
SENRI...

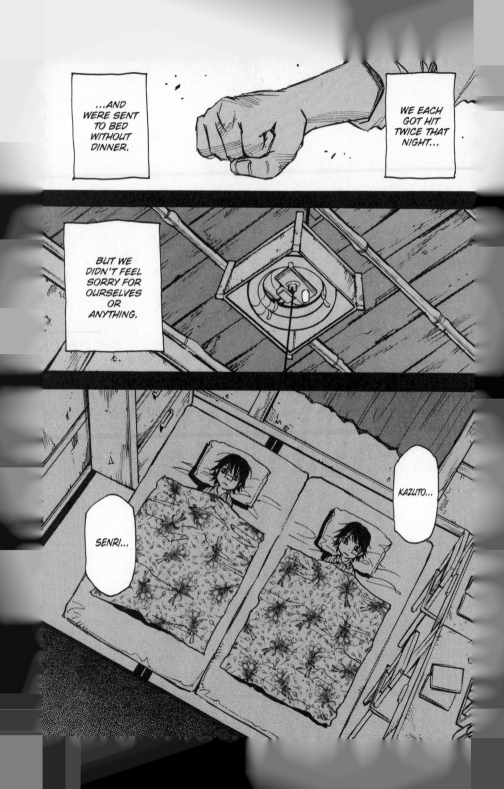

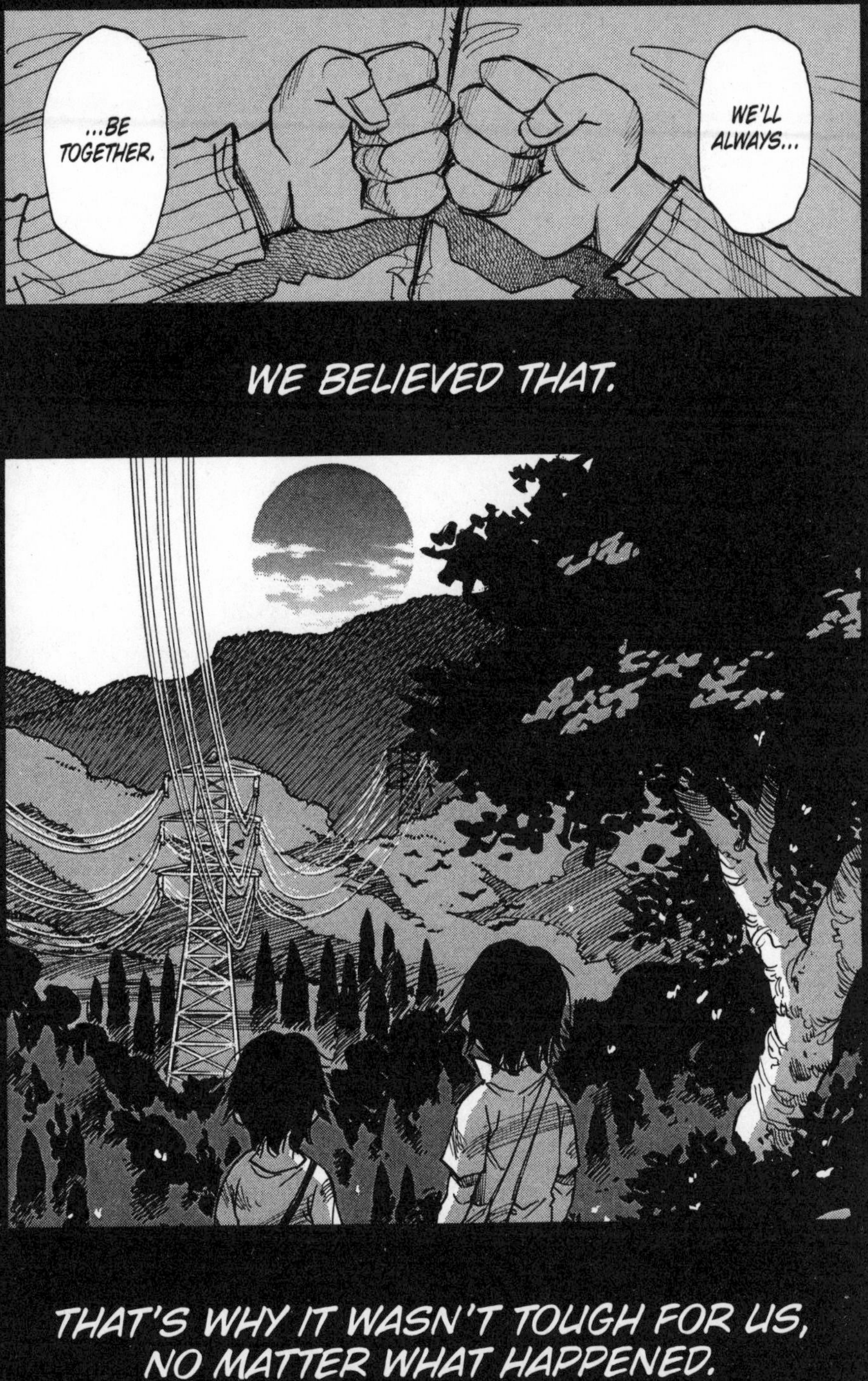
WE'LL ALWAYS...
...BE TOGETHER.
WE BELIEVED THAT.
THAT'S WHY IT WASN'T TOUGH FOR US, NO MATTER WHAT HAPPENED.

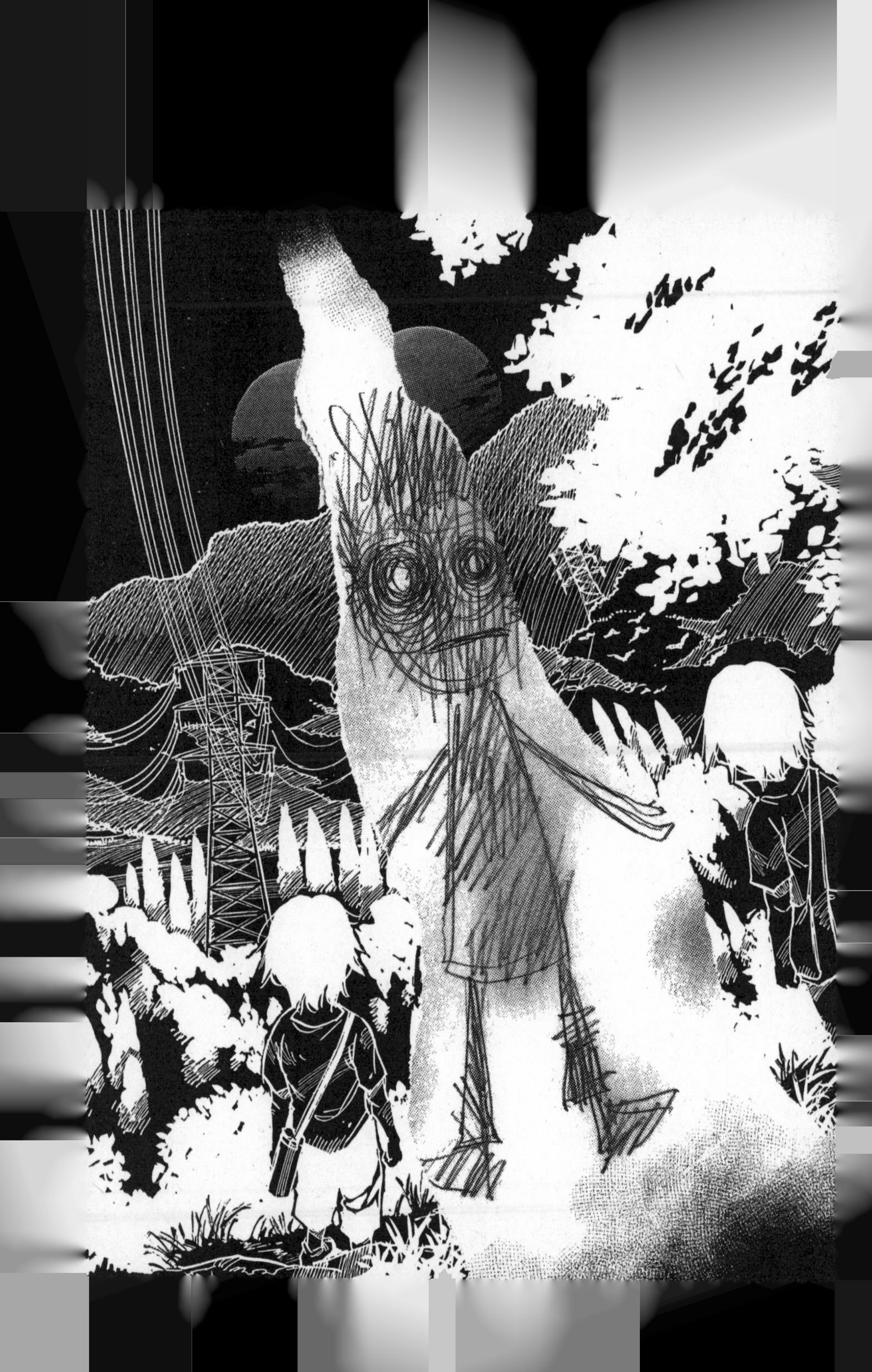

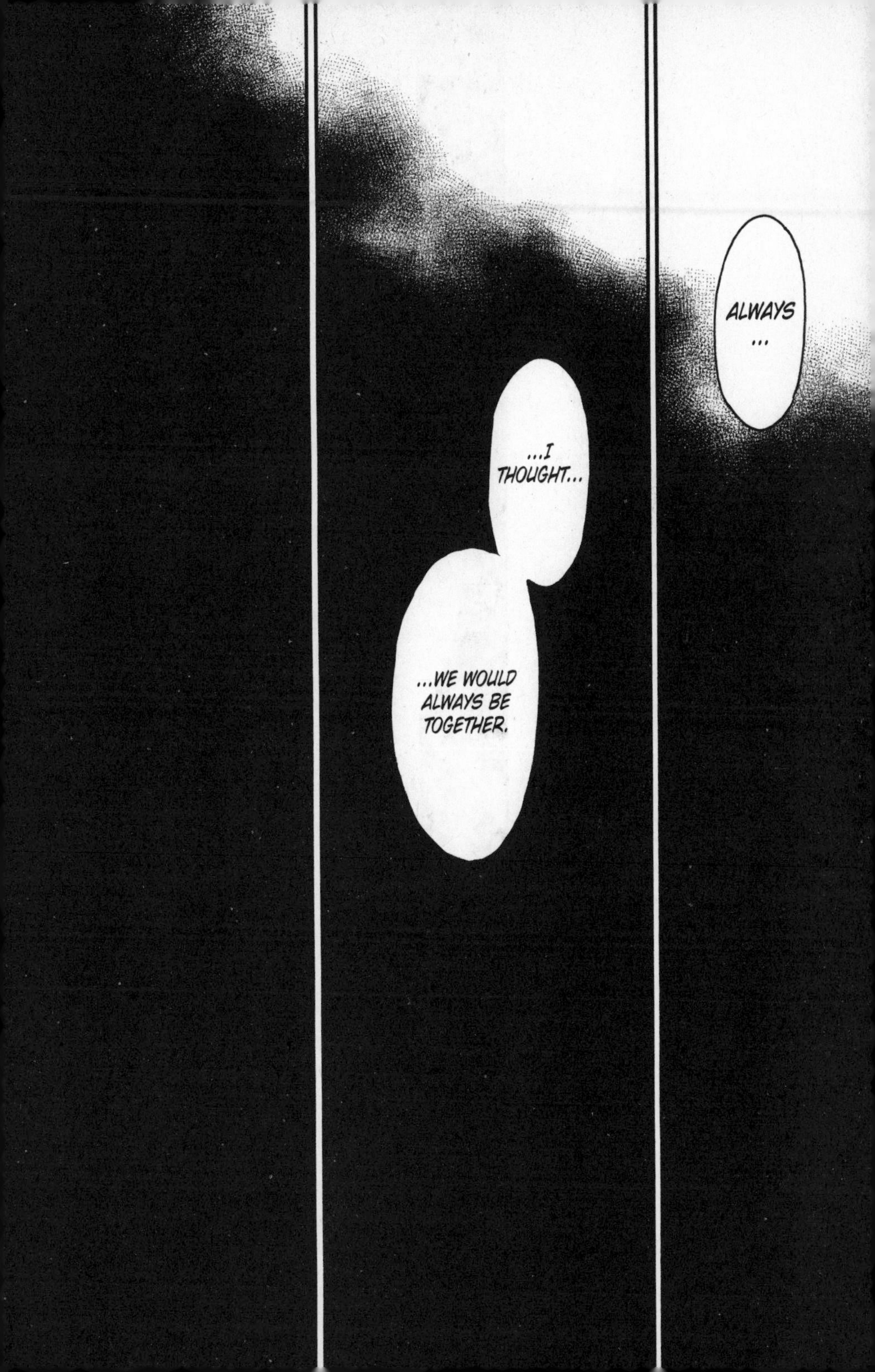
ALWAYS ...
...I THOUGHT...
...WE WOULD ALWAYS BE TOGETHER.

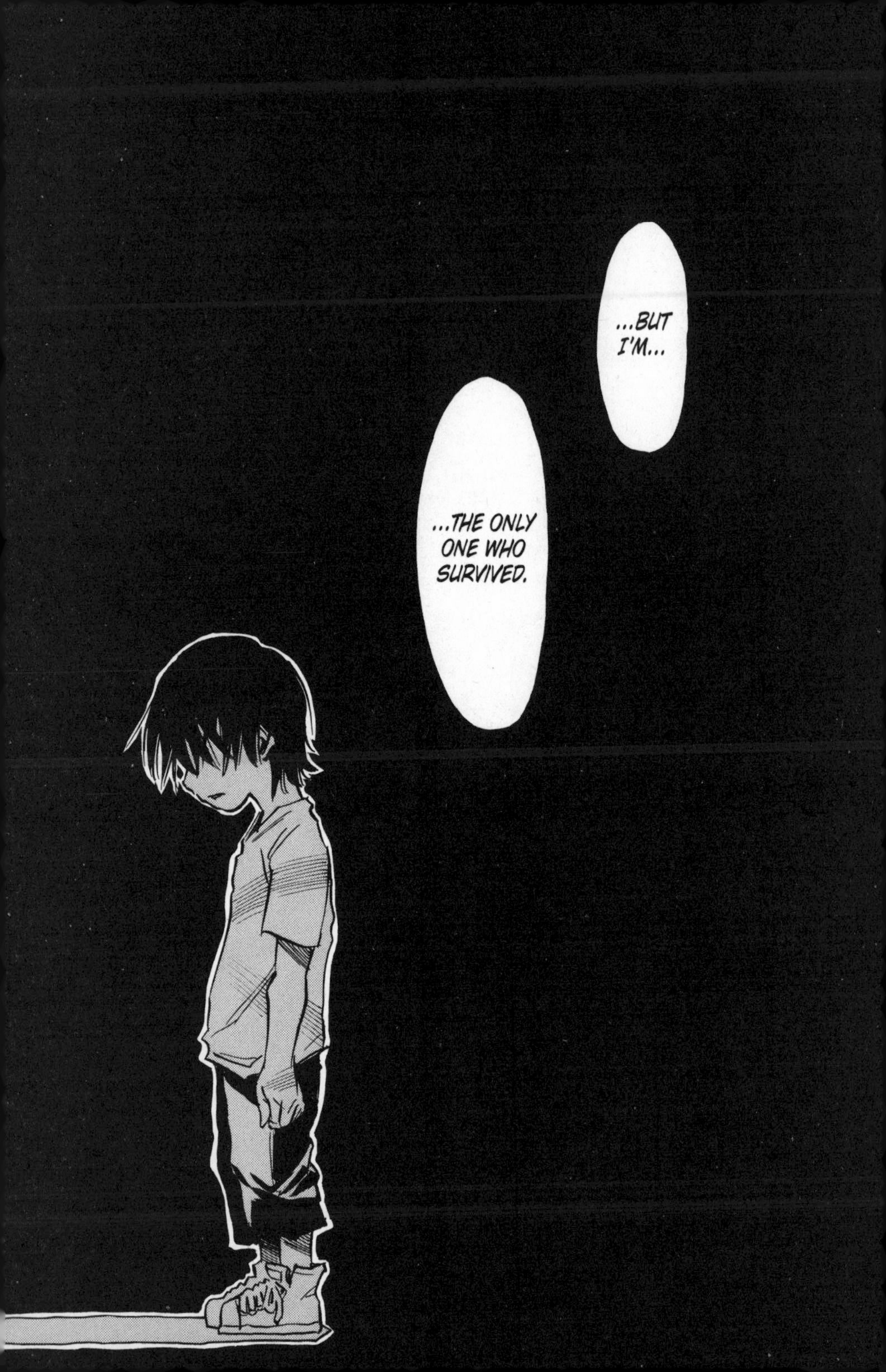
...BUT I'M...
...THE ONLY ONE WHO SURVIVED.

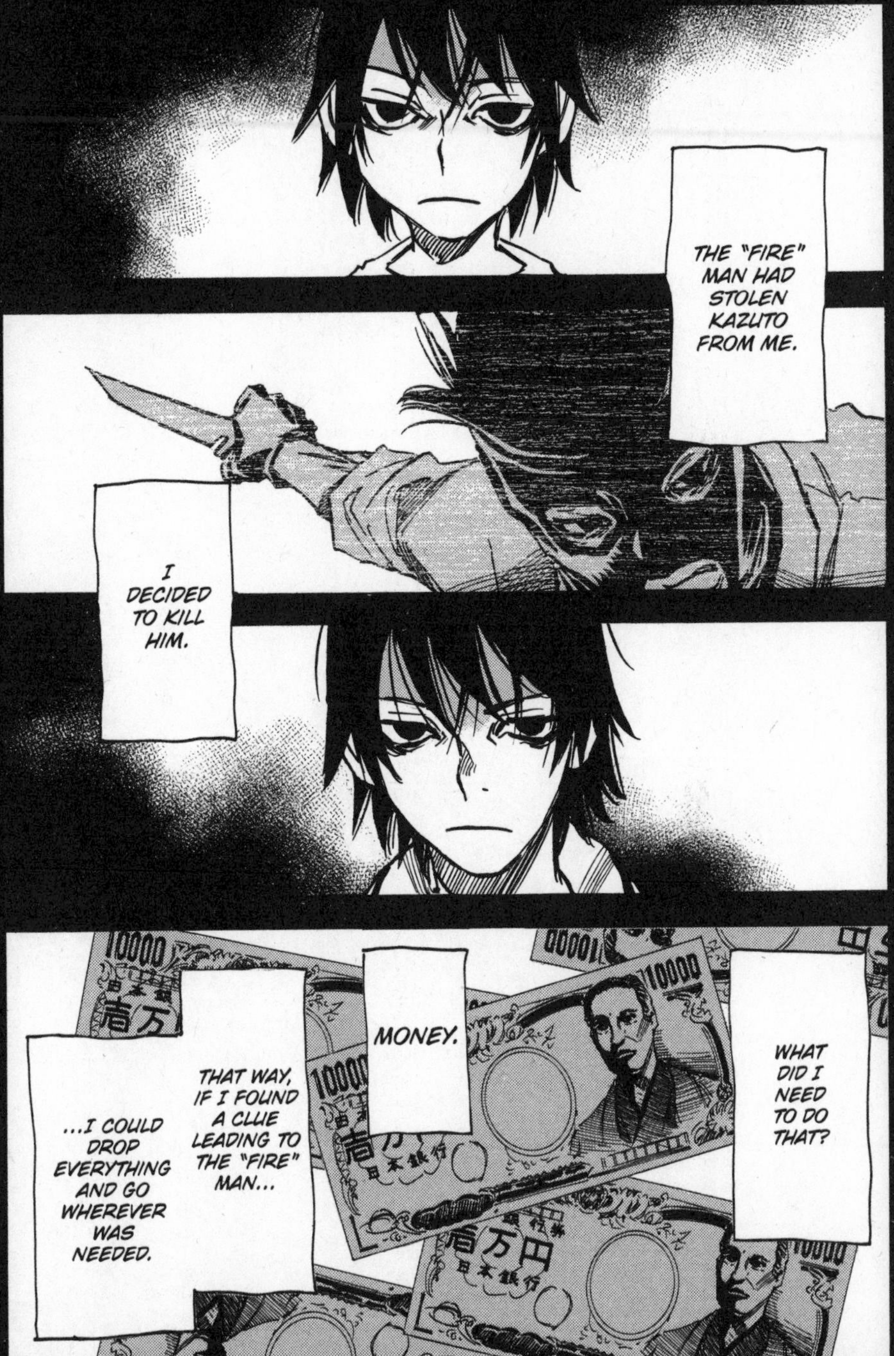
THE "FIRE" MAN HAD STOLEN KAZUTO FROM ME.
I DECIDED TO KILL HIM.
WHAT DID I NEED TO DO THAT?
MONEY.
THAT WAY, IF I FOUND A CLUE LEADING TO THE "FIRE" MAN...
...I COULD DROP EVERYTHING AND GO WHEREVER WAS NEEDED.

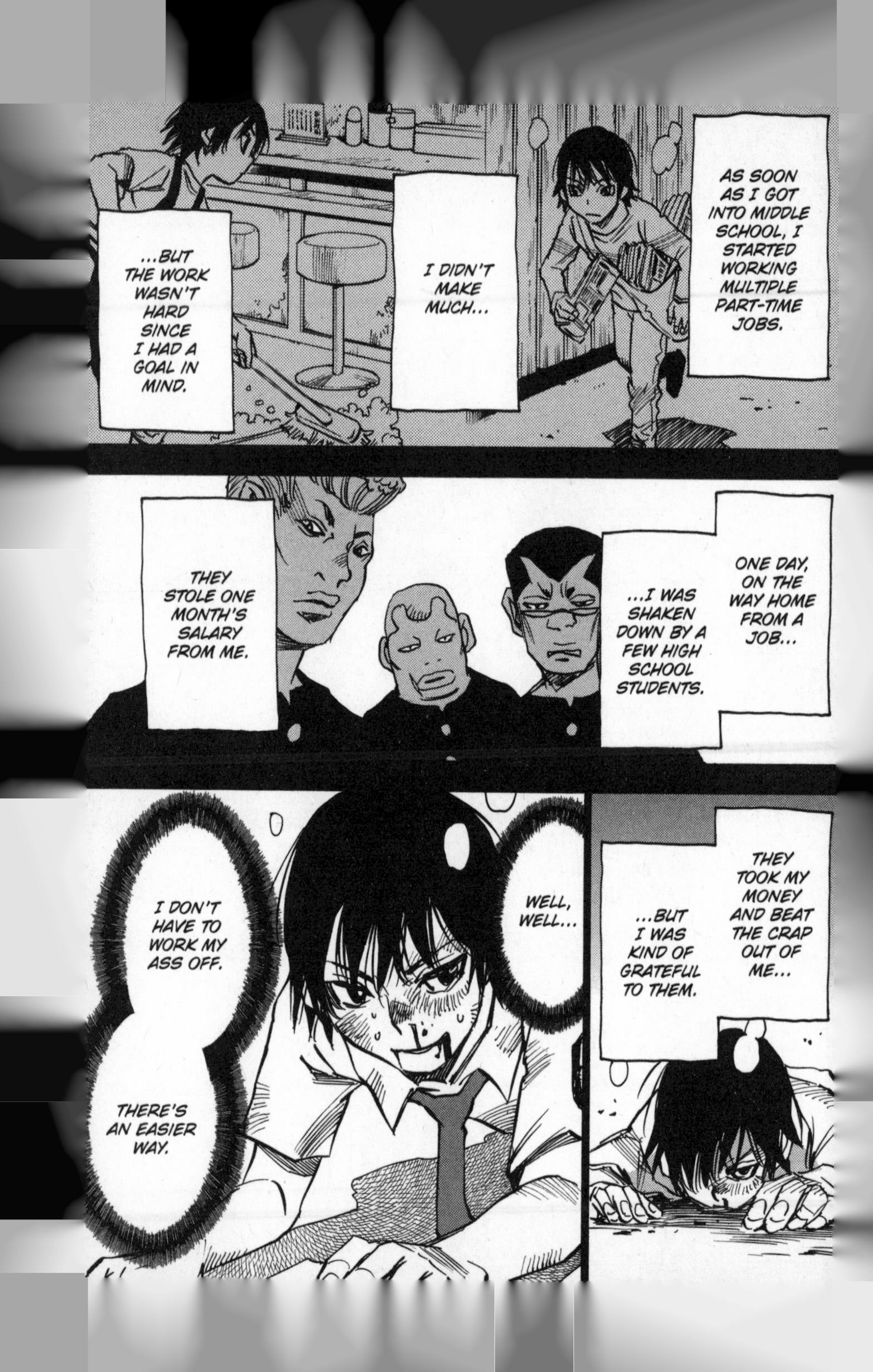
AS SOON AS I GOT INTO MIDDLE SCHOOL, I STARTED WORKING MULTIPLE PART-TIME JOBS.
I DIDN'T MAKE MUCH...
...BUT THE WORK WASN'T HARD SINCE I HAD A GOAL IN MIND.
ONE DAY, ON THE WAY HOME FROM A JOB...
...I WAS SHAKEN DOWN BY A FEW HIGH SCHOOL STUDENTS.
THEY STOLE ONE MONTH'S SALARY FROM ME.
THEY TOOK MY MONEY AND BEAT THE CRAP OUT OF ME...
...BUT I WAS KIND OF GRATEFUL TO THEM.
WELL, WELL...
I DON'T HAVE TO WORK MY ASS OFF.
THERE'S AN EASIER WAY.

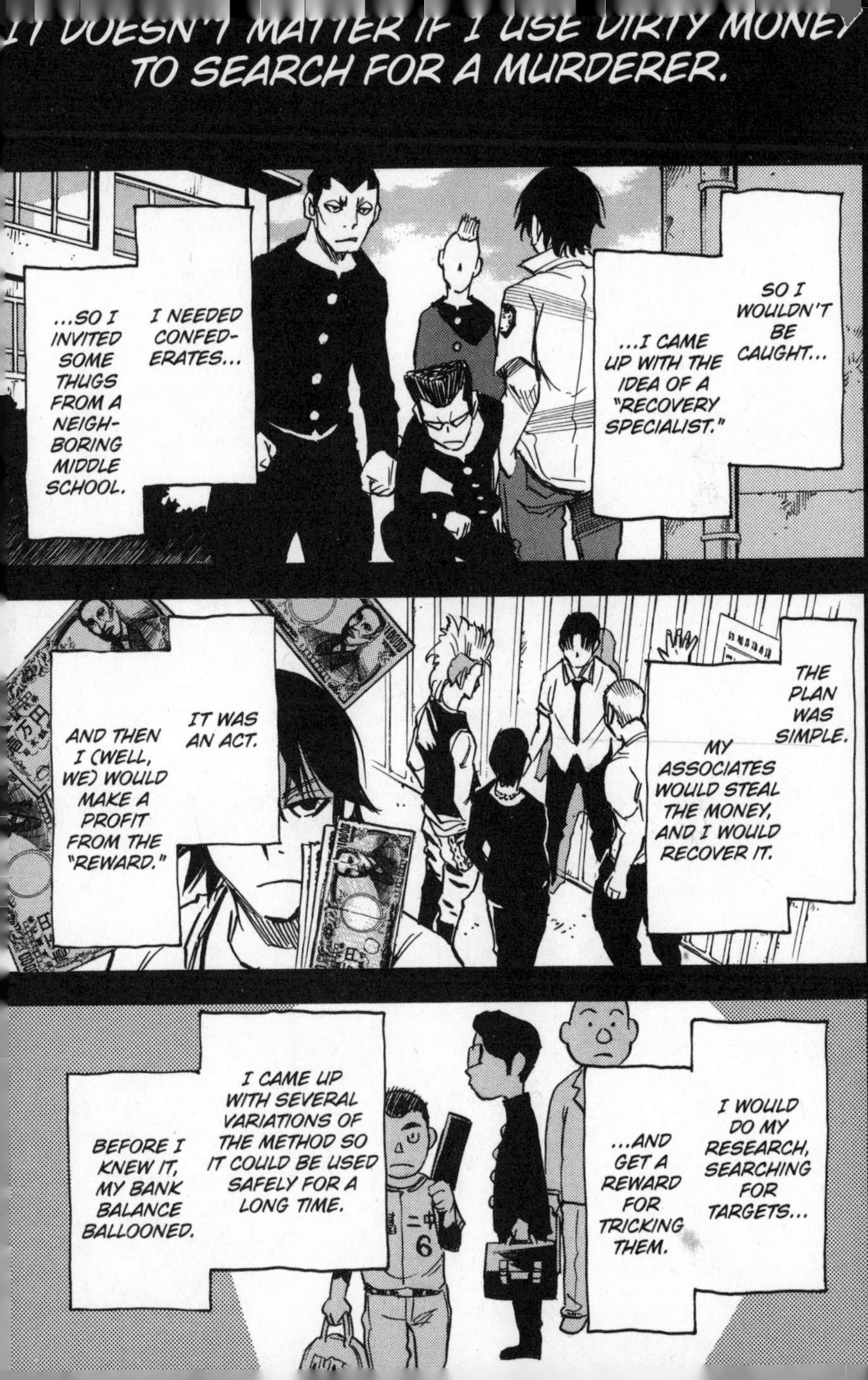
IT DOESN'T MATTER IF I USE DIRTY MONEY TO SEARCH FOR A MURDERER.
SO I WOULDN'T BE CAUGHT...
...I CAME UP WITH THE IDEA OF A "RECOVERY SPECIALIST."
I NEEDED CONFEDERATES...
...SO I INVITED SOME THUGS FROM A NEIGHBORING MIDDLE SCHOOL.
THE PLAN WAS SIMPLE.
MY ASSOCIATES WOULD STEAL THE MONEY, AND I WOULD RECOVER IT.
IT WAS AN ACT.
AND THEN I (WELL, WE) WOULD MAKE A PROFIT FROM THE "REWARD."
I WOULD DO MY RESEARCH, SEARCHING FOR TARGETS...
...AND GET A REWARD FOR TRICKING THEM.
I CAME UP WITH SEVERAL VARIATIONS OF THE METHOD SO IT COULD BE USED SAFELY FOR A LONG TIME.
BEFORE I KNEW IT, MY BANK BALANCE BALLOONED.

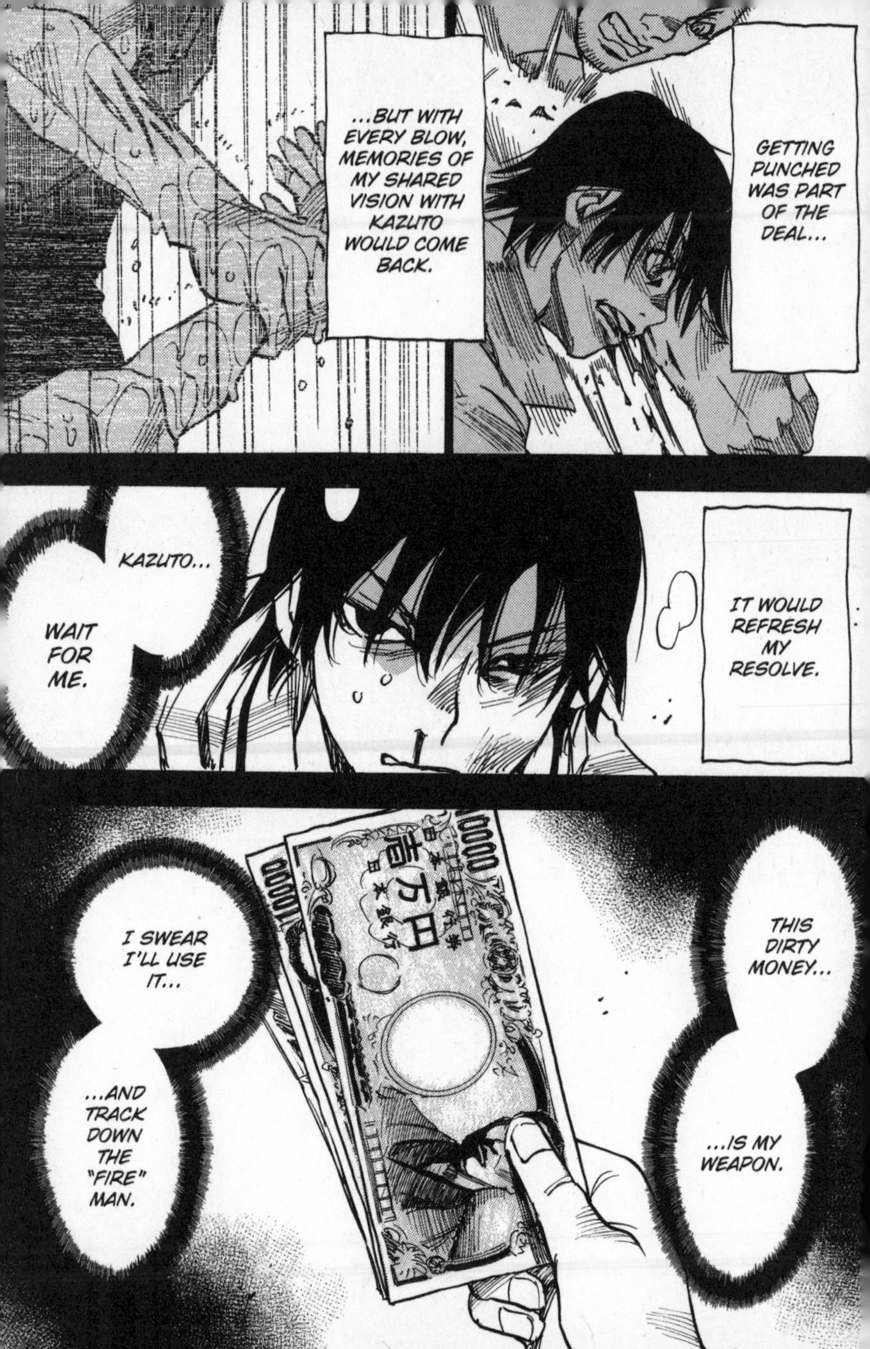
GETTING PUNCHED WAS PART OF THE DEAL...
...BUT WITH EVERY BLOW, MEMORIES OF MY SHARED VISION WITH KAZUTO WOULD COME BACK.
IT WOULD REFRESH MY RESOLVE.
KAZUTO...
WAIT FOR ME.
THIS DIRTY MONEY...
...IS MY WEAPON.
I SWEAR I'LL USE IT...
...AND TRACK DOWN THE "FIRE" MAN.

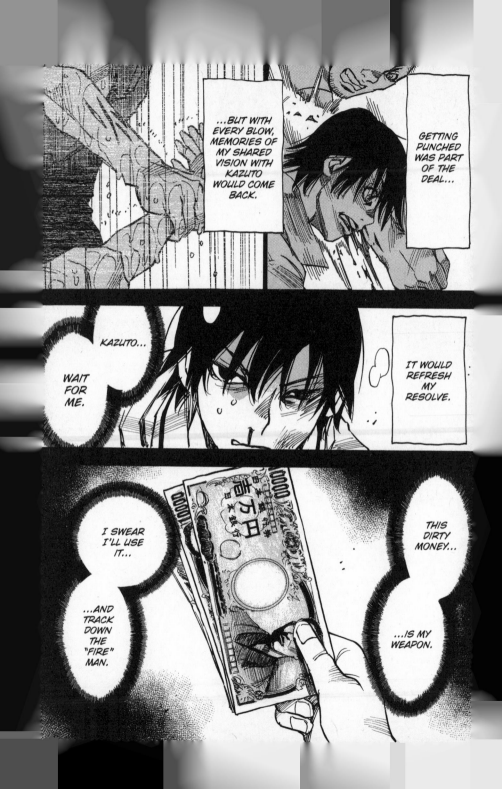

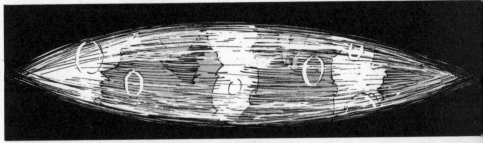

HI.

NAKAJOU-
KUN.

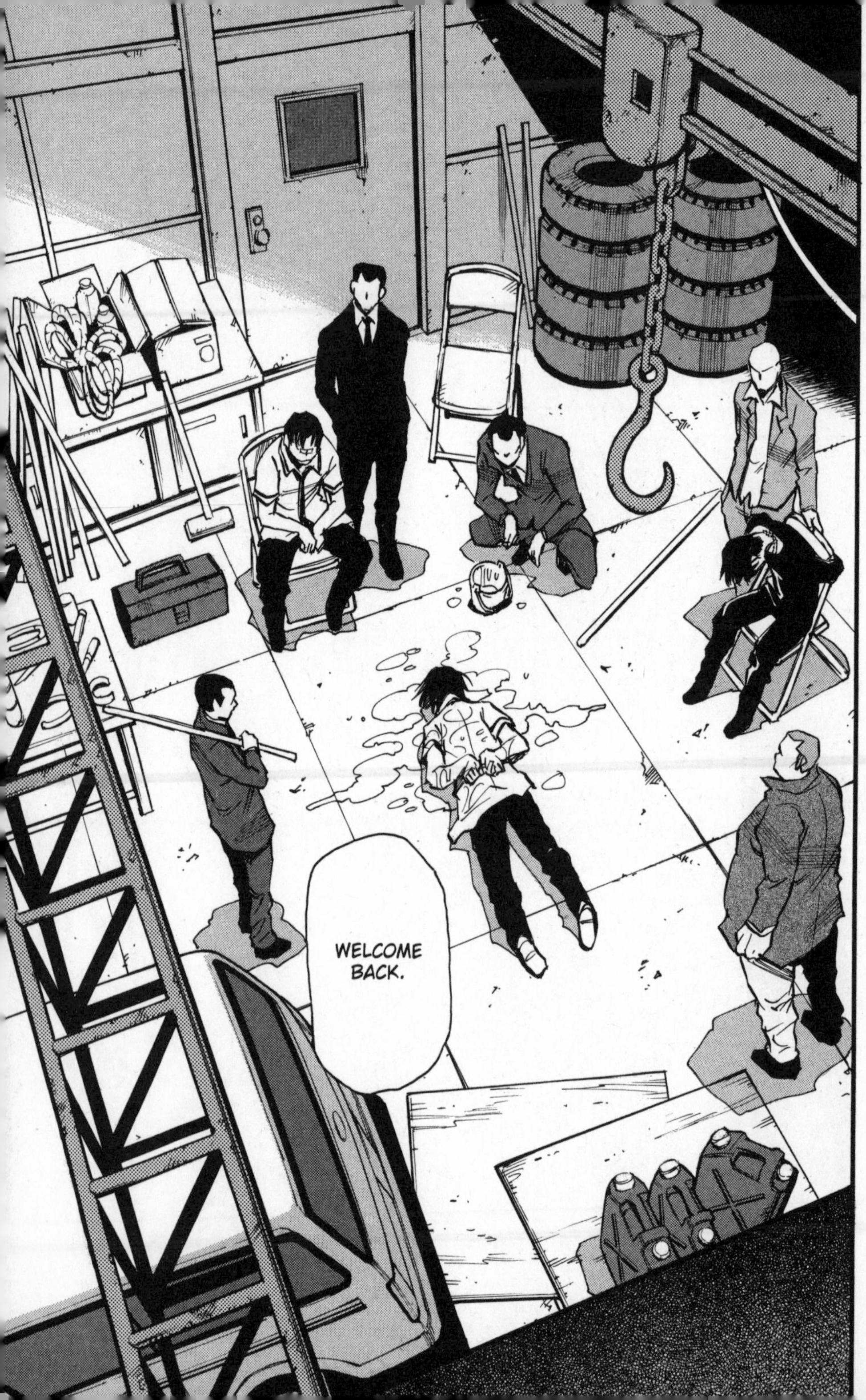
WELCOME BACK.

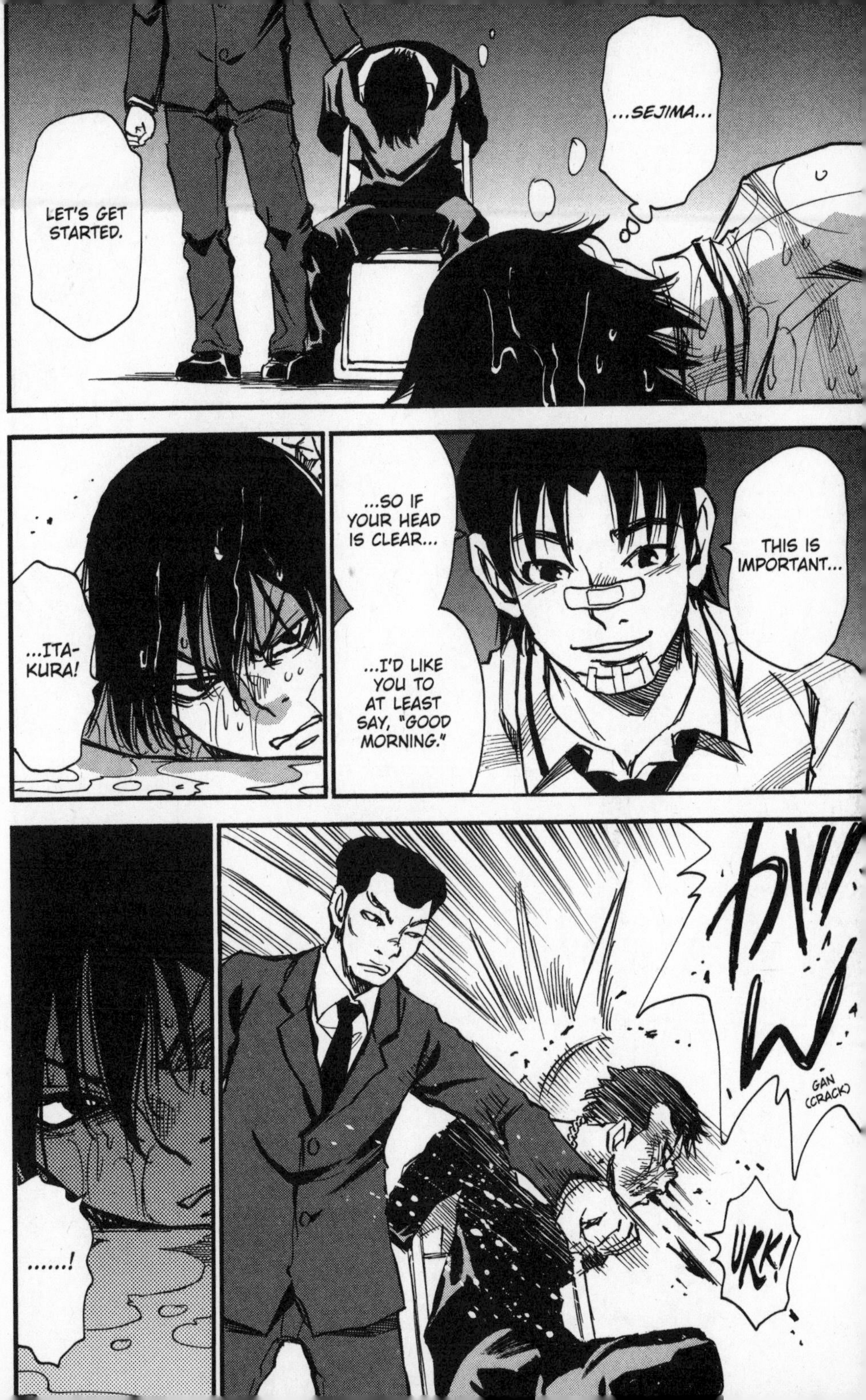
...SEJIMA...
LET'S GET STARTED.
THIS IS IMPORTANT...
...SO IF YOUR HEAD IS CLEAR...
...I'D LIKE YOU TO AT LEAST SAY, "GOOD MORNING."
...ITA-KURA!
GAN (CRACK)
URK!
......!

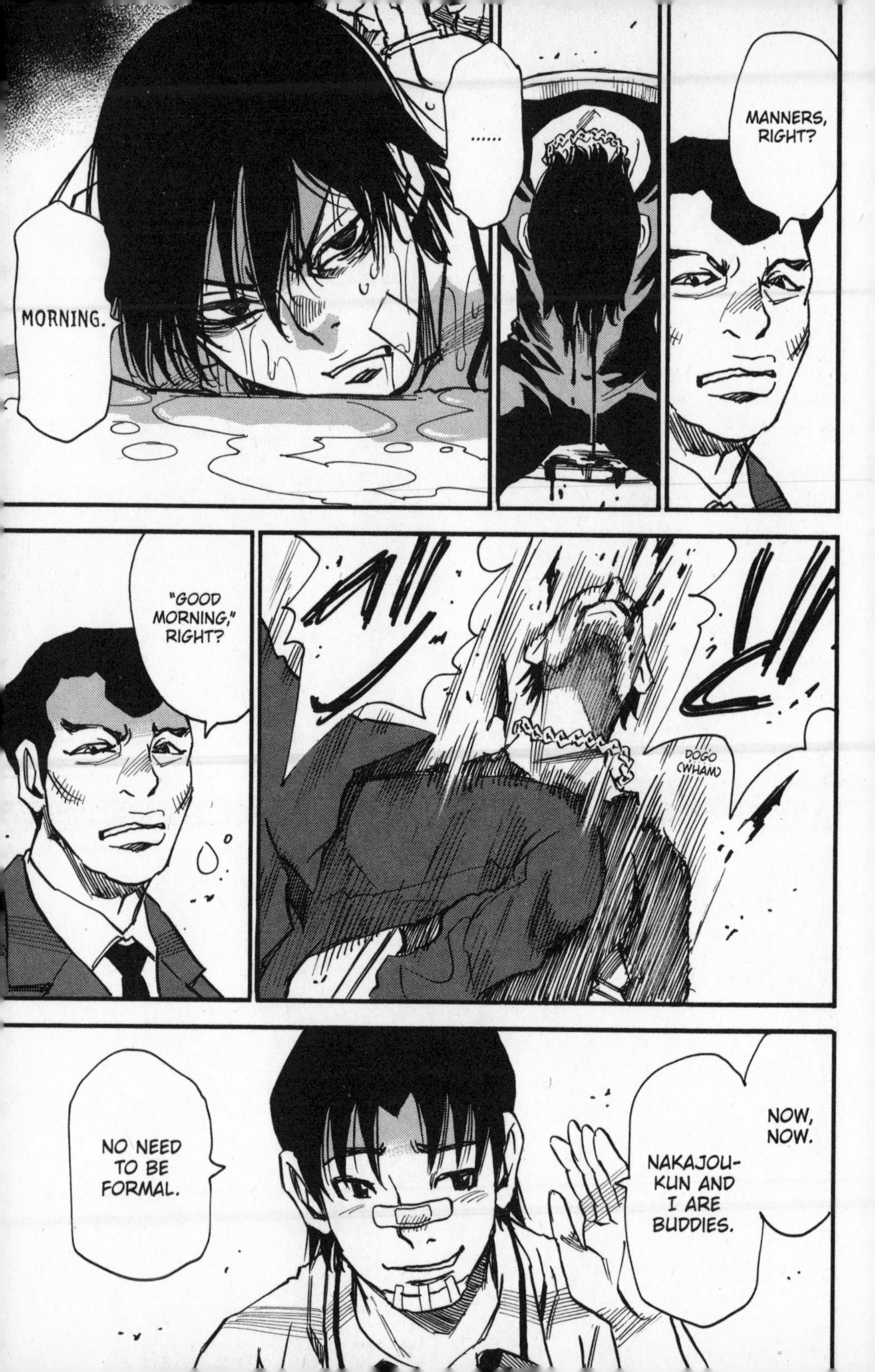
MANNERS, RIGHT?
......
MORNING.
DOGO (WHAM)
"GOOD MORNING," RIGHT?
NOW, NOW.
NAKAJOU-KUN AND I ARE BUDDIES.
NO NEED TO BE FORMAL.

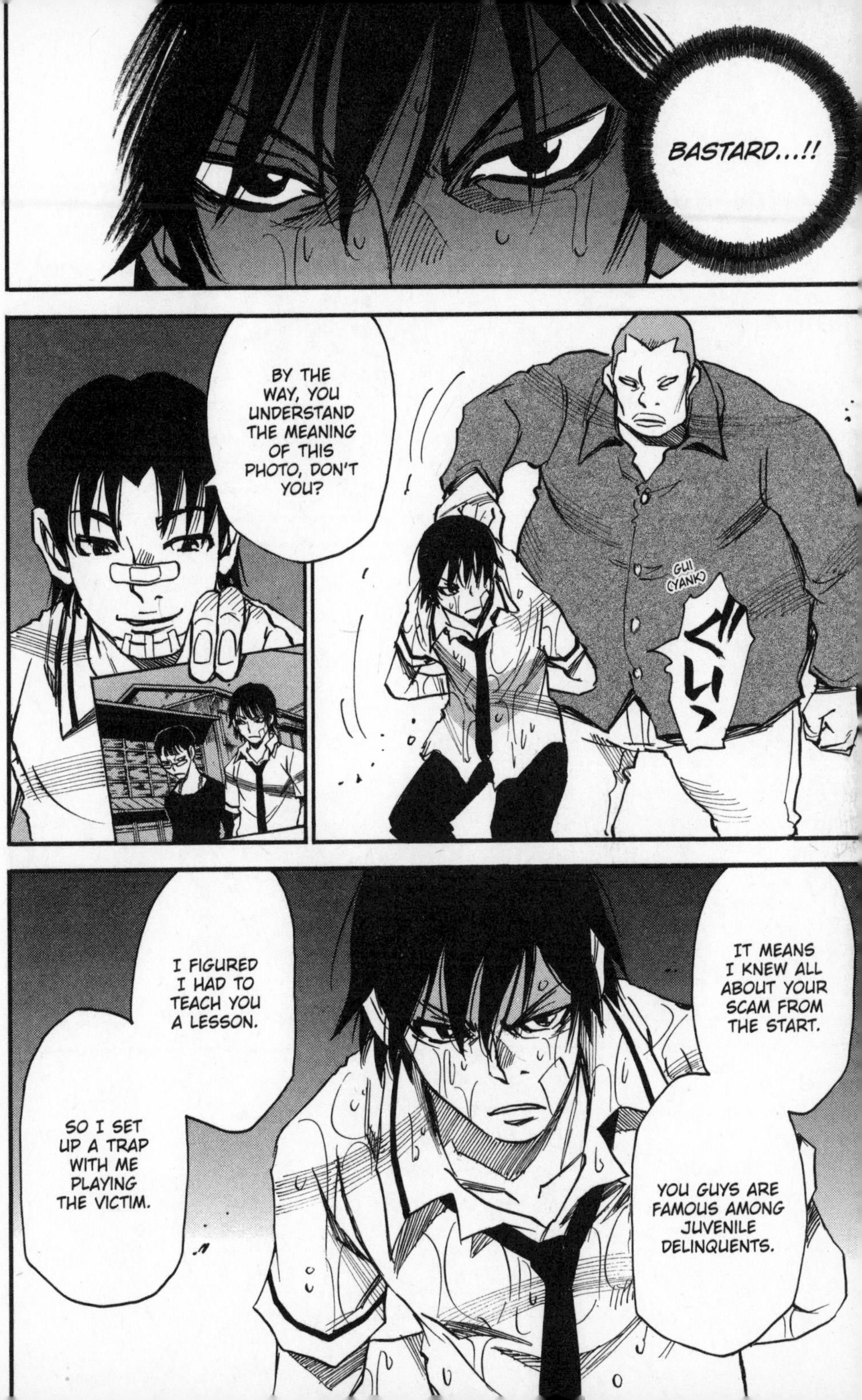
BASTARD...!!
GUI (YANK)
ぐいっ
BY THE WAY, YOU UNDERSTAND THE MEANING OF THIS PHOTO, DON'T YOU?
IT MEANS I KNEW ALL ABOUT YOUR SCAM FROM THE START.
YOU GUYS ARE FAMOUS AMONG JUVENILE DELINQUENTS.
I FIGURED I HAD TO TEACH YOU A LESSON.
SO I SET UP A TRAP WITH ME PLAYING THE VICTIM.

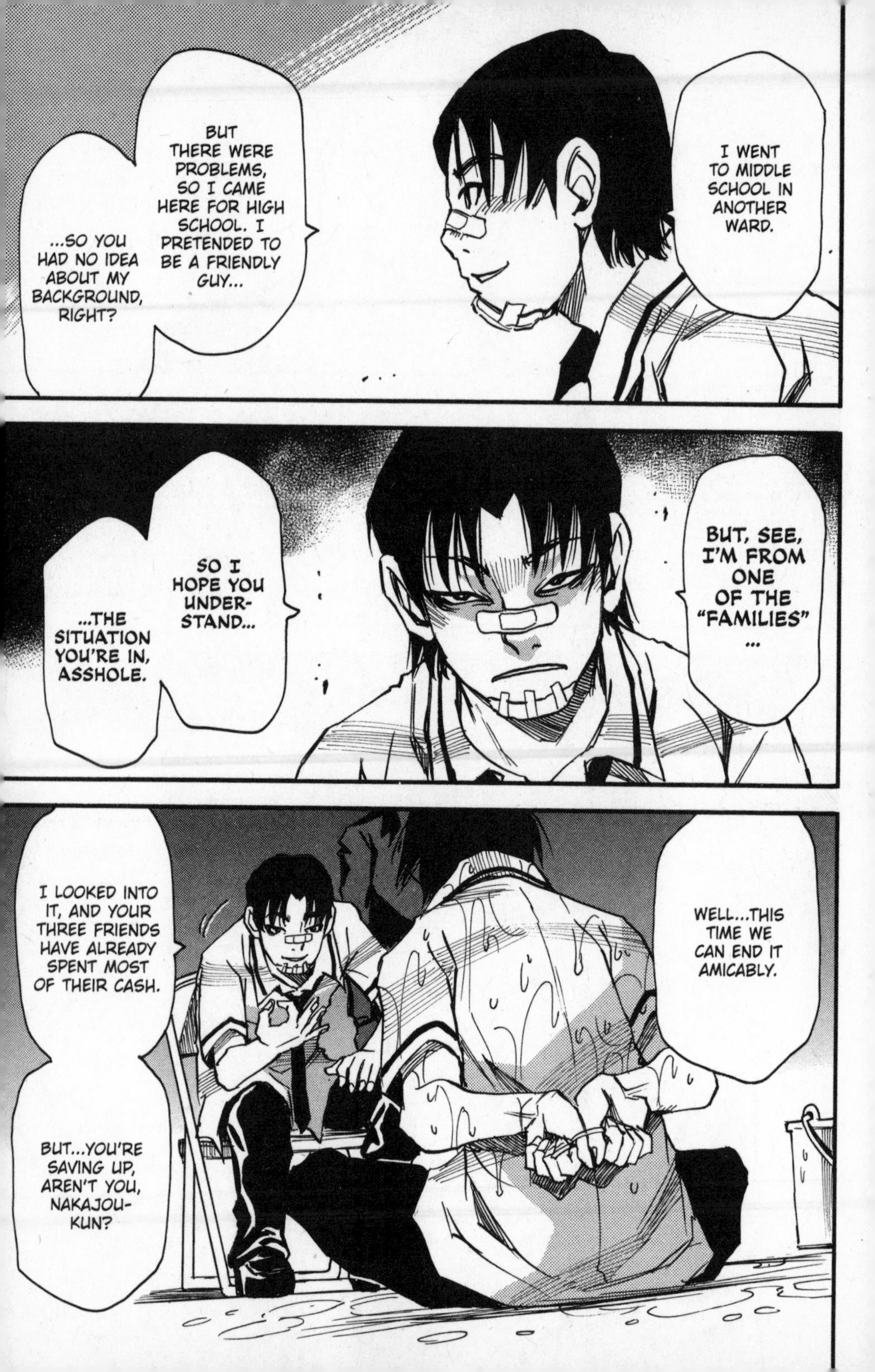
I WENT TO MIDDLE SCHOOL IN ANOTHER WARD.
BUT THERE WERE PROBLEMS, SO I CAME HERE FOR HIGH SCHOOL. I PRETENDED TO BE A FRIENDLY GUY...
...SO YOU HAD NO IDEA ABOUT MY BACKGROUND, RIGHT?
BUT, SEE, I'M FROM ONE OF THE "FAMILIES"...
SO I HOPE YOU UNDERSTAND...
...THE SITUATION YOU'RE IN, ASSHOLE.
WELL...THIS TIME WE CAN END IT AMICABLY.
I LOOKED INTO IT, AND YOUR THREE FRIENDS HAVE ALREADY SPENT MOST OF THEIR CASH.
BUT...YOU'RE SAVING UP, AREN'T YOU, NAKAJOU-KUN?

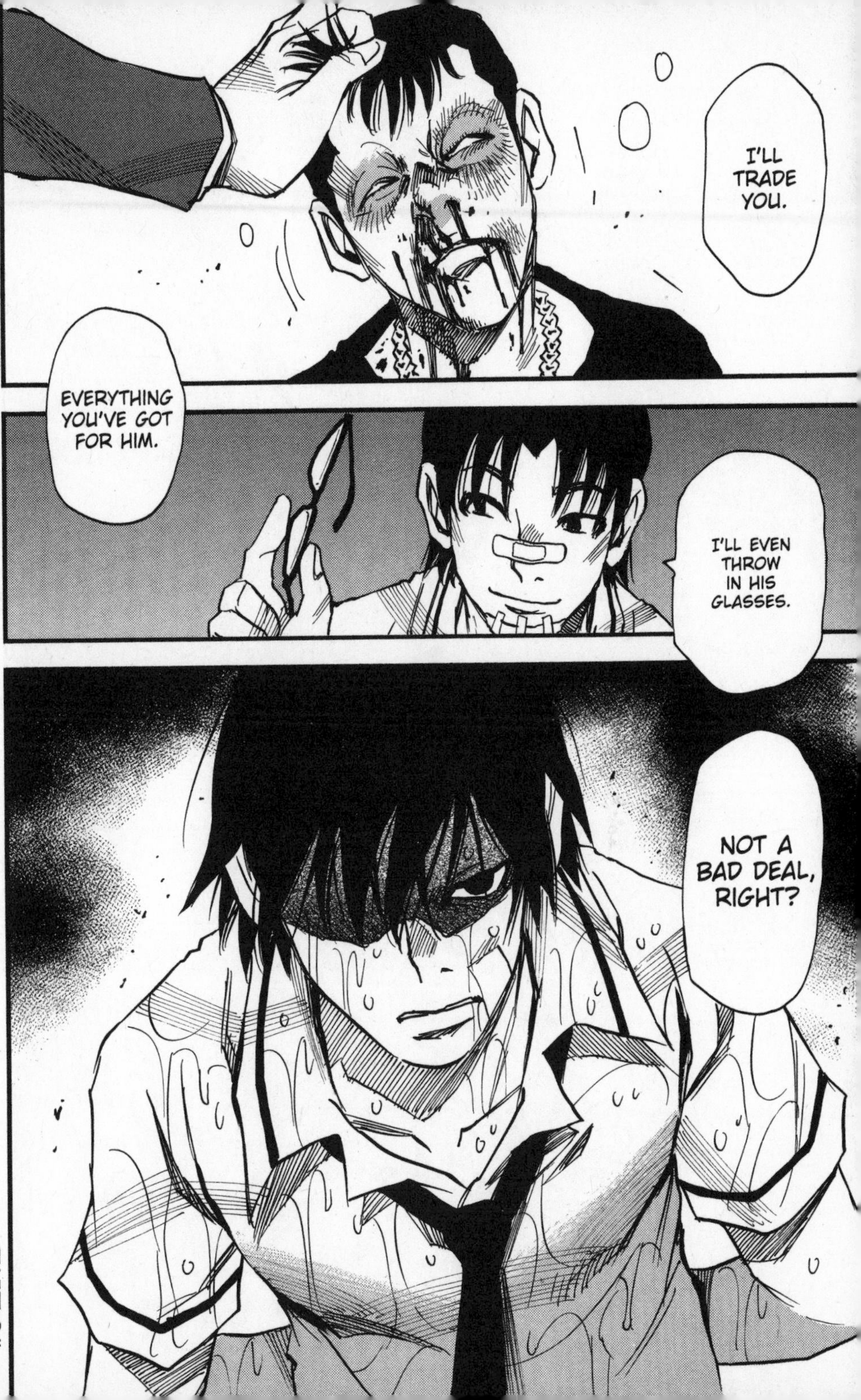
I'LL TRADE YOU.
EVERYTHING YOU'VE GOT FOR HIM.
I'LL EVEN THROW IN HIS GLASSES.
NOT A BAD DEAL, RIGHT?

#6 END

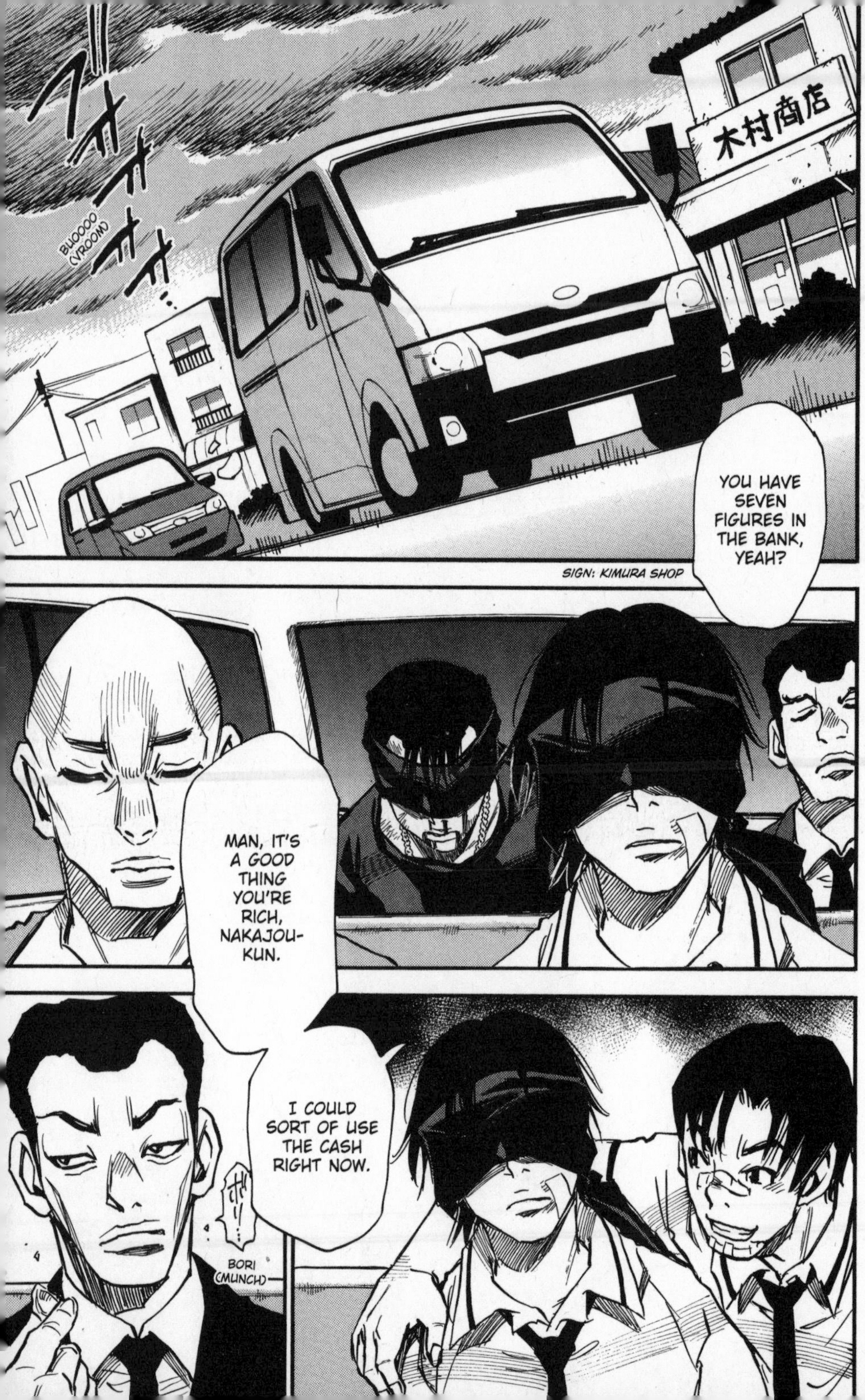
木村商店
BUOOOO (VROOM)
YOU HAVE SEVEN FIGURES IN THE BANK, YEAH?
SIGN: KIMURA SHOP
MAN, IT'S A GOOD THING YOU'RE RICH, NAKAJOU-KUN.
I COULD SORT OF USE THE CASH RIGHT NOW.
BORI (MUNCH)

#7 Tainted Weapon

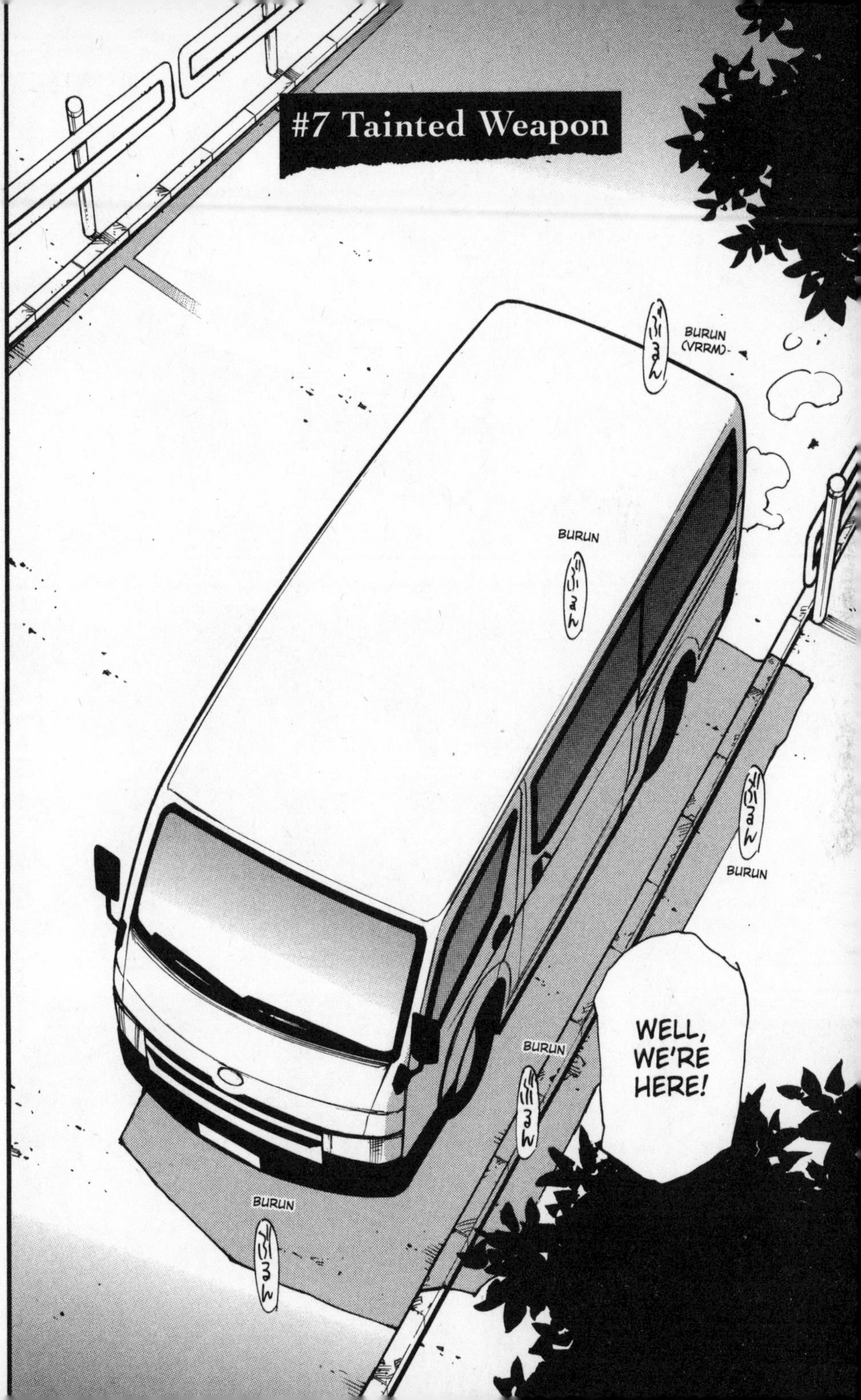
ぶるん
BURUN (VRRM)-
ぶるん
BURUN
ぶるん
BURUN
WELL, WE'RE HERE!
BURUN
ぶるん
BURUN
ぶるん

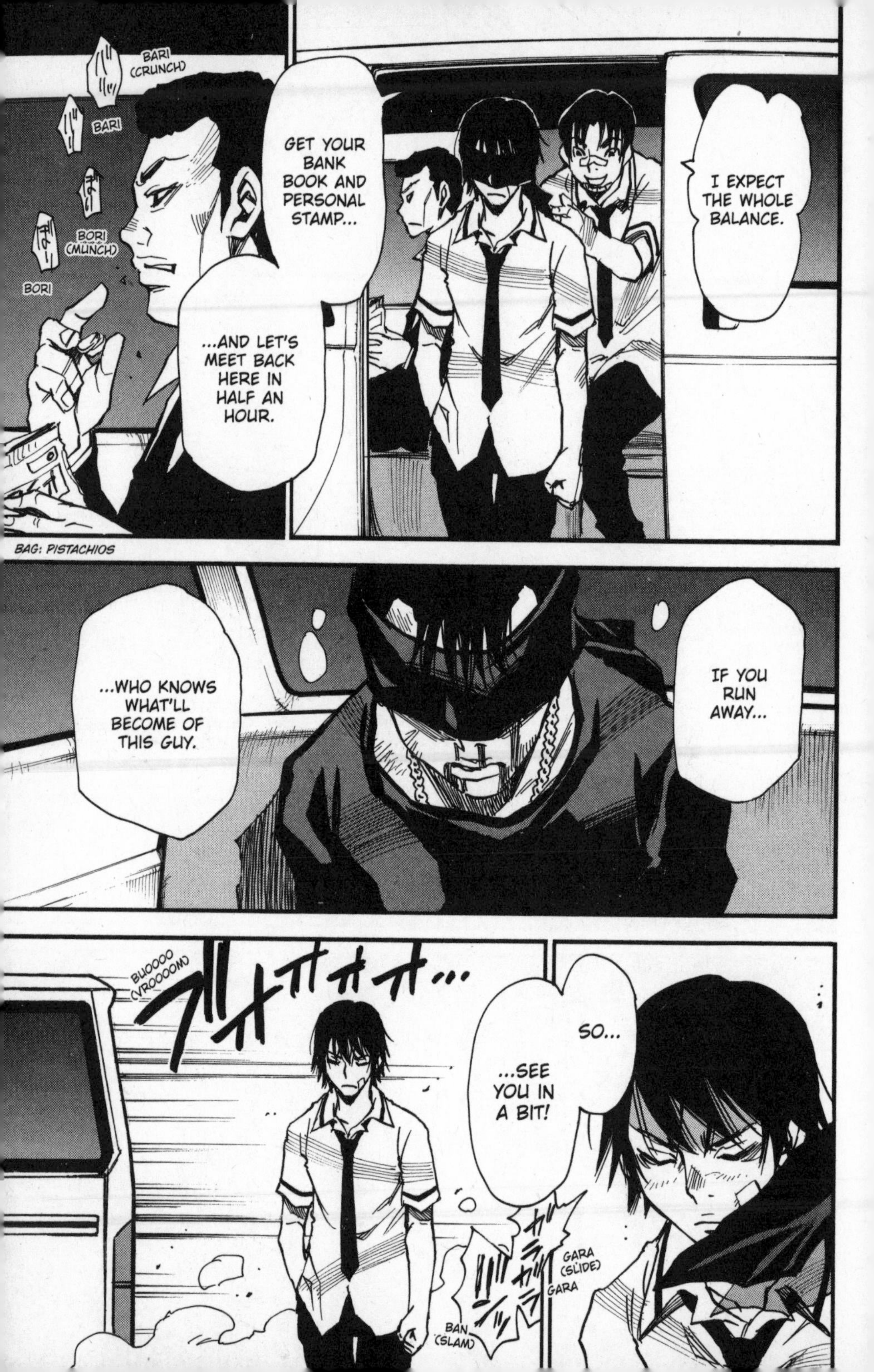
I EXPECT THE WHOLE BALANCE.
GET YOUR BANK BOOK AND PERSONAL STAMP...
...AND LET'S MEET BACK HERE IN HALF AN HOUR.
BARI (CRUNCH)
BARI
BORI (MUNCH)
BORI
BAG: PISTACHIOS
IF YOU RUN AWAY...
...WHO KNOWS WHAT'LL BECOME OF THIS GUY.
SO...
...SEE YOU IN A BIT!
GARA (SLIDE)
GARA
BAN (SLAM)
BUOOOO (VROOOOM)

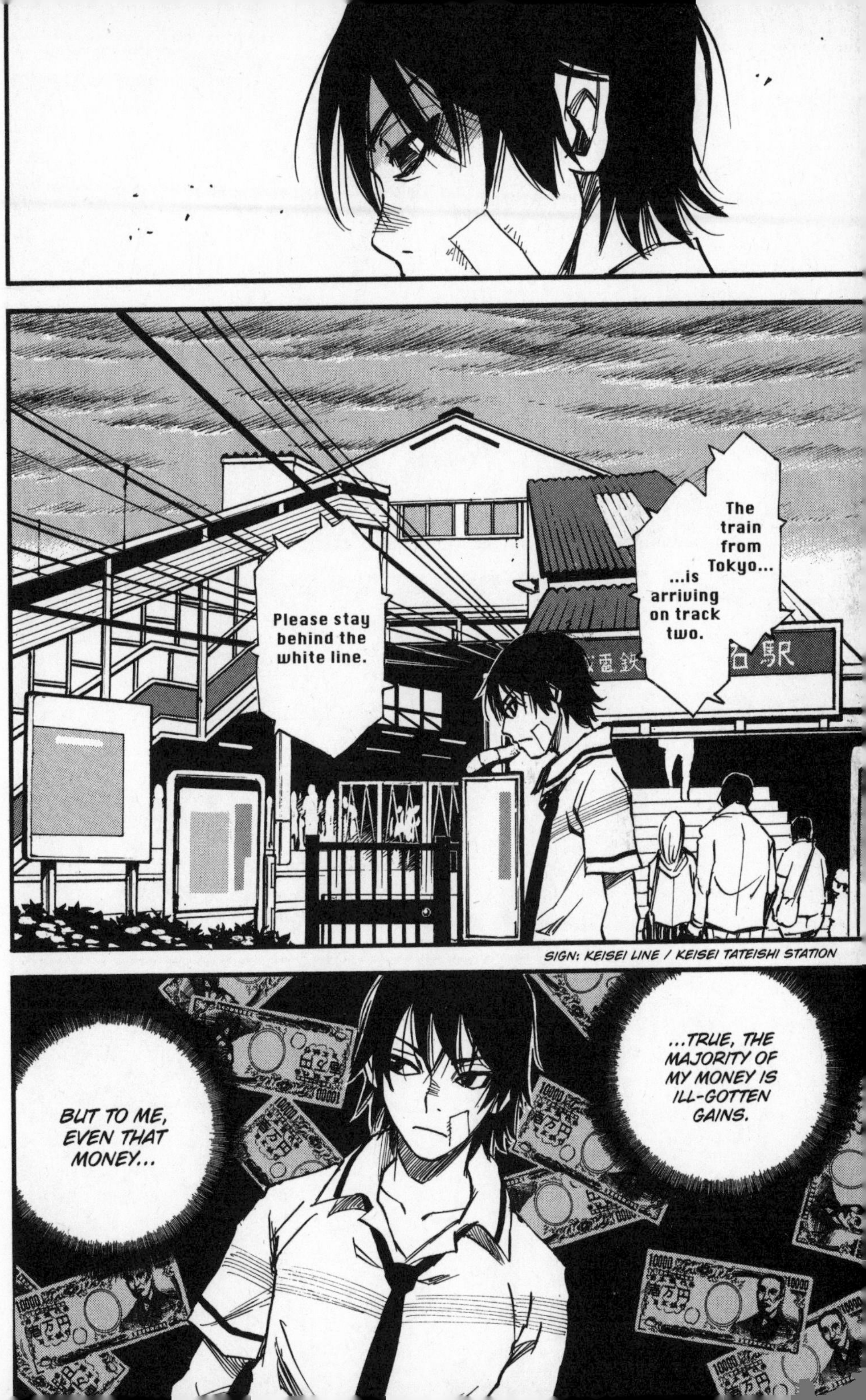
The train from Tokyo...
...is arriving on track two.
Please stay behind the white line.
SIGN: KEISEI LINE / KEISEI TATEISHI STATION
...TRUE, THE MAJORITY OF MY MONEY IS ILL-GOTTEN GAINS.
BUT TO ME, EVEN THAT MONEY...

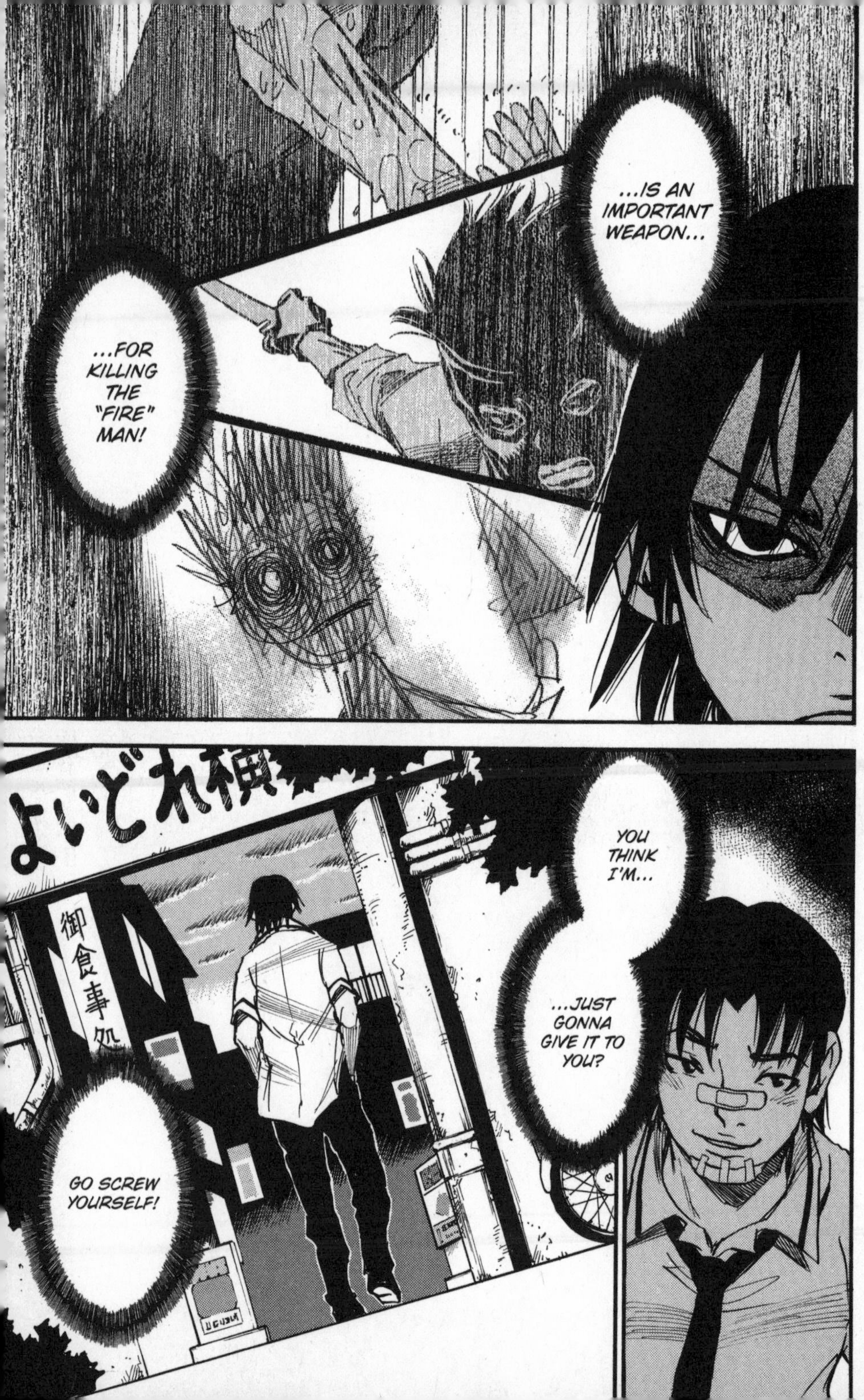
...IS AN IMPORTANT WEAPON...
...FOR KILLING THE "FIRE" MAN!
YOU THINK I'M...
...JUST GONNA GIVE IT TO YOU?
よいどれ横
御食事処
GO SCREW YOURSELF!

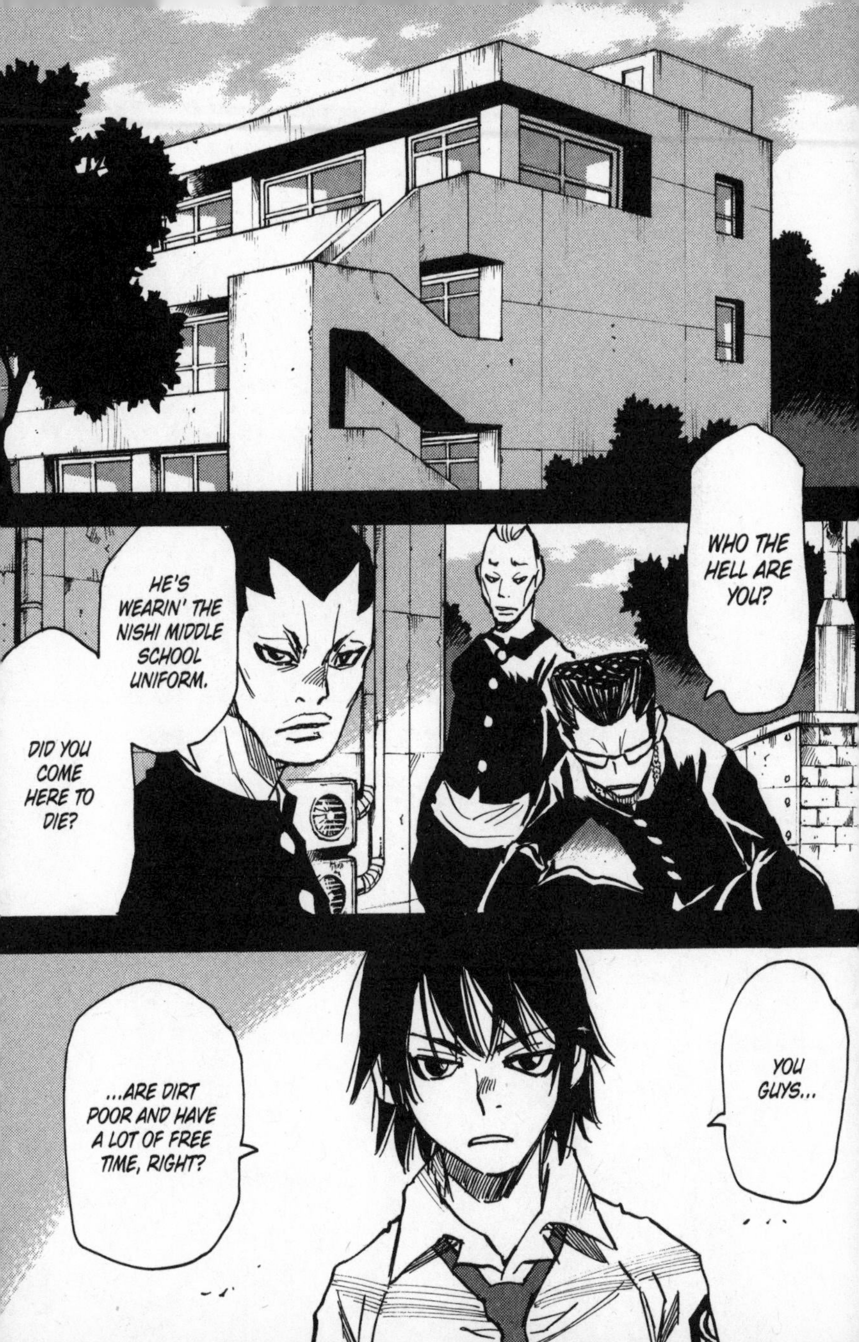
WHO THE HELL ARE YOU?
HE'S WEARIN' THE NISHI MIDDLE SCHOOL UNIFORM.
DID YOU COME HERE TO DIE?
YOU GUYS...
...ARE DIRT POOR AND HAVE A LOT OF FREE TIME, RIGHT?

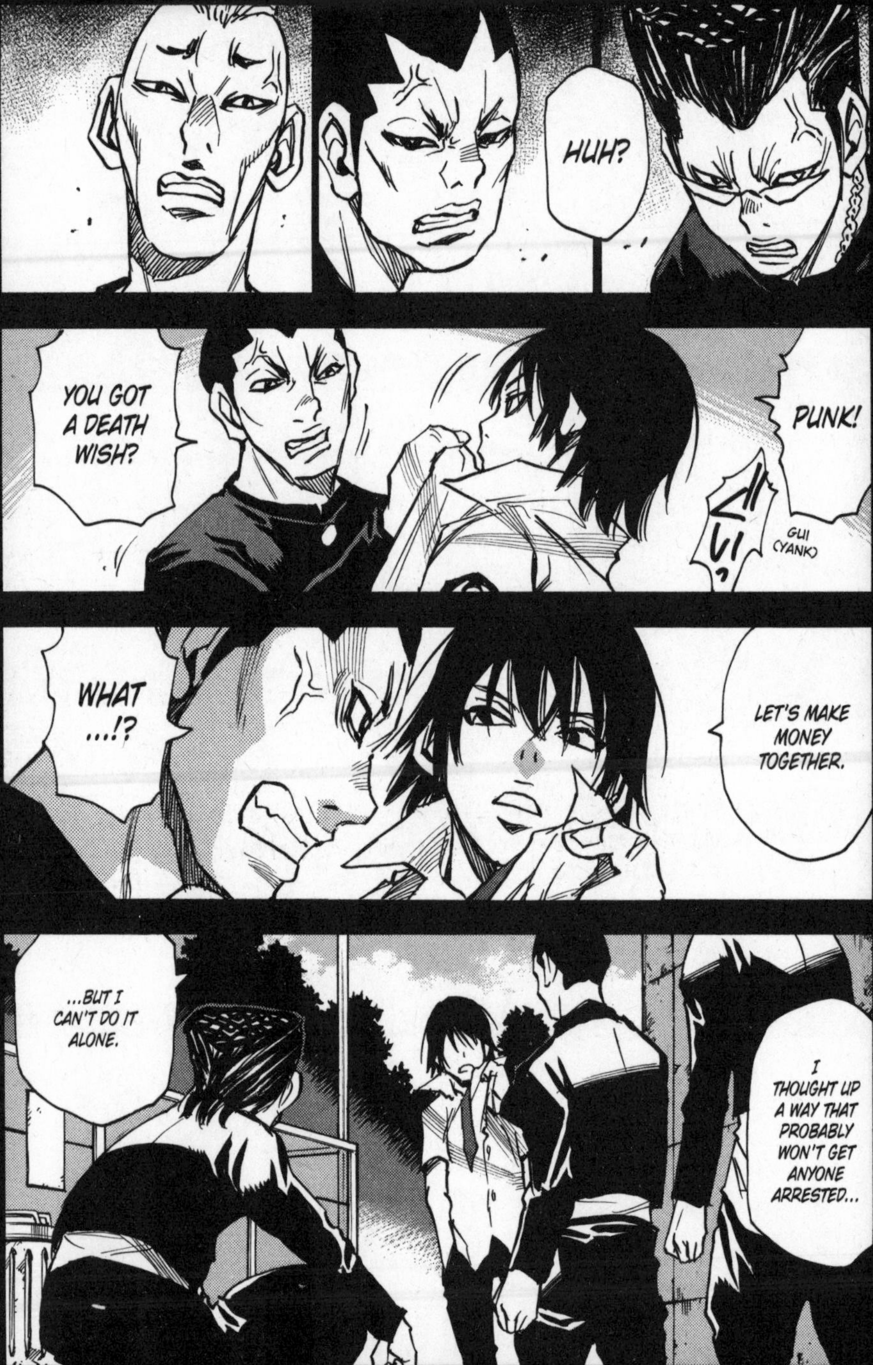
HUH?
PUNK!
GUI (YANK)
YOU GOT A DEATH WISH?
LET'S MAKE MONEY TOGETHER.
WHAT ...!?
I THOUGHT UP A WAY THAT PROBABLY WON'T GET ANYONE ARRESTED...
...BUT I CAN'T DO IT ALONE.

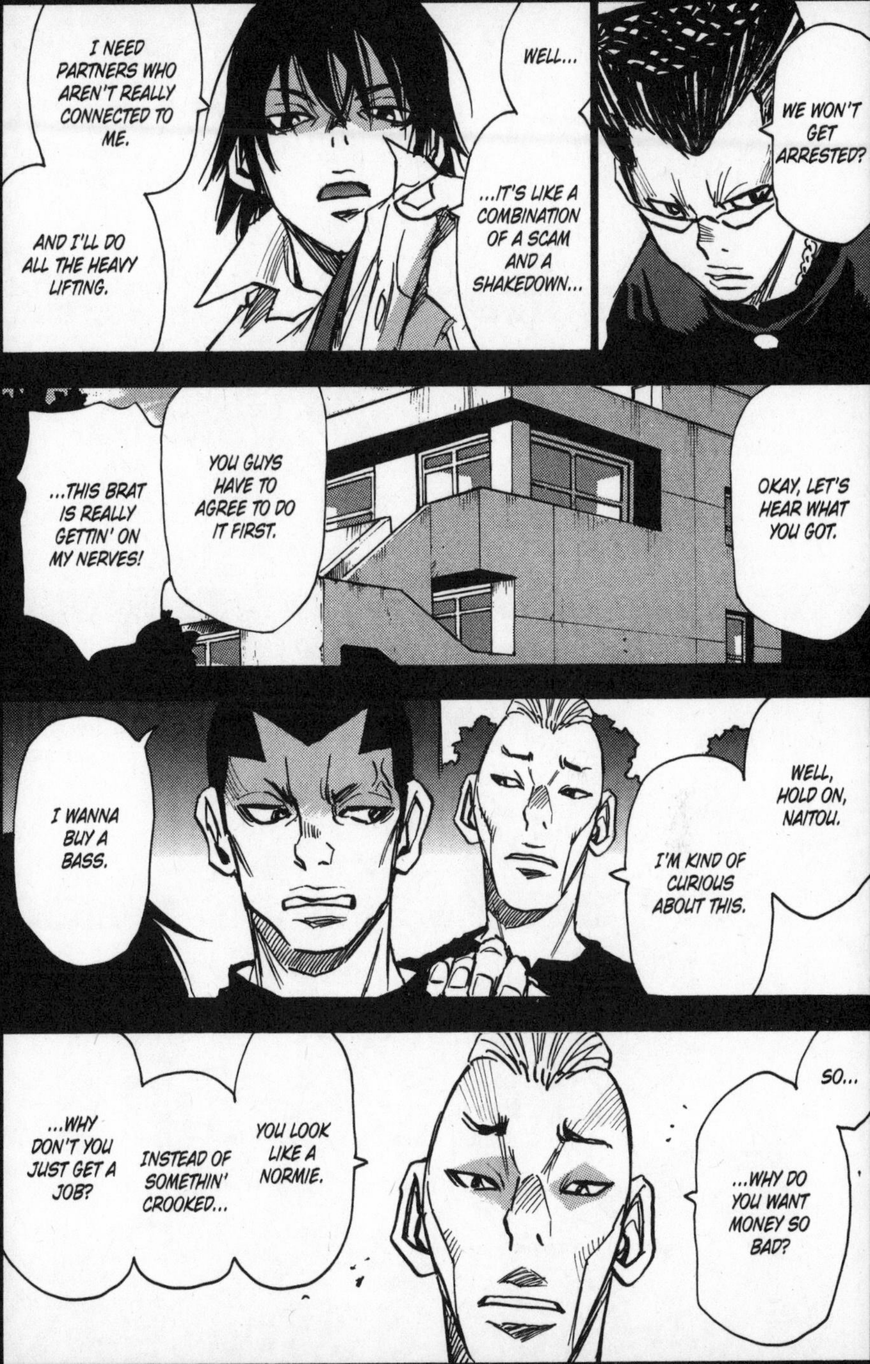
WE WON'T GET ARRESTED?
WELL...
...IT'S LIKE A COMBINATION OF A SCAM AND A SHAKEDOWN...
I NEED PARTNERS WHO AREN'T REALLY CONNECTED TO ME.
AND I'LL DO ALL THE HEAVY LIFTING.
OKAY, LET'S HEAR WHAT YOU GOT.
YOU GUYS HAVE TO AGREE TO DO IT FIRST.
...THIS BRAT IS REALLY GETTIN' ON MY NERVES!
WELL, HOLD ON, NAITOU.
I'M KIND OF CURIOUS ABOUT THIS.
I WANNA BUY A BASS.
SO...
...WHY DO YOU WANT MONEY SO BAD?
YOU LOOK LIKE A NORMIE.
INSTEAD OF SOMETHIN' CROOKED...
...WHY DON'T YOU JUST GET A JOB?

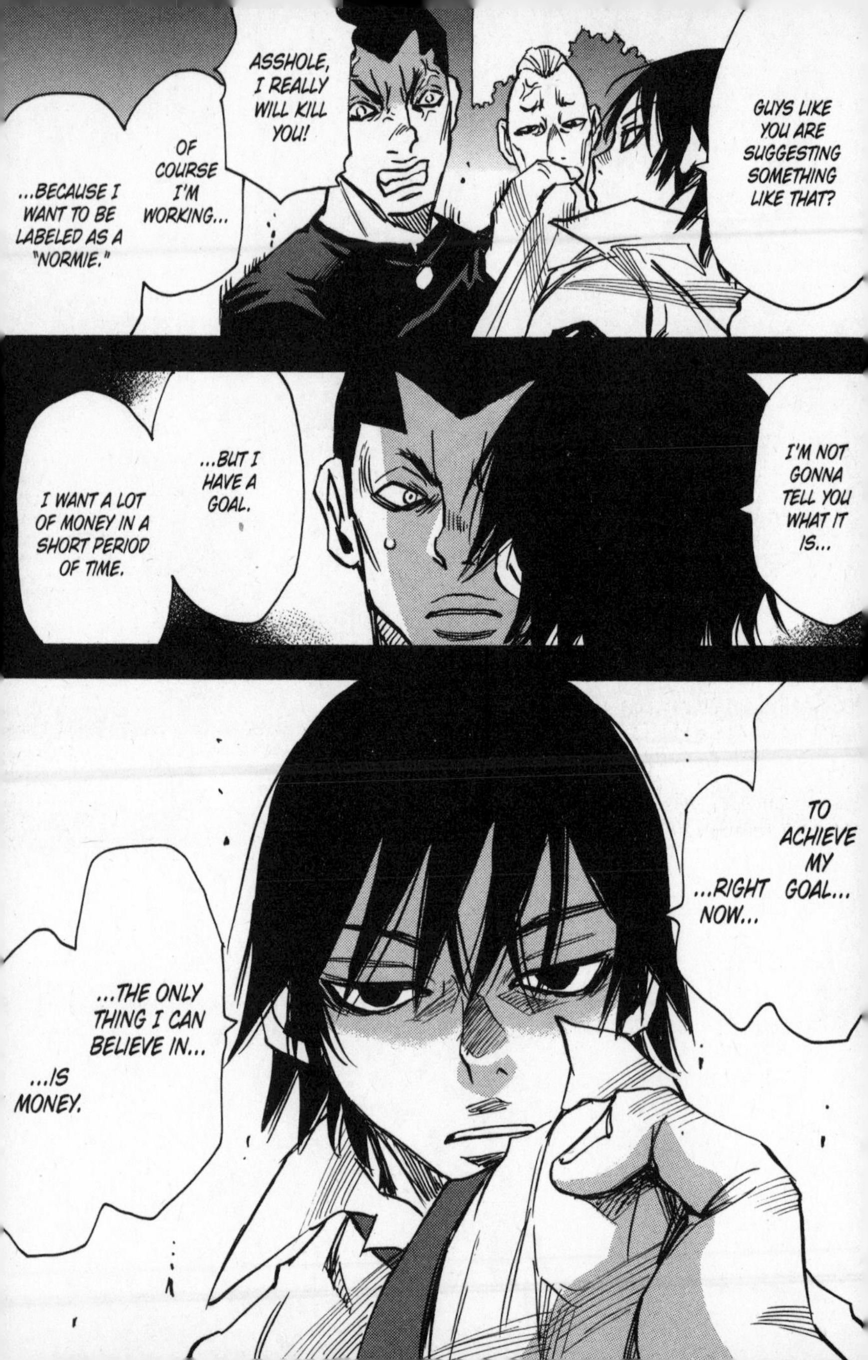
GUYS LIKE YOU ARE SUGGESTING SOMETHING LIKE THAT?
ASSHOLE, I REALLY WILL KILL YOU!
OF COURSE I'M WORKING...
...BECAUSE I WANT TO BE LABELED AS A "NORMIE."
I'M NOT GONNA TELL YOU WHAT IT IS...
...BUT I HAVE A GOAL.
I WANT A LOT OF MONEY IN A SHORT PERIOD OF TIME.
TO ACHIEVE MY GOAL...
...RIGHT NOW...
...THE ONLY THING I CAN BELIEVE IN...
...IS MONEY.

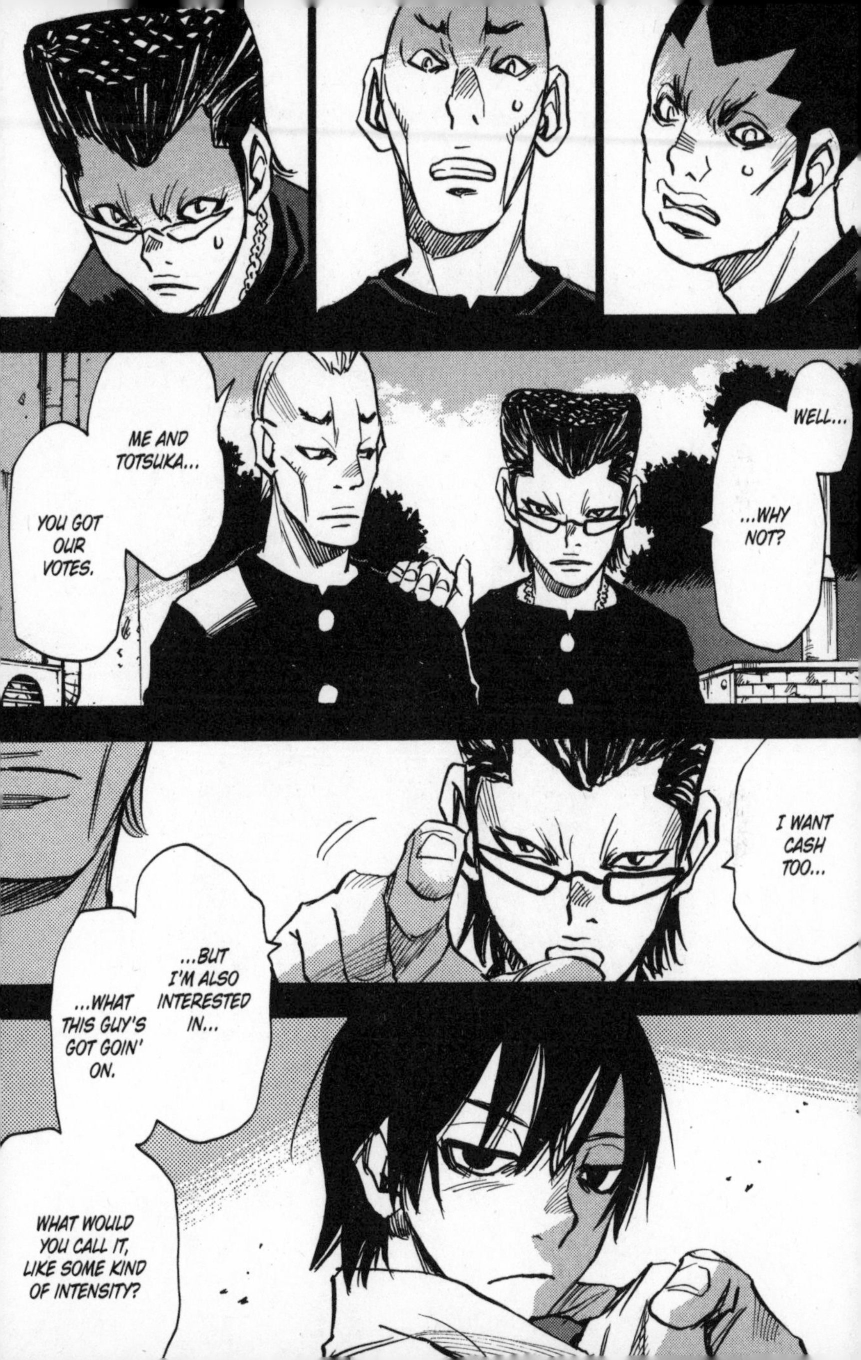
WELL... ...WHY NOT?
ME AND TOTSUKA... YOU GOT OUR VOTES.
I WANT CASH TOO...
...BUT I'M ALSO INTERESTED IN...
...WHAT THIS GUY'S GOT GOIN' ON.
WHAT WOULD YOU CALL IT, LIKE SOME KIND OF INTENSITY?

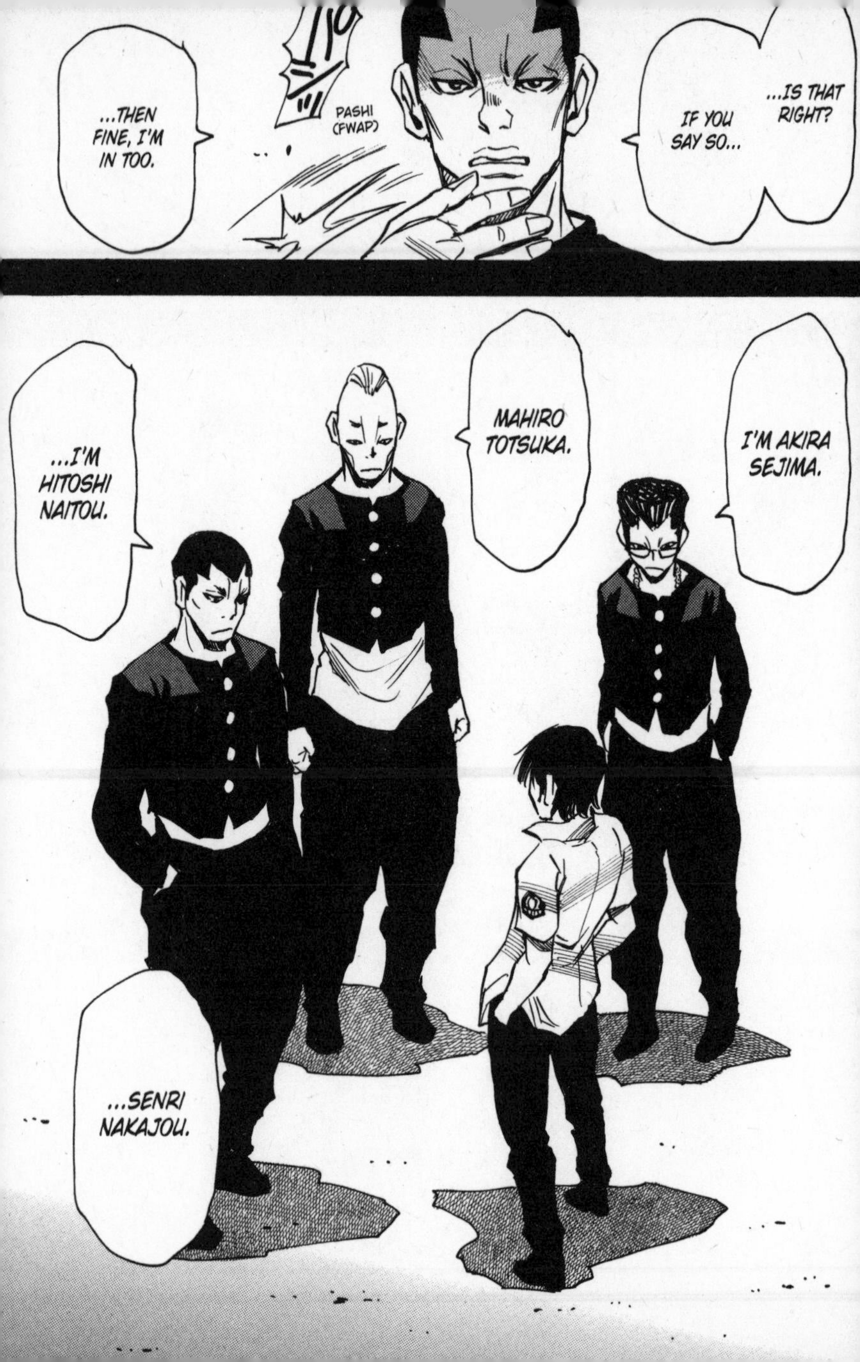
...IS THAT RIGHT?
IF YOU SAY SO...
PASHI (FWAP)
...THEN FINE, I'M IN TOO.
I'M AKIRA SEJIMA.
MAHIRO TOTSUKA.
...I'M HITOSHI NAITOU.
...SENRI NAKAJOU.

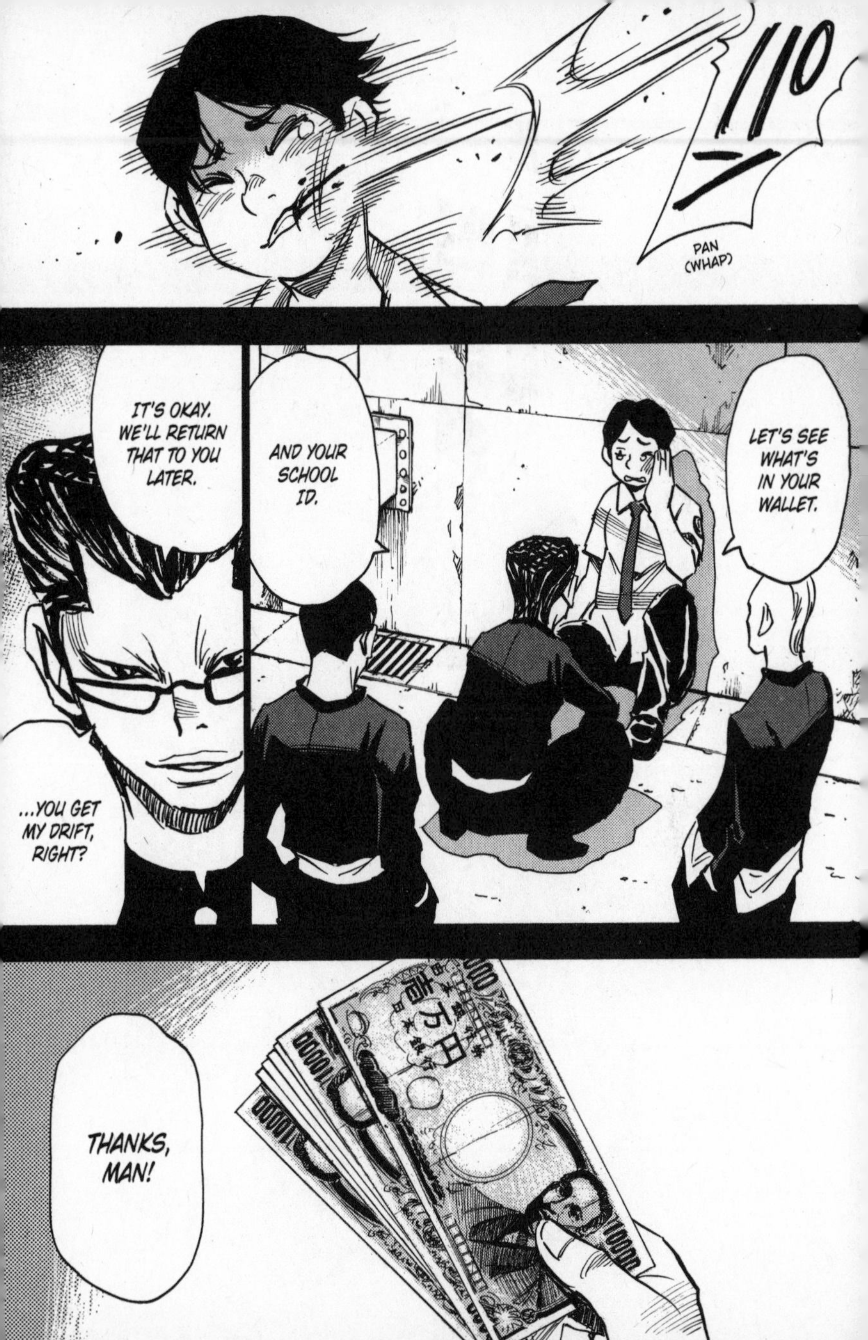
PAN
(WHAP)
LET'S SEE WHAT'S IN YOUR WALLET.
AND YOUR SCHOOL ID.
IT'S OKAY. WE'LL RETURN THAT TO YOU LATER.
...YOU GET MY DRIFT, RIGHT?
THANKS, MAN!

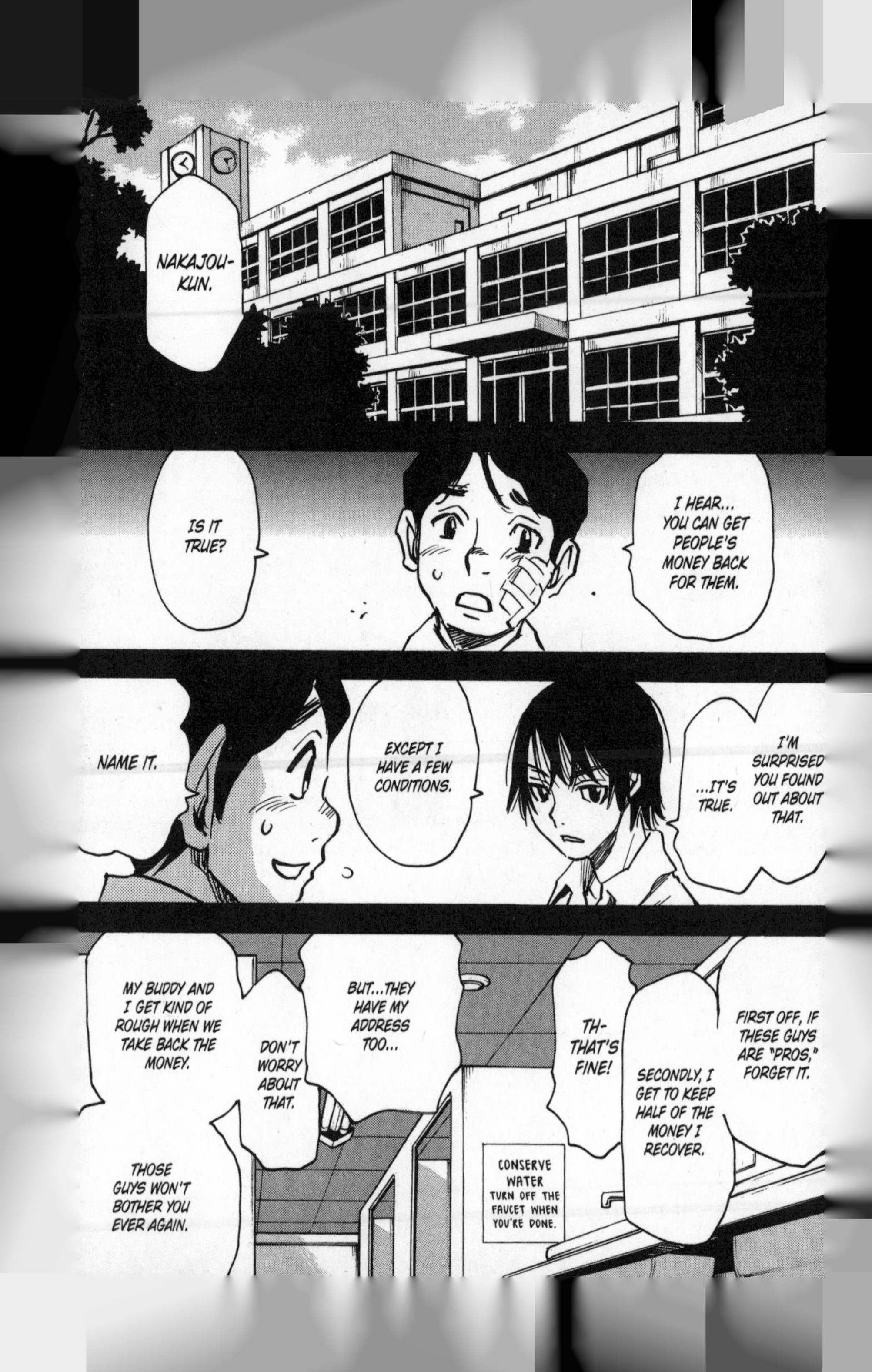
NAKAJOU-KUN.
I HEAR... YOU CAN GET PEOPLE'S MONEY BACK FOR THEM.
IS IT TRUE?
I'M SURPRISED YOU FOUND OUT ABOUT THAT.
...IT'S TRUE.
EXCEPT I HAVE A FEW CONDITIONS.
NAME IT.
FIRST OFF, IF THESE GUYS ARE "PROS," FORGET IT.
SECONDLY, I GET TO KEEP HALF OF THE MONEY I RECOVER.
TH-THAT'S FINE!
CONSERVE WATER
TURN OFF THE FAUCET WHEN YOU'RE DONE.
BUT...THEY HAVE MY ADDRESS TOO...
DON'T WORRY ABOUT THAT.
MY BUDDY AND I GET KIND OF ROUGH WHEN WE TAKE BACK THE MONEY.
THOSE GUYS WON'T BOTHER YOU EVER AGAIN.

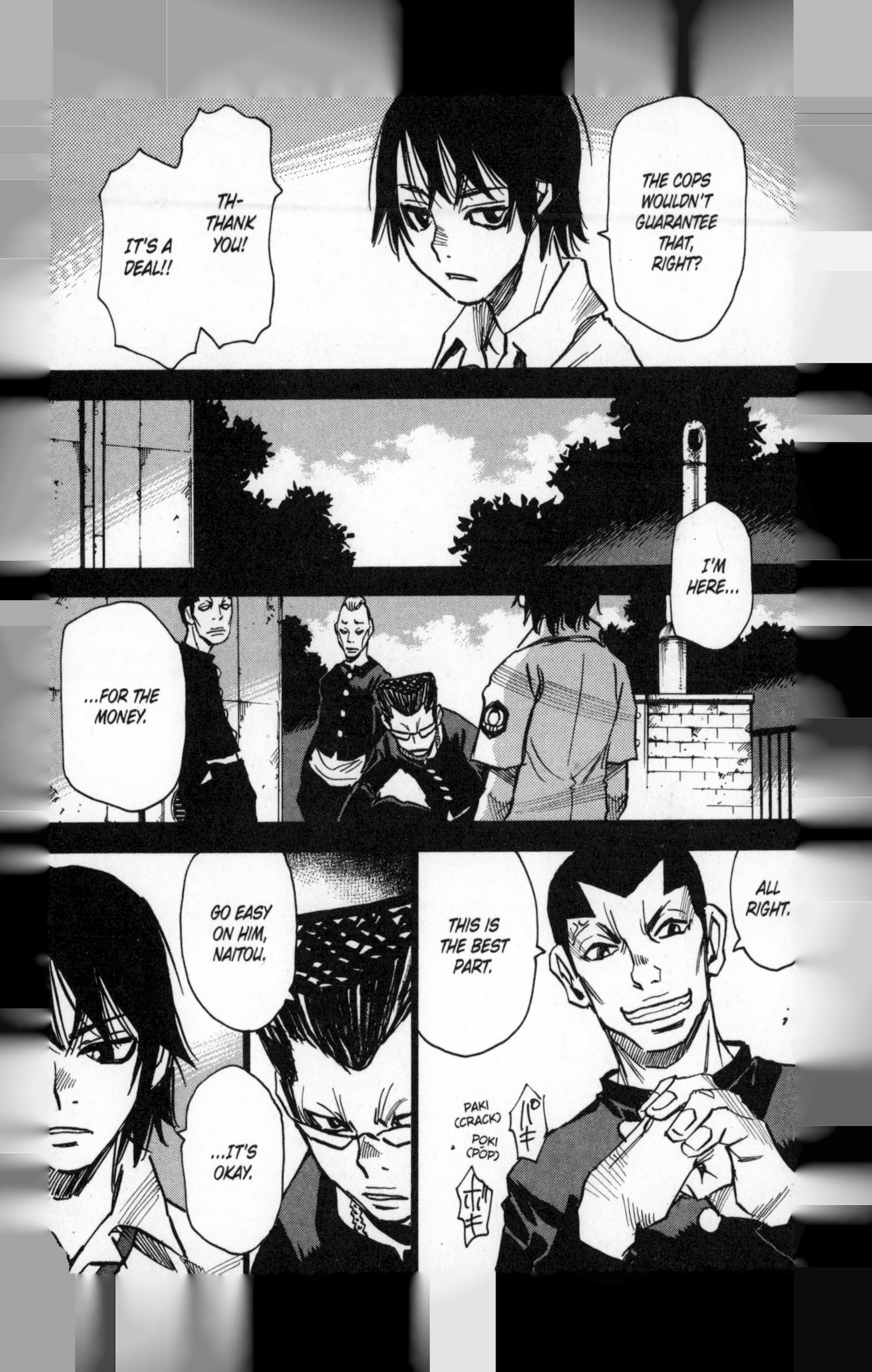
THE COPS WOULDN'T GUARANTEE THAT, RIGHT?
TH- THANK YOU!
IT'S A DEAL!!
I'M HERE...
...FOR THE MONEY.
ALL RIGHT.
THIS IS THE BEST PART.
パキ
PAKI (CRACK)
ポキ
POKI (POP)
GO EASY ON HIM, NAITOU.
...IT'S OKAY.

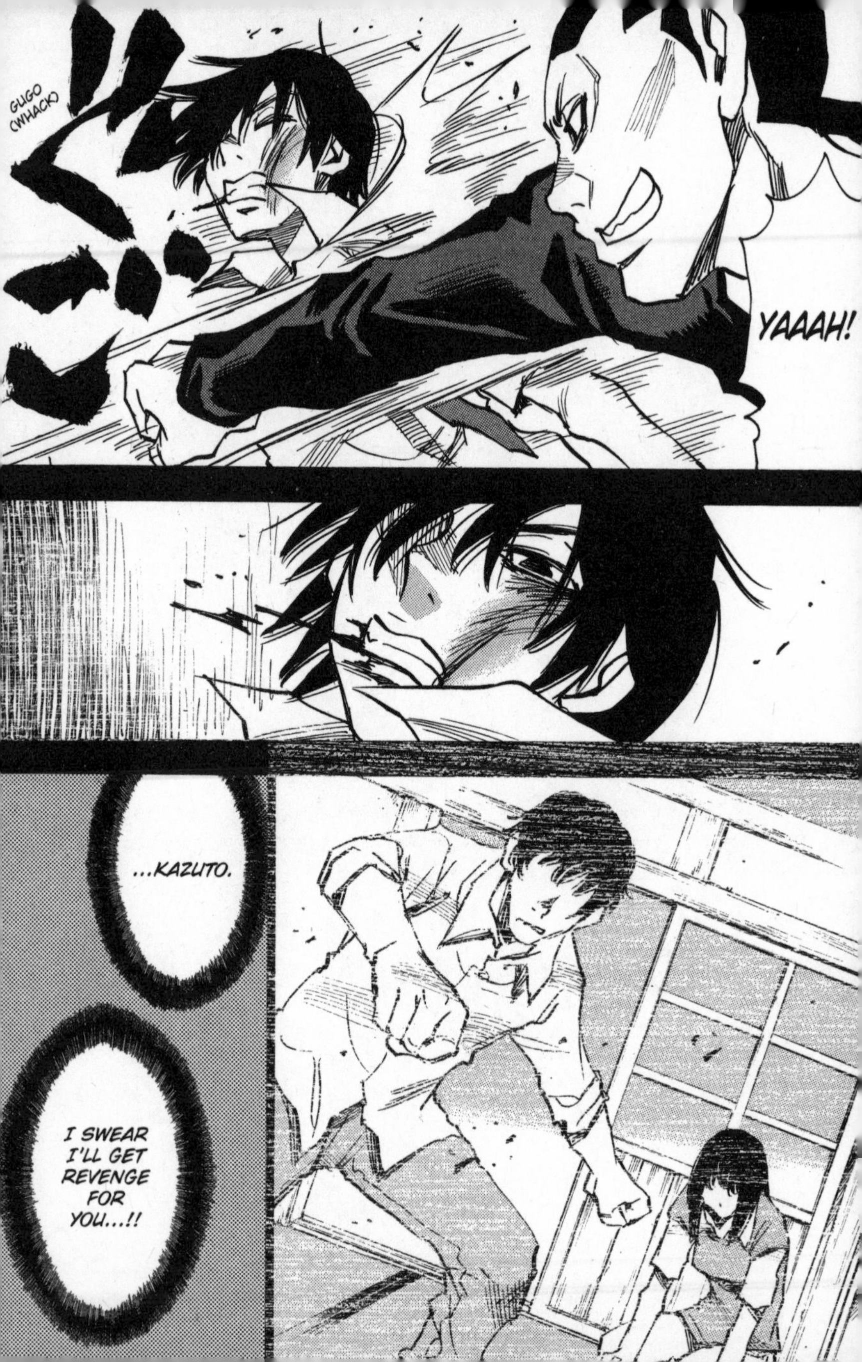
YAAAH!
GUGO (WHACK)
...KAZUTO.
I SWEAR I'LL GET REVENGE FOR YOU...!!

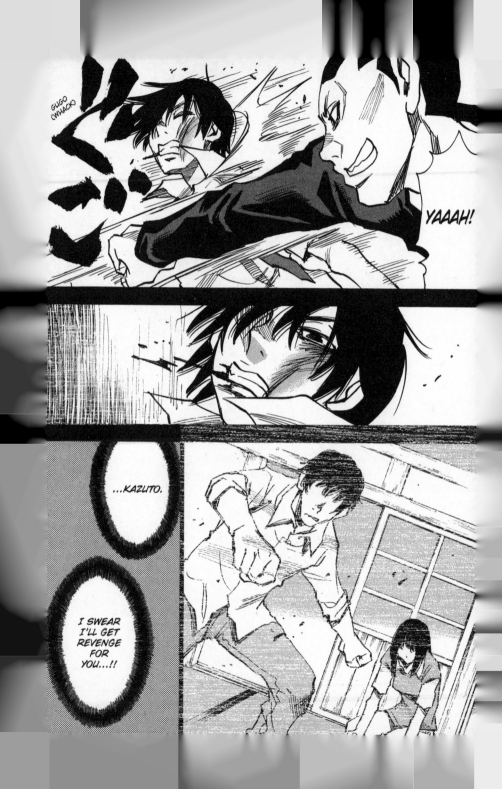

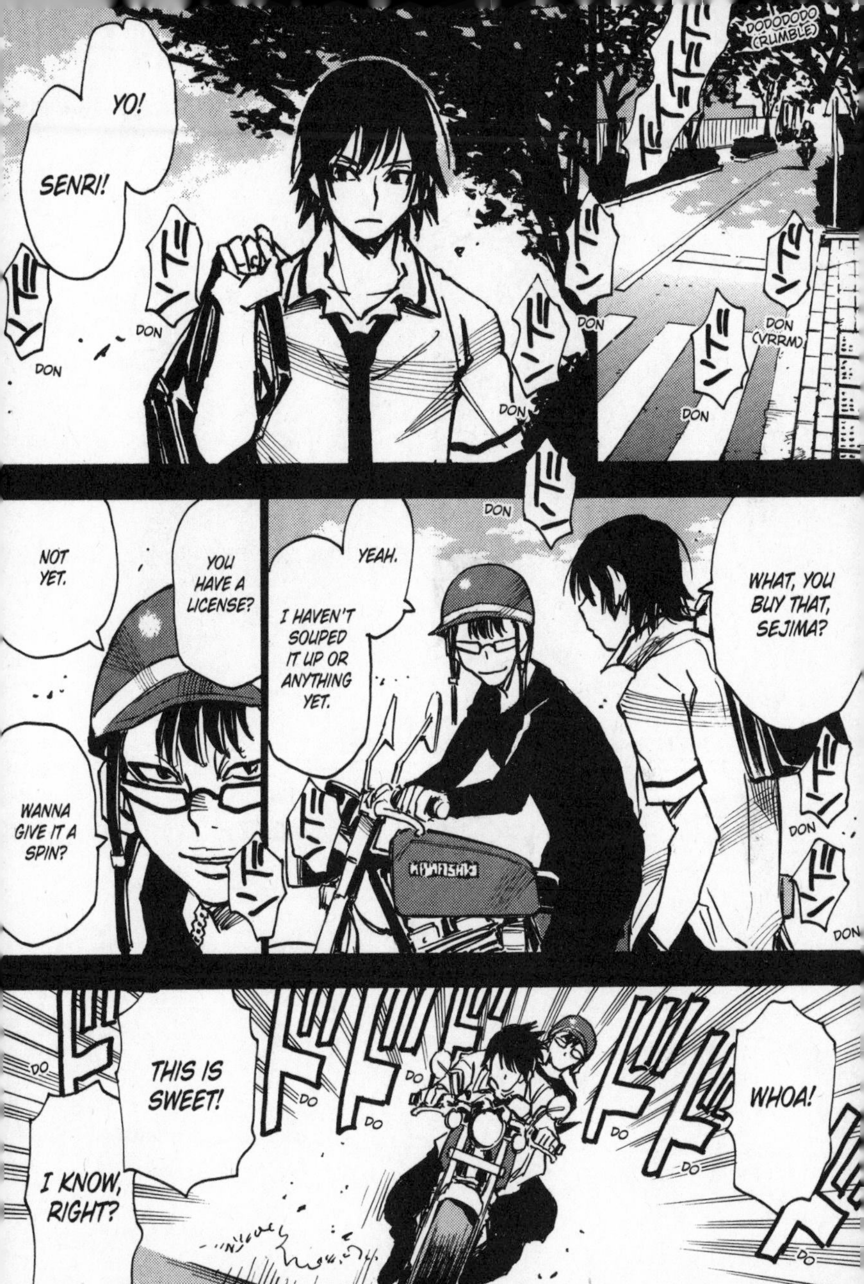
DODODODO (RUMBLE)
DON
DON (VRRM)
DON
DON
YO! SENRI!
DON
DON
DON
WHAT, YOU BUY THAT, SEJIMA?
DON
YEAH.
I HAVEN'T SOUPED IT UP OR ANYTHING YET.
DON
DON
YOU HAVE A LICENSE?
NOT YET.
WANNA GIVE IT A SPIN?
DO
WHOA!
DO
DO
DO
DO
THIS IS SWEET!
I KNOW, RIGHT?
DO

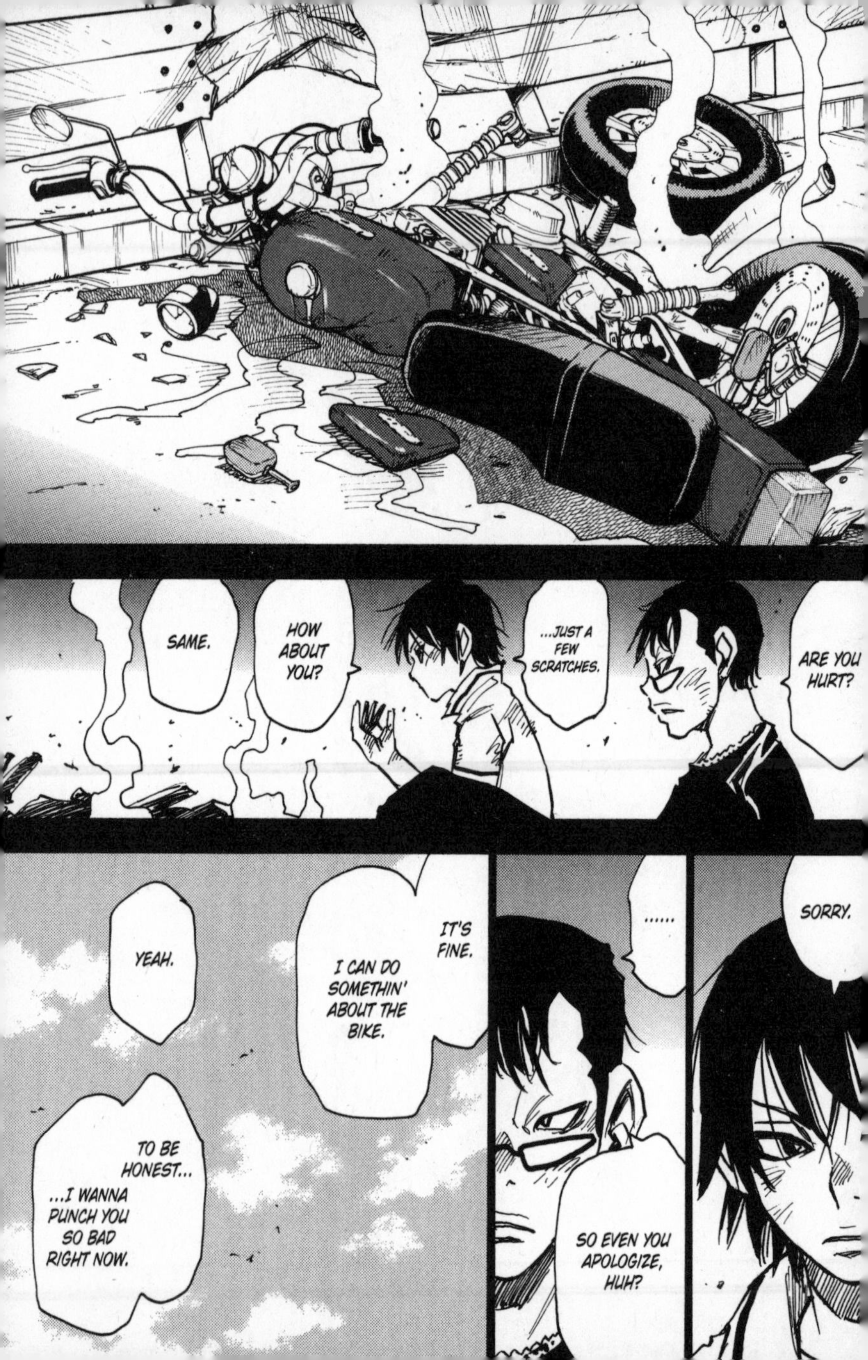
ARE YOU HURT?
...JUST A FEW SCRATCHES.
HOW ABOUT YOU?
SAME.
SORRY.
......
SO EVEN YOU APOLOGIZE, HUH?
IT'S FINE.
I CAN DO SOMETHIN' ABOUT THE BIKE.
YEAH.
TO BE HONEST...
...I WANNA PUNCH YOU SO BAD RIGHT NOW.

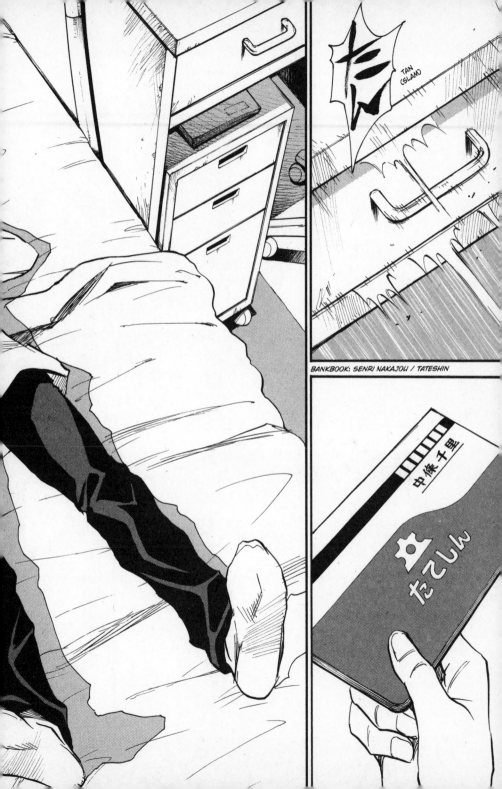

TAN
(SLAM)

BANKBOOK: SENRI NAKAJOU / TATESHIN

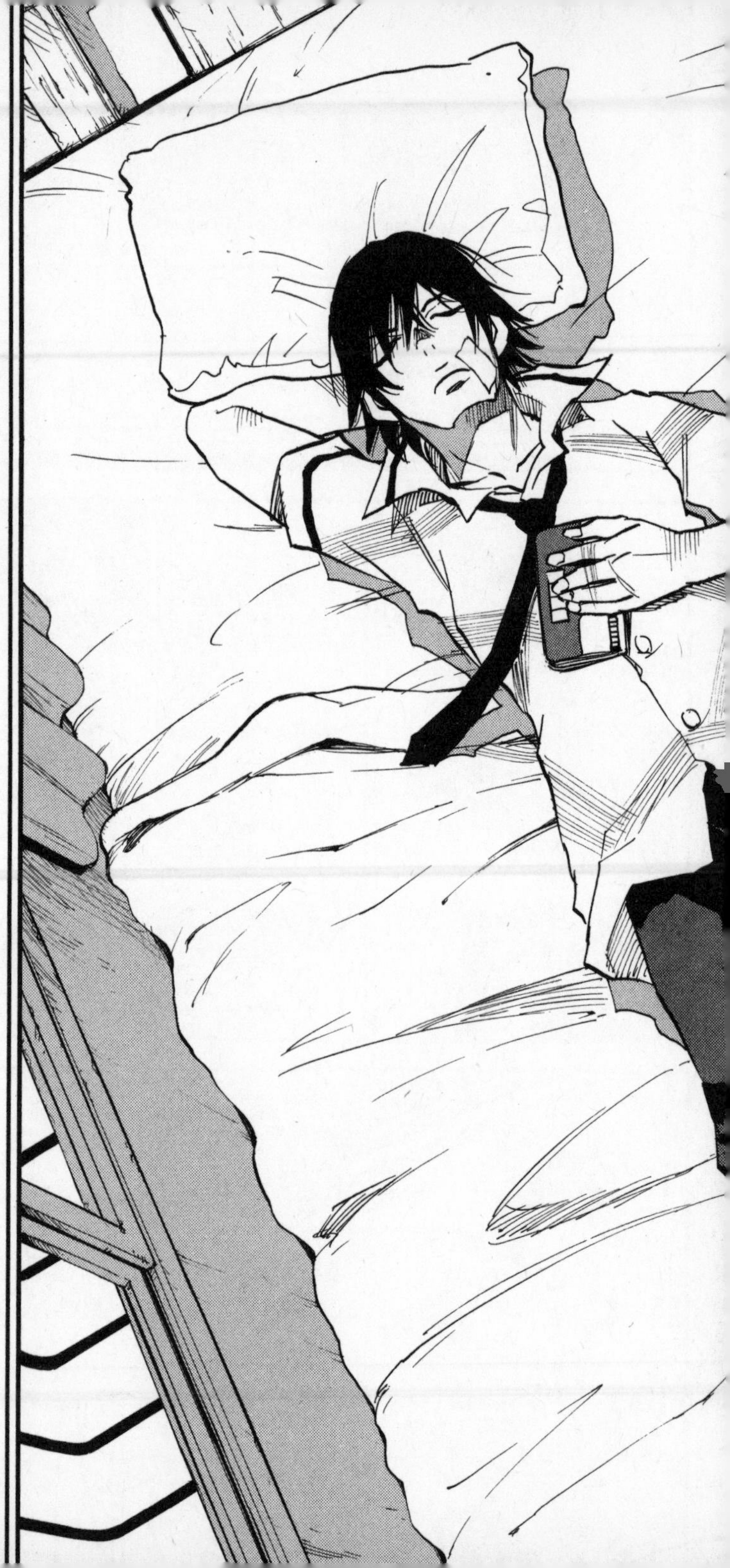

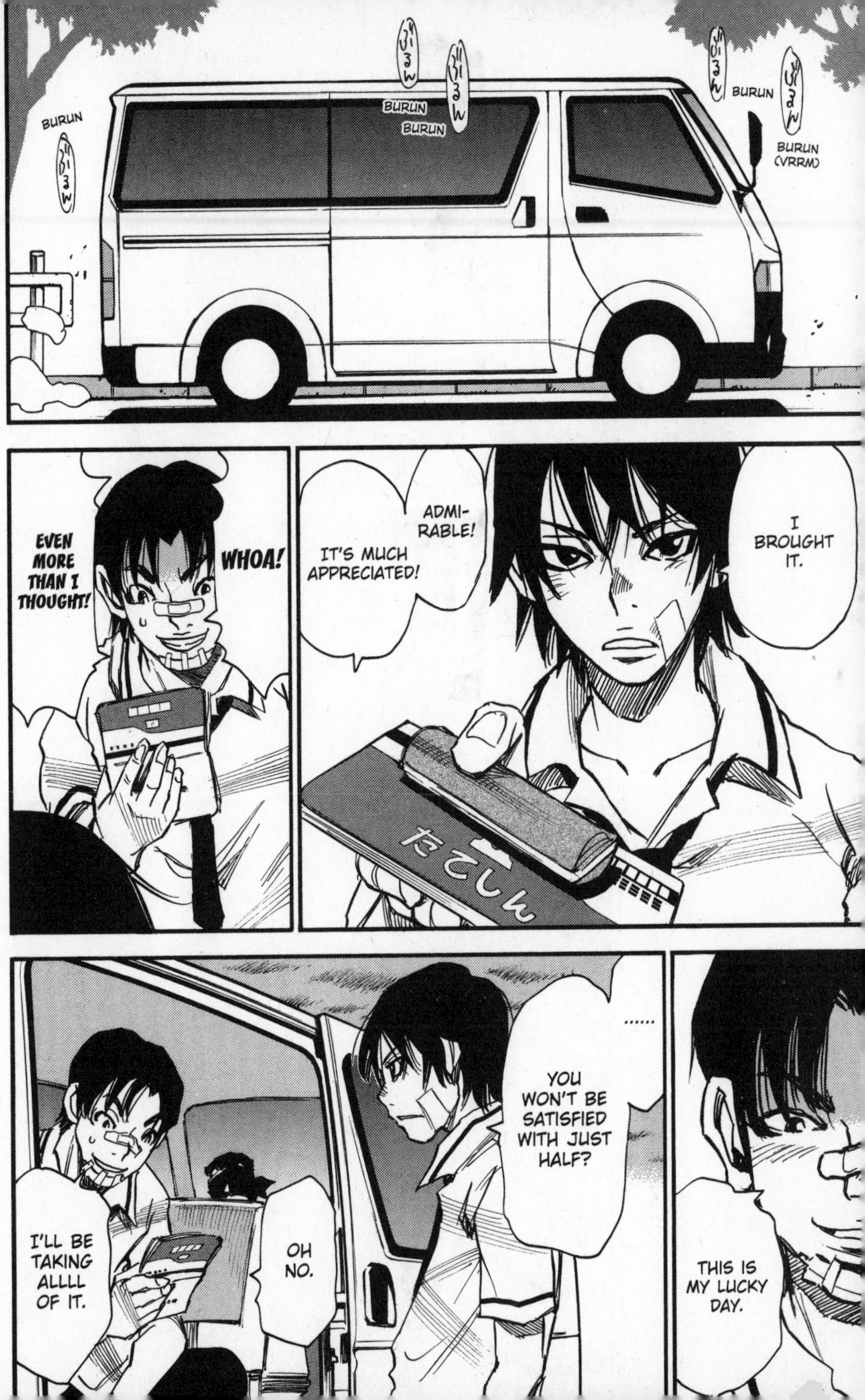
BURUN (VRRM)
BURUN
BURUN
BURUN
BURUN
I BROUGHT IT.
ADMIRABLE!
IT'S MUCH APPRECIATED!
WHOA!
EVEN MORE THAN I THOUGHT!
THIS IS MY LUCKY DAY.
......
YOU WON'T BE SATISFIED WITH JUST HALF?
OH NO.
I'LL BE TAKING ALLLL OF IT.

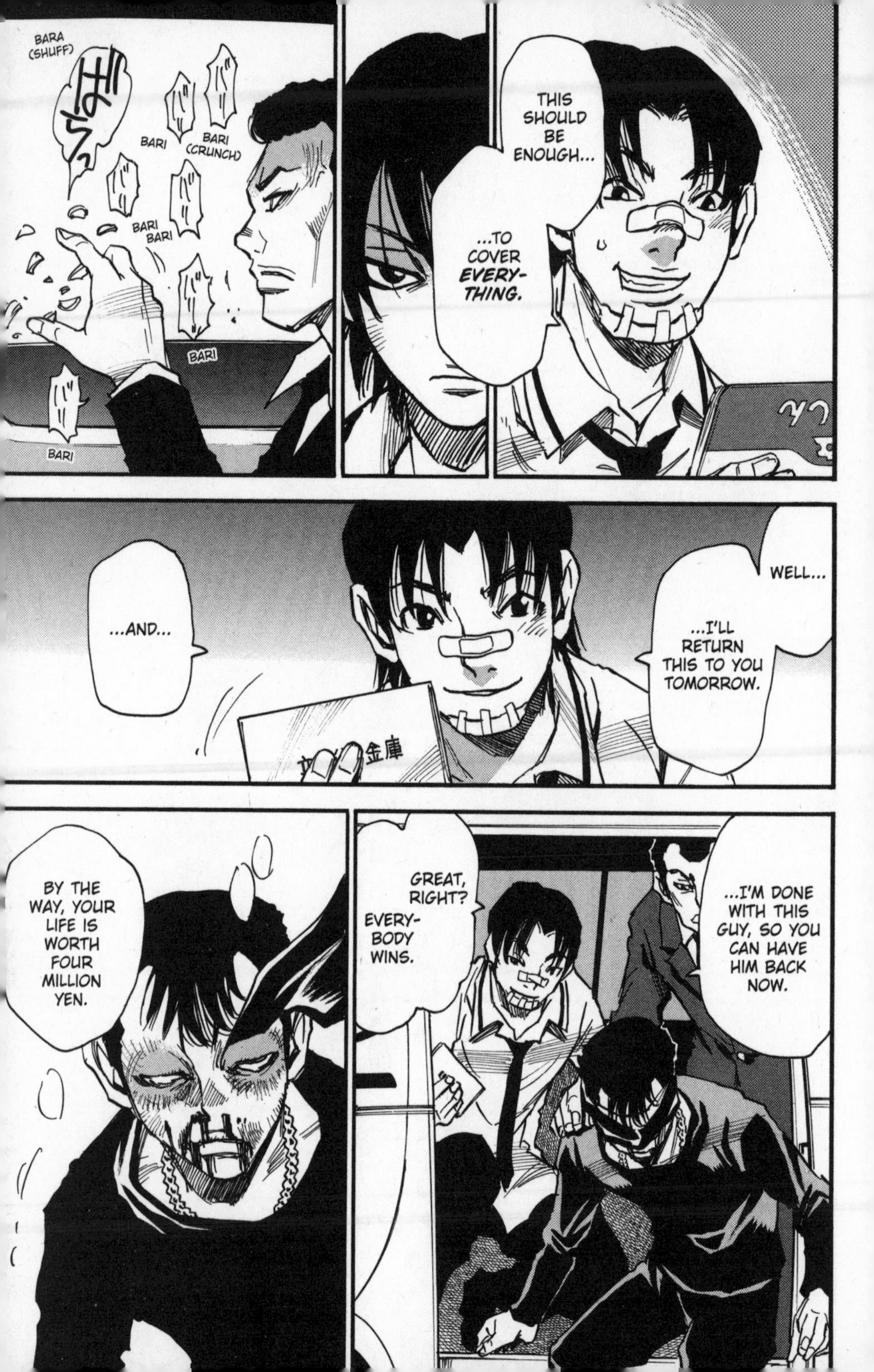
THIS SHOULD BE ENOUGH...
...TO COVER *EVERYTHING.*
BARA (SHUFF)
BARI
BARI (CRUNCH)
BARI BARI
BARI
BARI
WELL...
...I'LL RETURN THIS TO YOU TOMORROW.
...AND...
金庫
...I'M DONE WITH THIS GUY, SO YOU CAN HAVE HIM BACK NOW.
GREAT, RIGHT?
EVERYBODY WINS.
BY THE WAY, YOUR LIFE IS WORTH FOUR MILLION YEN.

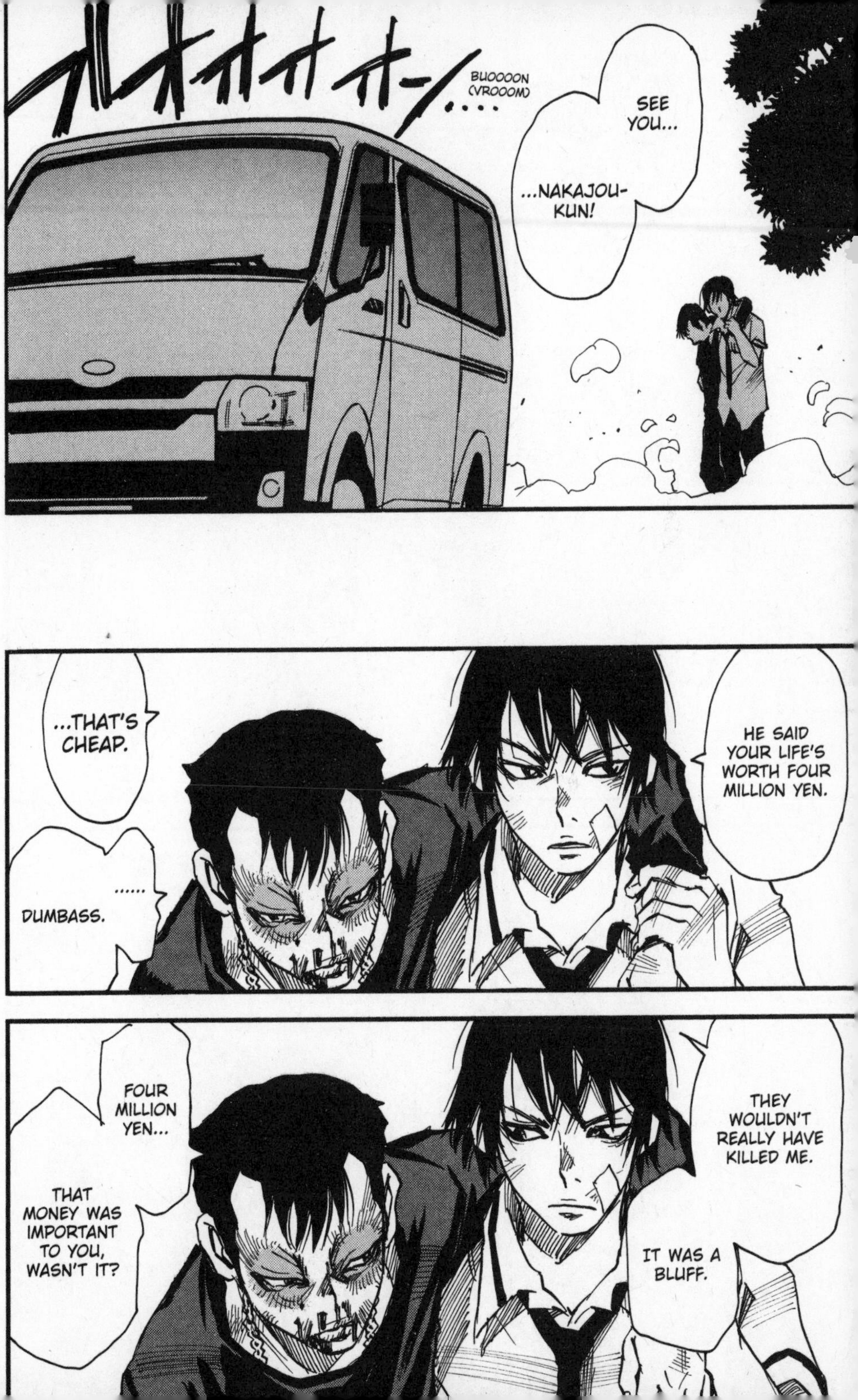
SEE YOU... ...NAKAJOU-KUN!
BUOOOON (VROOOM)....
HE SAID YOUR LIFE'S WORTH FOUR MILLION YEN.
...THAT'S CHEAP.
......
DUMBASS.
THEY WOULDN'T REALLY HAVE KILLED ME.
IT WAS A BLUFF.
FOUR MILLION YEN...
THAT MONEY WAS IMPORTANT TO YOU, WASN'T IT?

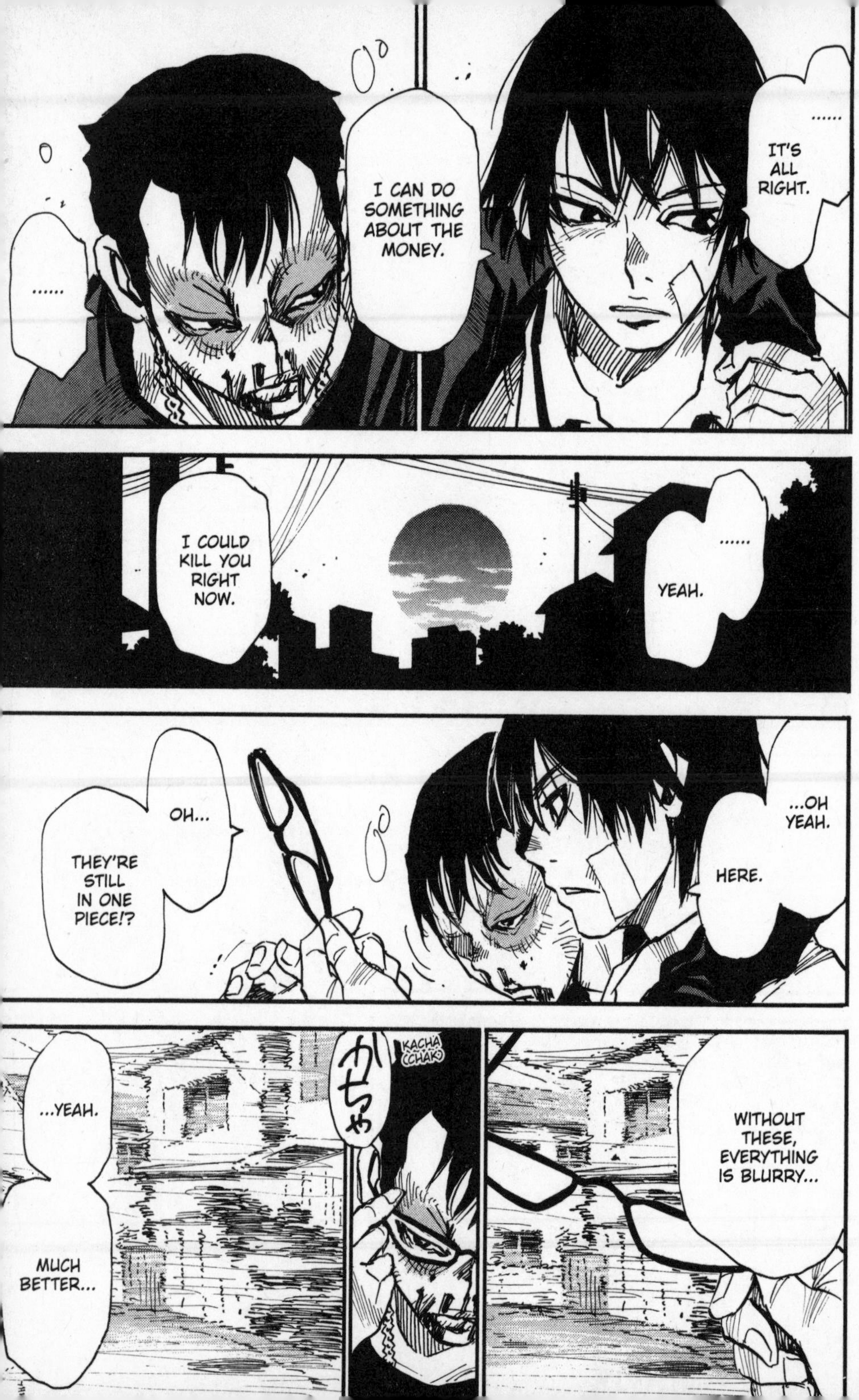
......
IT'S ALL RIGHT.
I CAN DO SOMETHING ABOUT THE MONEY.
......
...... YEAH.
I COULD KILL YOU RIGHT NOW.
...OH YEAH. HERE.
OH... THEY'RE STILL IN ONE PIECE!?
WITHOUT THESE, EVERYTHING IS BLURRY...
かちゃ
KACHA (CHAK)
...YEAH. MUCH BETTER...

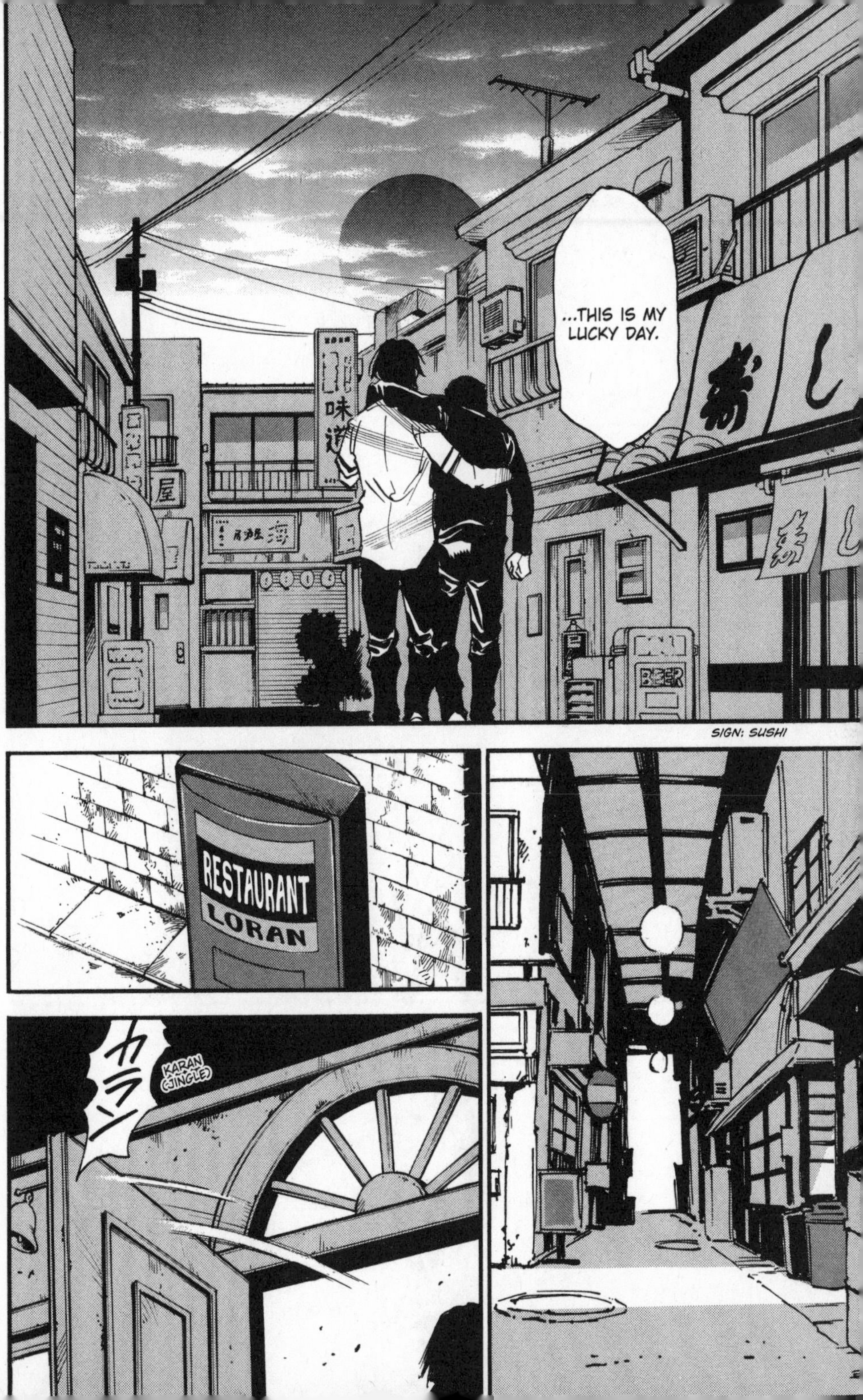
...THIS IS MY LUCKY DAY.
BEER
SIGN: SUSHI
RESTAURANT
LORAN
カラン
KARAN (JINGLE)

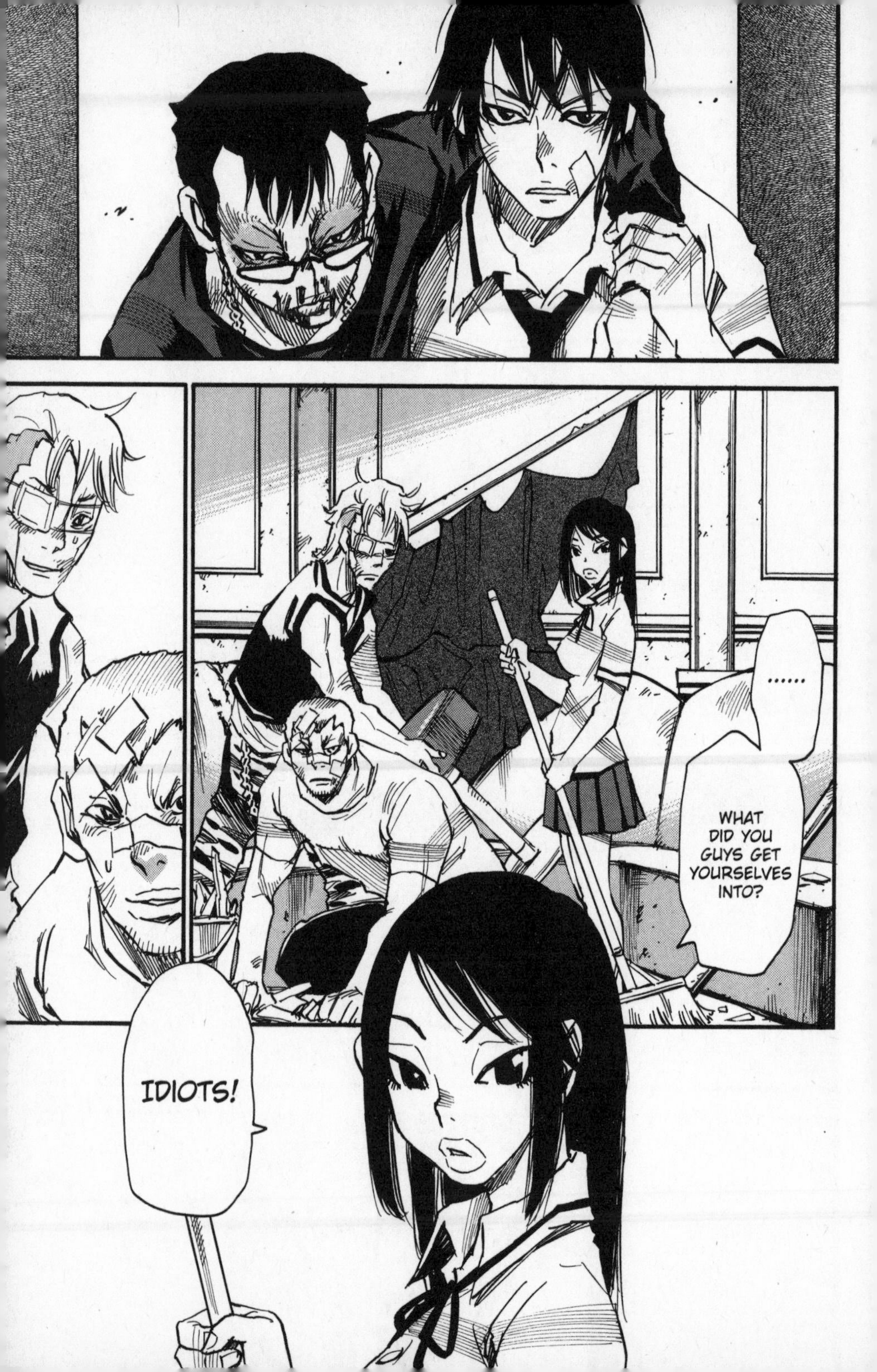
......
WHAT DID YOU GUYS GET YOURSELVES INTO?
IDIOTS!

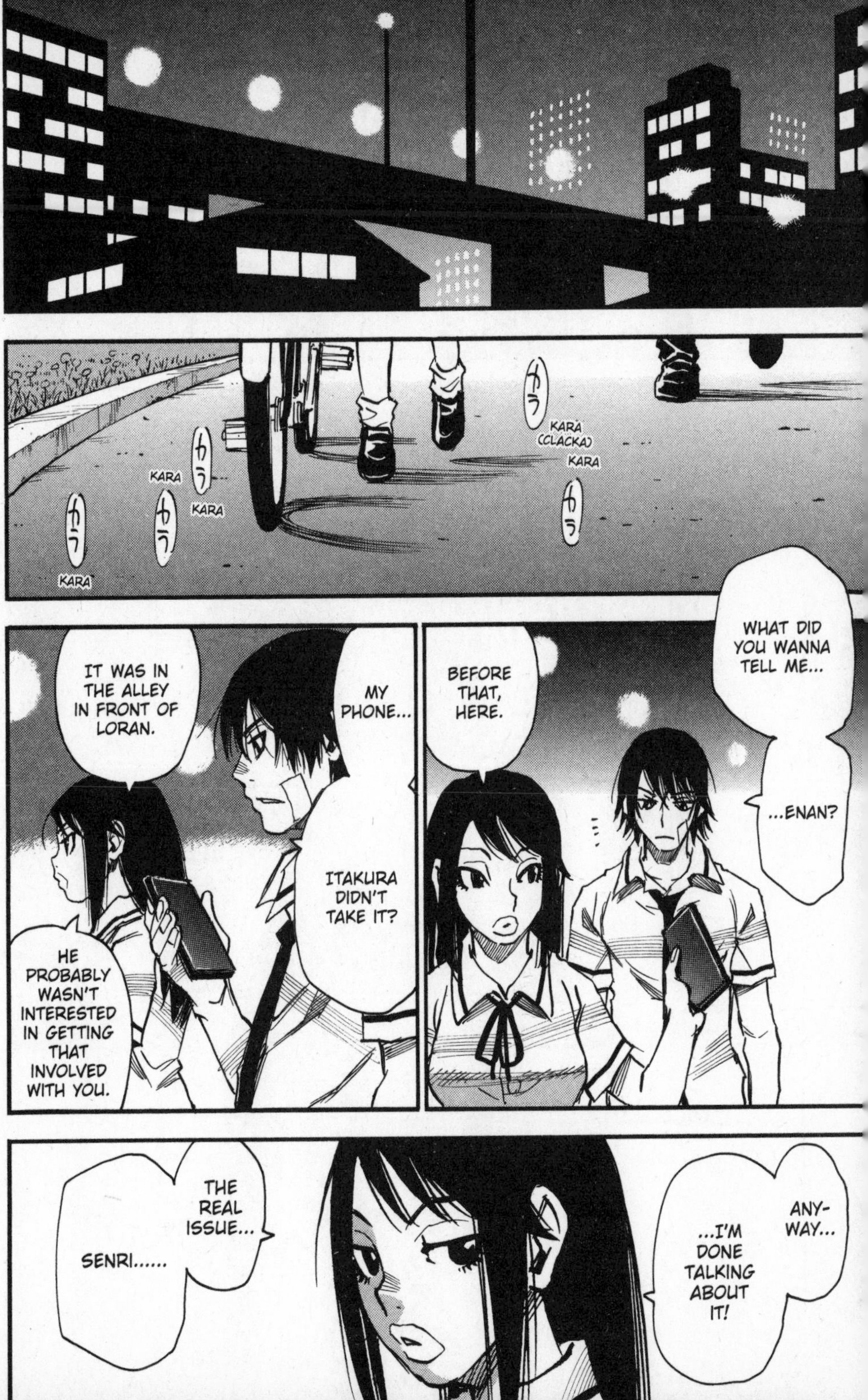
カラ
KARA (CLACKA)
カラ
KARA
カラ
KARA
カラ
KARA
カラ
KARA
WHAT DID YOU WANNA TELL ME...
...ENAN?
BEFORE THAT, HERE.
...
MY PHONE...
IT WAS IN THE ALLEY IN FRONT OF LORAN.
ITAKURA DIDN'T TAKE IT?
HE PROBABLY WASN'T INTERESTED IN GETTING THAT INVOLVED WITH YOU.
ANY-WAY...
...I'M DONE TALKING ABOUT IT!
THE REAL ISSUE...
SENRI......

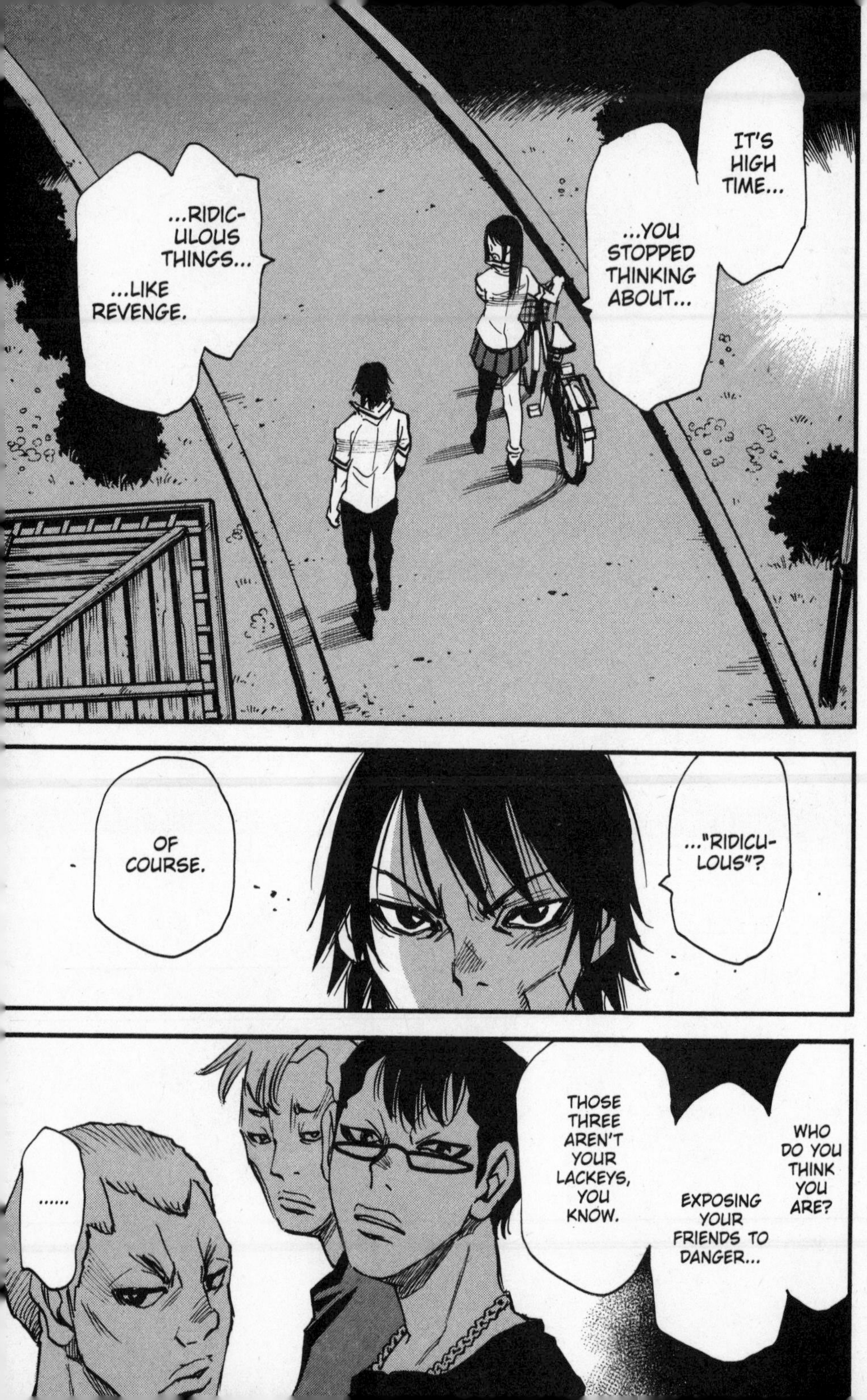
IT'S HIGH TIME...
...YOU STOPPED THINKING ABOUT...
...RIDIC-ULOUS THINGS...
...LIKE REVENGE.
..."RIDICU-LOUS"?
OF COURSE.
WHO DO YOU THINK YOU ARE?
EXPOSING YOUR FRIENDS TO DANGER...
THOSE THREE AREN'T YOUR LACKEYS, YOU KNOW.
......

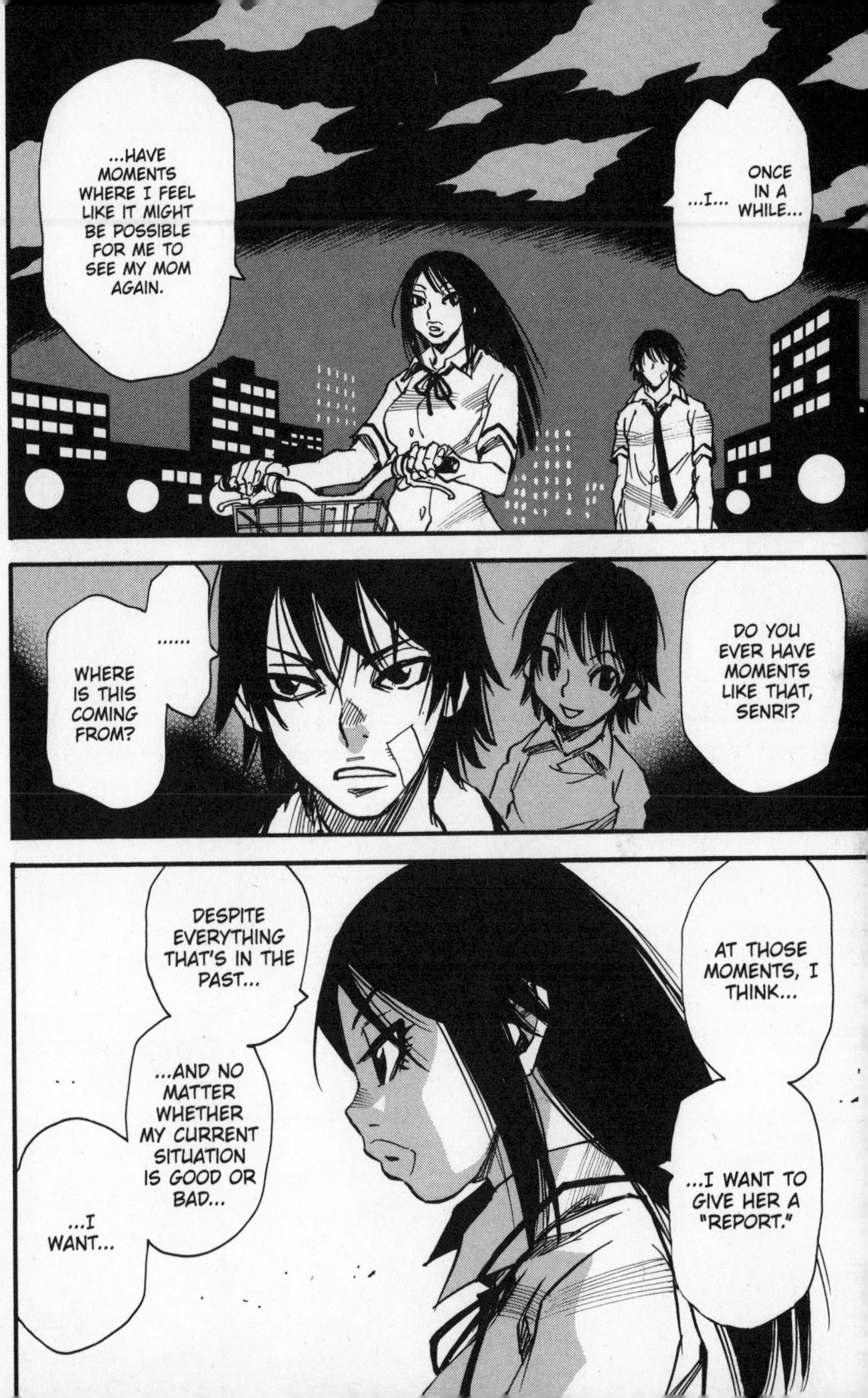
ONCE IN A WHILE...
...I...
...HAVE MOMENTS WHERE I FEEL LIKE IT MIGHT BE POSSIBLE FOR ME TO SEE MY MOM AGAIN.
DO YOU EVER HAVE MOMENTS LIKE THAT, SENRI?
......
WHERE IS THIS COMING FROM?
AT THOSE MOMENTS, I THINK...
DESPITE EVERYTHING THAT'S IN THE PAST...
...AND NO MATTER WHETHER MY CURRENT SITUATION IS GOOD OR BAD...
...I WANT...
...I WANT TO GIVE HER A "REPORT."

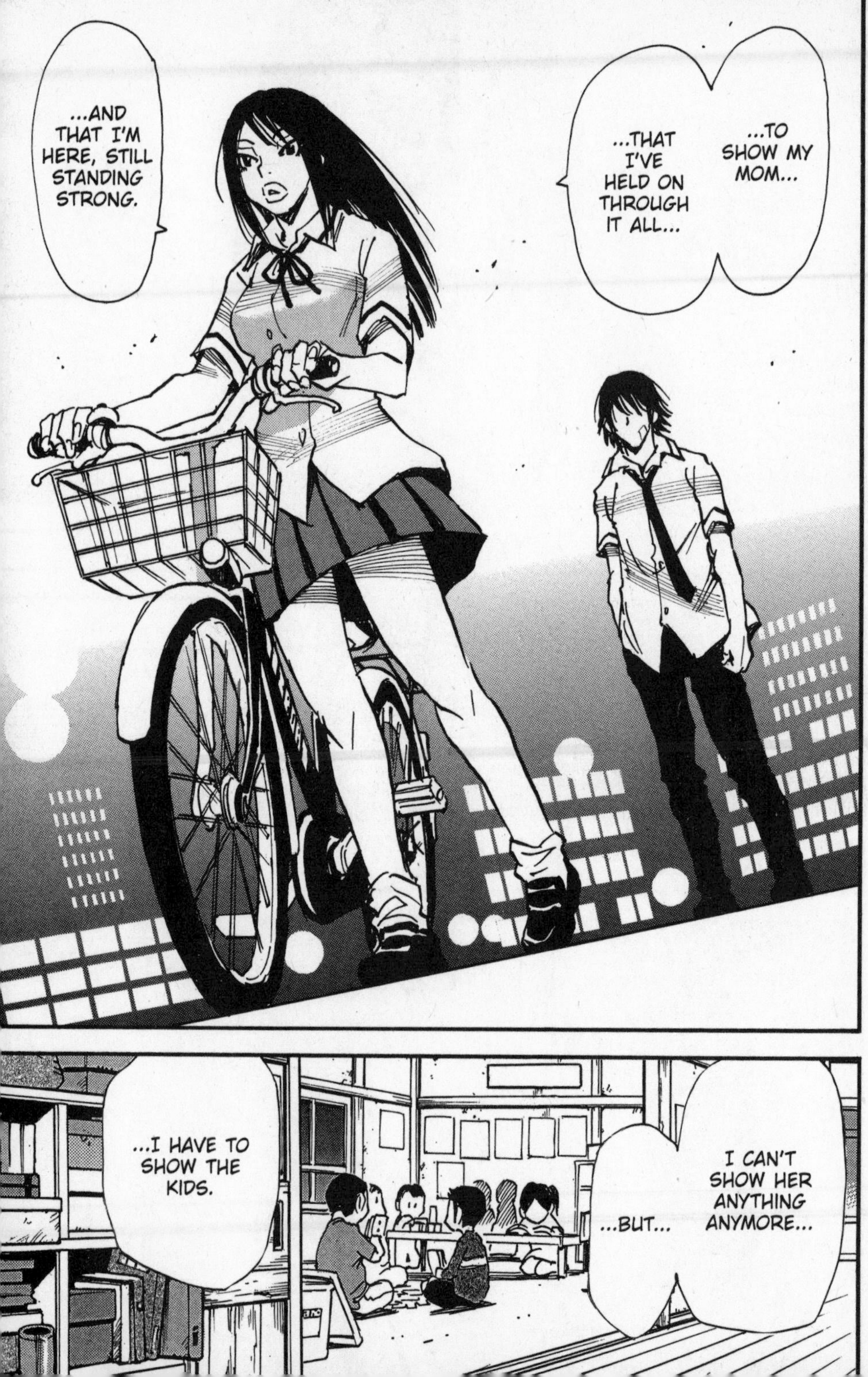
...TO SHOW MY MOM...
...THAT I'VE HELD ON THROUGH IT ALL...
...AND THAT I'M HERE, STILL STANDING STRONG.
I CAN'T SHOW HER ANYTHING ANYMORE...
...BUT...
...I HAVE TO SHOW THE KIDS.

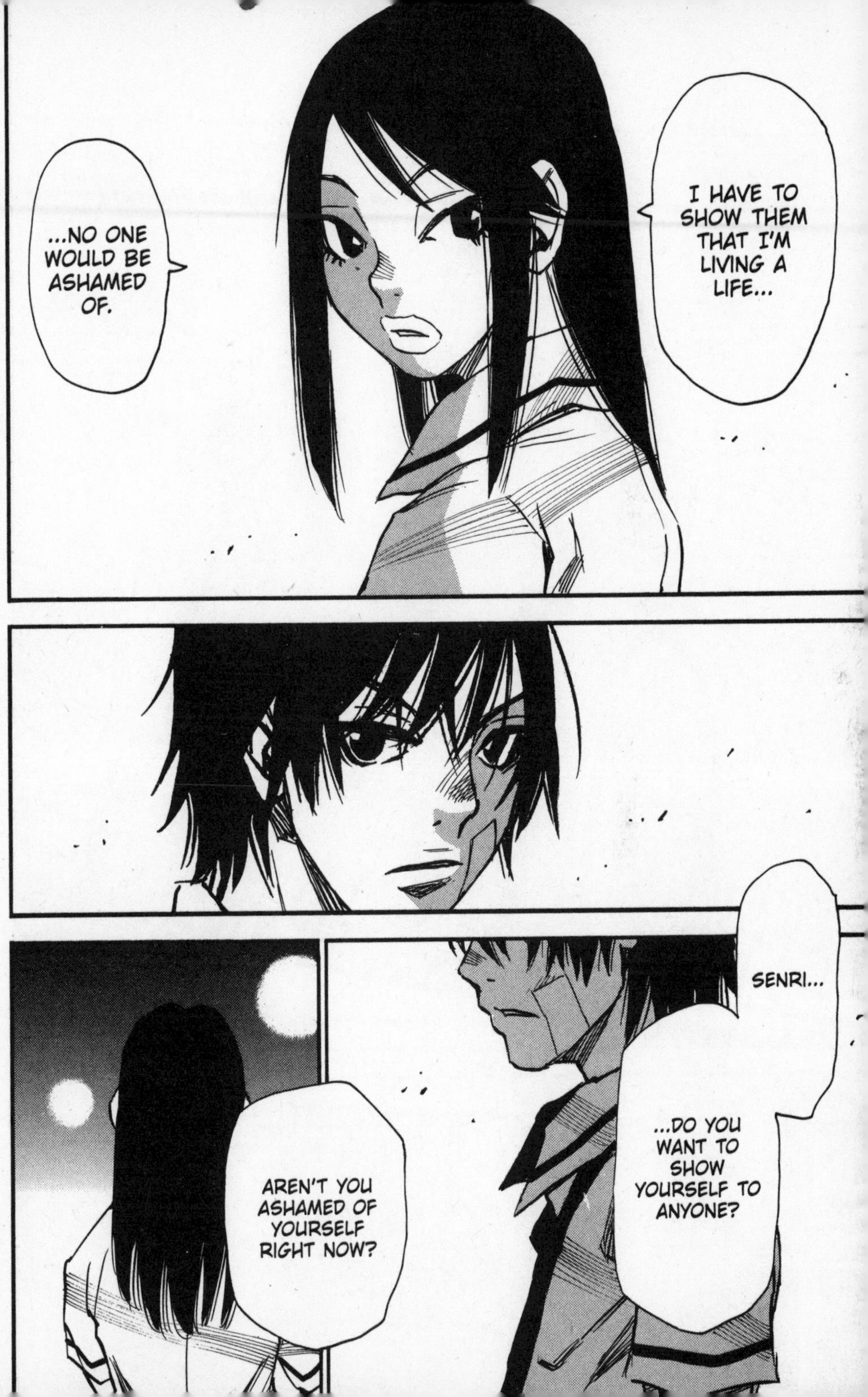
I HAVE TO SHOW THEM THAT I'M LIVING A LIFE...
...NO ONE WOULD BE ASHAMED OF.
SENRI...
...DO YOU WANT TO SHOW YOURSELF TO ANYONE?
AREN'T YOU ASHAMED OF YOURSELF RIGHT NOW?

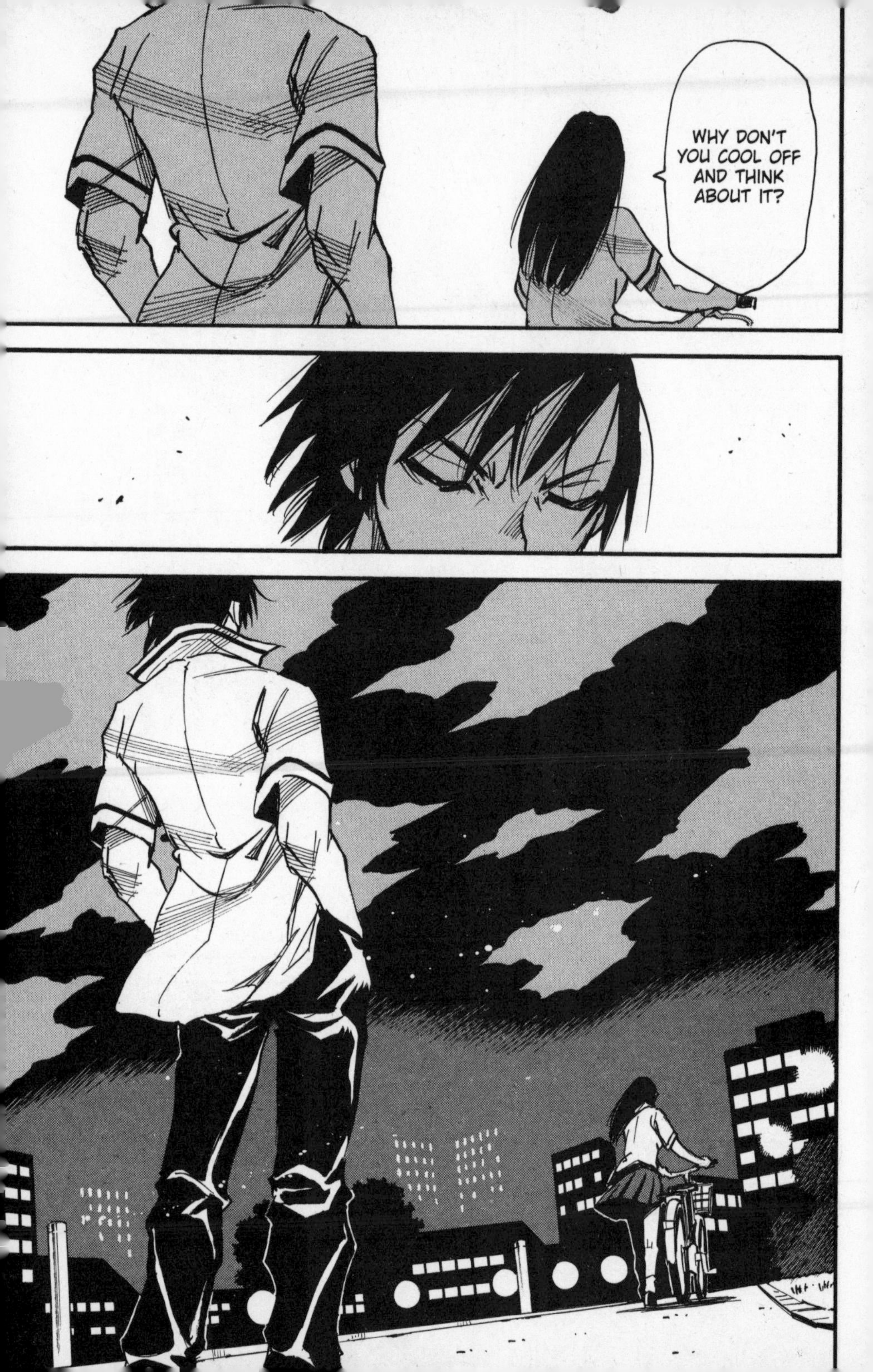
WHY DON'T YOU COOL OFF AND THINK ABOUT IT?

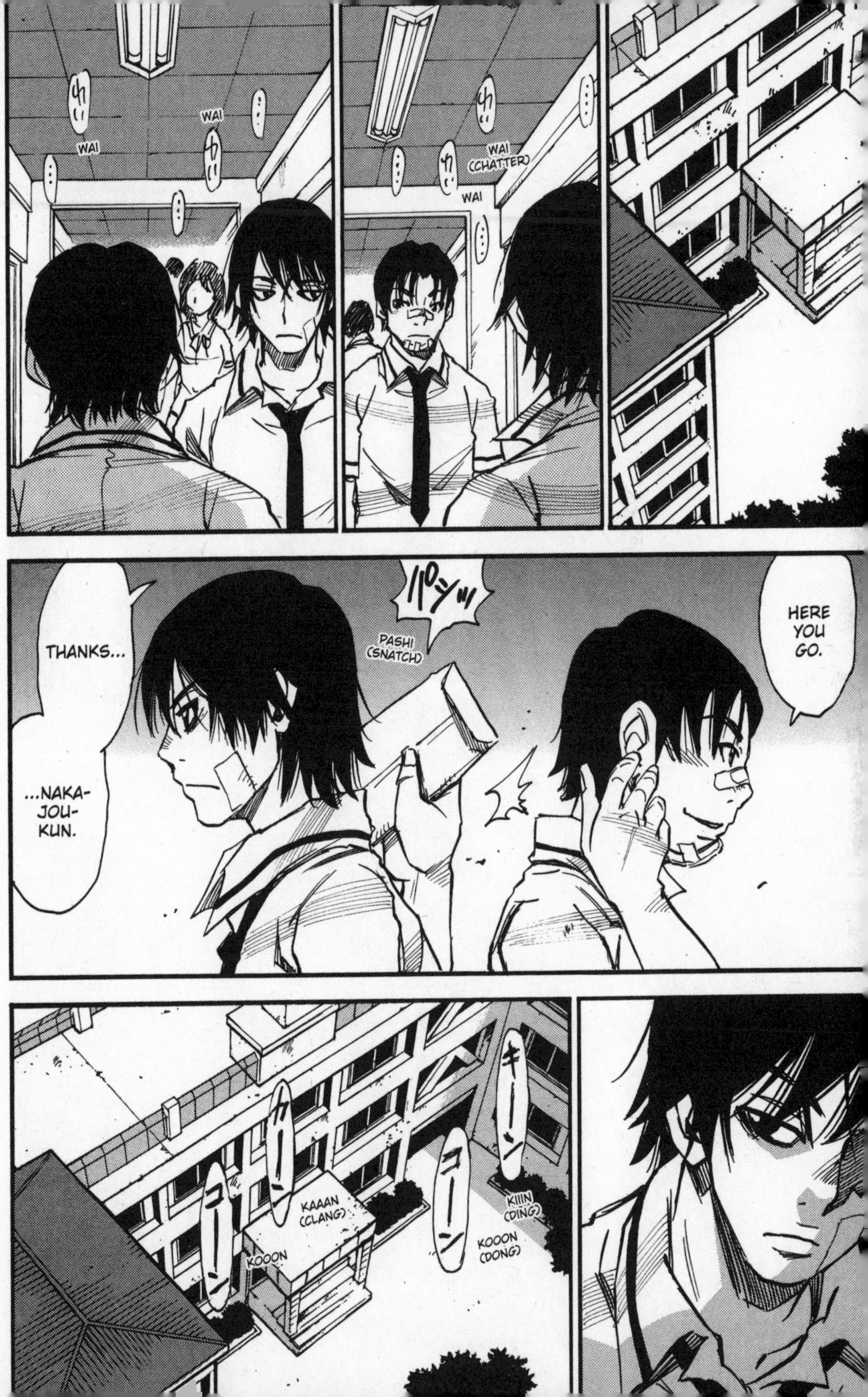
わい
WAI (CHATTER)
わい
WAI
わい
WAI
わい
WAI
HERE YOU GO.
パシッ
PASHI (SNATCH)
THANKS...
...NAKA-JOU-KUN.
キーン
KIIN (DING)
コーン
KOOON (DONG)
カーン
KAAAN (CLANG)
コーン
KOOON

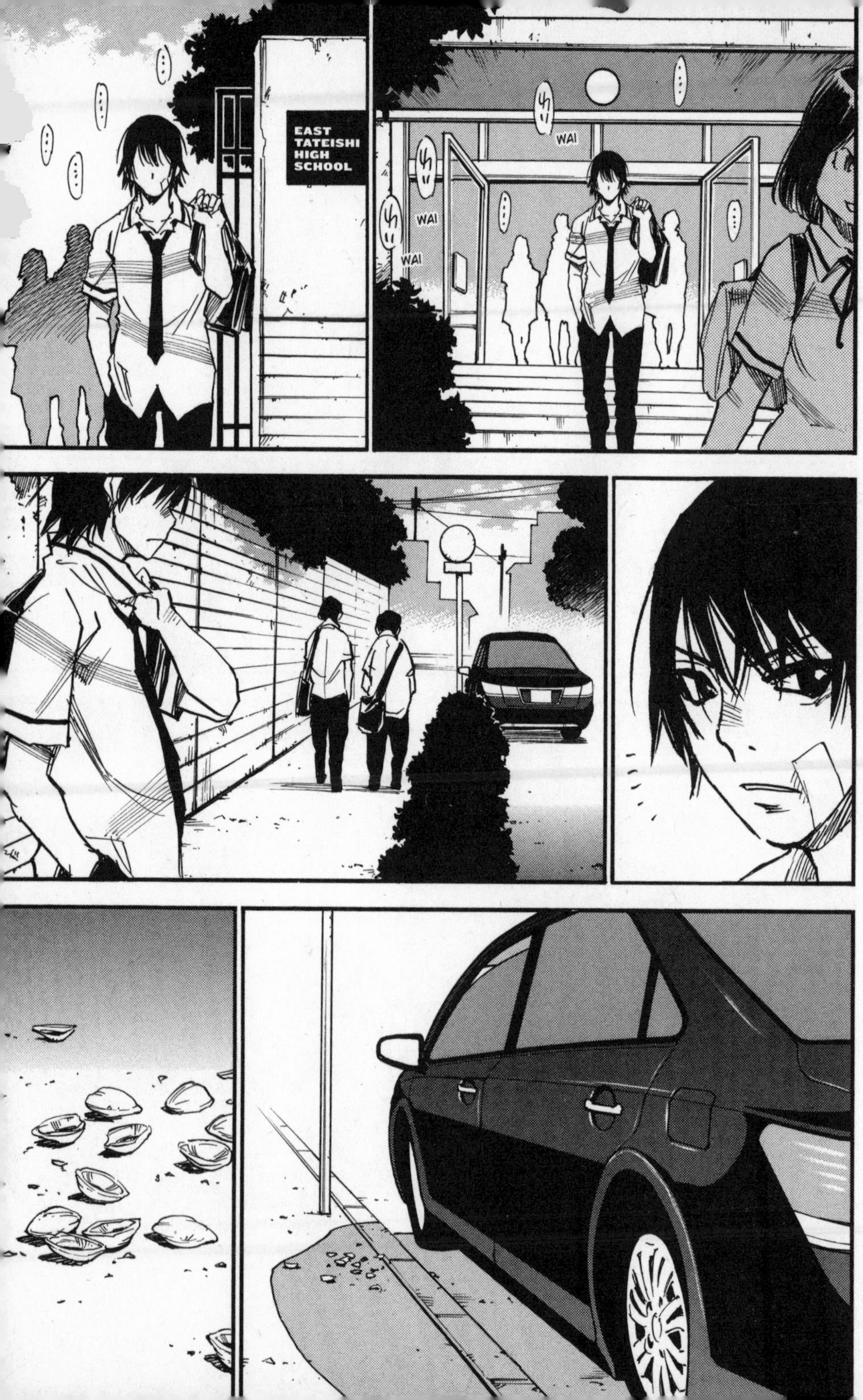
WAI
WAI
WAI
EAST TATEISHI HIGH SCHOOL

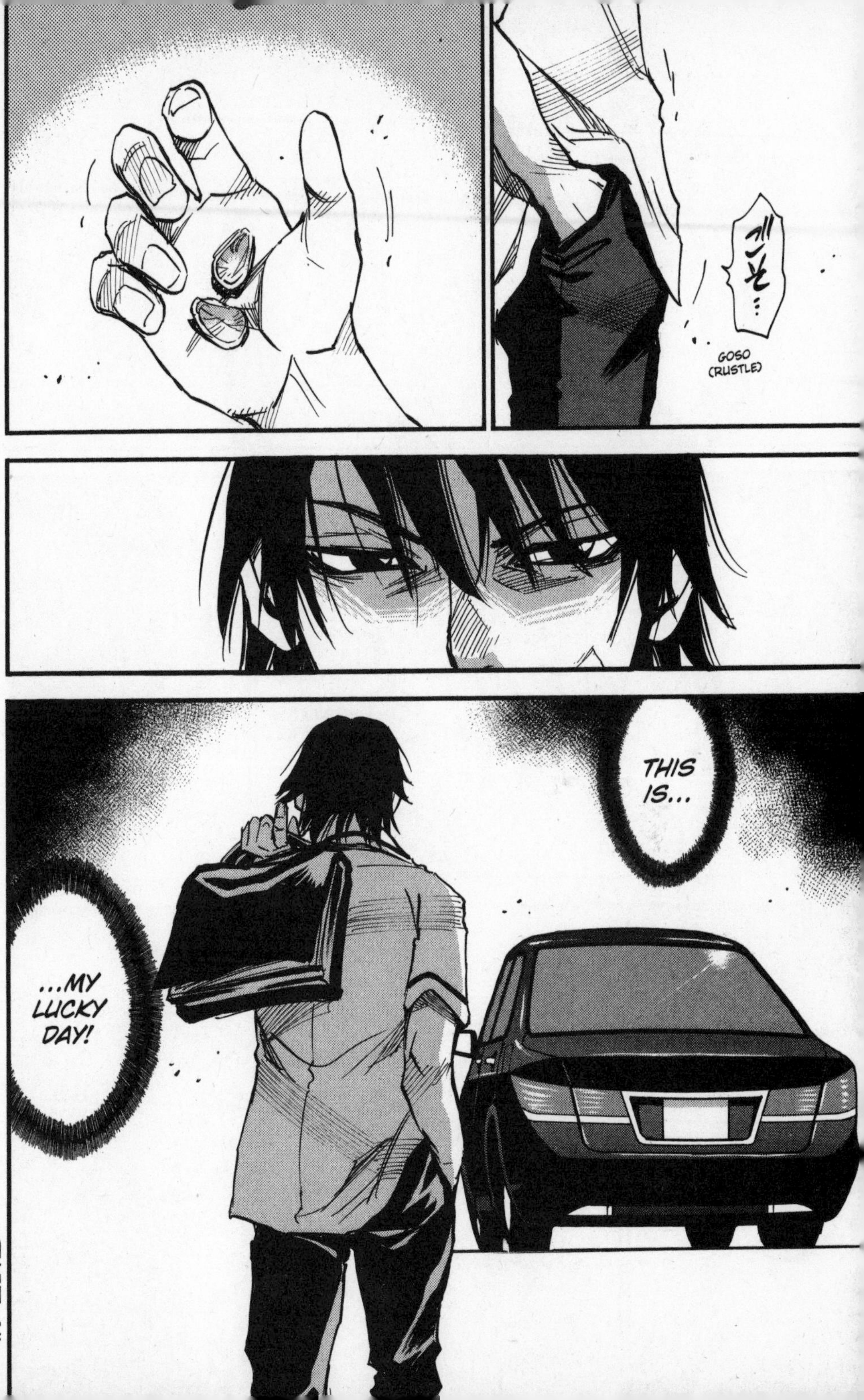
ゴソ…
GOSO (RUSTLE)
THIS IS...
...MY LUCKY DAY!

#7 END

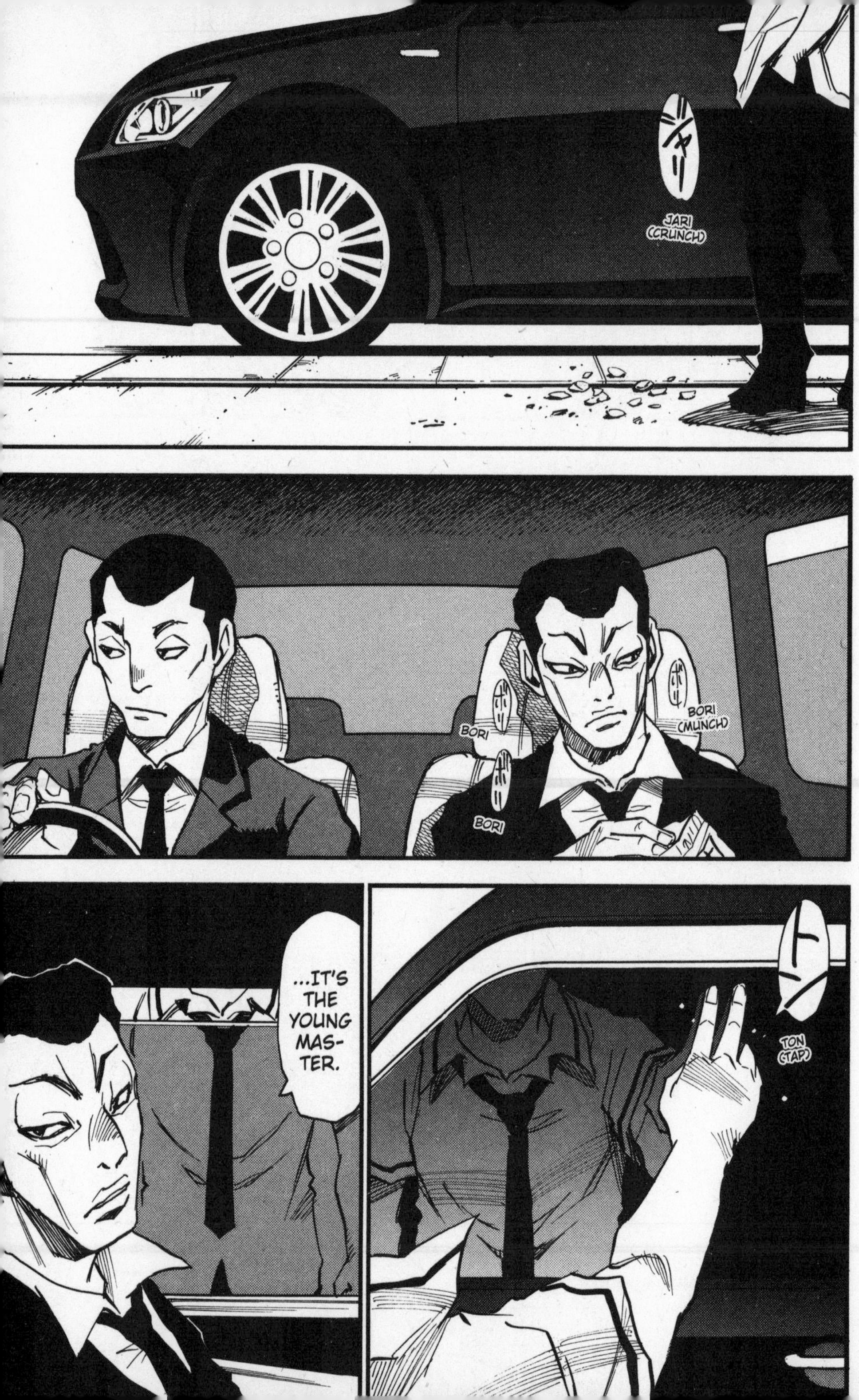
JARI (CRUNCH)
BORI (MUNCH)
BORI
BORI
TON (TAP)
...IT'S THE YOUNG MAS-TER.

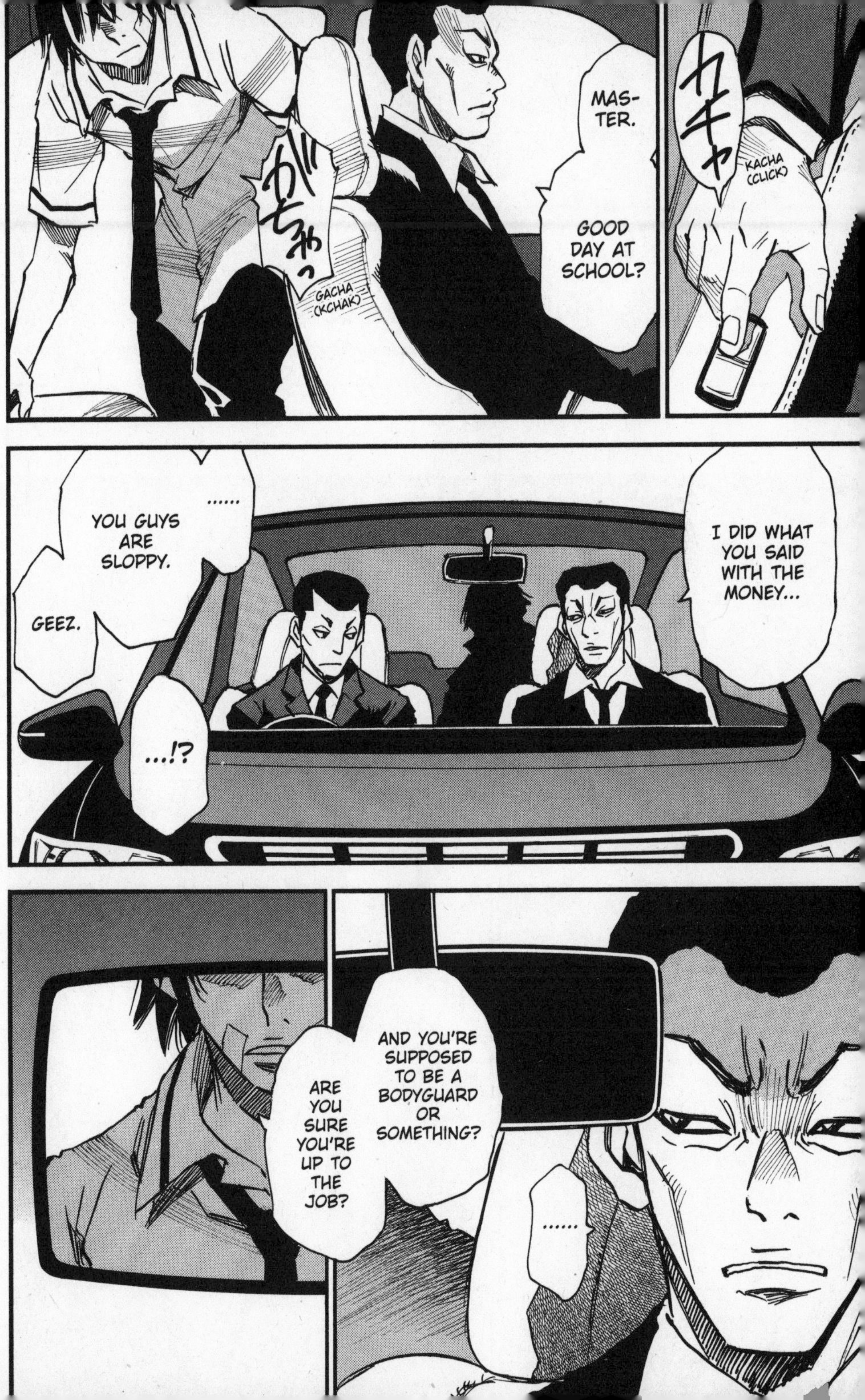
カチャ
KACHA (CLICK)
MAS-TER.
GOOD DAY AT SCHOOL?
がちゃっ
GACHA (KCHAK)
I DID WHAT YOU SAID WITH THE MONEY...
......
YOU GUYS ARE SLOPPY.
GEEZ.
...!?
AND YOU'RE SUPPOSED TO BE A BODYGUARD OR SOMETHING?
ARE YOU SURE YOU'RE UP TO THE JOB?
......

#8 Trap

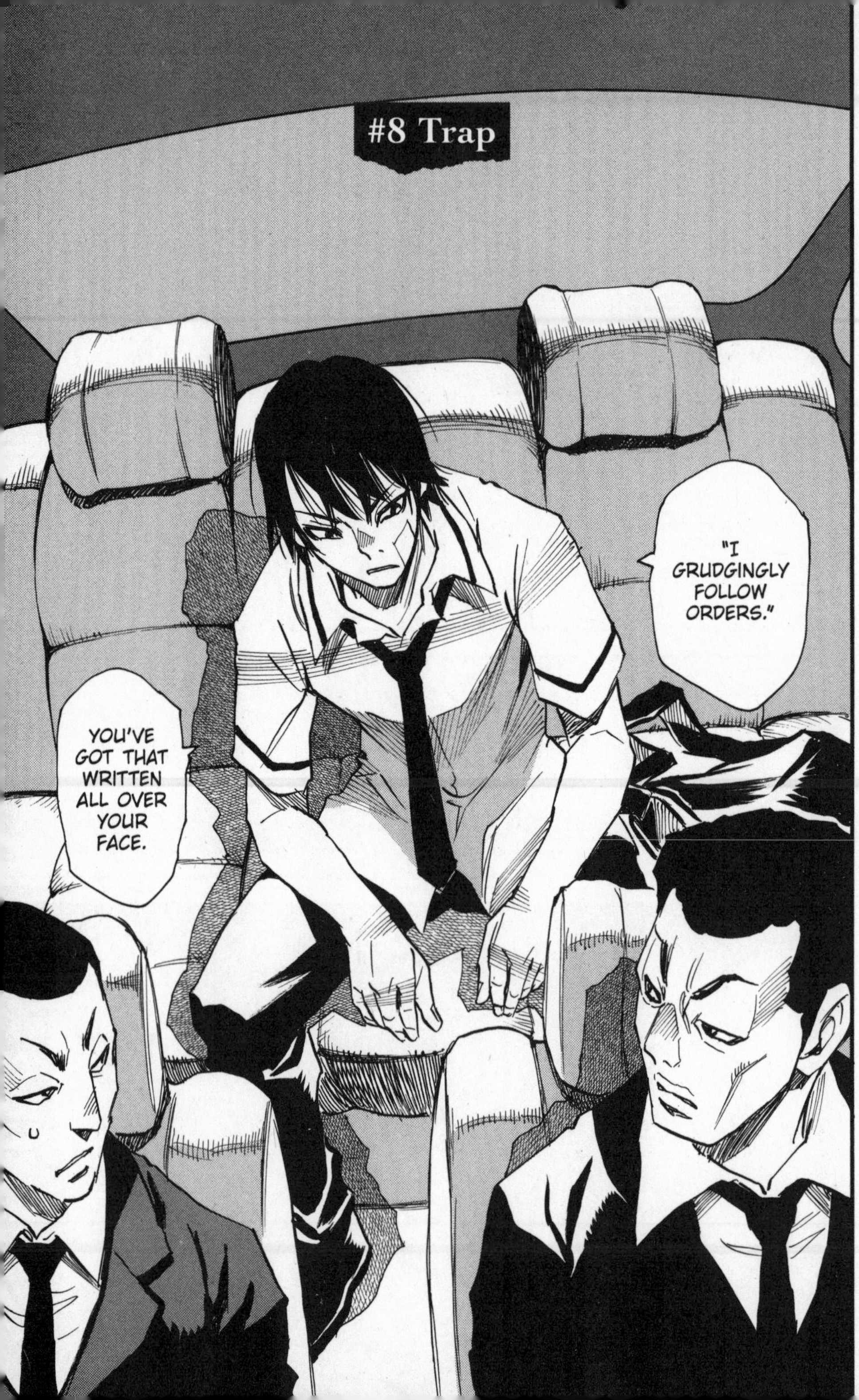
"I GRUDGINGLY FOLLOW ORDERS."
YOU'VE GOT THAT WRITTEN ALL OVER YOUR FACE.

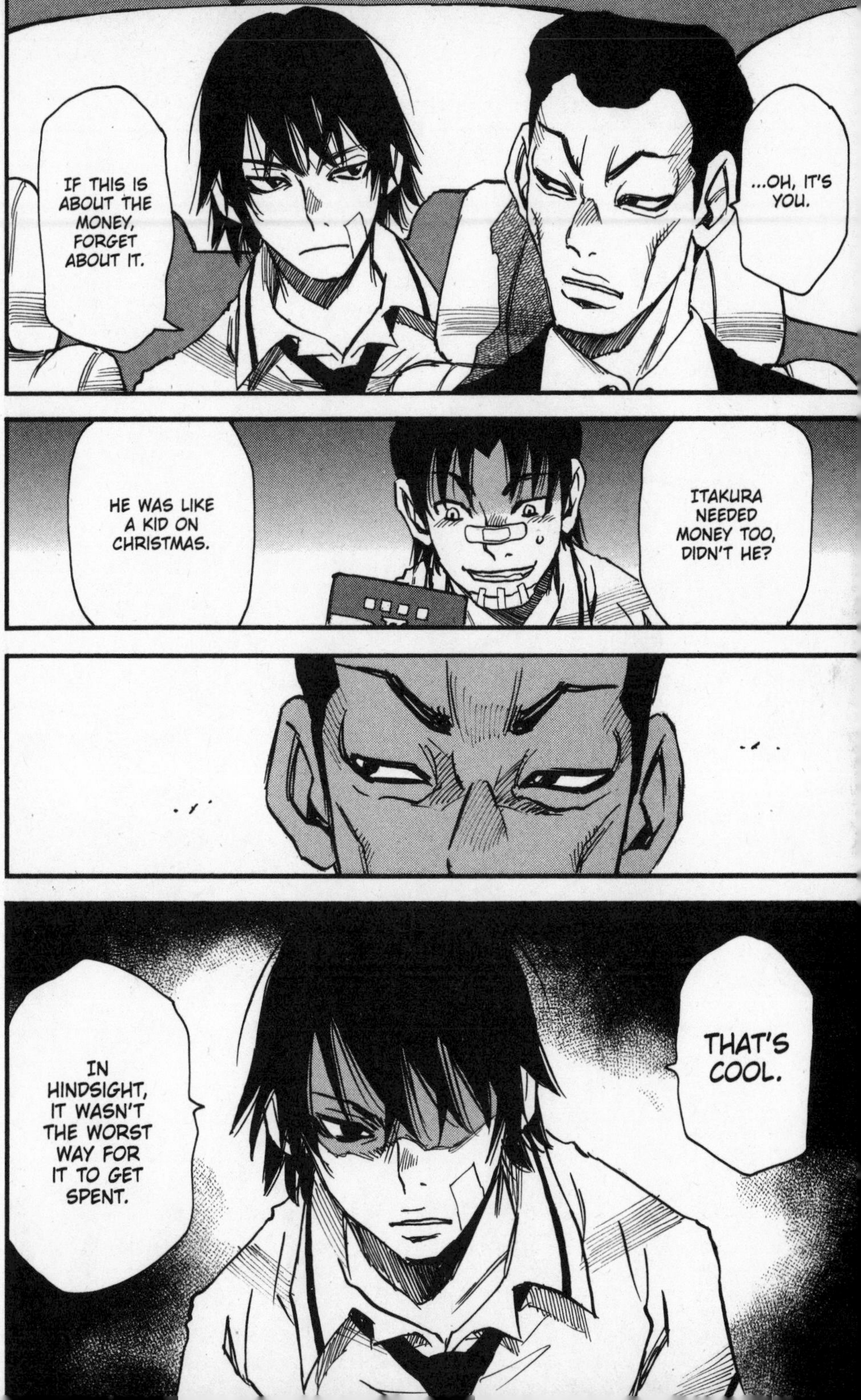
...OH, IT'S YOU.
IF THIS IS ABOUT THE MONEY, FORGET ABOUT IT.
ITAKURA NEEDED MONEY TOO, DIDN'T HE?
HE WAS LIKE A KID ON CHRISTMAS.
THAT'S COOL.
IN HINDSIGHT, IT WASN'T THE WORST WAY FOR IT TO GET SPENT.

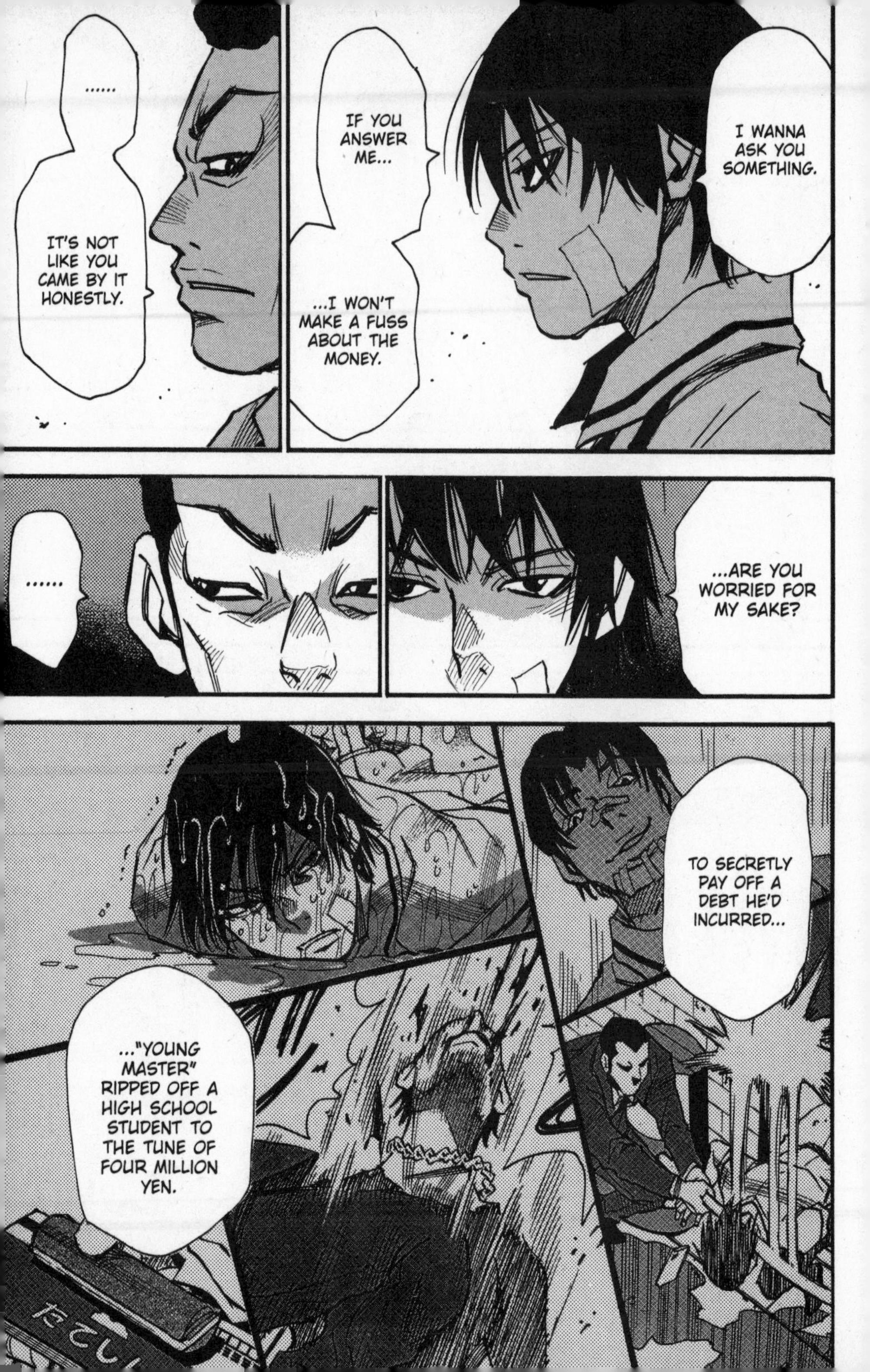
I WANNA ASK YOU SOMETHING.
IF YOU ANSWER ME...
...I WON'T MAKE A FUSS ABOUT THE MONEY.
......
IT'S NOT LIKE YOU CAME BY IT HONESTLY.
...ARE YOU WORRIED FOR MY SAKE?
......
TO SECRETLY PAY OFF A DEBT HE'D INCURRED...
..."YOUNG MASTER" RIPPED OFF A HIGH SCHOOL STUDENT TO THE TUNE OF FOUR MILLION YEN.

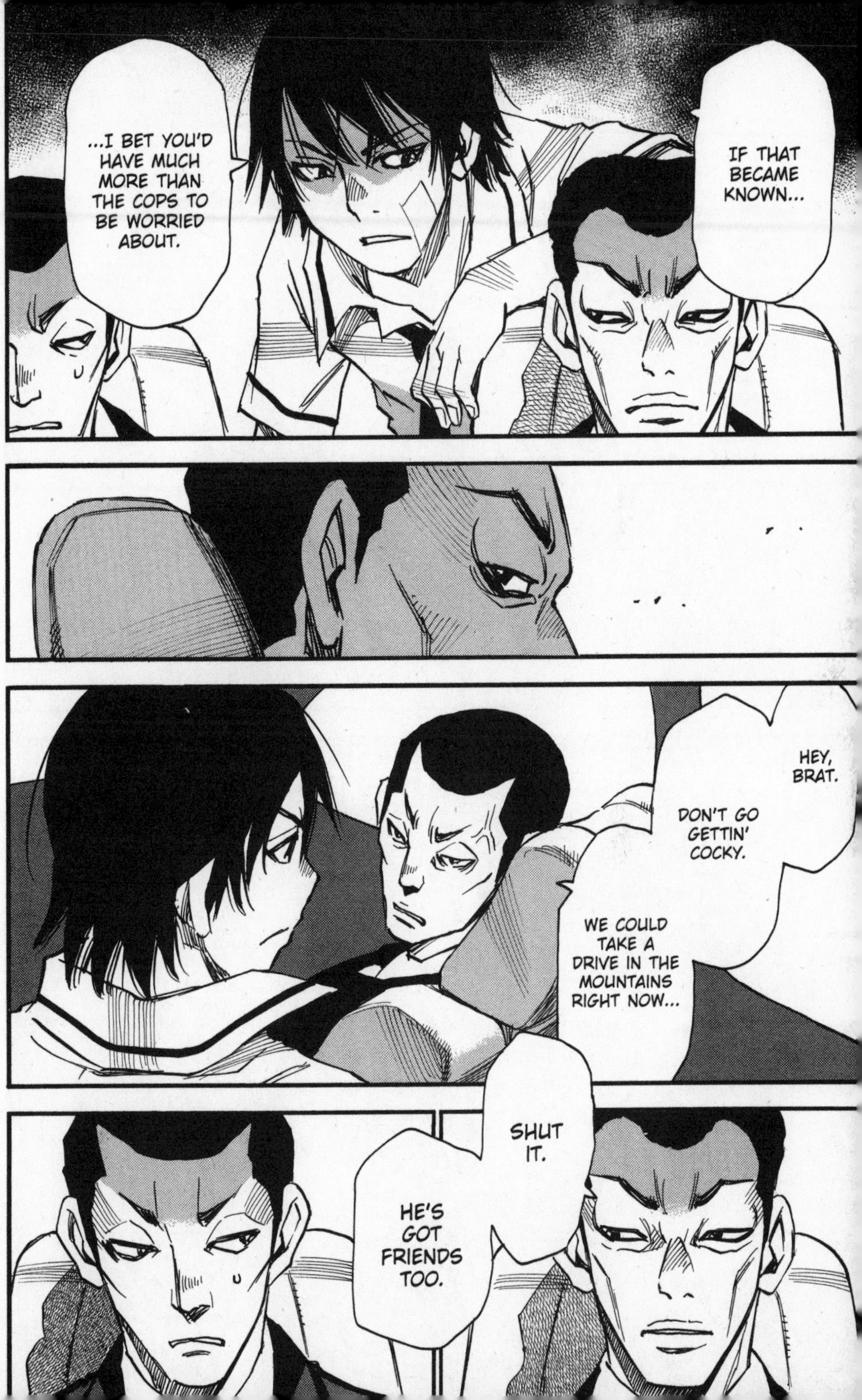
IF THAT BECAME KNOWN...
...I BET YOU'D HAVE MUCH MORE THAN THE COPS TO BE WORRIED ABOUT.
HEY, BRAT.
DON'T GO GETTIN' COCKY.
WE COULD TAKE A DRIVE IN THE MOUNTAINS RIGHT NOW...
SHUT IT.
HE'S GOT FRIENDS TOO.

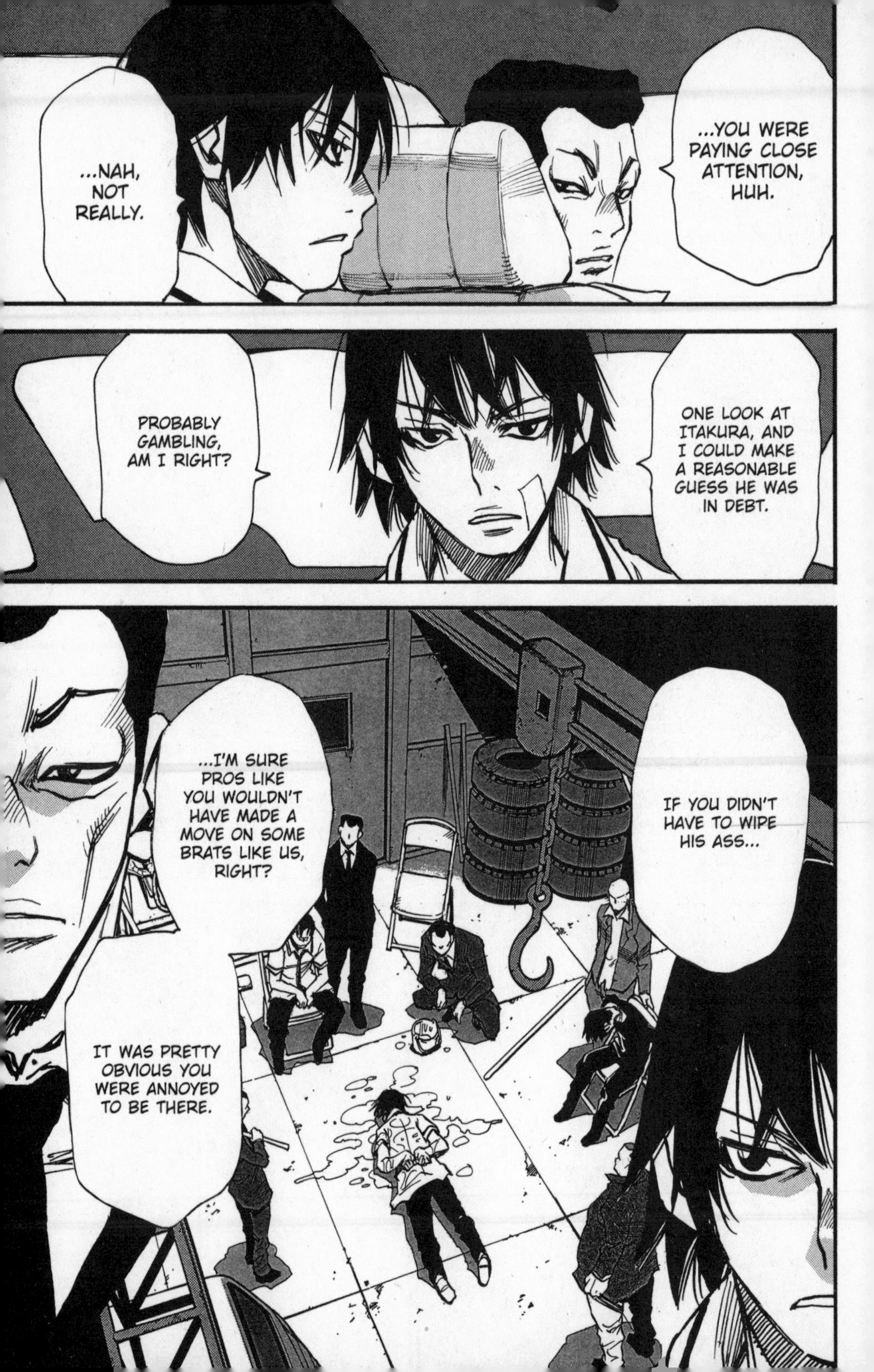
...YOU WERE PAYING CLOSE ATTENTION, HUH.
...NAH, NOT REALLY.
ONE LOOK AT ITAKURA, AND I COULD MAKE A REASONABLE GUESS HE WAS IN DEBT.
PROBABLY GAMBLING, AM I RIGHT?
IF YOU DIDN'T HAVE TO WIPE HIS ASS...
...I'M SURE PROS LIKE YOU WOULDN'T HAVE MADE A MOVE ON SOME BRATS LIKE US, RIGHT?
IT WAS PRETTY OBVIOUS YOU WERE ANNOYED TO BE THERE.

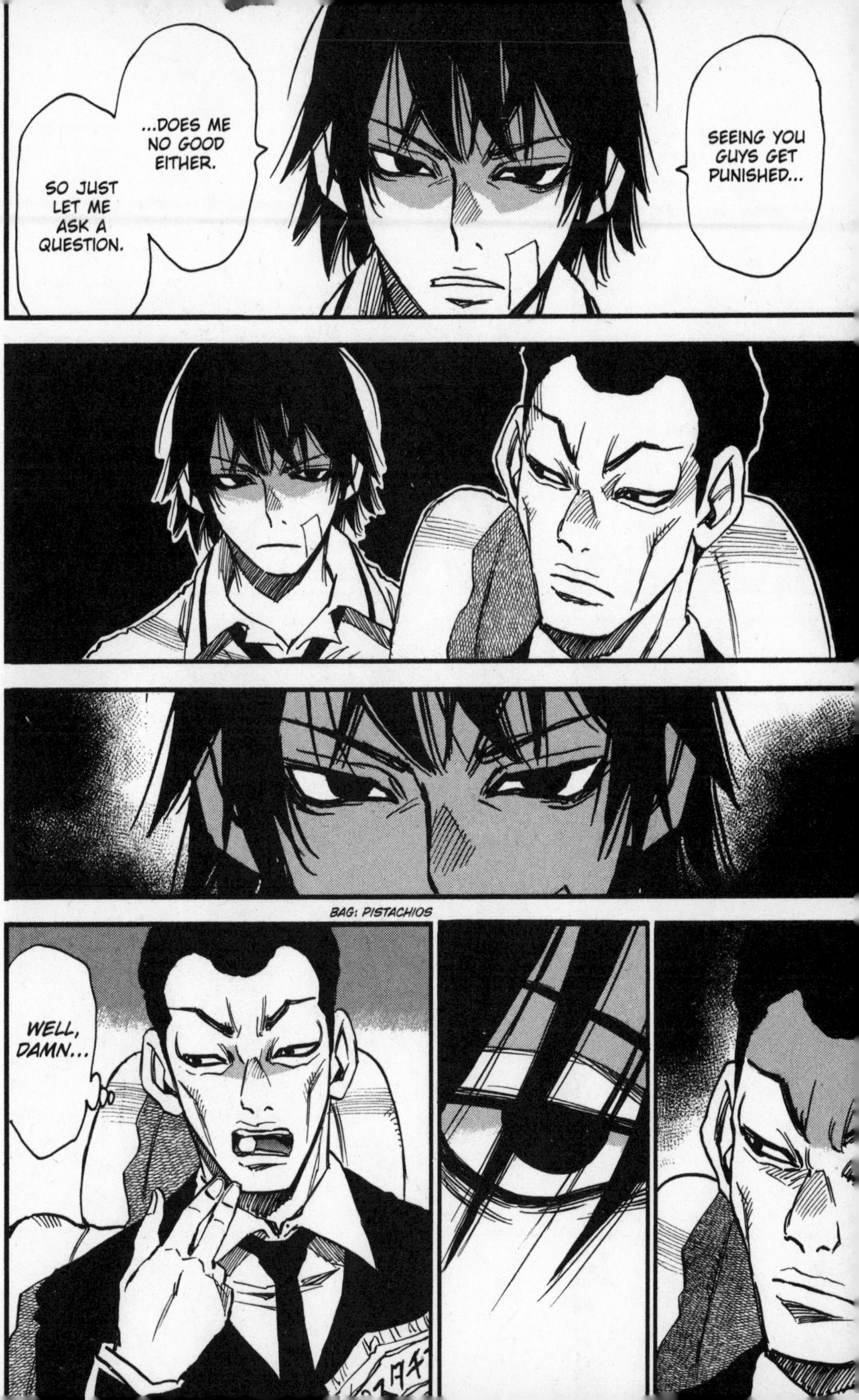
SEEING YOU GUYS GET PUNISHED...
...DOES ME NO GOOD EITHER.
SO JUST LET ME ASK A QUESTION.
BAG: PISTACHIOS
WELL, DAMN...

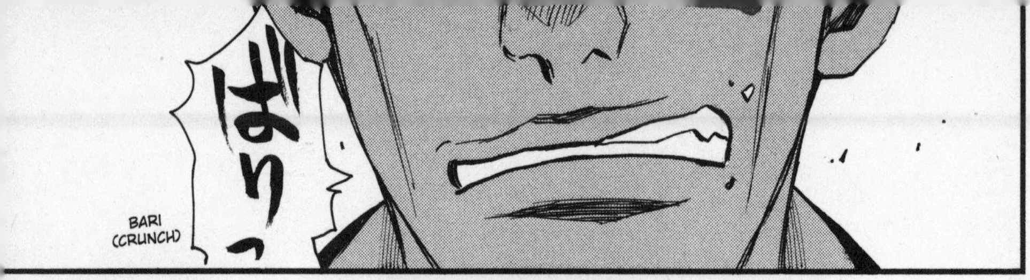
ばりっ
BARI (CRUNCH)

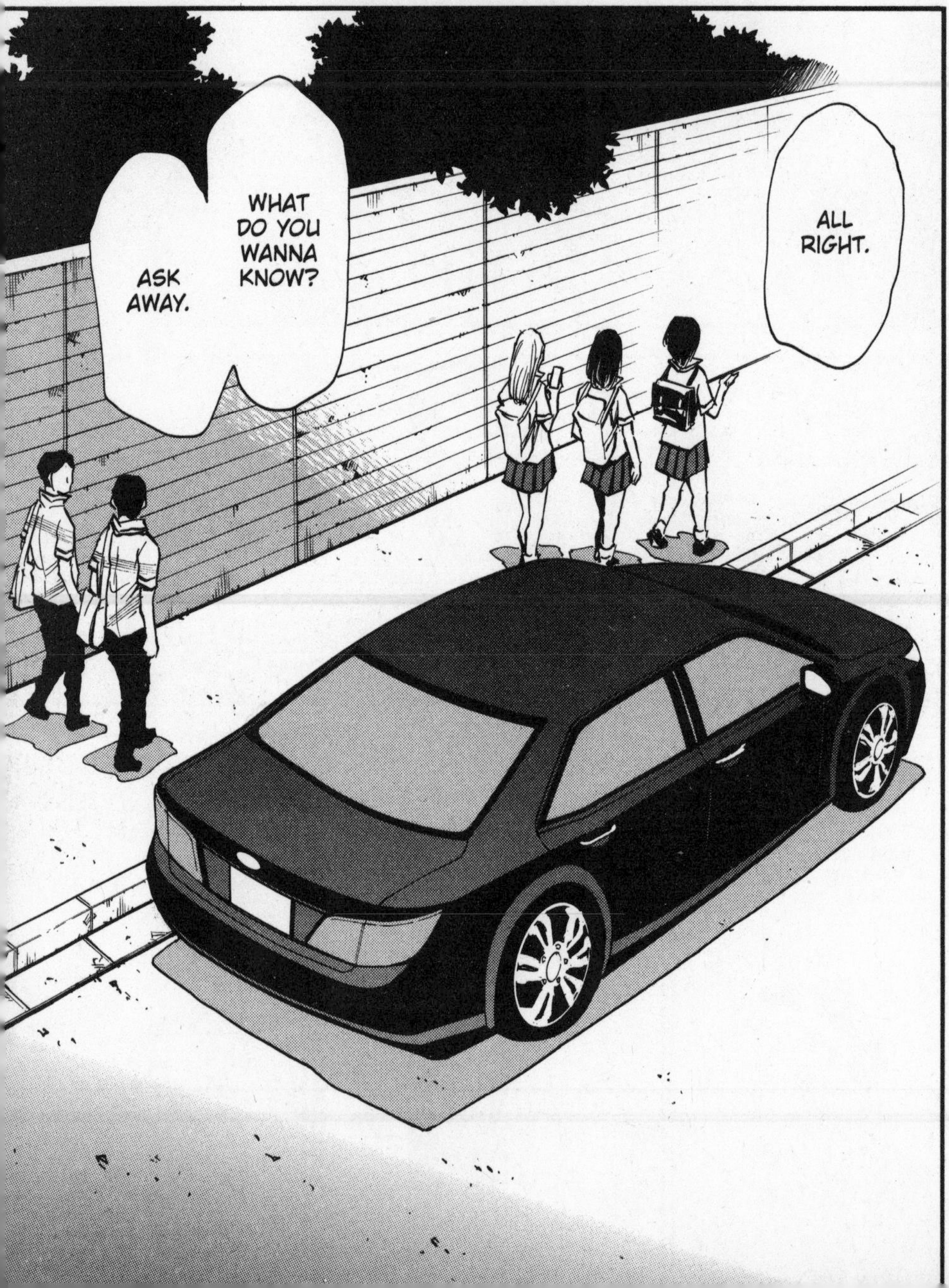
ALL RIGHT.
WHAT DO YOU WANNA KNOW?
ASK AWAY.

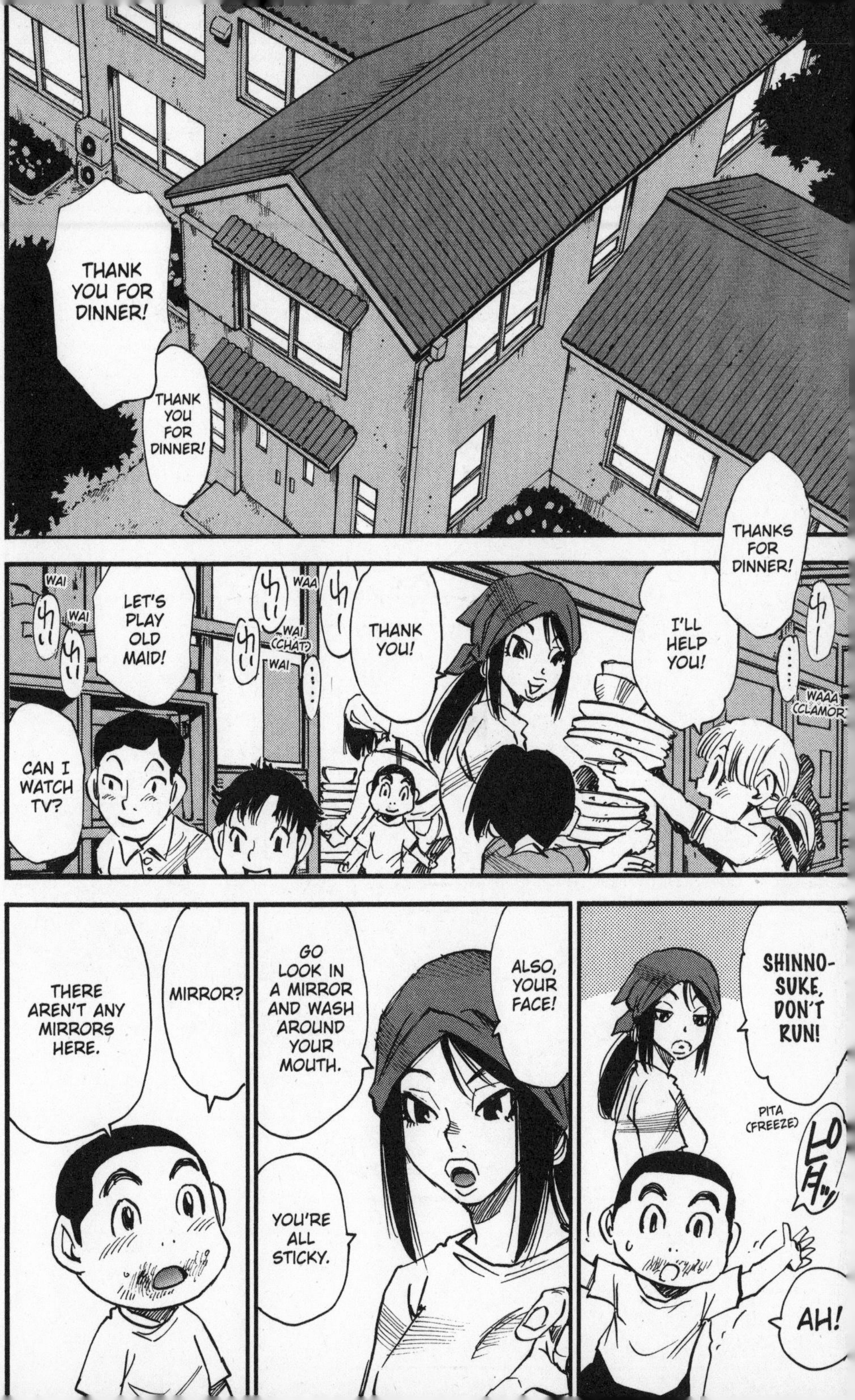
THANK YOU FOR DINNER!
THANK YOU FOR DINNER!
THANKS FOR DINNER!
WAAA (CLAMOR)
I'LL HELP YOU!
......
THANK YOU!
WAA
WAI (CHAT)
WAI
......
LET'S PLAY OLD MAID!
WAI
WAI
CAN I WATCH TV?
SHINNO-SUKE, DON'T RUN!
PITA (FREEZE)
AH!
ALSO, YOUR FACE!
GO LOOK IN A MIRROR AND WASH AROUND YOUR MOUTH.
YOU'RE ALL STICKY.
MIRROR?
THERE AREN'T ANY MIRRORS HERE.

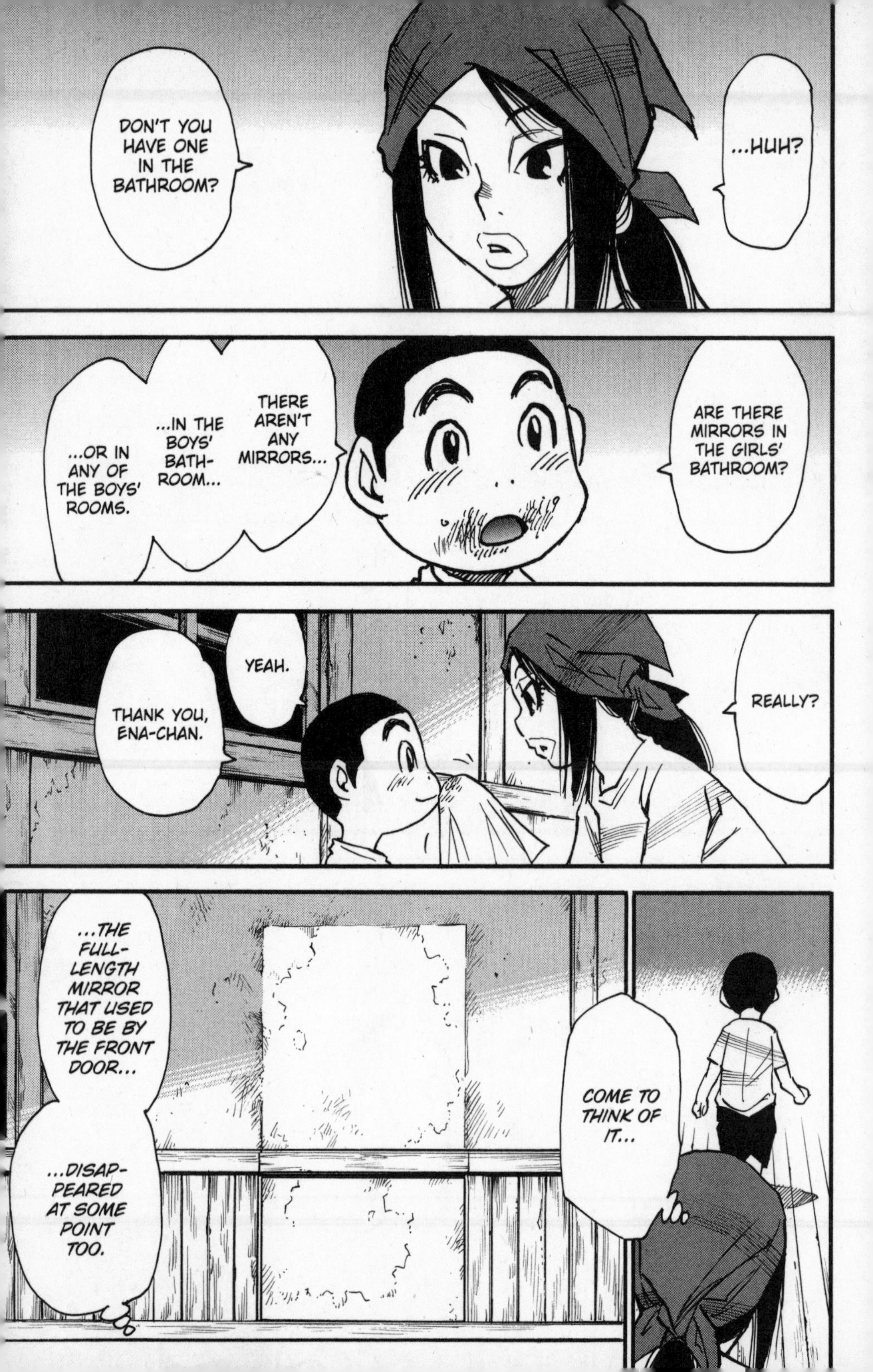
...HUH?
DON'T YOU HAVE ONE IN THE BATHROOM?
ARE THERE MIRRORS IN THE GIRLS' BATHROOM?
THERE AREN'T ANY MIRRORS...
...IN THE BOYS' BATHROOM...
...OR IN ANY OF THE BOYS' ROOMS.
REALLY?
YEAH.
THANK YOU, ENA-CHAN.
COME TO THINK OF IT...
...THE FULL-LENGTH MIRROR THAT USED TO BE BY THE FRONT DOOR...
...DISAPPEARED AT SOME POINT TOO.

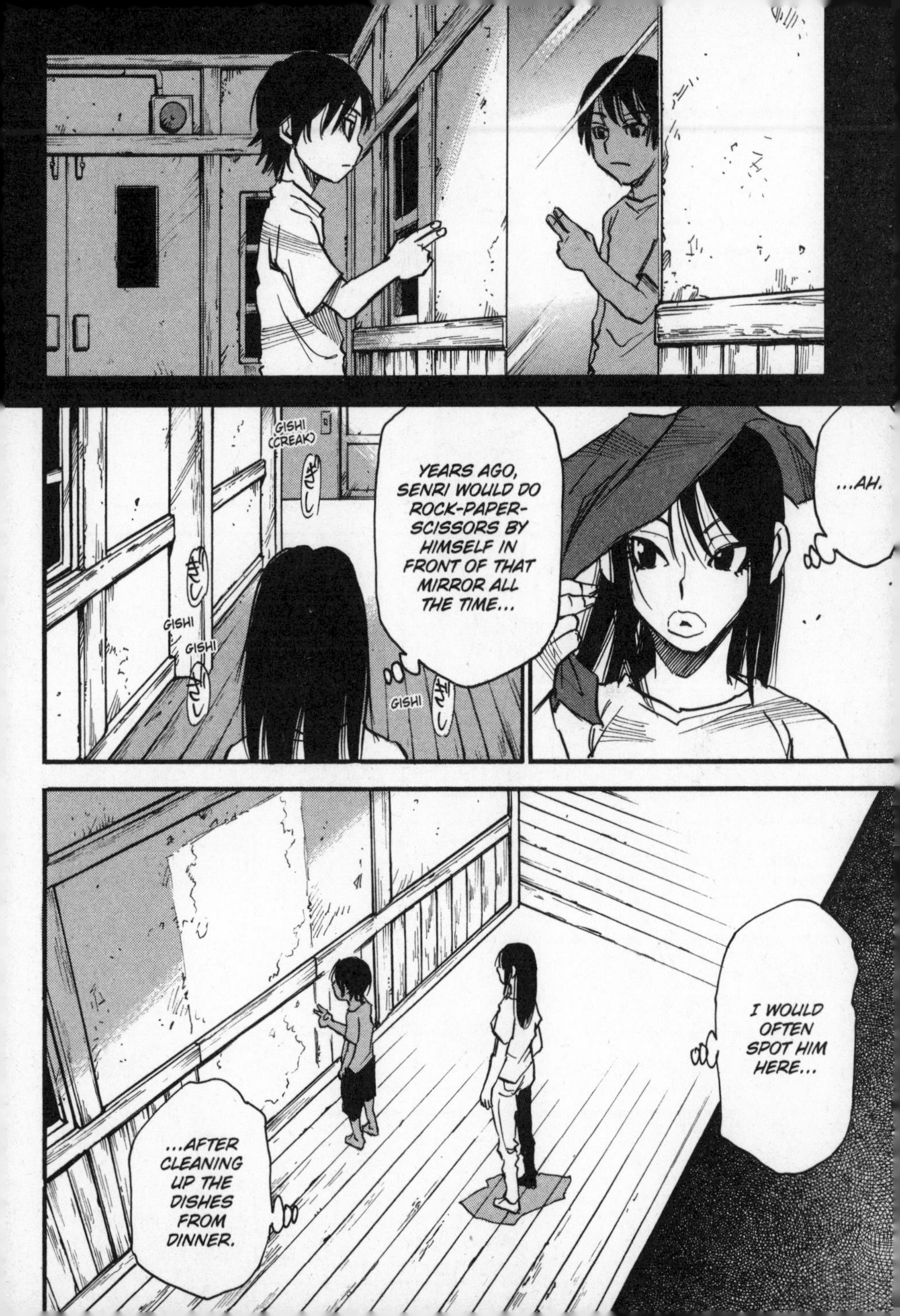
...AH.
YEARS AGO, SENRI WOULD DO ROCK-PAPER-SCISSORS BY HIMSELF IN FRONT OF THAT MIRROR ALL THE TIME...
GISHI (CREAK)
GISHI
GISHI
GISHI
I WOULD OFTEN SPOT HIM HERE...
...AFTER CLEANING UP THE DISHES FROM DINNER.

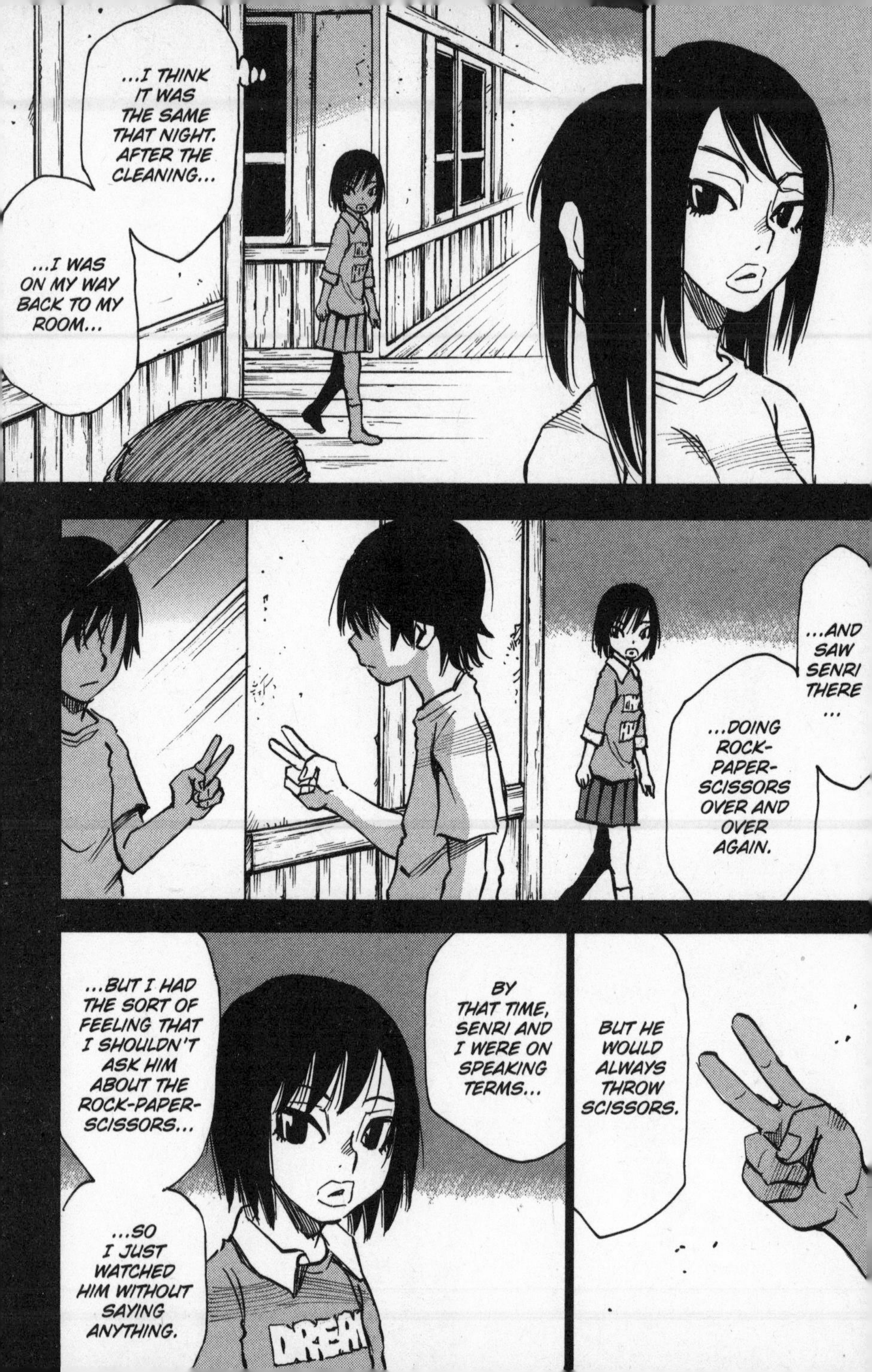
...I THINK IT WAS THE SAME THAT NIGHT. AFTER THE CLEANING...
...I WAS ON MY WAY BACK TO MY ROOM...
...AND SAW SENRI THERE...
...DOING ROCK-PAPER-SCISSORS OVER AND OVER AGAIN.
BUT HE WOULD ALWAYS THROW SCISSORS.
BY THAT TIME, SENRI AND I WERE ON SPEAKING TERMS...
...BUT I HAD THE SORT OF FEELING THAT I SHOULDN'T ASK HIM ABOUT THE ROCK-PAPER-SCISSORS...
...SO I JUST WATCHED HIM WITHOUT SAYING ANYTHING.

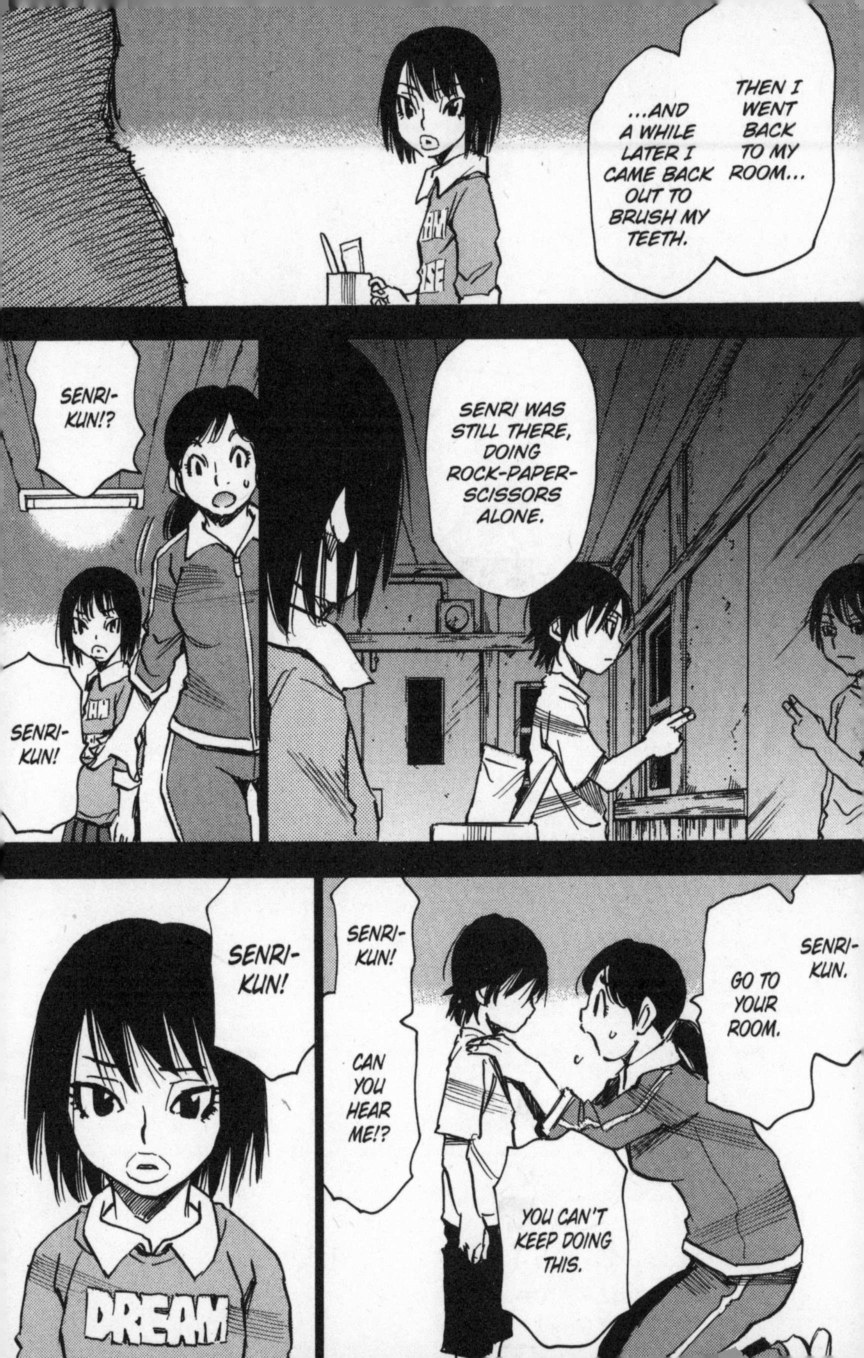
THEN I WENT BACK TO MY ROOM...
...AND A WHILE LATER I CAME BACK OUT TO BRUSH MY TEETH.
SENRI WAS STILL THERE, DOING ROCK-PAPER-SCISSORS ALONE.
SENRI-KUN!?
SENRI-KUN!
SENRI-KUN.
GO TO YOUR ROOM.
SENRI-KUN!
CAN YOU HEAR ME!?
YOU CAN'T KEEP DOING THIS.
SENRI-KUN!
DREAM

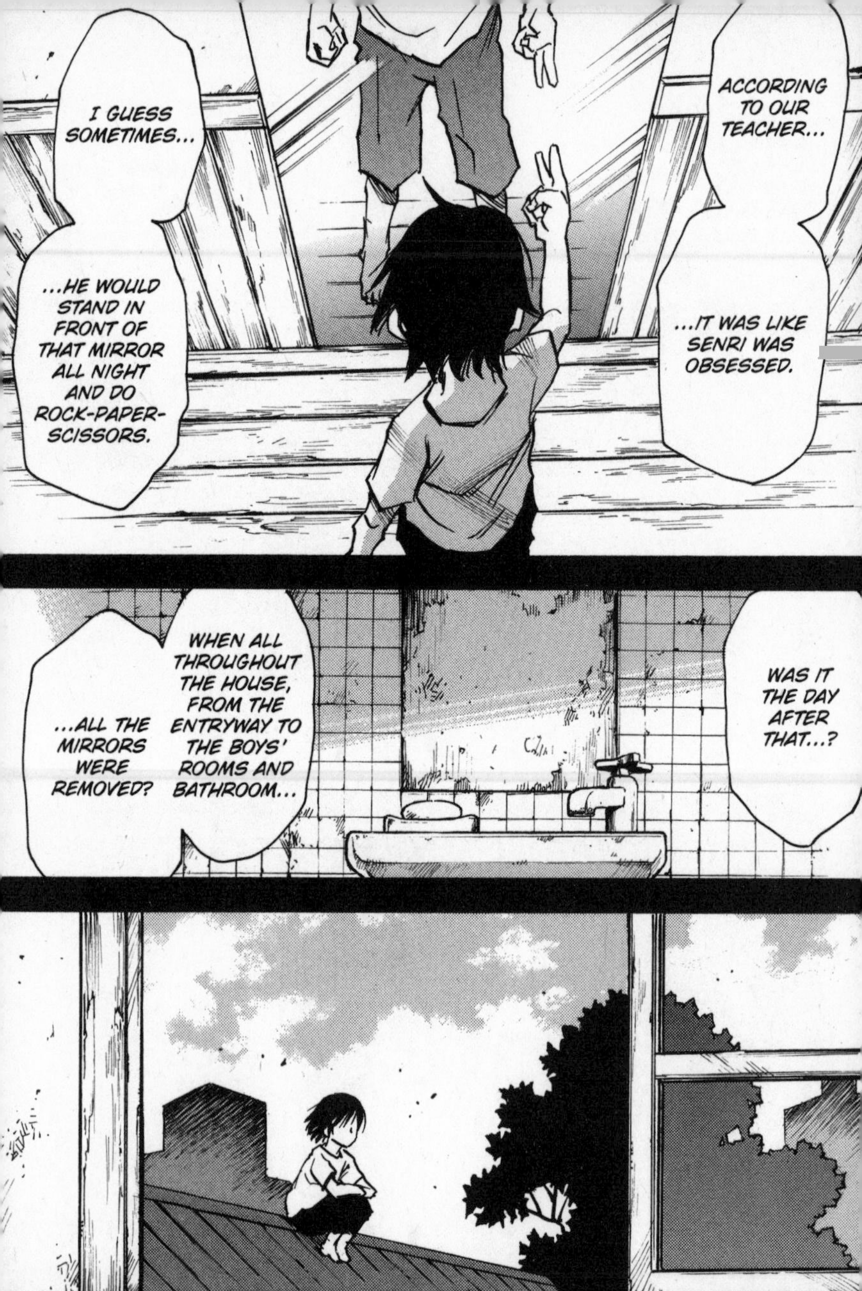
ACCORDING TO OUR TEACHER...
...IT WAS LIKE SENRI WAS OBSESSED.
I GUESS SOMETIMES...
...HE WOULD STAND IN FRONT OF THAT MIRROR ALL NIGHT AND DO ROCK-PAPER-SCISSORS.
WAS IT THE DAY AFTER THAT...?
WHEN ALL THROUGHOUT THE HOUSE, FROM THE ENTRYWAY TO THE BOYS' ROOMS AND BATHROOM...
...ALL THE MIRRORS WERE REMOVED?

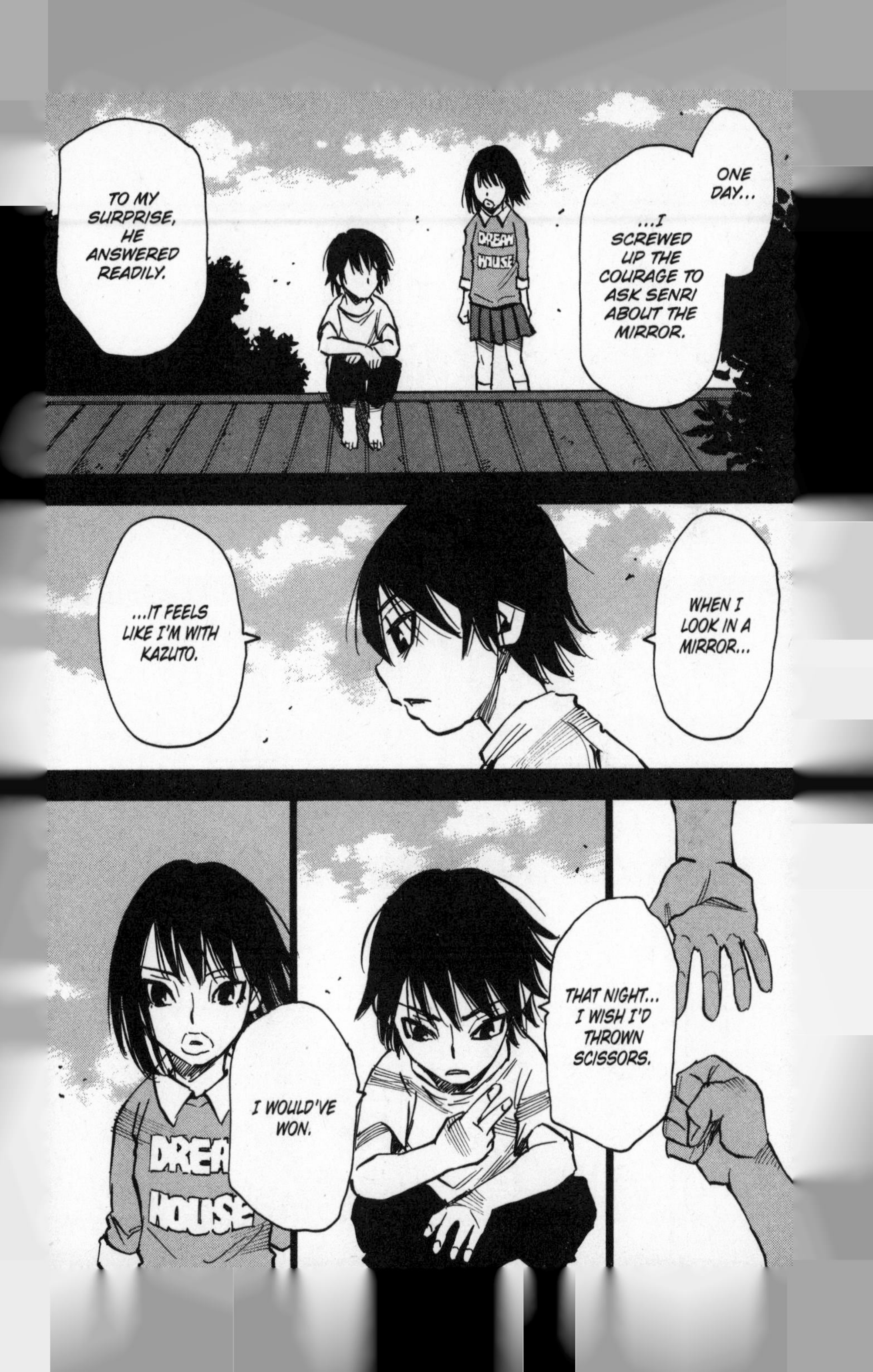
ONE DAY...
...I SCREWED UP THE COURAGE TO ASK SENRI ABOUT THE MIRROR.
DREAM HOUSE
TO MY SURPRISE, HE ANSWERED READILY.
WHEN I LOOK IN A MIRROR...
...IT FEELS LIKE I'M WITH KAZUTO.
THAT NIGHT... I WISH I'D THROWN SCISSORS.
I WOULD'VE WON.

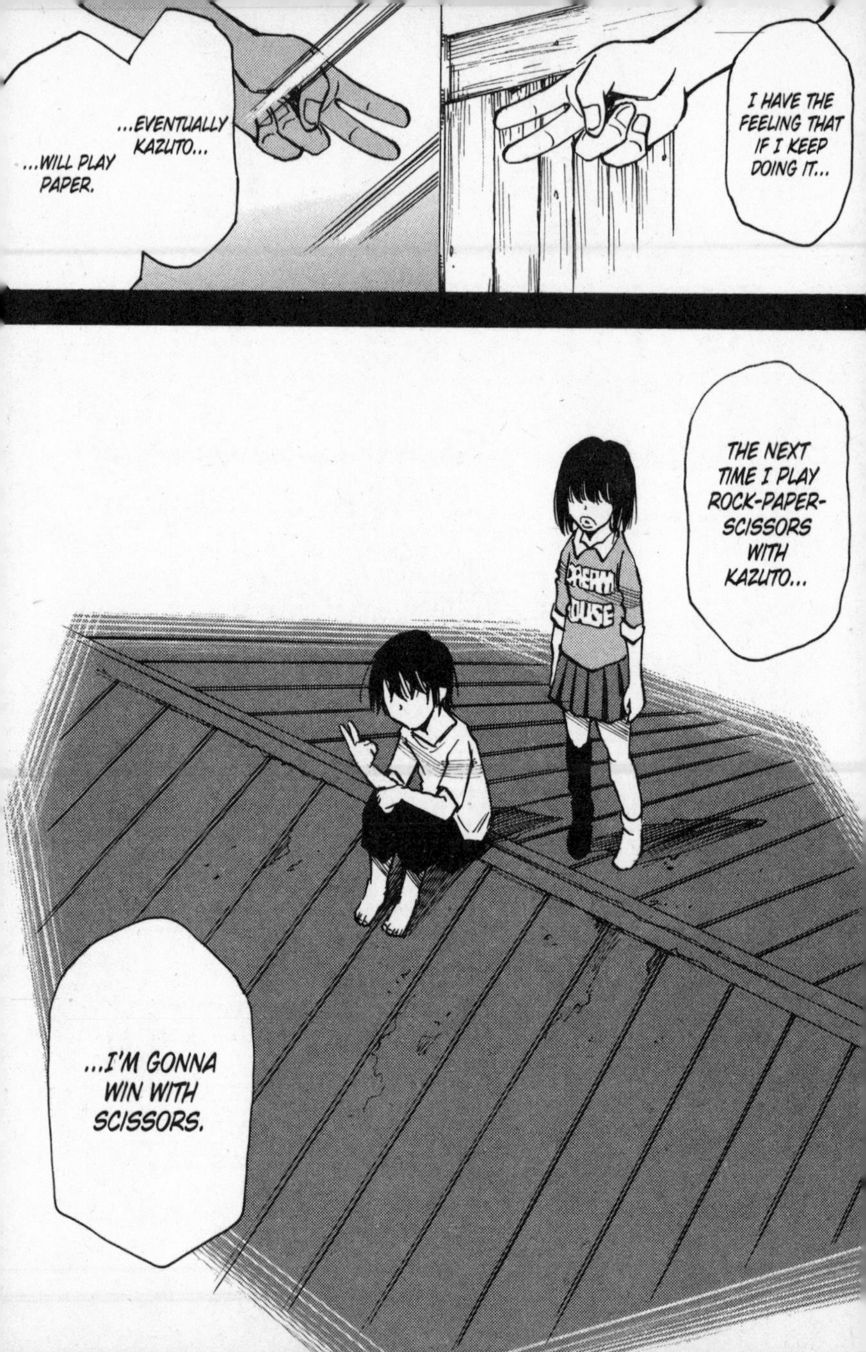
I HAVE THE FEELING THAT IF I KEEP DOING IT...
...EVENTUALLY KAZUTO...
...WILL PLAY PAPER.
THE NEXT TIME I PLAY ROCK-PAPER-SCISSORS WITH KAZUTO...
...I'M GONNA WIN WITH SCISSORS.

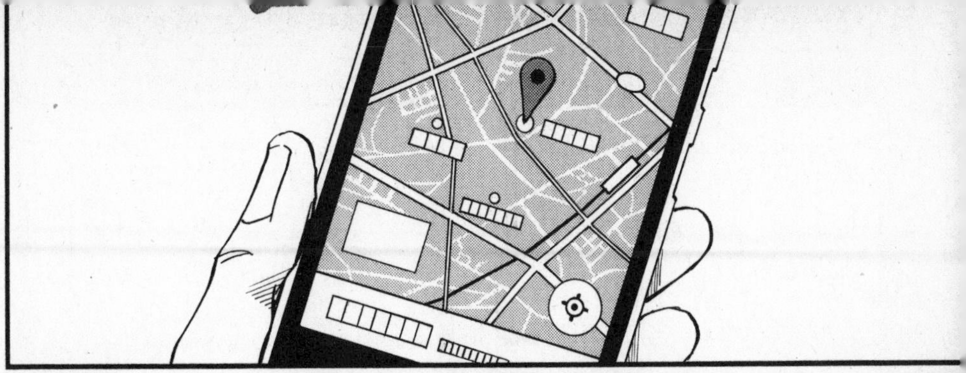

SIGN: MOMOMIYA LOANS / BOTTOM SIGN: KONAKAZAWA DENTISTRY

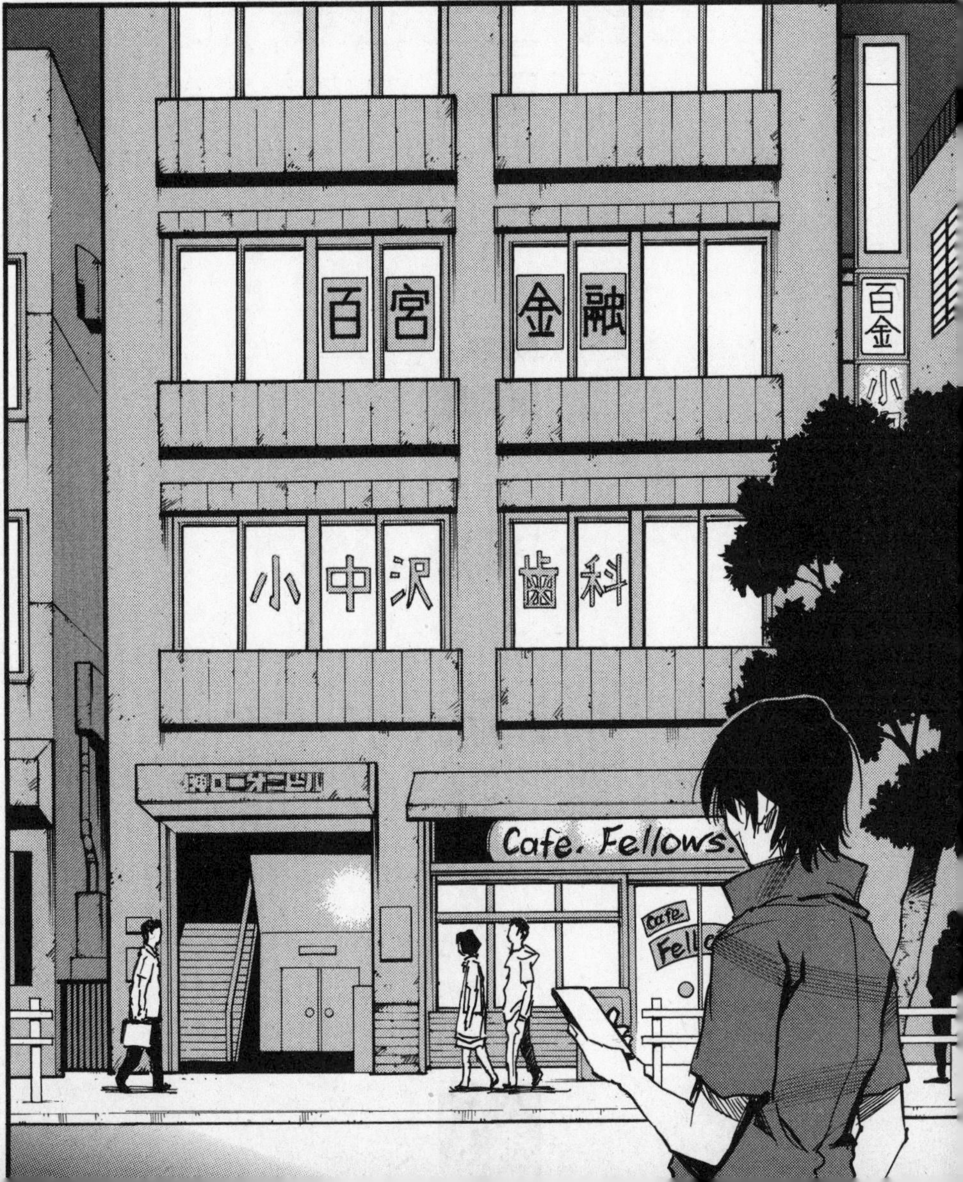
百宮金融
小中沢歯科
Cafe. Fellows.

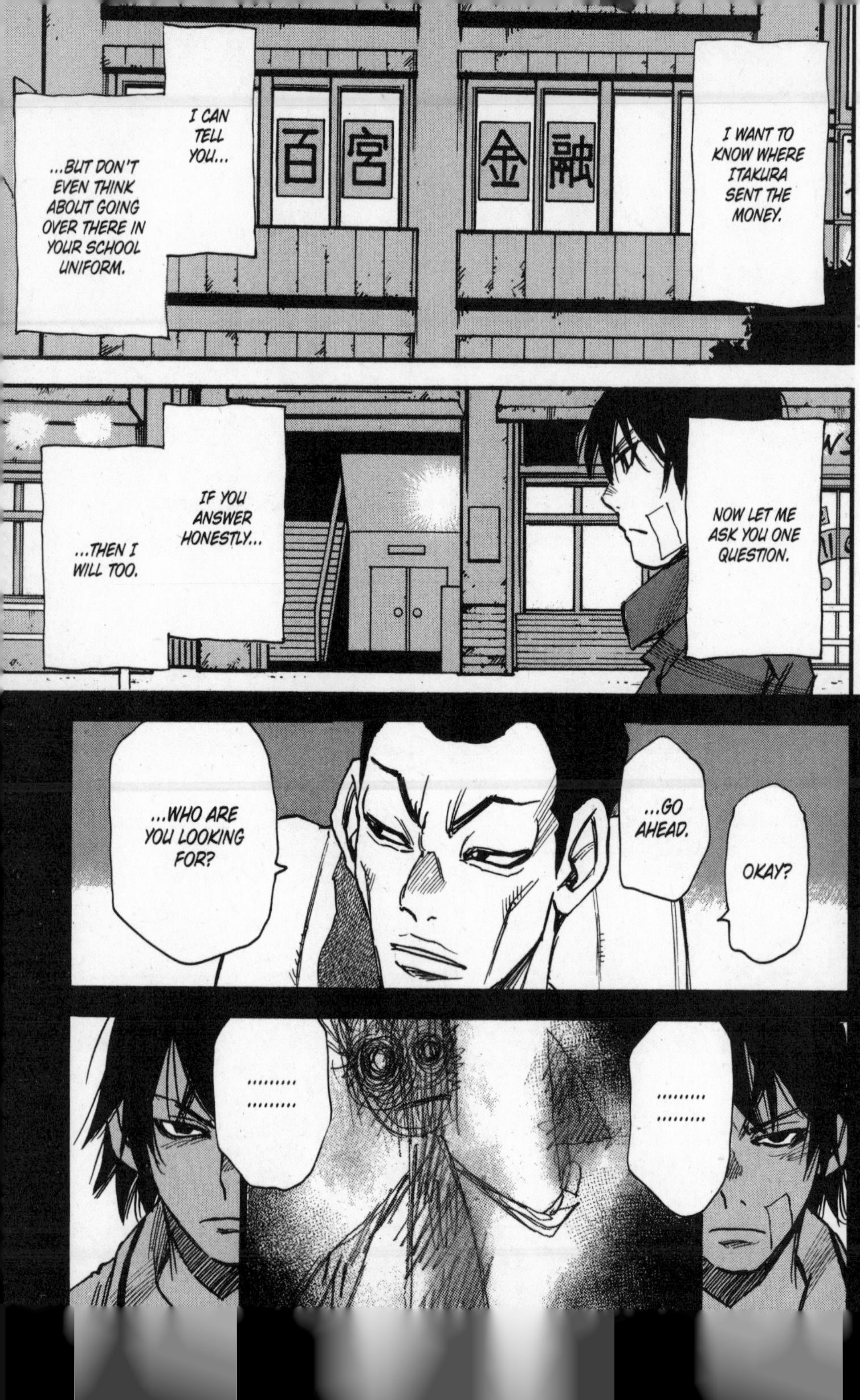
百宮金融
I WANT TO KNOW WHERE ITAKURA SENT THE MONEY.
I CAN TELL YOU...
...BUT DON'T EVEN THINK ABOUT GOING OVER THERE IN YOUR SCHOOL UNIFORM.
NOW LET ME ASK YOU ONE QUESTION.
IF YOU ANSWER HONESTLY...
...THEN I WILL TOO.
OKAY?
...GO AHEAD.
...WHO ARE YOU LOOKING FOR?
....
....
....
....

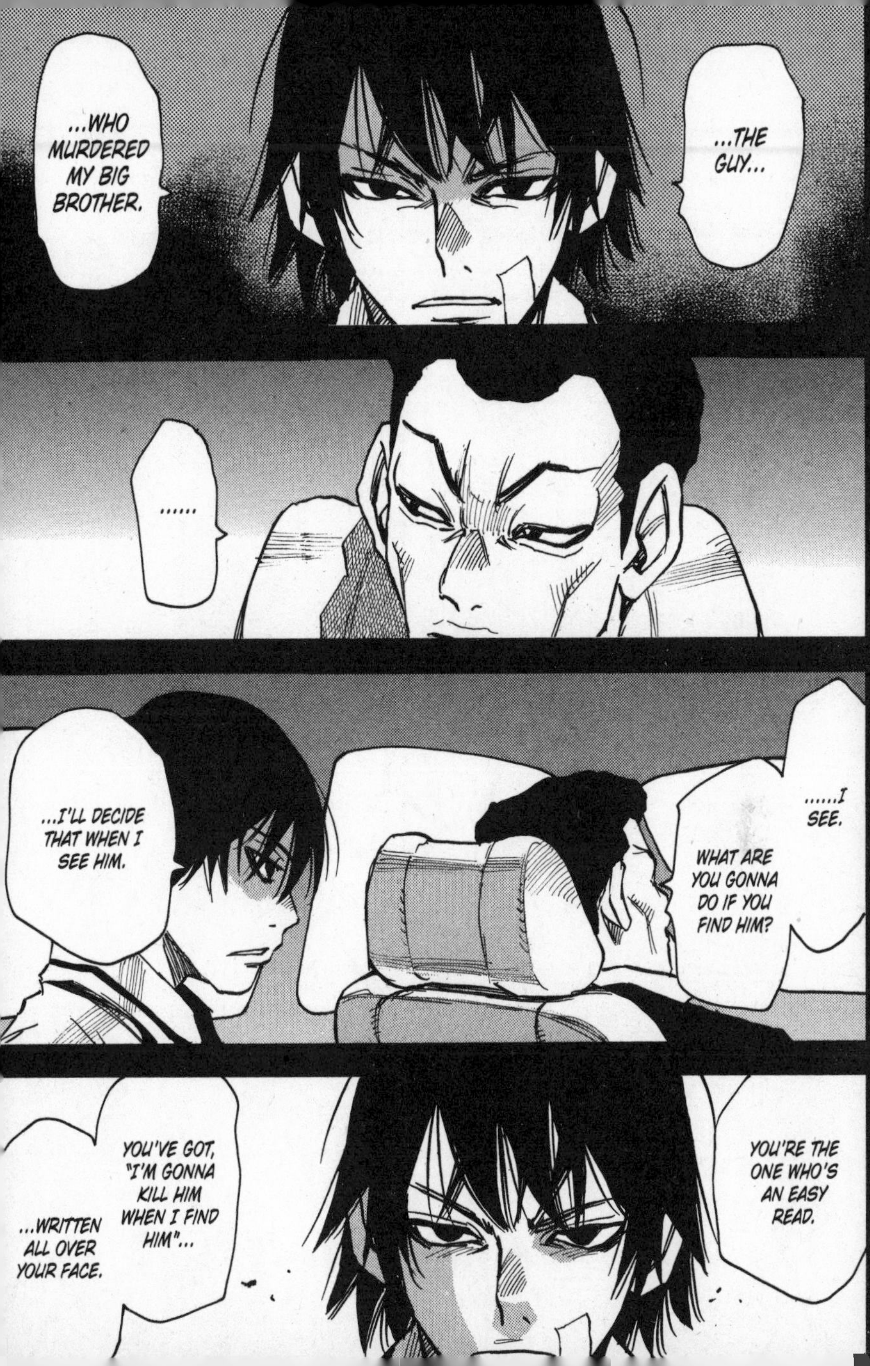
...THE GUY...
...WHO MURDERED MY BIG BROTHER.
......
......I SEE.
WHAT ARE YOU GONNA DO IF YOU FIND HIM?
...I'LL DECIDE THAT WHEN I SEE HIM.
YOU'RE THE ONE WHO'S AN EASY READ.
YOU'VE GOT, "I'M GONNA KILL HIM WHEN I FIND HIM"...
...WRITTEN ALL OVER YOUR FACE.

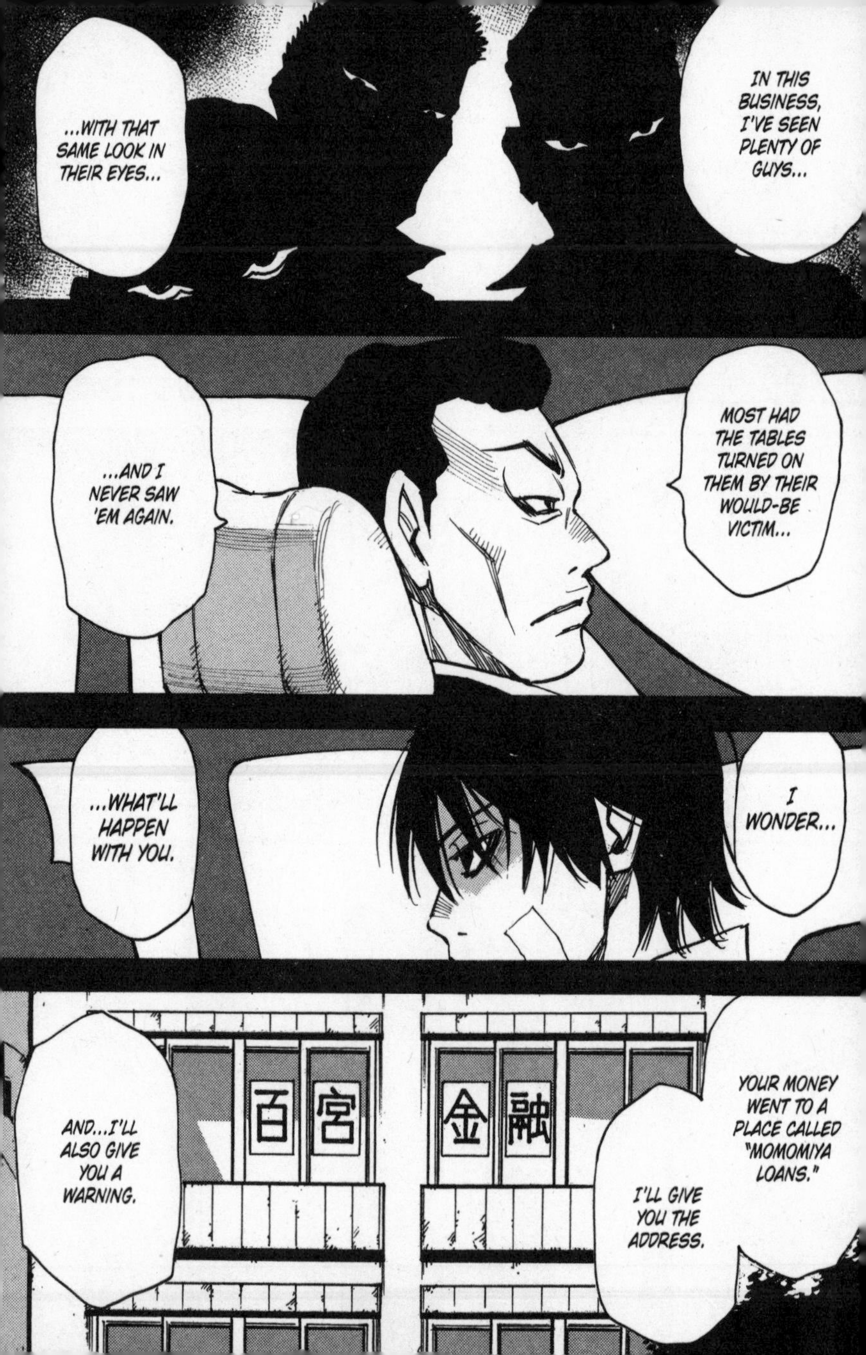
IN THIS BUSINESS, I'VE SEEN PLENTY OF GUYS...
...WITH THAT SAME LOOK IN THEIR EYES...
MOST HAD THE TABLES TURNED ON THEM BY THEIR WOULD-BE VICTIM...
...AND I NEVER SAW 'EM AGAIN.
I WONDER...
...WHAT'LL HAPPEN WITH YOU.
YOUR MONEY WENT TO A PLACE CALLED "MOMOMIYA LOANS."
I'LL GIVE YOU THE ADDRESS.
百宮金融
AND...I'LL ALSO GIVE YOU A WARNING.

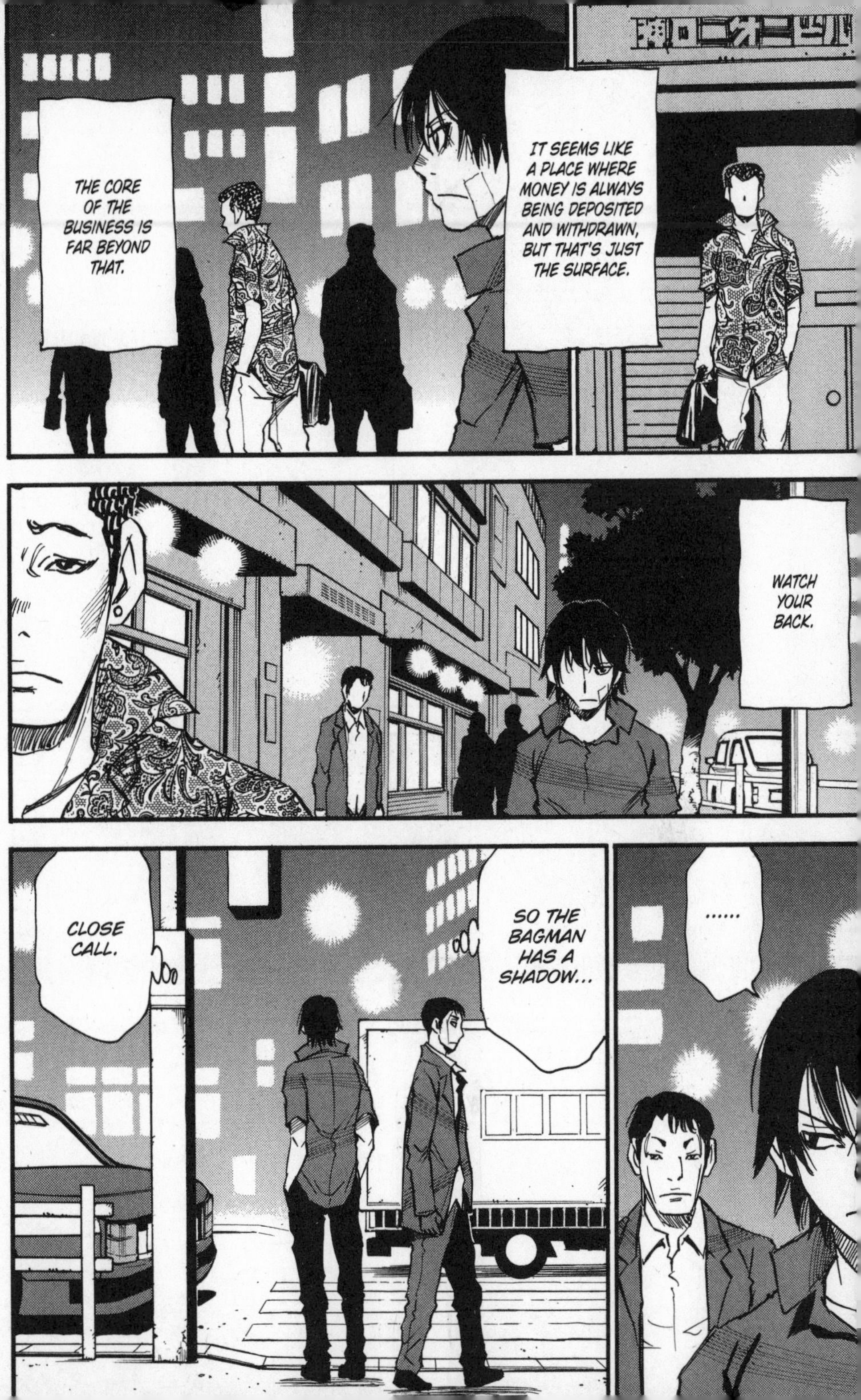
IT SEEMS LIKE A PLACE WHERE MONEY IS ALWAYS BEING DEPOSITED AND WITHDRAWN, BUT THAT'S JUST THE SURFACE.
THE CORE OF THE BUSINESS IS FAR BEYOND THAT.
WATCH YOUR BACK.
......
SO THE BAGMAN HAS A SHADOW...
CLOSE CALL.

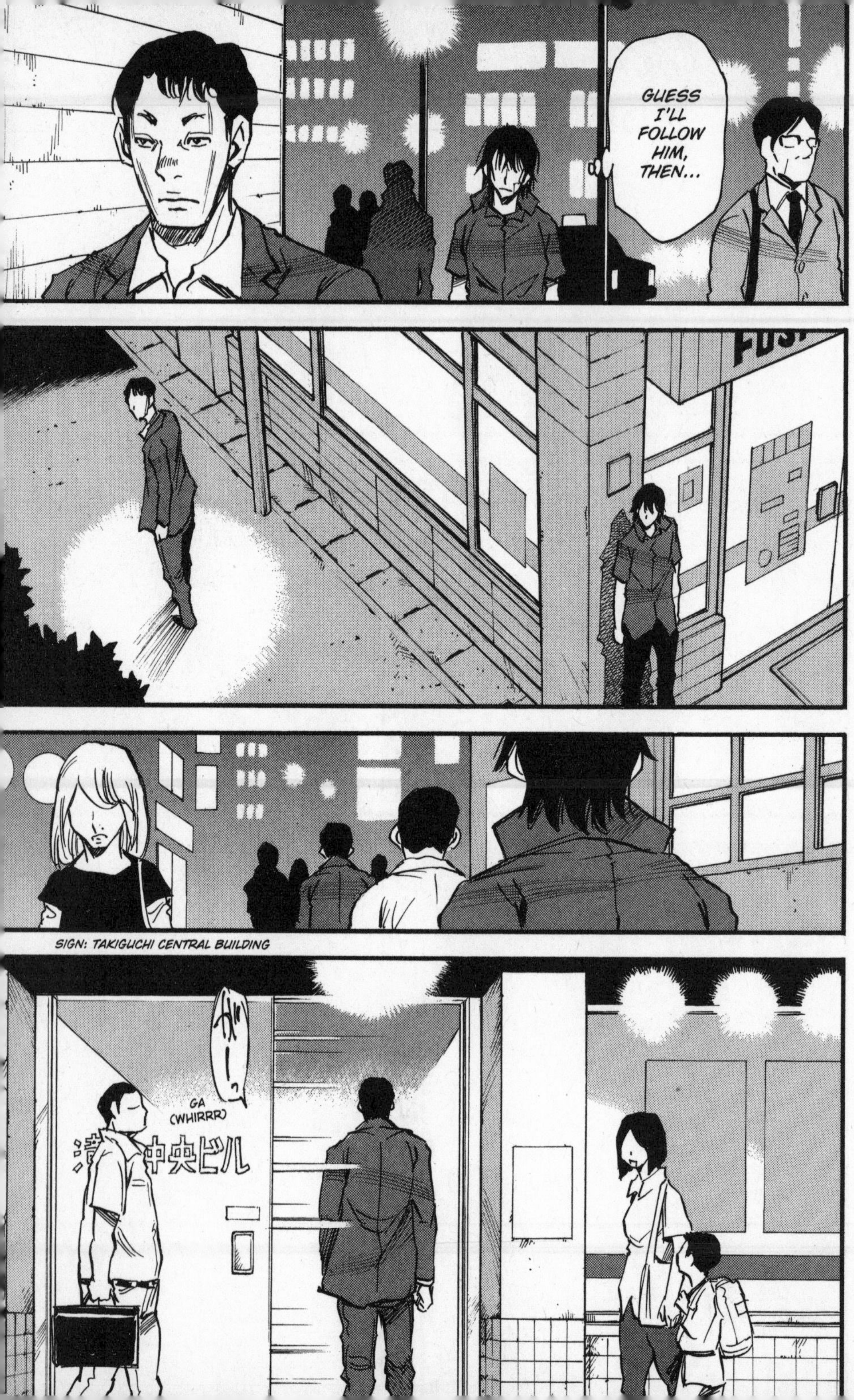
GUESS I'LL FOLLOW HIM, THEN...
SIGN: TAKIGUCHI CENTRAL BUILDING
ガー
GA (WHIRRR)

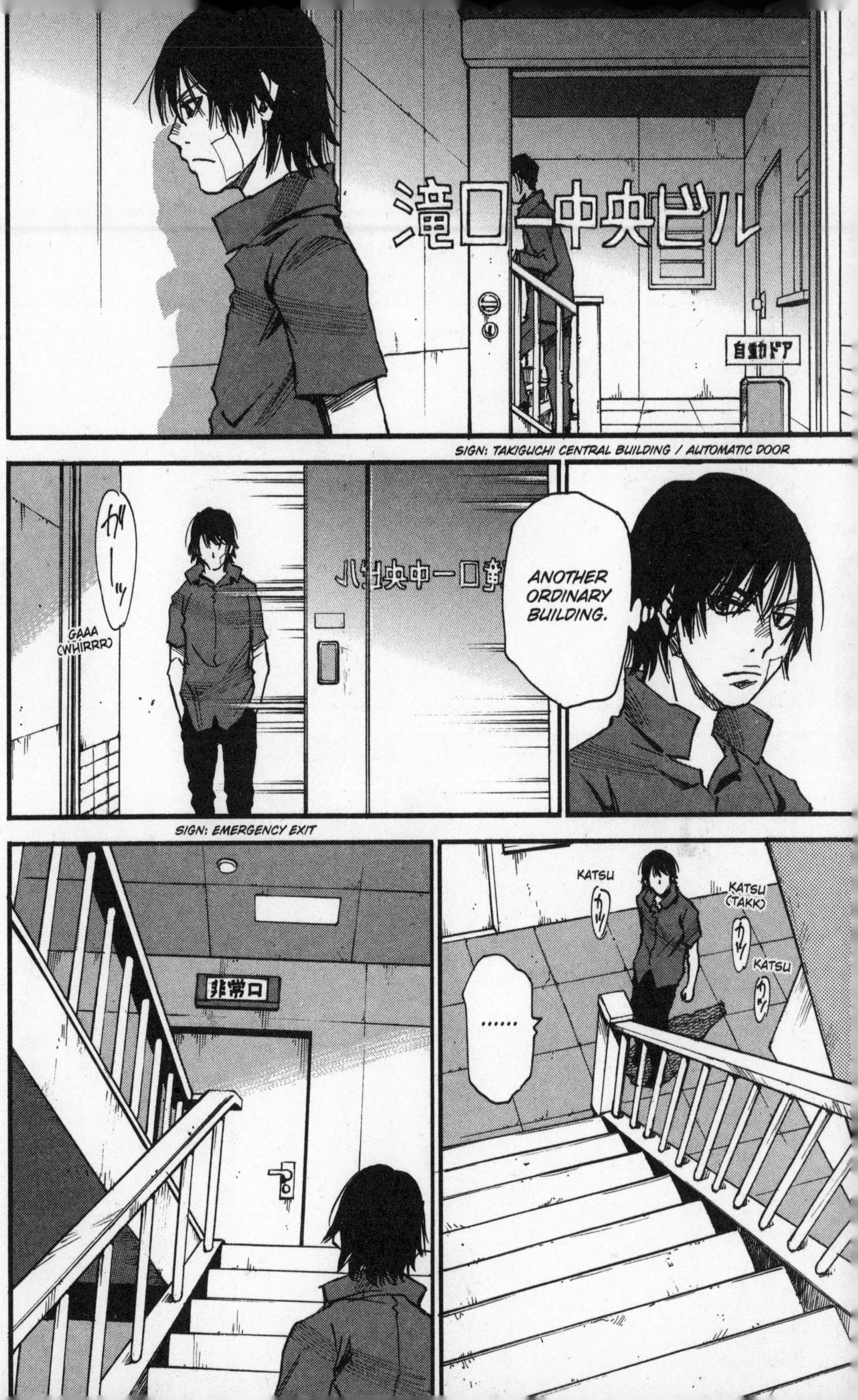
滝口中央ビル
自動ドア
SIGN: TAKIGUCHI CENTRAL BUILDING / AUTOMATIC DOOR
ANOTHER ORDINARY BUILDING.
がーッ
GAAA (WHIRRR)
SIGN: EMERGENCY EXIT
カッ
KATSU
カッ
KATSU (TAKK)
カッ
KATSU
......
非常口

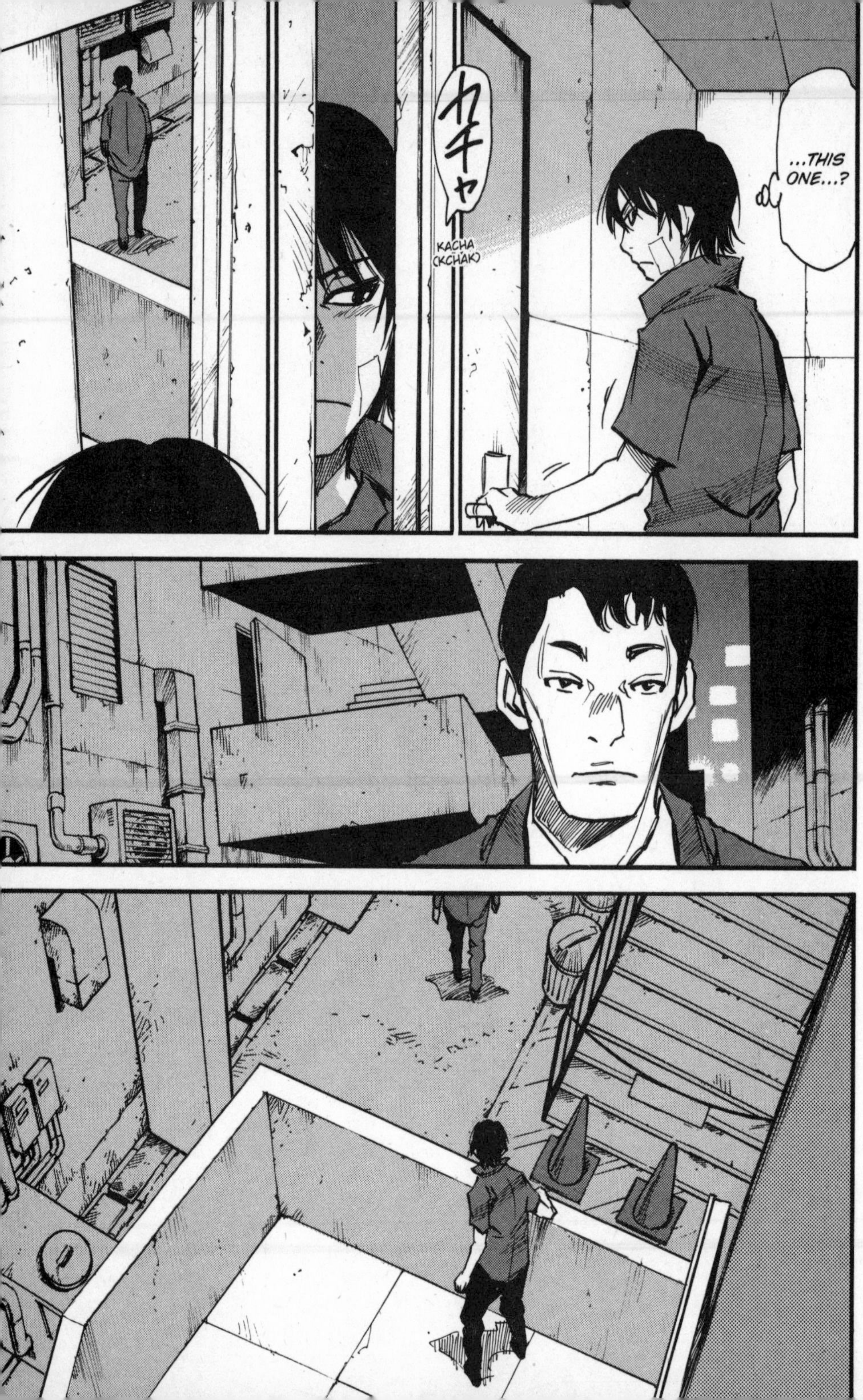
...THIS ONE...?
カチャ
KACHA (KCHAK)

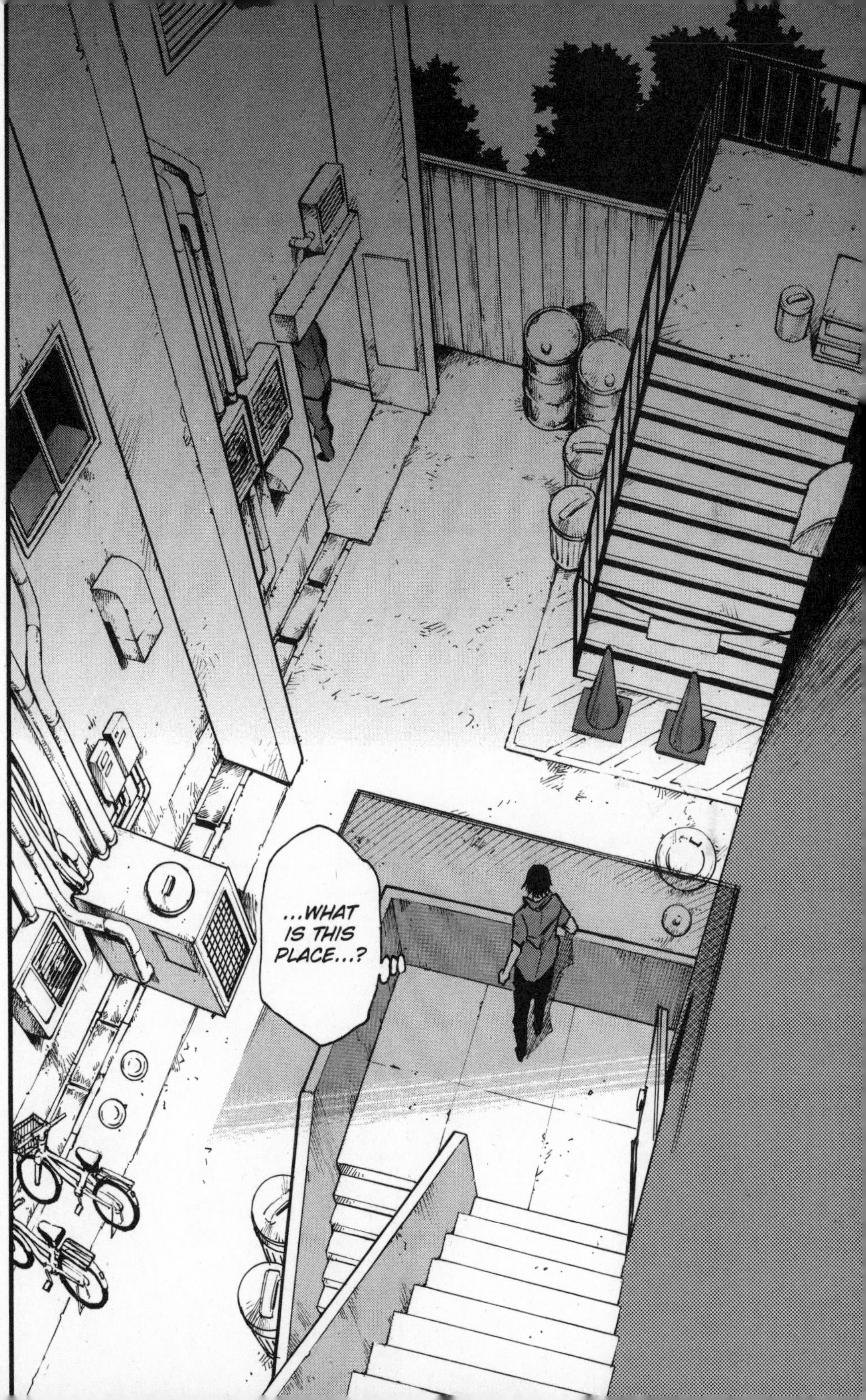
...WHAT IS THIS PLACE...?

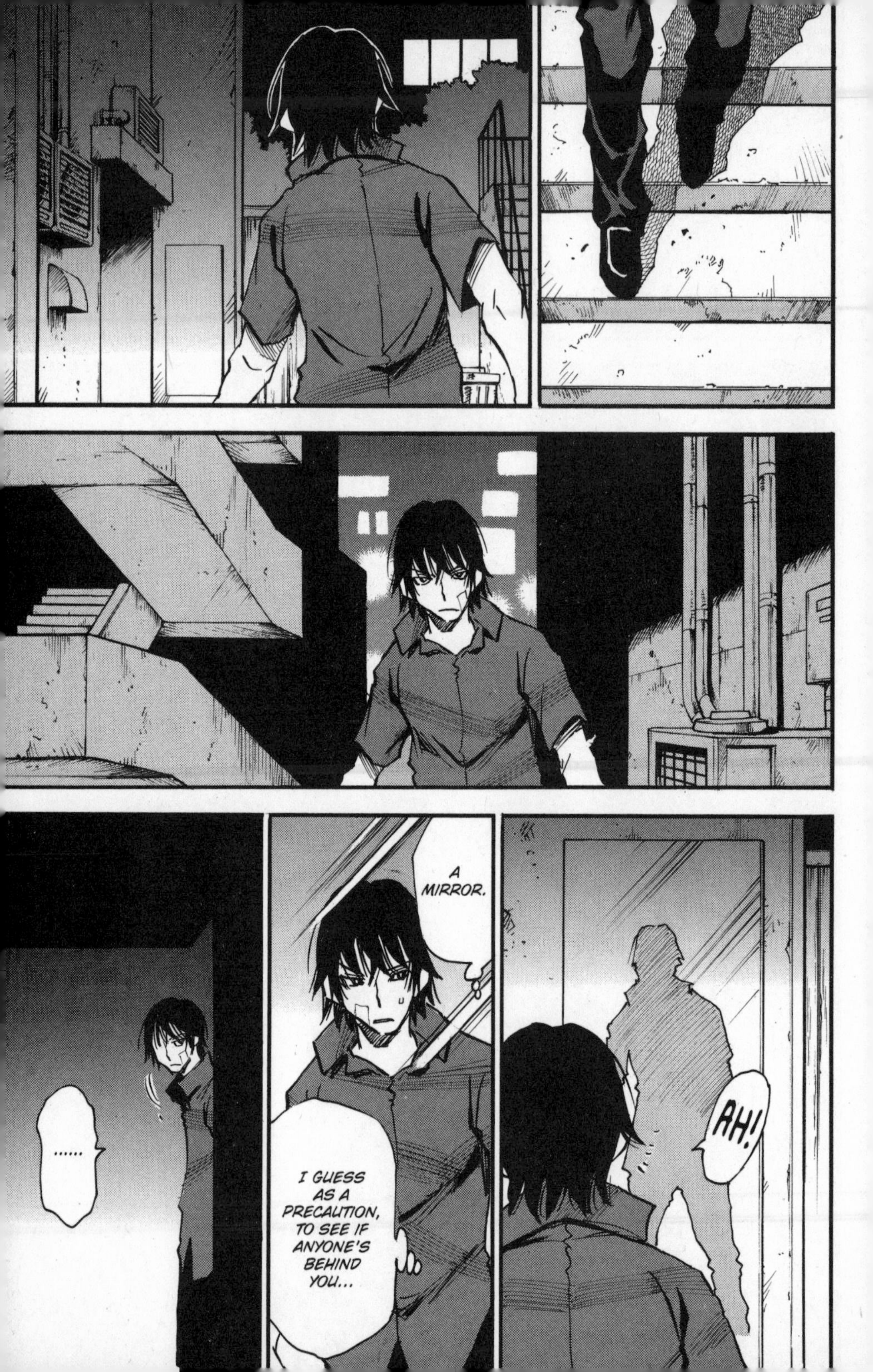
RH!
A MIRROR.
I GUESS AS A PRECAUTION, TO SEE IF ANYONE'S BEHIND YOU...
......

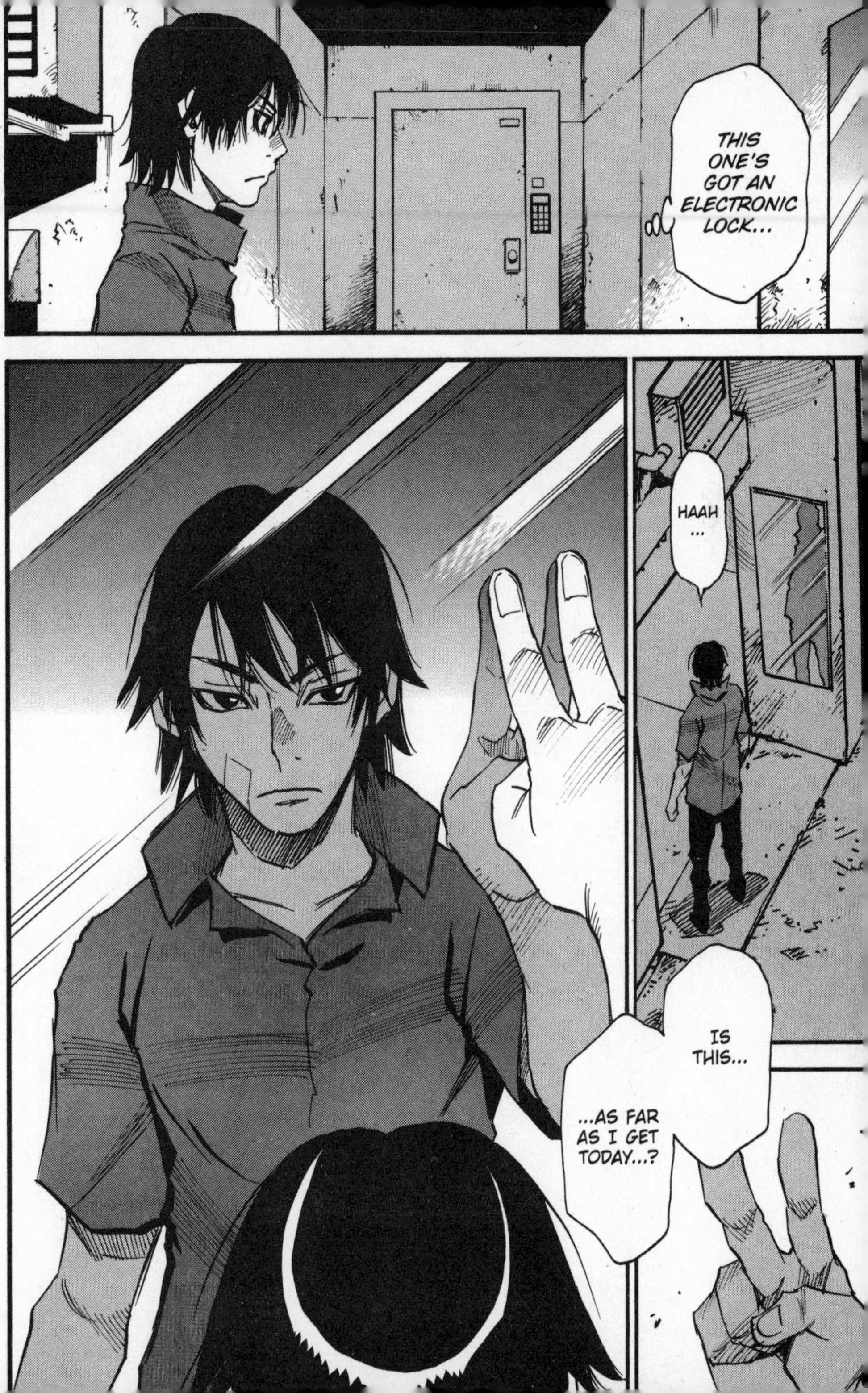
THIS ONE'S GOT AN ELECTRONIC LOCK...
HAAH ...
IS THIS...
...AS FAR AS I GET TODAY...?

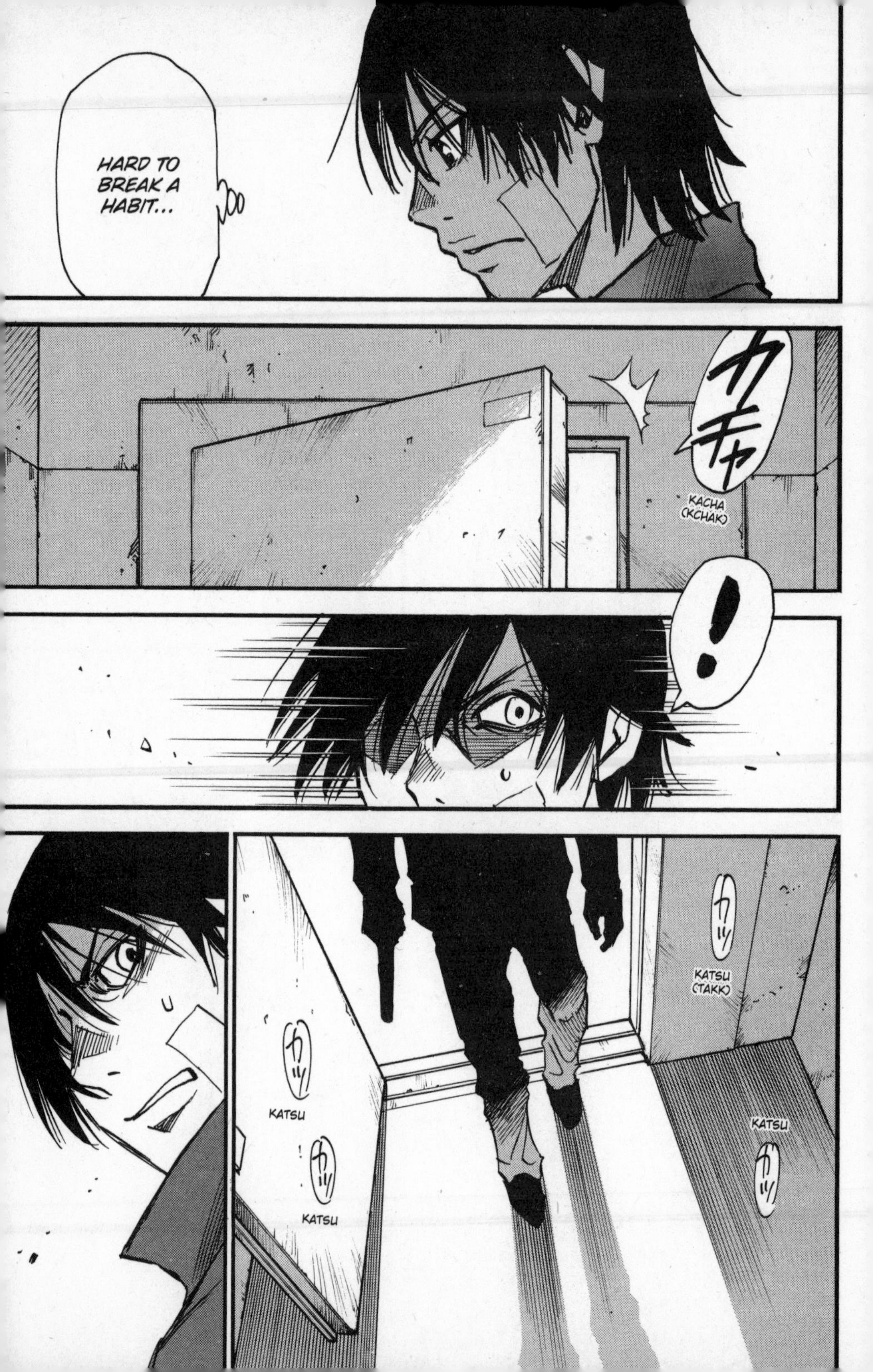
HARD TO BREAK A HABIT...
カチャ
KACHA (KCHAK)
!
カツ
KATSU (TAKK)
KATSU
カツ
カツ
KATSU
カツ
KATSU

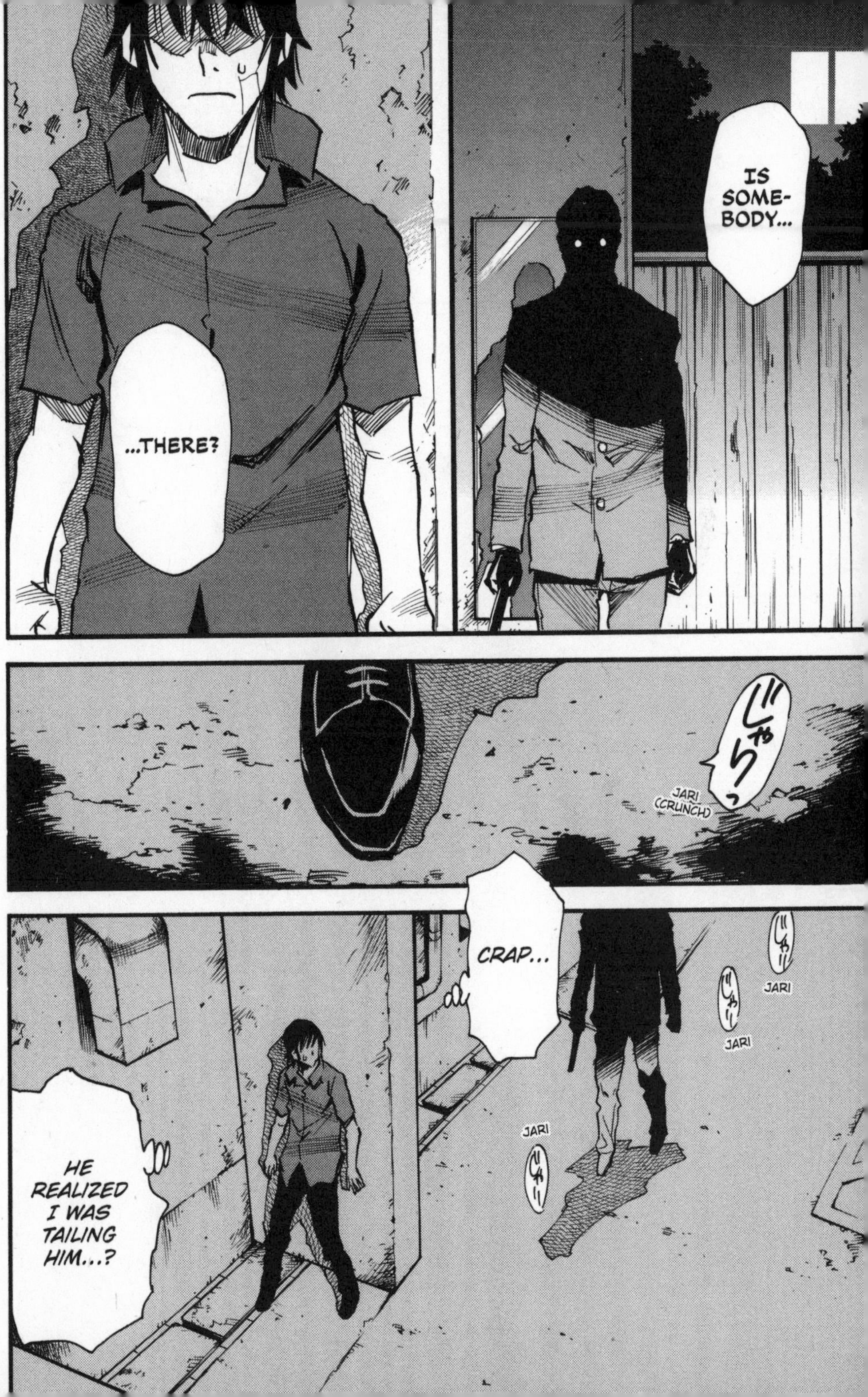
IS SOMEBODY...
...THERE?
じゃりっ
JARI (CRUNCH)
じゃり
JARI
じゃり
JARI
CRAP...
JARI
じゃり
HE REALIZED I WAS TAILING HIM...?

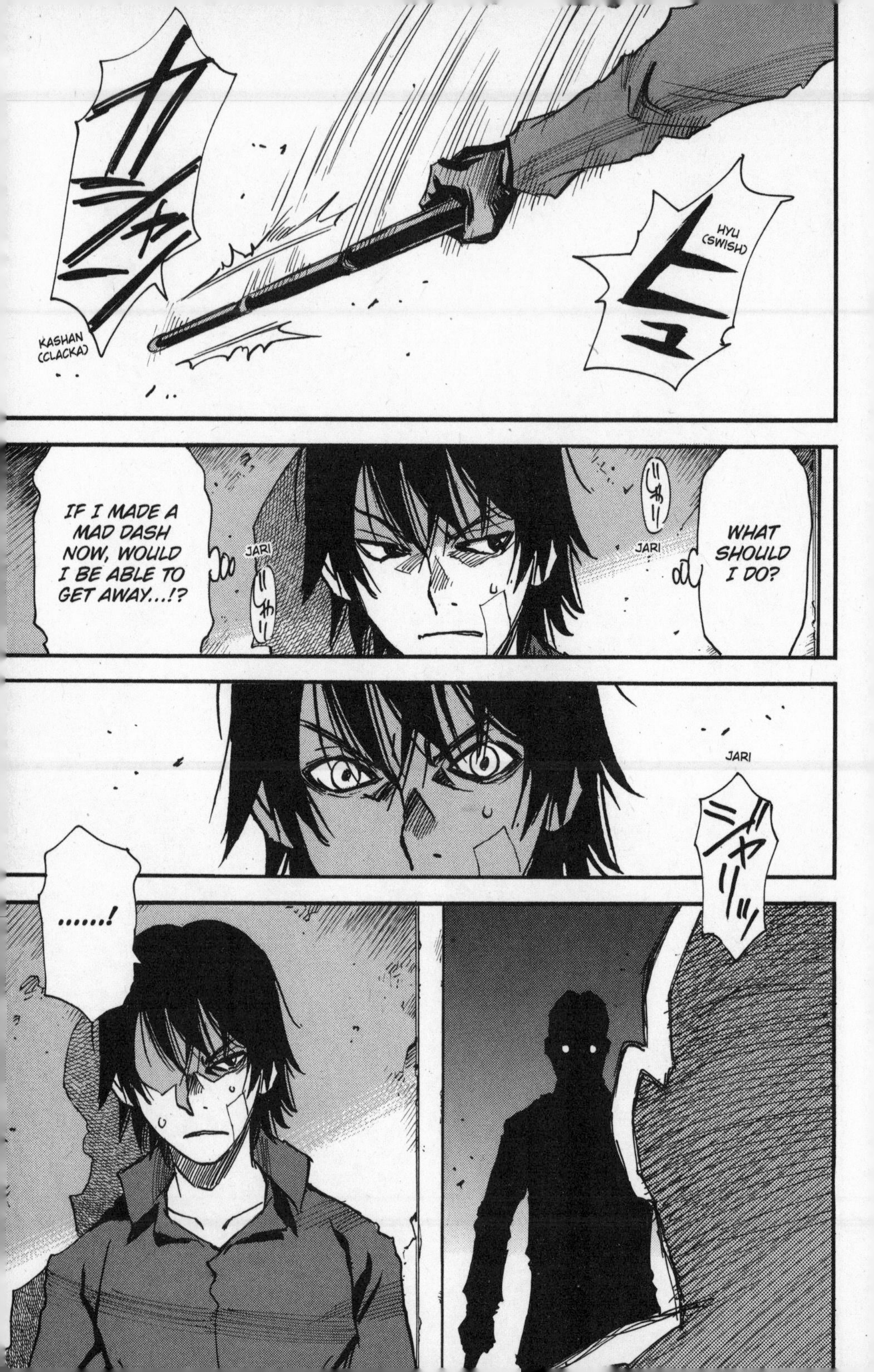
ヒュ
HYU (SWISH)
カシャン
KASHAN (CLACKA)
WHAT SHOULD I DO?
じゃり
JARI
じゃり
JARI
IF I MADE A MAD DASH NOW, WOULD I BE ABLE TO GET AWAY...!?
ジャリッ
JARI
......!

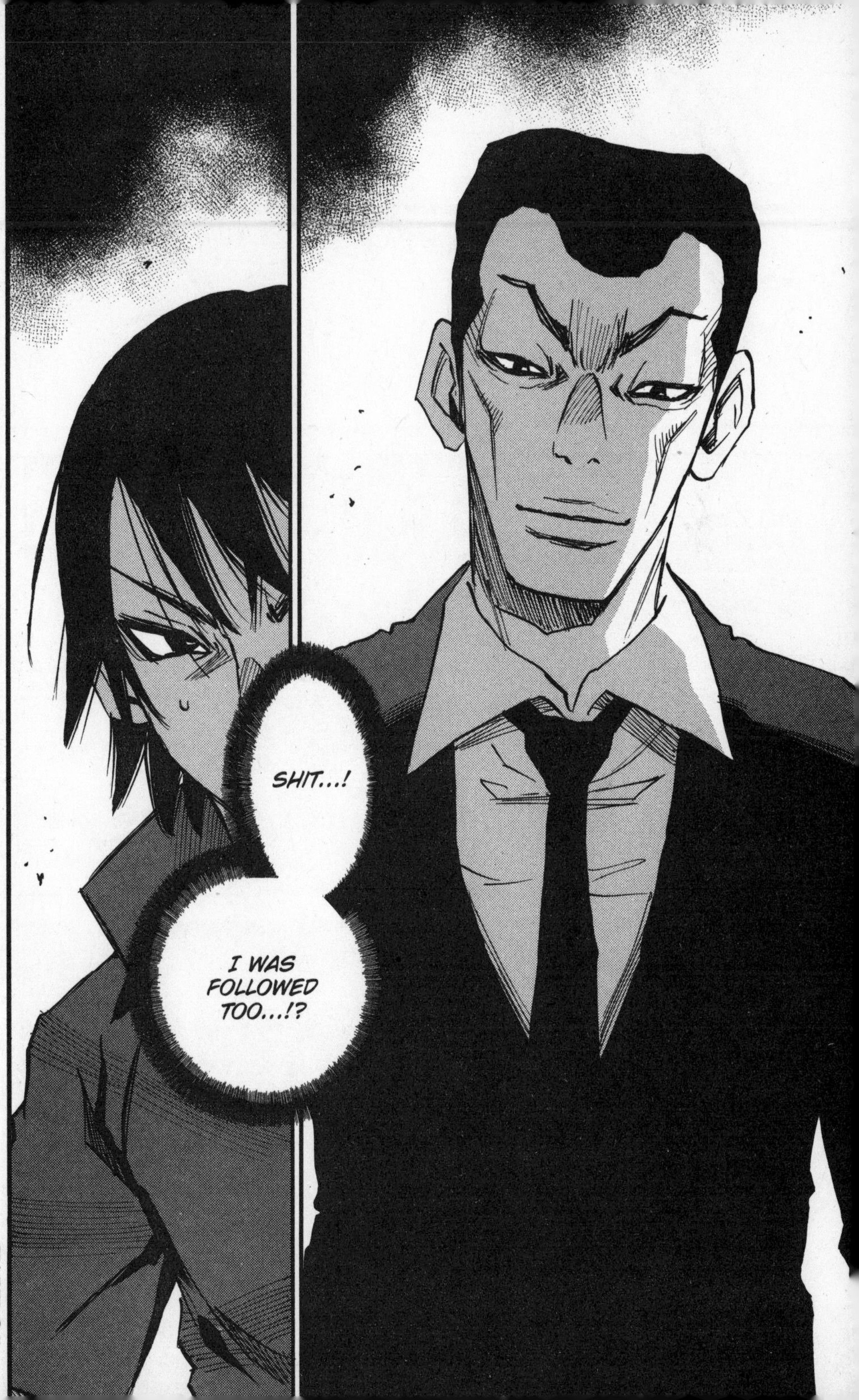
SHIT...!
I WAS FOLLOWED TOO...!?

#8 END

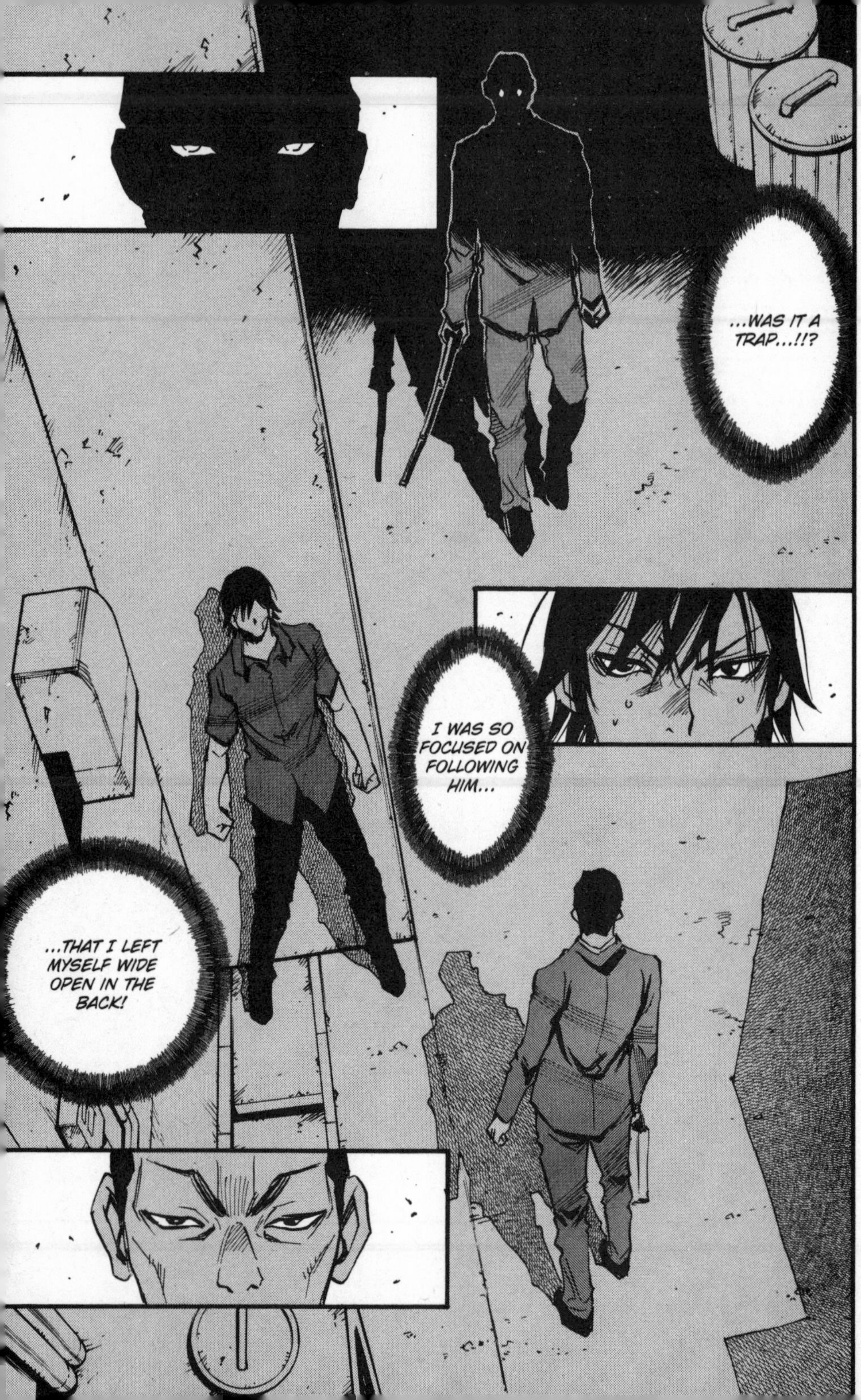
...WAS IT A TRAP...!!?
I WAS SO FOCUSED ON FOLLOWING HIM...
...THAT I LEFT MYSELF WIDE OPEN IN THE BACK!

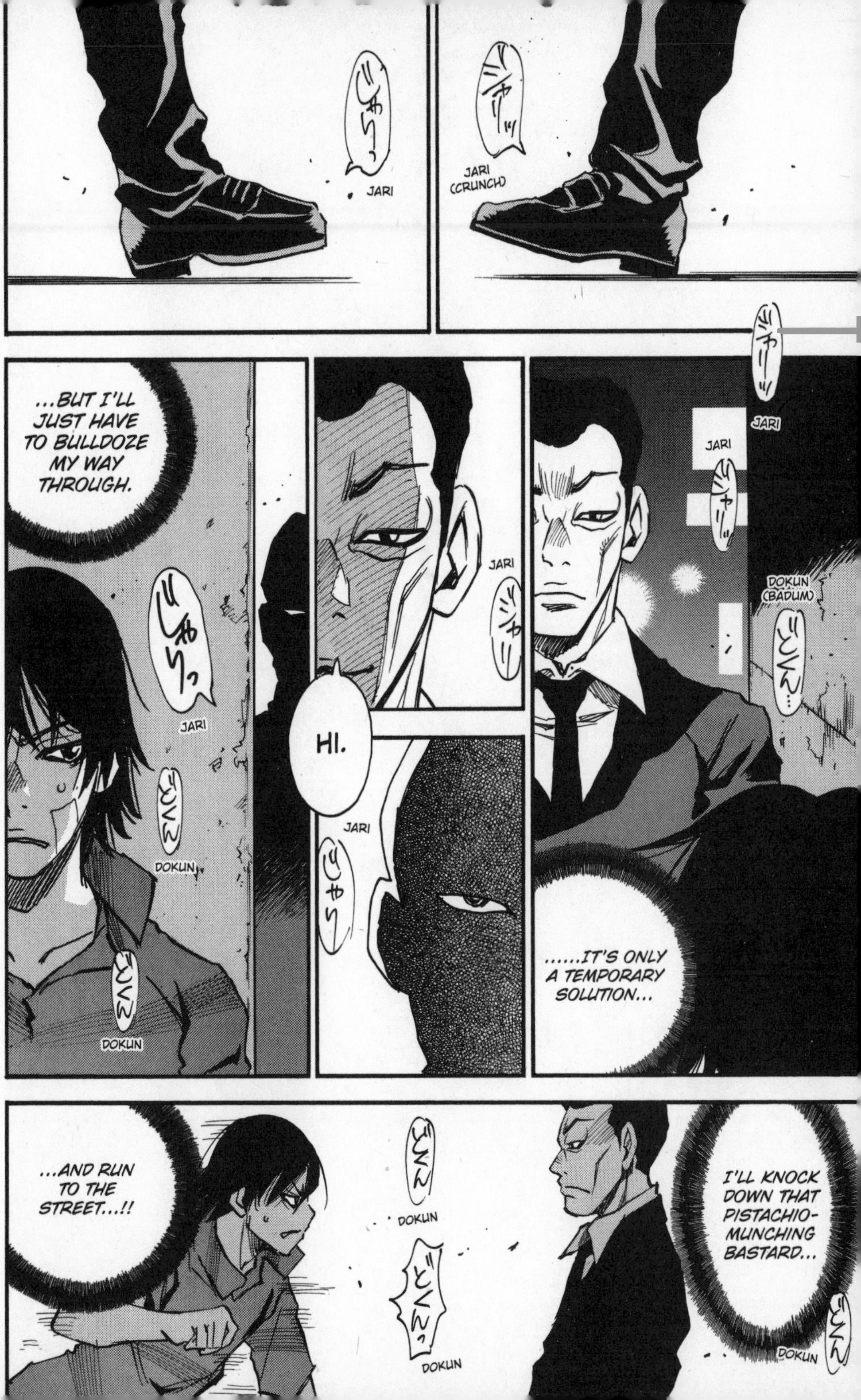

ジャリッ
JARI (CRUNCH)
じゃりっ
JARI
ジャリッ
JARI
じゃりっ
JARI
DOKUN (BADUM)
どくん…
……IT'S ONLY A TEMPORARY SOLUTION…
ジャリ
JARI
HI.
じゃり
JARI
…BUT I'LL JUST HAVE TO BULLDOZE MY WAY THROUGH.
じゃりっ
JARI
どくん
DOKUN
どくん
DOKUN
I'LL KNOCK DOWN THAT PISTACHIO-MUNCHING BASTARD…
どくん
DOKUN
どくんっ
DOKUN
どくん
DOKUN
…AND RUN TO THE STREET…!!

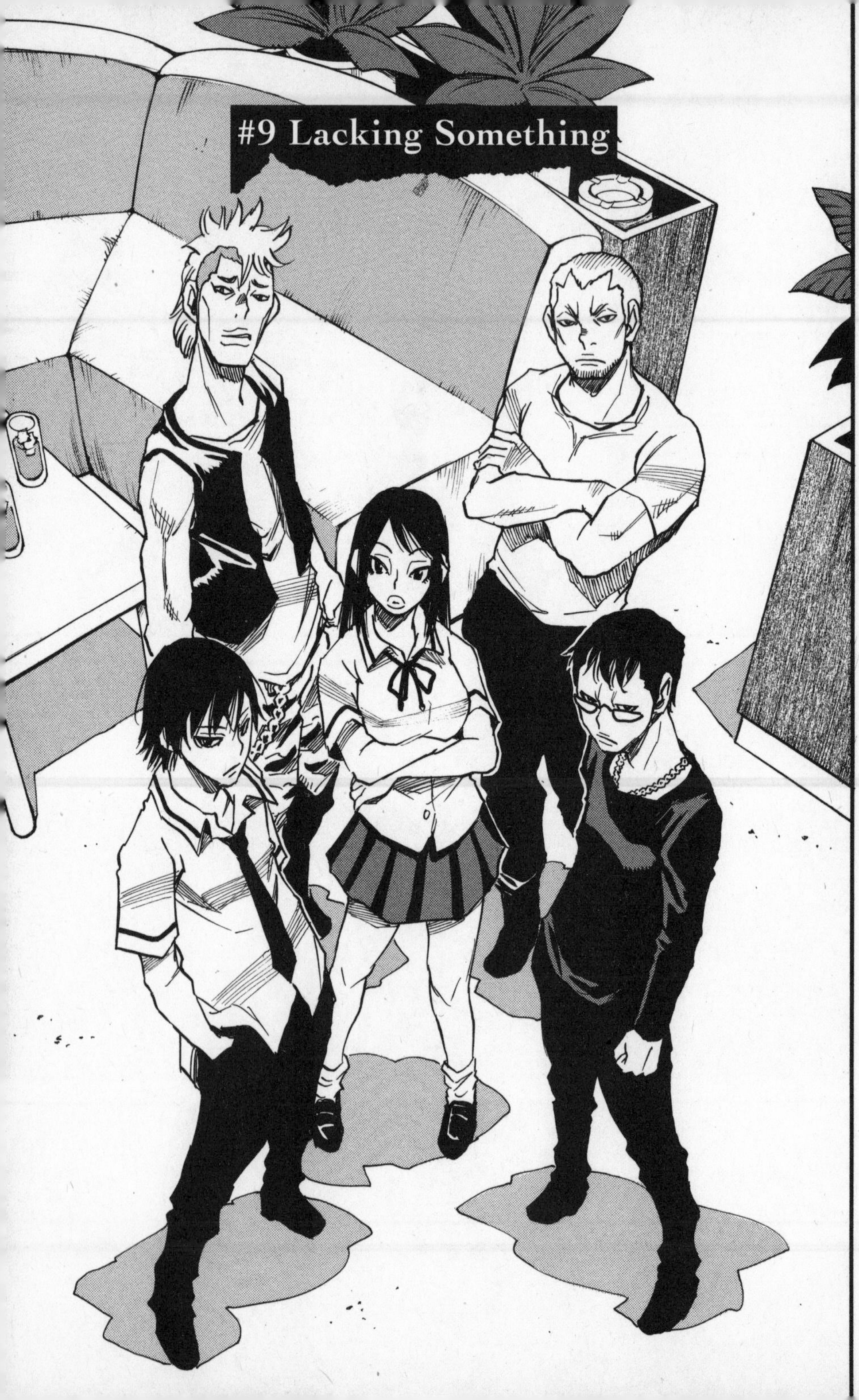
#9 Lacking Something

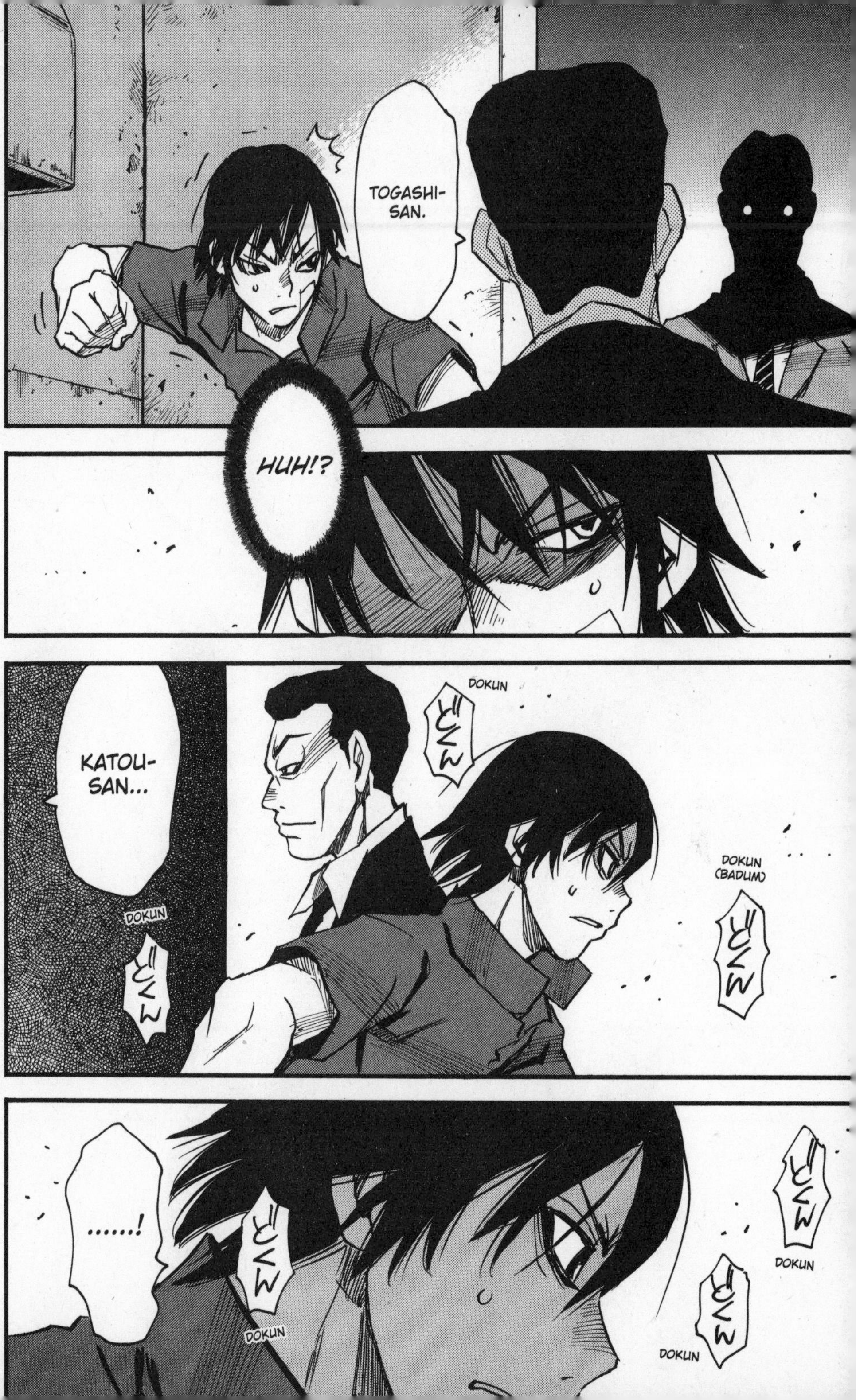
TOGASHI-SAN.
HUH!?
DOKUN
DOKUN (BADUM)
KATOU-SAN...
DOKUN
DOKUN
DOKUN
......!
DOKUN

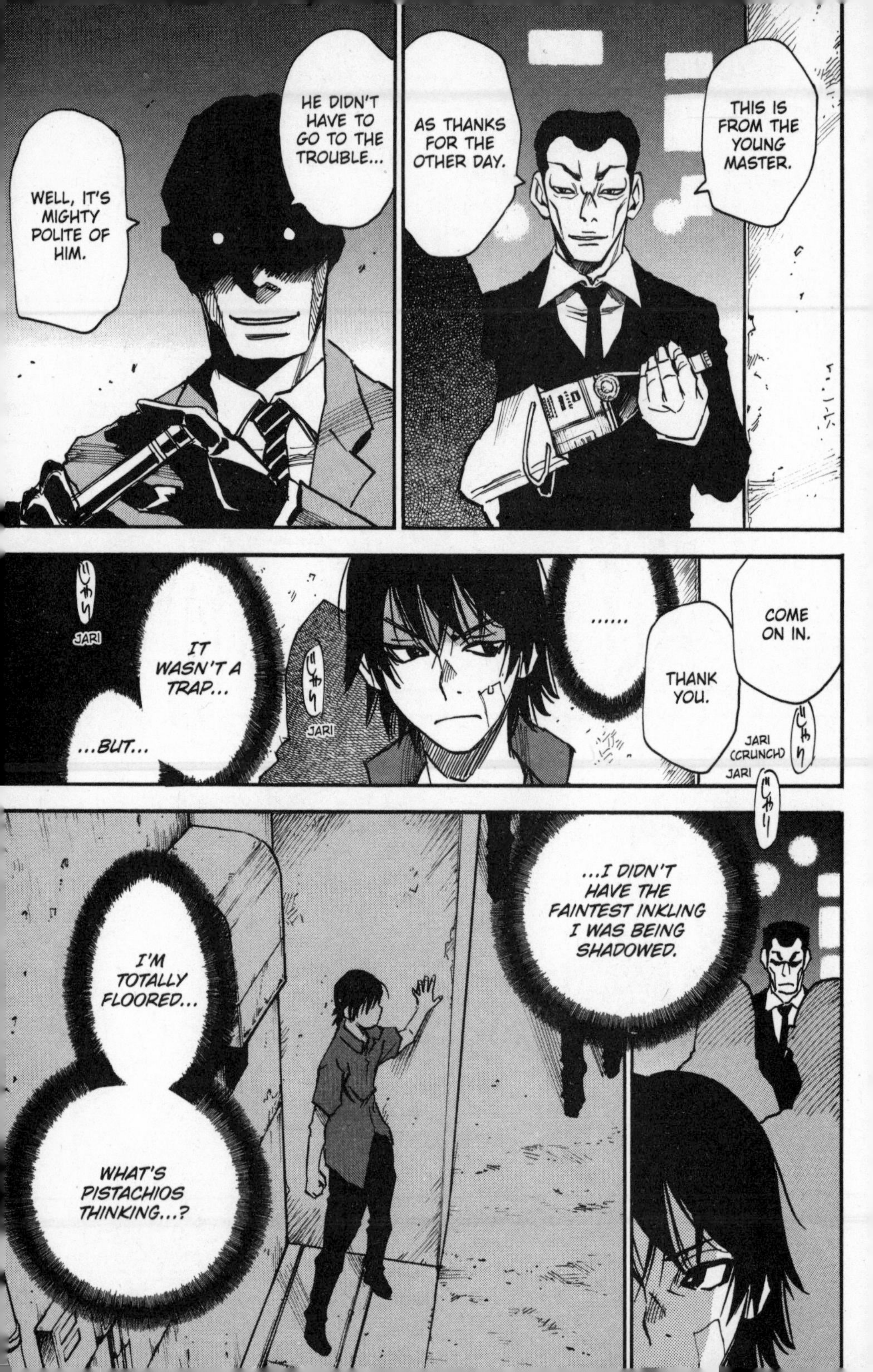
THIS IS FROM THE YOUNG MASTER.
AS THANKS FOR THE OTHER DAY.
HE DIDN'T HAVE TO GO TO THE TROUBLE...
WELL, IT'S MIGHTY POLITE OF HIM.
COME ON IN.
THANK YOU.
じゃり
JARI
じゃり
JARI (CRUNCH)
......
じゃり
JARI
IT WASN'T A TRAP...
...BUT...
じゃり
JARI
...I DIDN'T HAVE THE FAINTEST INKLING I WAS BEING SHADOWED.
I'M TOTALLY FLOORED...
WHAT'S PISTACHIOS THINKING...?

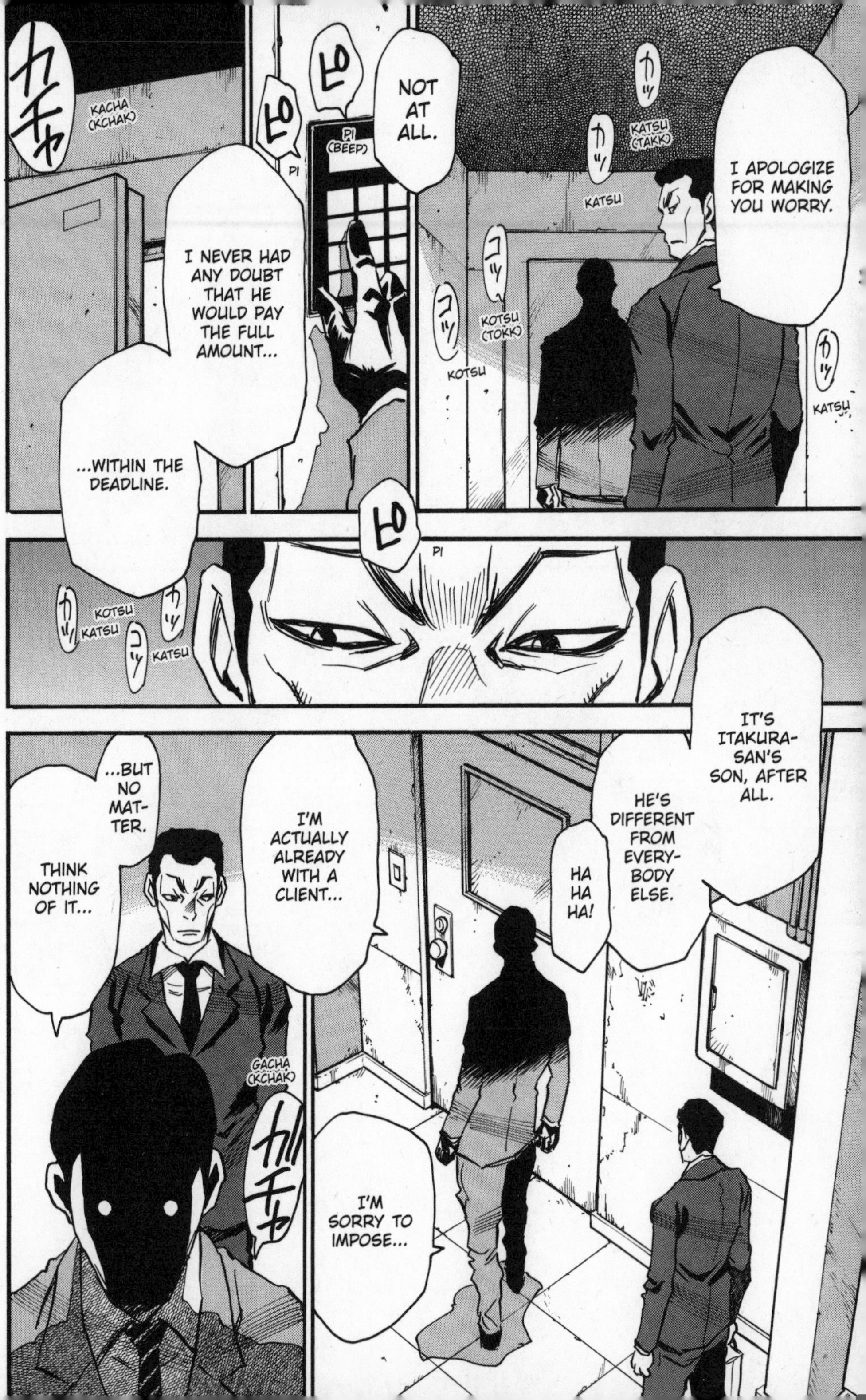
I APOLOGIZE FOR MAKING YOU WORRY.
カッ
KATSU (TAKK)
カッ
KATSU
カッ
KATSU
コッ
コッ
KOTSU (TOKK)
KOTSU
NOT AT ALL.
ピ
ピ
PI (BEEP)
PI
I NEVER HAD ANY DOUBT THAT HE WOULD PAY THE FULL AMOUNT...
...WITHIN THE DEADLINE.
カチャ
KACHA (KCHAK)
ピ
PI
カッ
KOTSU
KATSU
コッ
カッ
KATSU
IT'S ITAKURA-SAN'S SON, AFTER ALL.
HE'S DIFFERENT FROM EVERY-BODY ELSE.
HA HA HA!
I'M ACTUALLY ALREADY WITH A CLIENT...
I'M SORRY TO IMPOSE...
...BUT NO MAT-TER.
THINK NOTHING OF IT...
GACHA (KCHAK)
ガチャ

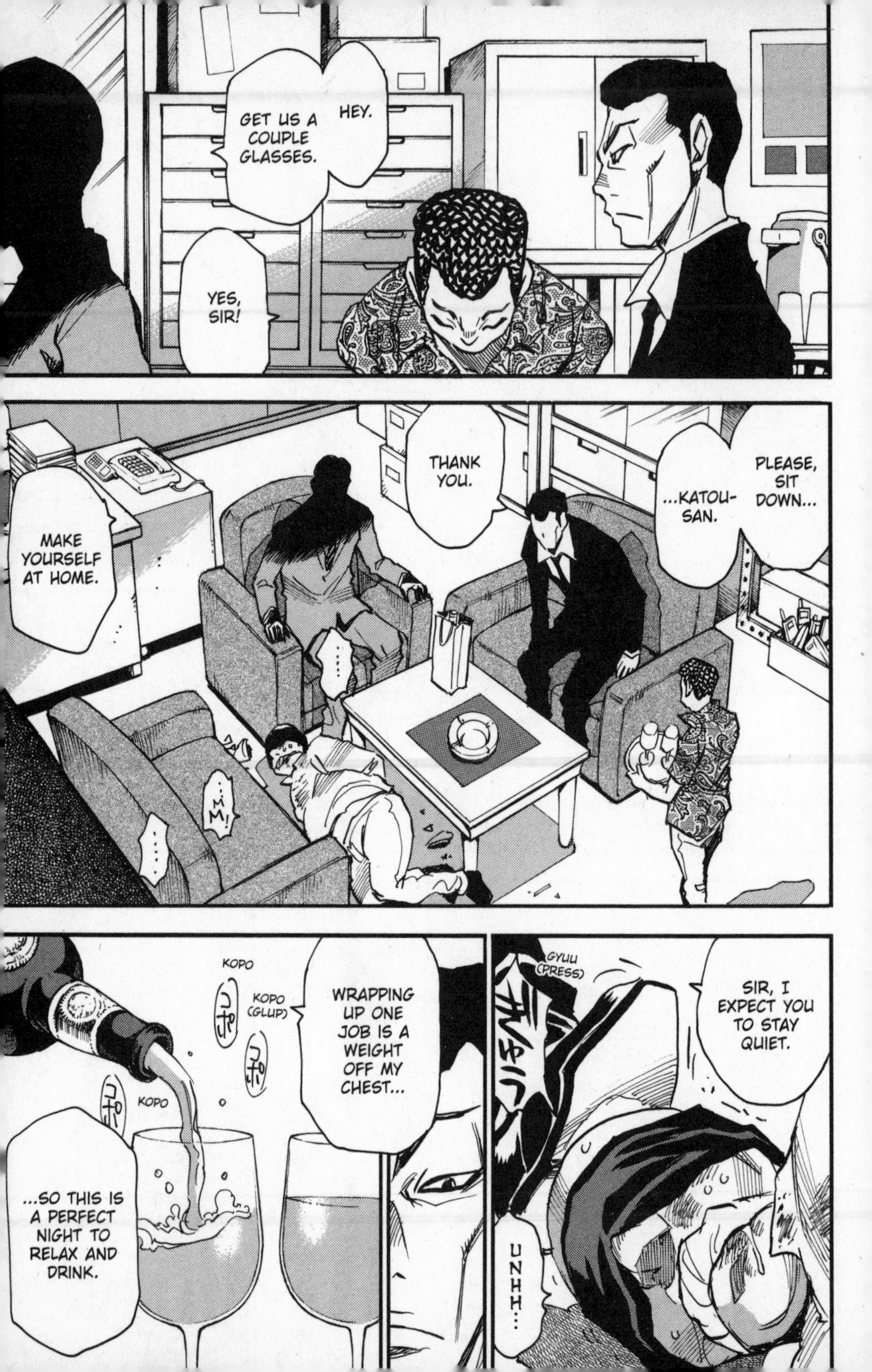

HEY.
GET US A COUPLE GLASSES.
YES, SIR!
PLEASE, SIT DOWN...
...KATOU-SAN.
THANK YOU.
MAKE YOURSELF AT HOME.
...MM!
GYUU (PRESS)
SIR, I EXPECT YOU TO STAY QUIET.
UNHH...
WRAPPING UP ONE JOB IS A WEIGHT OFF MY CHEST...
KOPO
KOPO (GLUP)
KOPO
...SO THIS IS A PERFECT NIGHT TO RELAX AND DRINK.

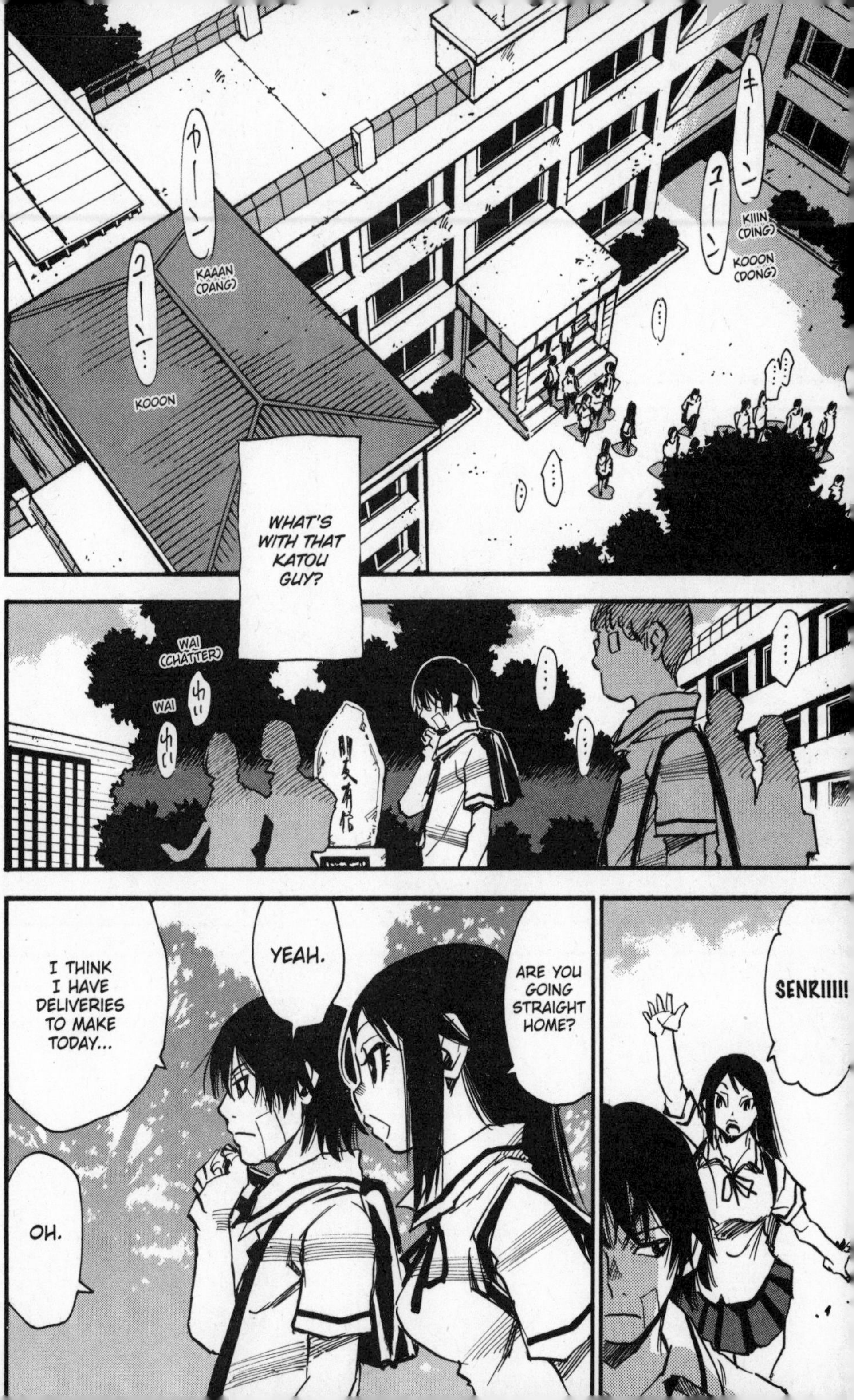
キーン
KIIN (DING)
コーン
KOOON (DONG)
カーン
KAAAN (DANG)
コーン…
KOOON
…
…
…
…
WHAT'S WITH THAT KATOU GUY?
……
…
…
WAI (CHATTER)
わい
WAI
わい
SENRIIII!
ARE YOU GOING STRAIGHT HOME?
YEAH.
I THINK I HAVE DELIVERIES TO MAKE TODAY...
OH.

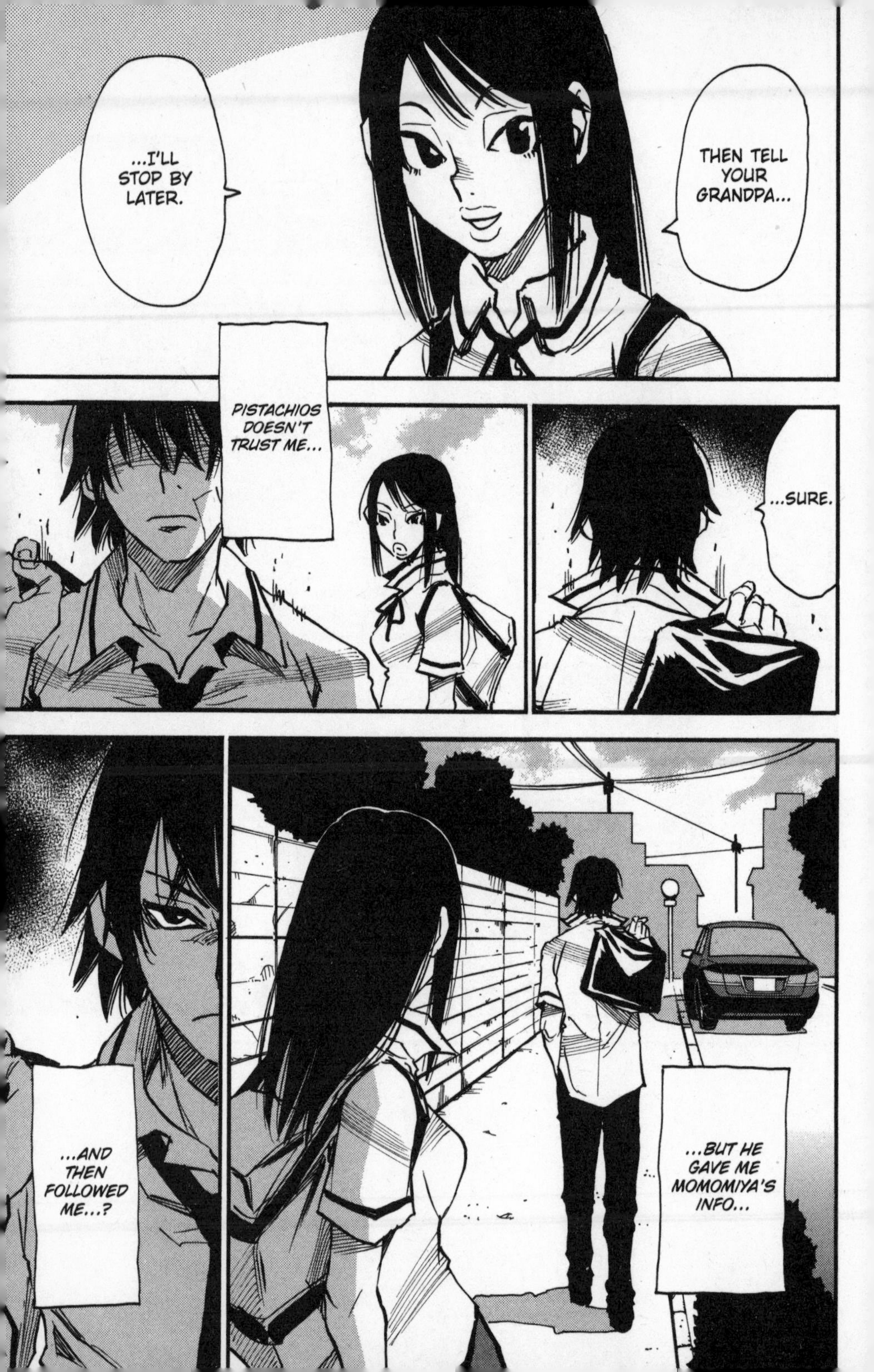
THEN TELL YOUR GRANDPA...
...I'LL STOP BY LATER.
...SURE.
PISTACHIOS DOESN'T TRUST ME...
...BUT HE GAVE ME MOMOMIYA'S INFO...
...AND THEN FOLLOWED ME...?

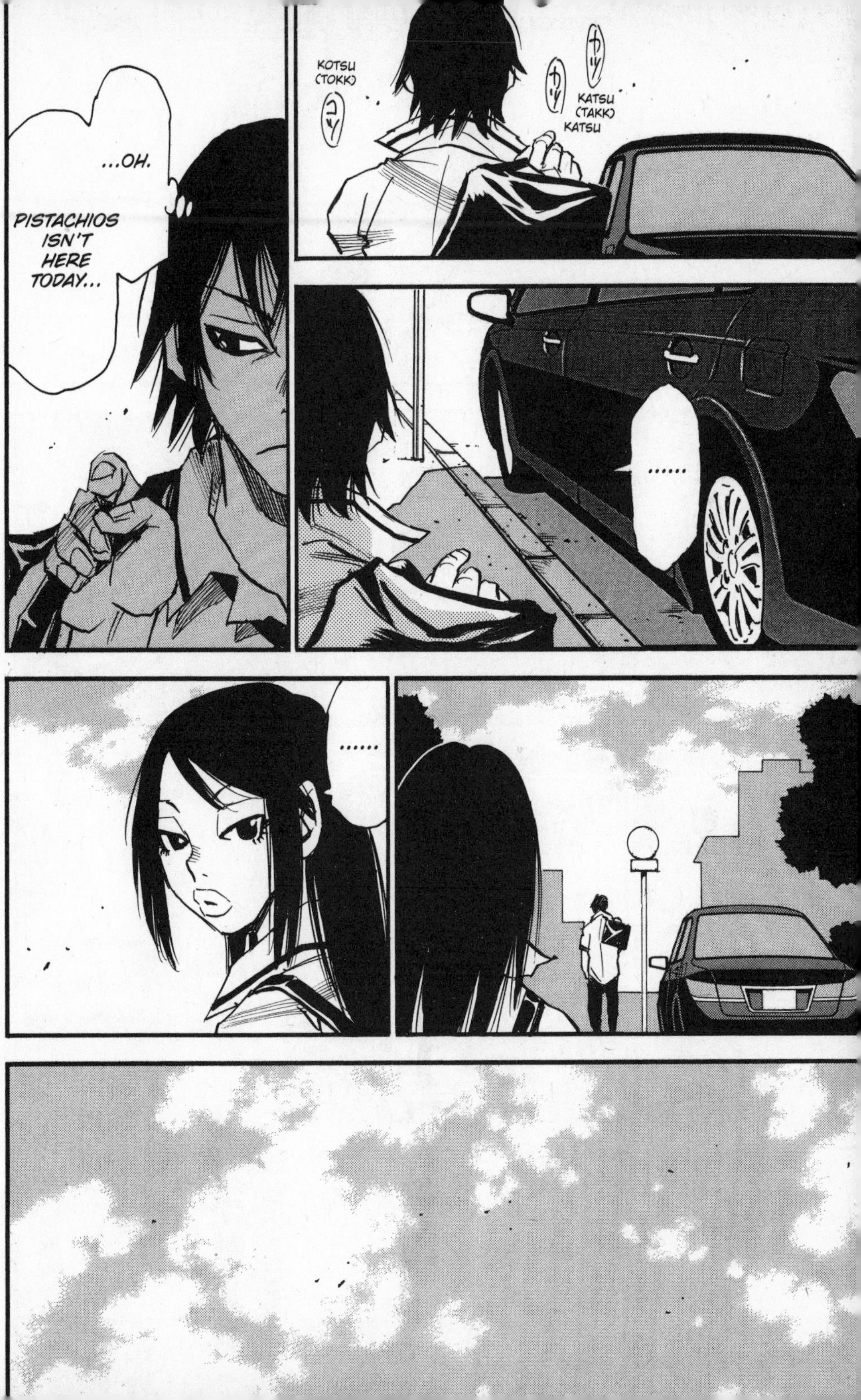
KOTSU (TOKK)
KATSU (TAKK) KATSU
......
...OH.
PISTACHIOS ISN'T HERE TODAY...
......

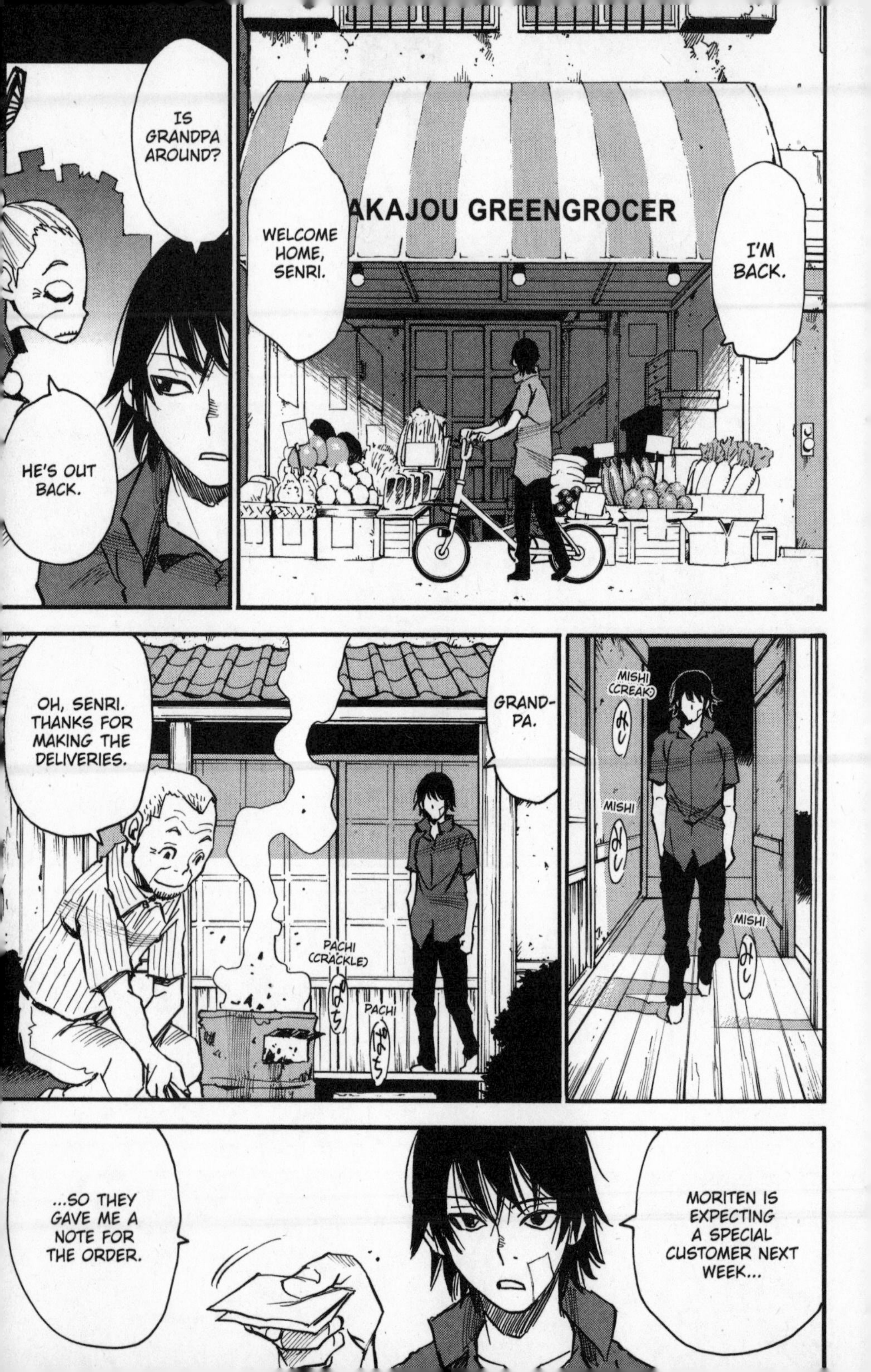
I'M BACK.
AKAJOU GREENGROCER
WELCOME HOME, SENRI.
IS GRANDPA AROUND?
HE'S OUT BACK.
MISHI (CREAK)
みし
MISHI
みし
MISHI
みし
GRAND-PA.
OH, SENRI. THANKS FOR MAKING THE DELIVERIES.
PACHI (CRACKLE)
ぱち
PACHI
ぱち
MORITEN IS EXPECTING A SPECIAL CUSTOMER NEXT WEEK...
...SO THEY GAVE ME A NOTE FOR THE ORDER.

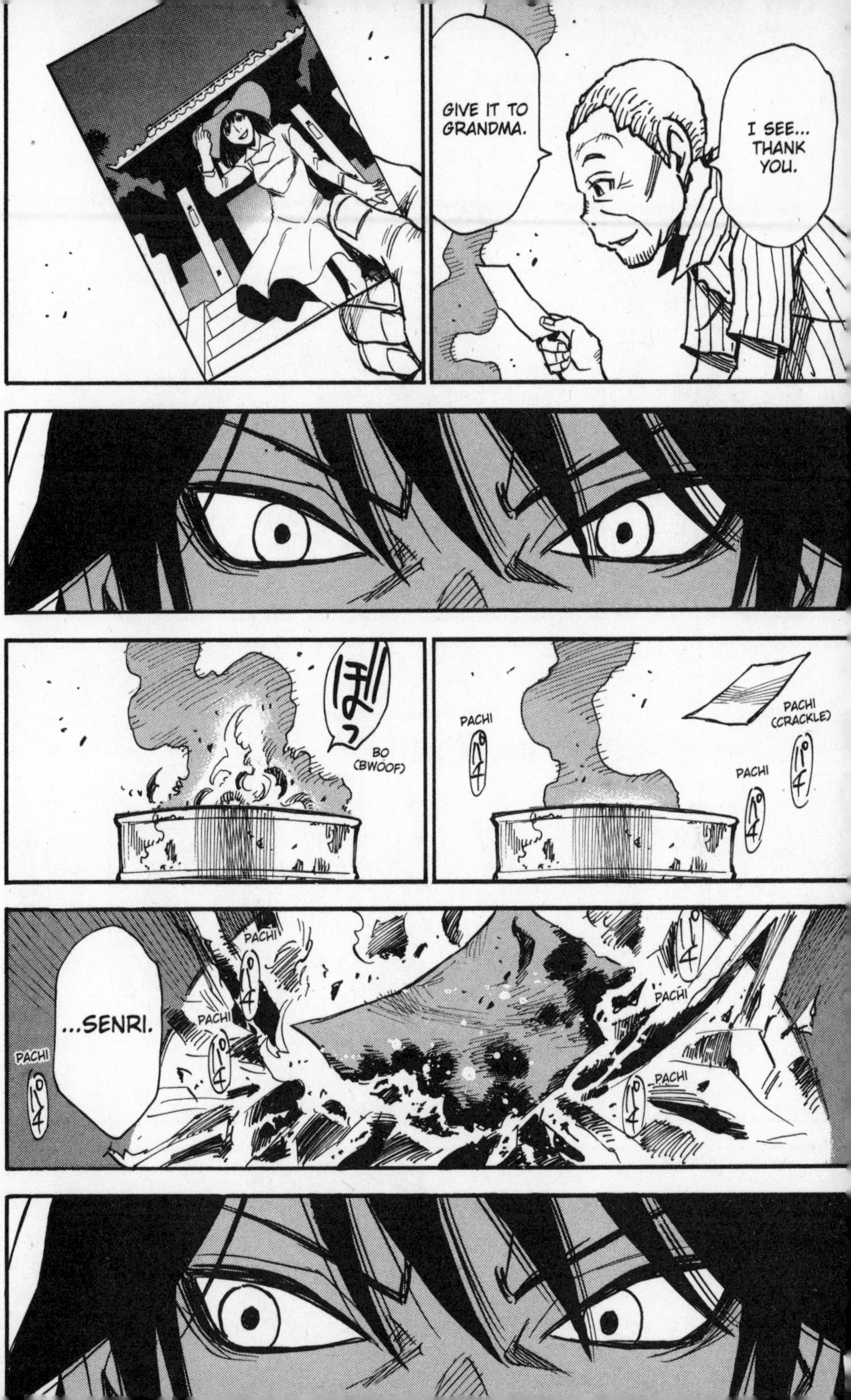

GIVE IT TO GRANDMA.
I SEE... THANK YOU.
PACHI (CRACKLE)
パチ
PACHI
パチ
PACHI
パチ
ぼっ
BO (BWOOF)
PACHI
PACHI
PACHI
PACHI
PACHI
...SENRI.
PACHI

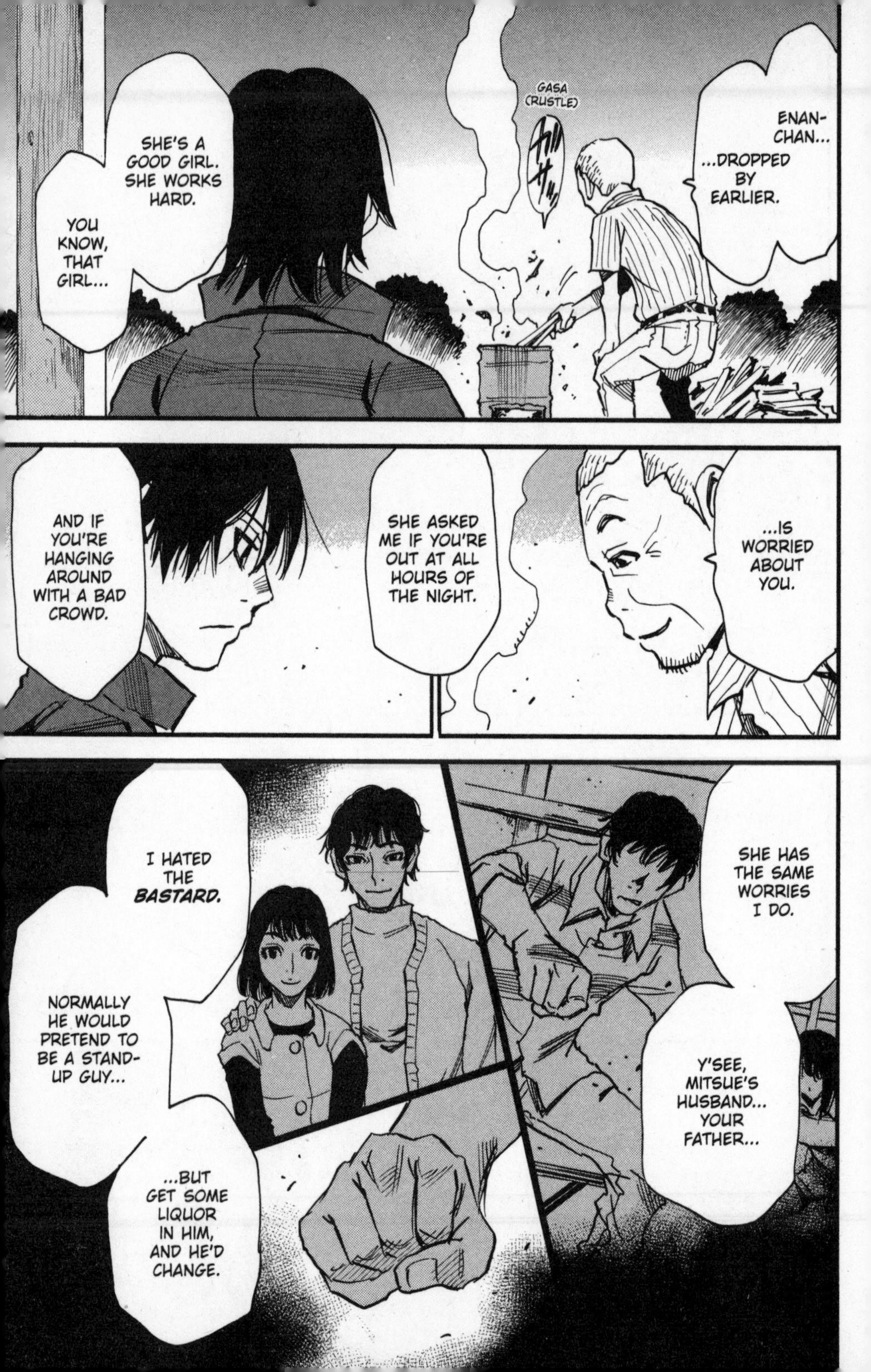
ENAN-CHAN... ...DROPPED BY EARLIER.
GASA (RUSTLE)
SHE'S A GOOD GIRL. SHE WORKS HARD.
YOU KNOW, THAT GIRL...
...IS WORRIED ABOUT YOU.
SHE ASKED ME IF YOU'RE OUT AT ALL HOURS OF THE NIGHT.
AND IF YOU'RE HANGING AROUND WITH A BAD CROWD.
SHE HAS THE SAME WORRIES I DO.
Y'SEE, MITSUE'S HUSBAND... YOUR FATHER...
I HATED THE ***BASTARD.***
NORMALLY HE WOULD PRETEND TO BE A STAND-UP GUY...
...BUT GET SOME LIQUOR IN HIM, AND HE'D CHANGE.

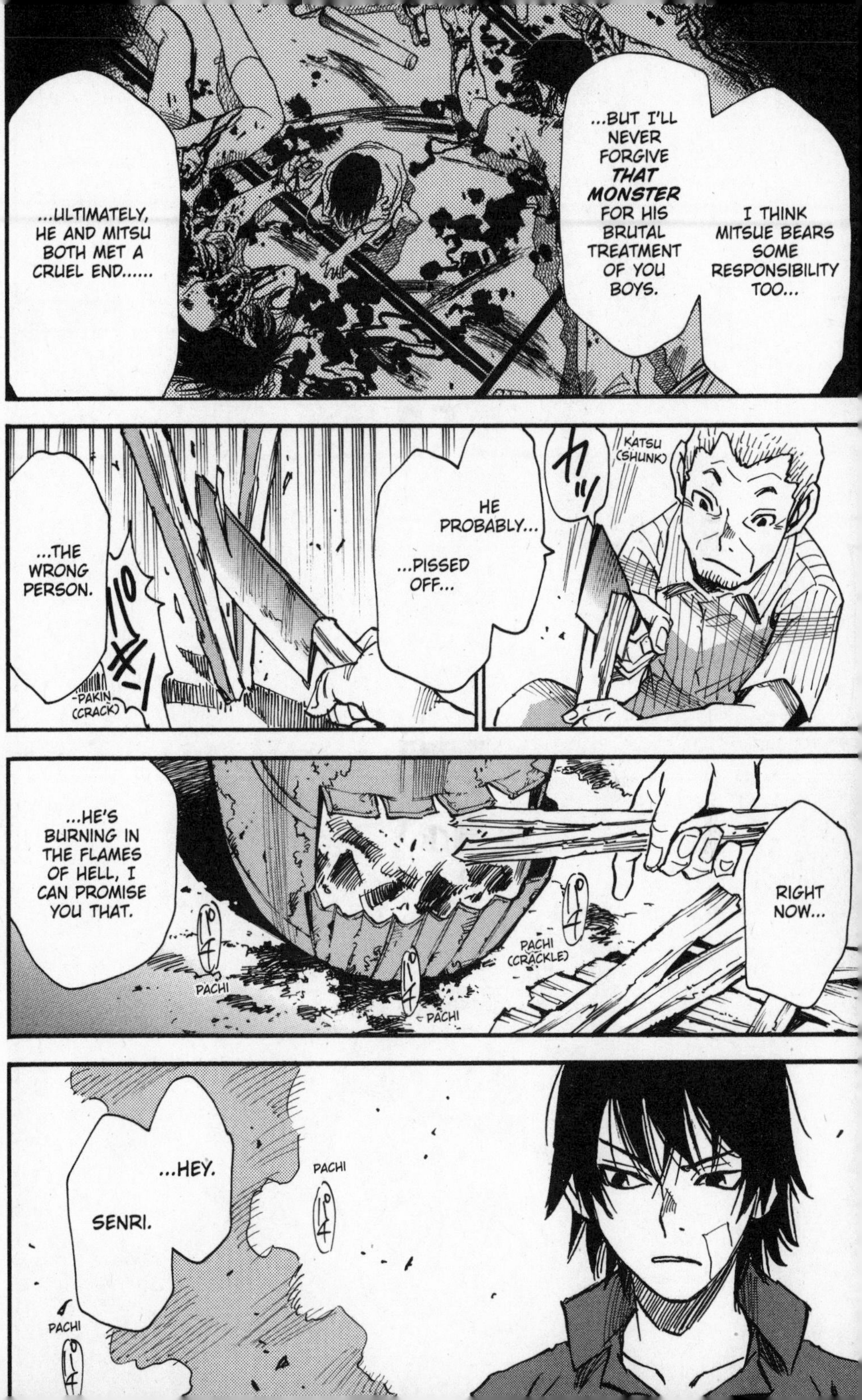

I THINK MITSUE BEARS SOME RESPONSIBILITY TOO...
...BUT I'LL NEVER FORGIVE ***THAT MONSTER*** FOR HIS BRUTAL TREATMENT OF YOU BOYS.
...ULTIMATELY, HE AND MITSU BOTH MET A CRUEL END......
KATSU (SHUNK)
HE PROBABLY...
...PISSED OFF...
...THE WRONG PERSON.
PAKIN (CRACK)
RIGHT NOW...
PACHI (CRACKLE)
...HE'S BURNING IN THE FLAMES OF HELL, I CAN PROMISE YOU THAT.
PACHI
PACHI
PACHI
...HEY.
SENRI.
PACHI

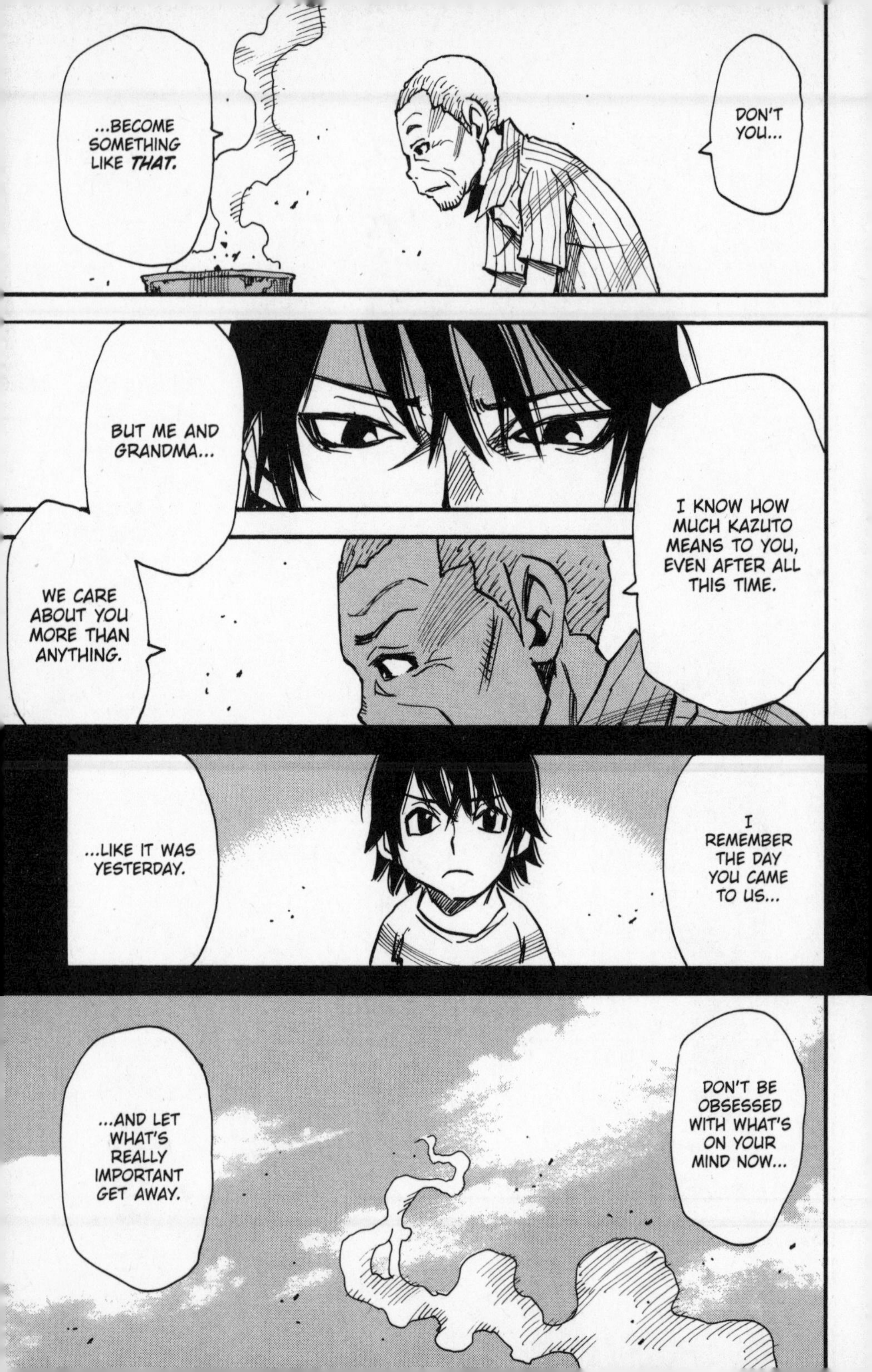
DON'T YOU...
...BECOME SOMETHING LIKE *THAT.*
I KNOW HOW MUCH KAZUTO MEANS TO YOU, EVEN AFTER ALL THIS TIME.
BUT ME AND GRANDMA...
WE CARE ABOUT YOU MORE THAN ANYTHING.
I REMEMBER THE DAY YOU CAME TO US...
...LIKE IT WAS YESTERDAY.
DON'T BE OBSESSED WITH WHAT'S ON YOUR MIND NOW...
...AND LET WHAT'S REALLY IMPORTANT GET AWAY.

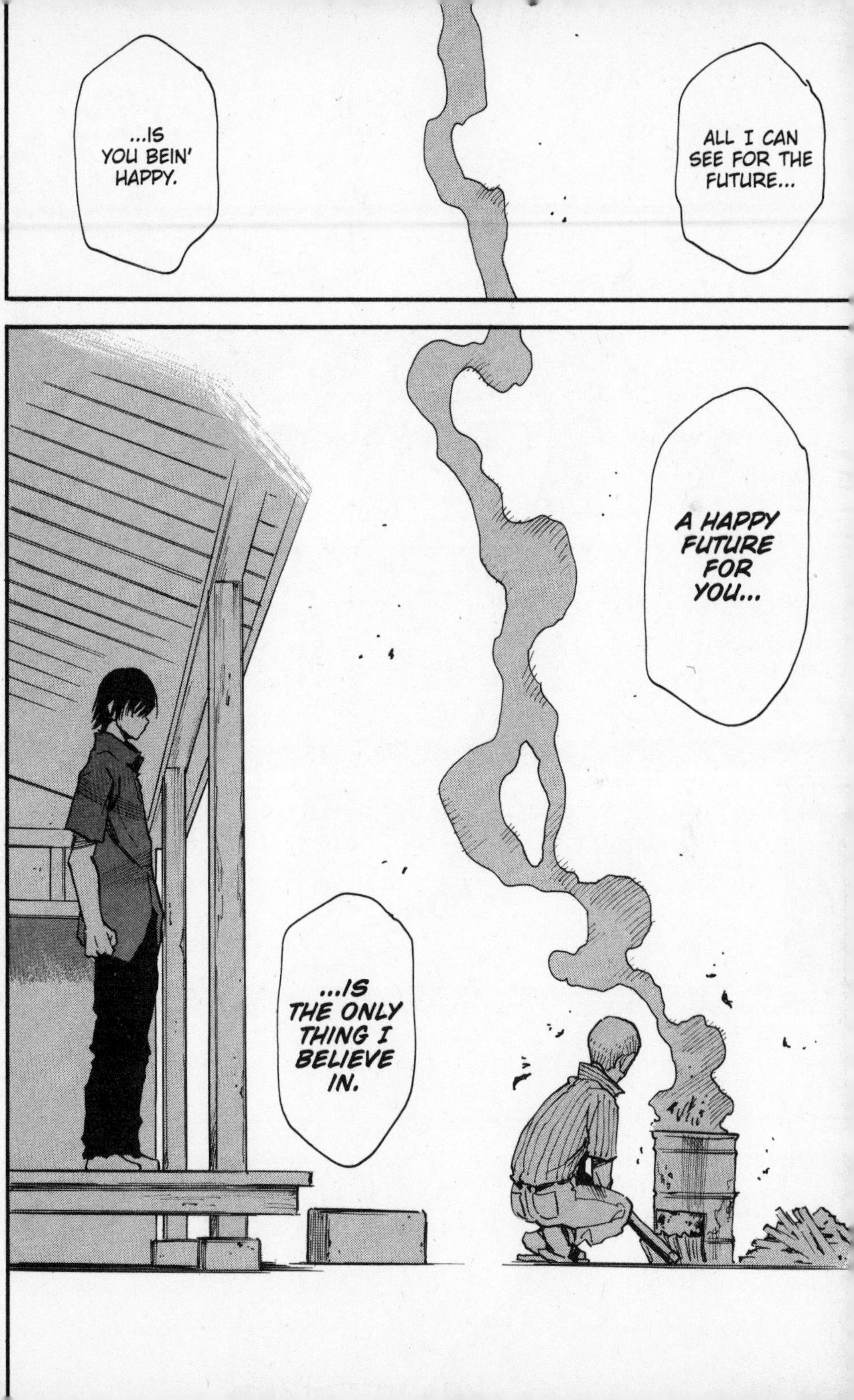
ALL I CAN SEE FOR THE FUTURE...
...IS YOU BEIN' HAPPY.
A HAPPY FUTURE FOR YOU...
...IS THE ONLY THING I BELIEVE IN.

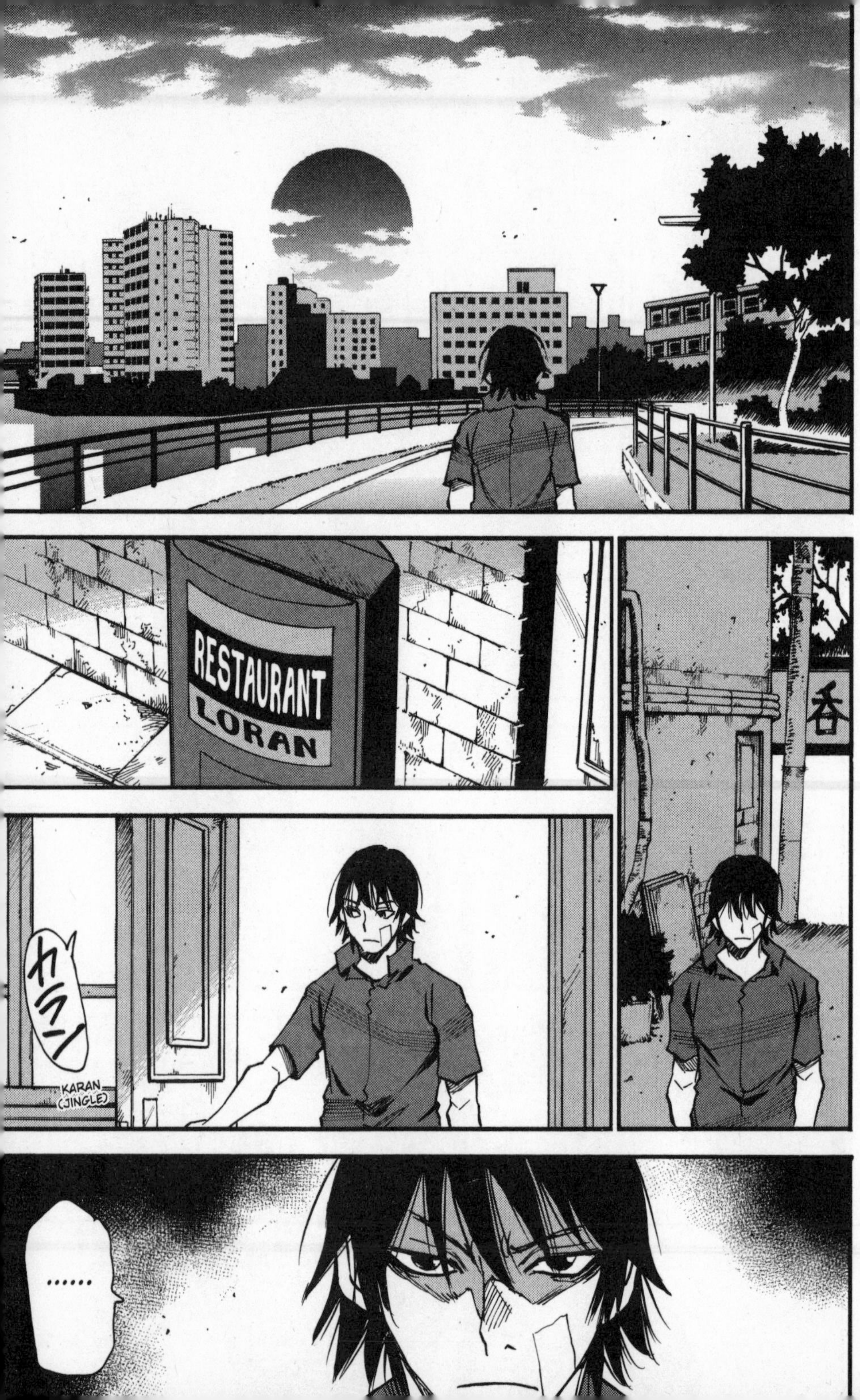

RESTAURANT
LORAN
香
カラン
KARAN (JINGLE)
......

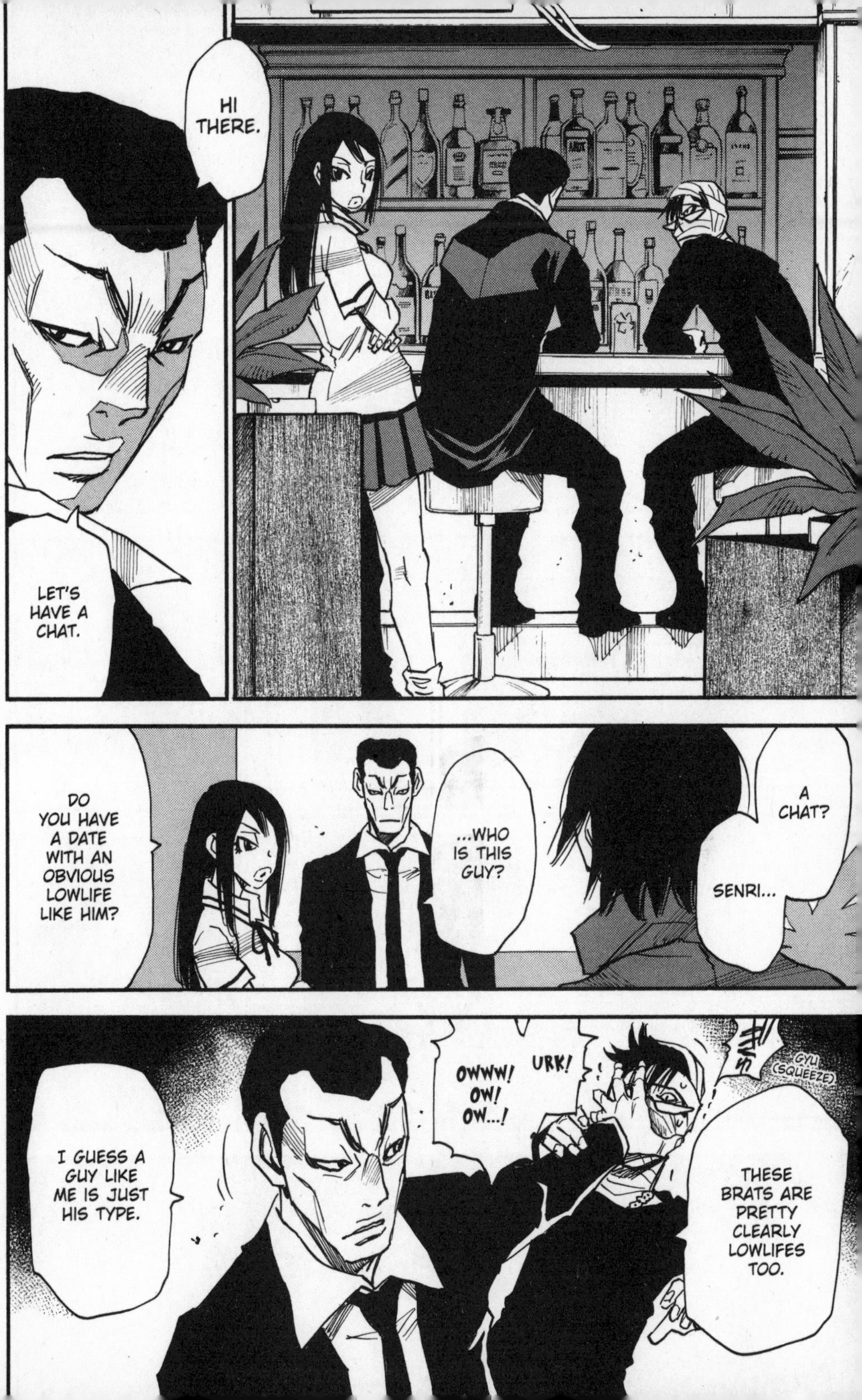
HI THERE.
LET'S HAVE A CHAT.
A CHAT?
SENRI...
...WHO IS THIS GUY?
DO YOU HAVE A DATE WITH AN OBVIOUS LOWLIFE LIKE HIM?
GYU (SQUEEZE)
THESE BRATS ARE PRETTY CLEARLY LOWLIFES TOO.
URK!
OWWW! OW! OW...!
I GUESS A GUY LIKE ME IS JUST HIS TYPE.

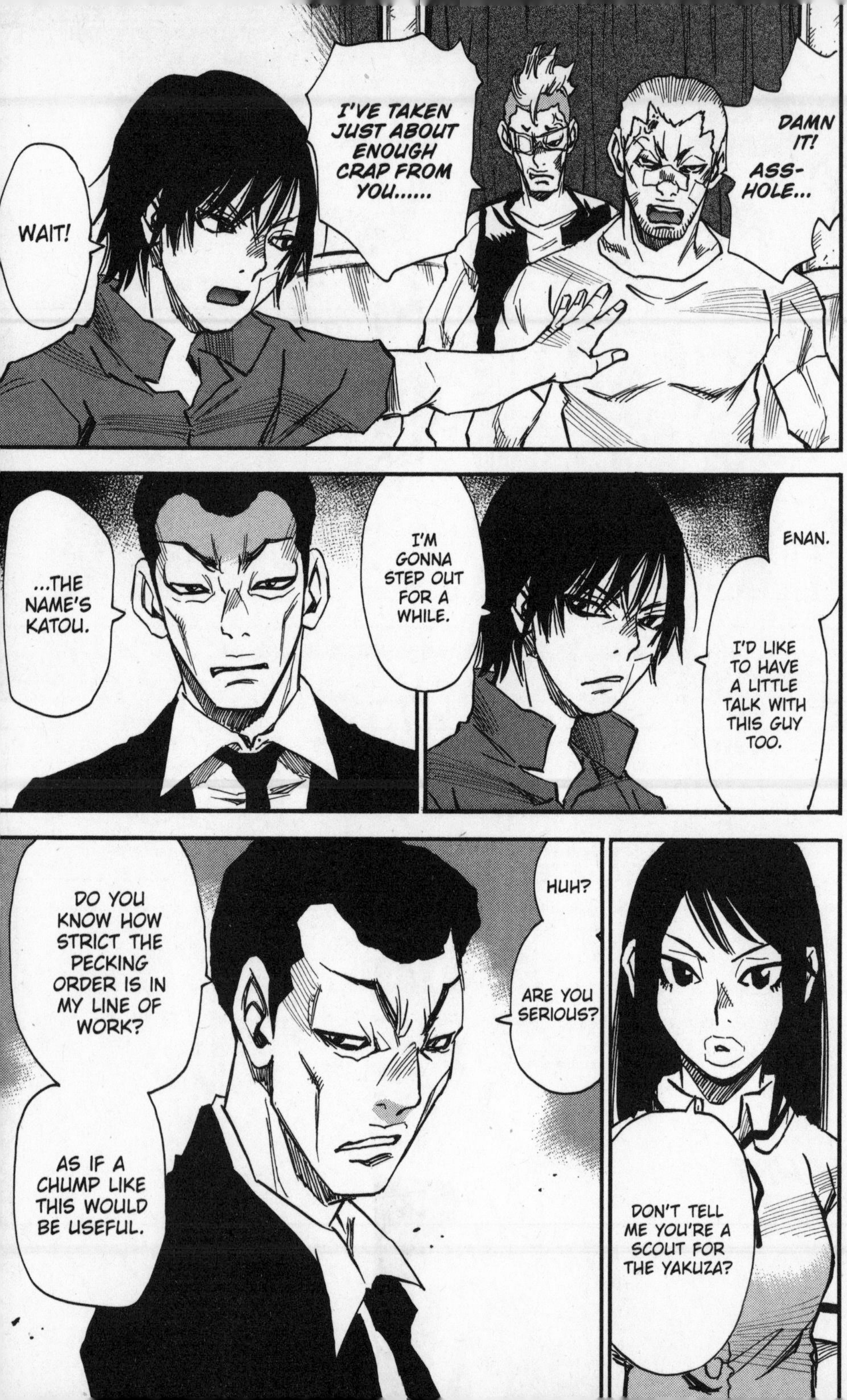
DAMN IT! ASS-HOLE...
I'VE TAKEN JUST ABOUT ENOUGH CRAP FROM YOU......
WAIT!
ENAN.
I'D LIKE TO HAVE A LITTLE TALK WITH THIS GUY TOO.
I'M GONNA STEP OUT FOR A WHILE.
...THE NAME'S KATOU.
HUH?
ARE YOU SERIOUS?
DON'T TELL ME YOU'RE A SCOUT FOR THE YAKUZA?
DO YOU KNOW HOW STRICT THE PECKING ORDER IS IN MY LINE OF WORK?
AS IF A CHUMP LIKE THIS WOULD BE USEFUL.

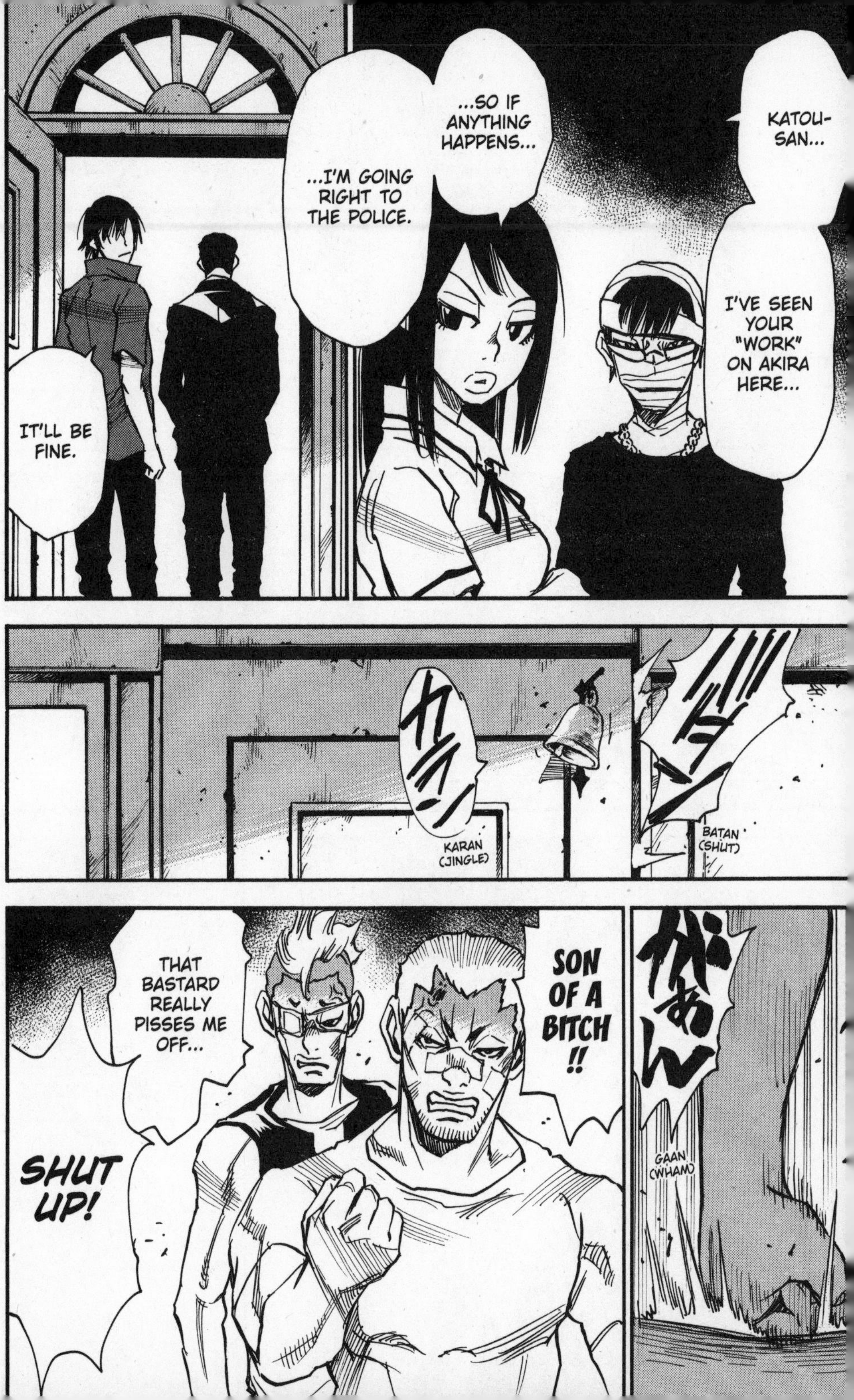
KATOU-SAN...
I'VE SEEN YOUR "WORK" ON AKIRA HERE...
...SO IF ANYTHING HAPPENS...
...I'M GOING RIGHT TO THE POLICE.
IT'LL BE FINE.
BATAN (SHUT)
KARAN (JINGLE)
GAAN (WHAM)
SON OF A BITCH!!
THAT BASTARD REALLY PISSES ME OFF...
SHUT UP!

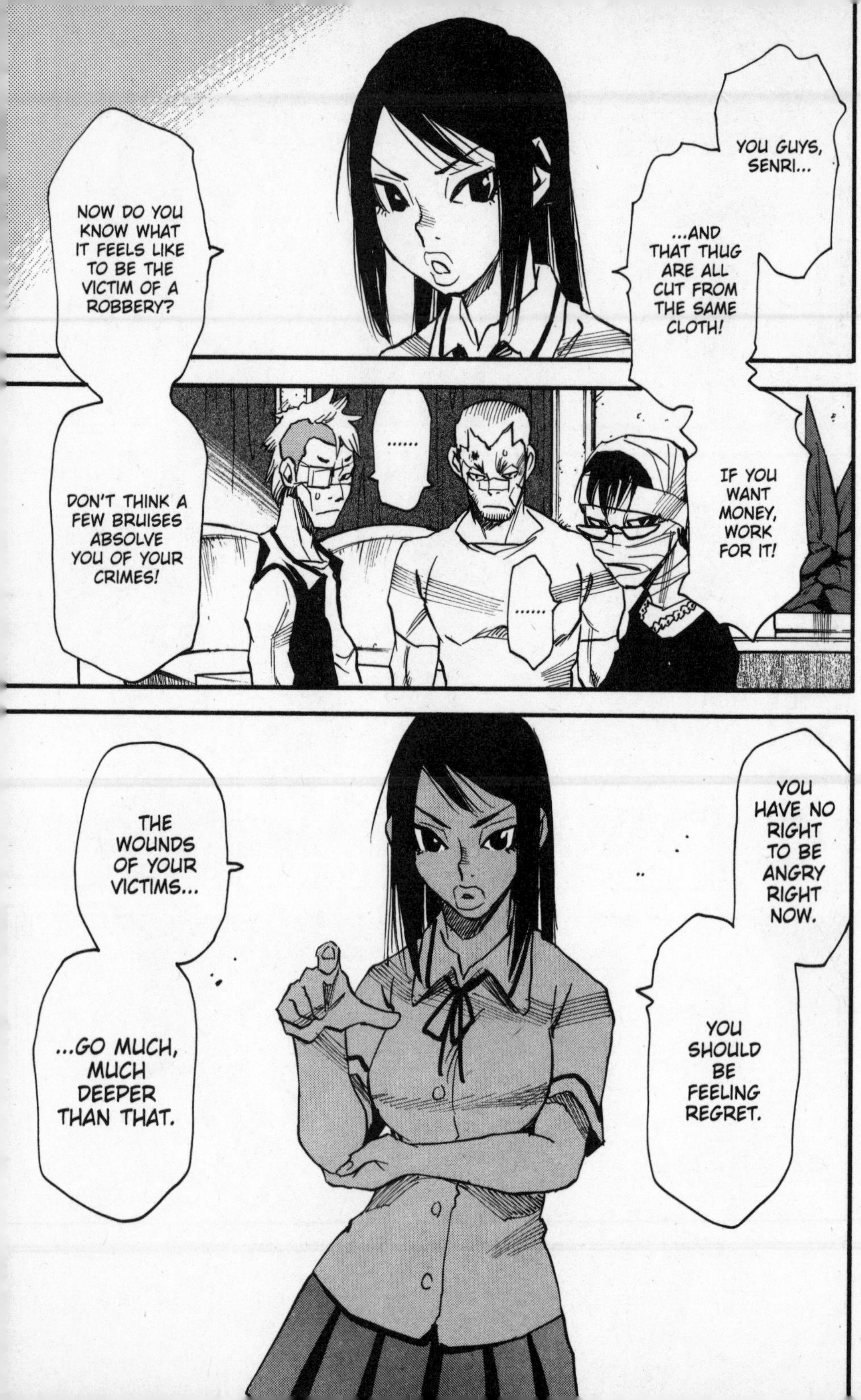
YOU GUYS, SENRI...
...AND THAT THUG ARE ALL CUT FROM THE SAME CLOTH!
NOW DO YOU KNOW WHAT IT FEELS LIKE TO BE THE VICTIM OF A ROBBERY?
IF YOU WANT MONEY, WORK FOR IT!
......
......
DON'T THINK A FEW BRUISES ABSOLVE YOU OF YOUR CRIMES!
YOU HAVE NO RIGHT TO BE ANGRY RIGHT NOW.
YOU SHOULD BE FEELING REGRET.
THE WOUNDS OF YOUR VICTIMS...
...GO MUCH, MUCH DEEPER THAN THAT.

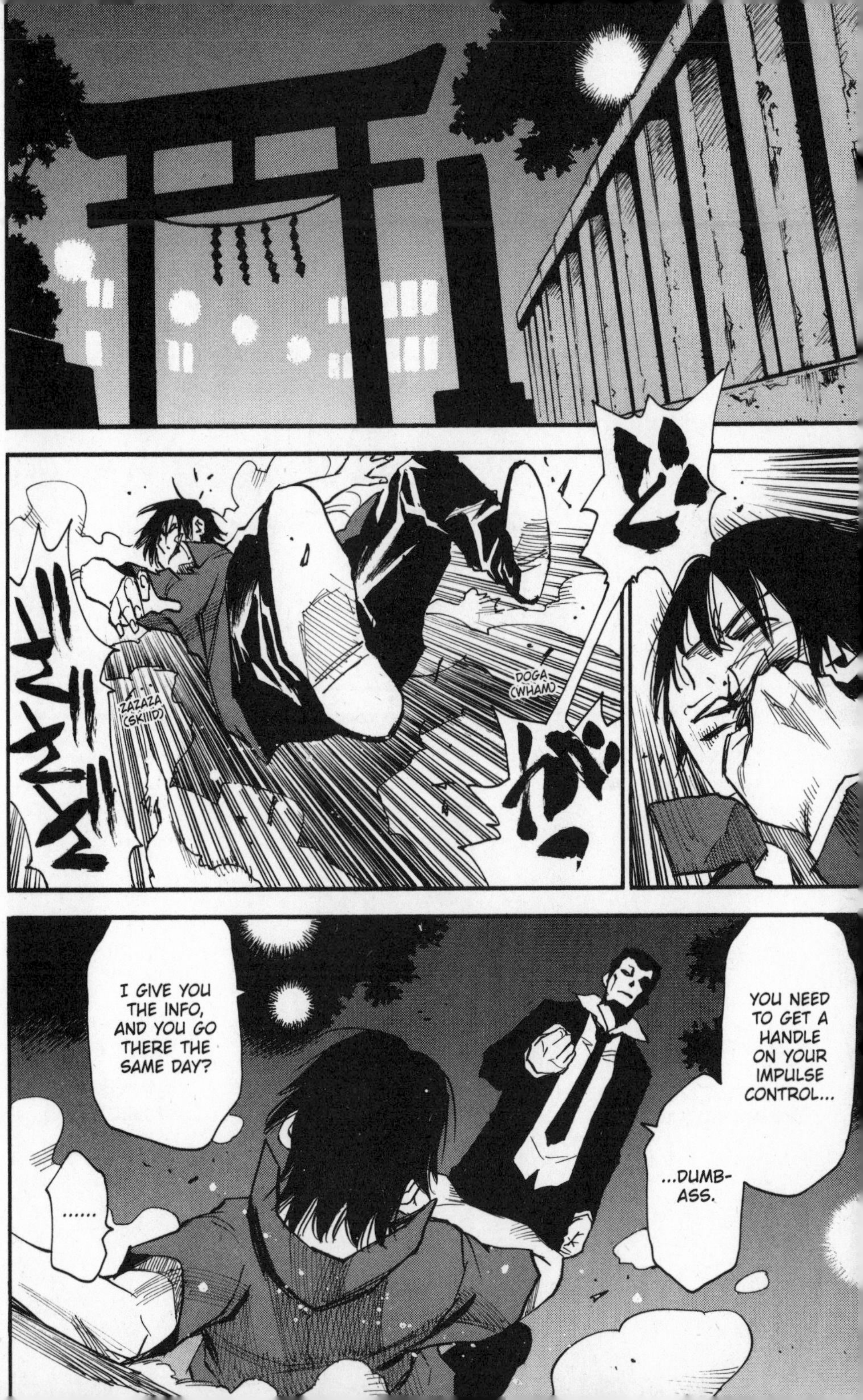
DOGA (WHAM)
ZAZAZA (SKIIID)
YOU NEED TO GET A HANDLE ON YOUR IMPULSE CONTROL...
...DUMB-ASS.
I GIVE YOU THE INFO, AND YOU GO THERE THE SAME DAY?
......

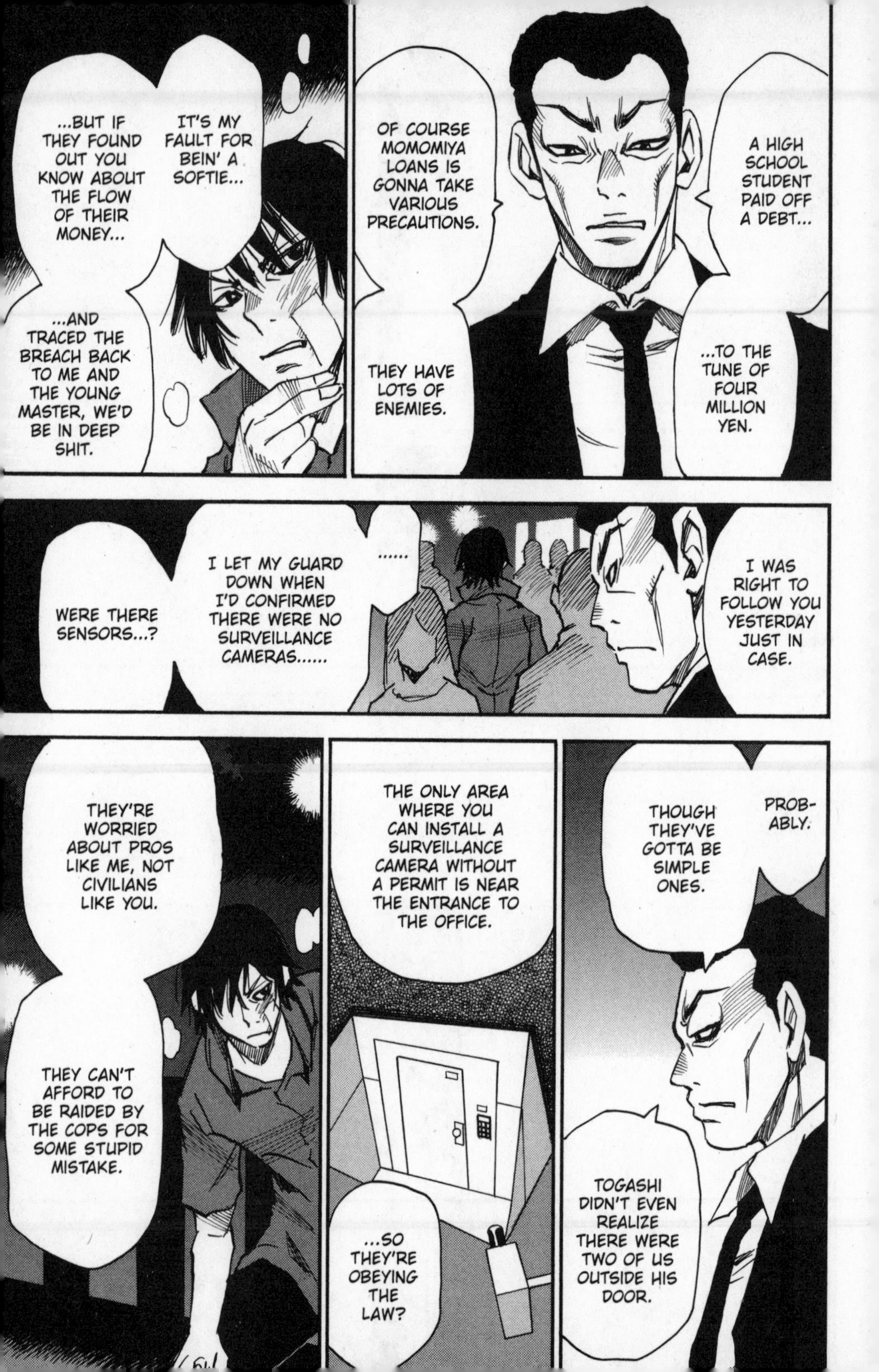
A HIGH SCHOOL STUDENT PAID OFF A DEBT...
...TO THE TUNE OF FOUR MILLION YEN.
OF COURSE MOMOMIYA LOANS IS GONNA TAKE VARIOUS PRECAUTIONS.
THEY HAVE LOTS OF ENEMIES.
IT'S MY FAULT FOR BEIN' A SOFTIE...
...BUT IF THEY FOUND OUT YOU KNOW ABOUT THE FLOW OF THEIR MONEY...
...AND TRACED THE BREACH BACK TO ME AND THE YOUNG MASTER, WE'D BE IN DEEP SHIT.
I WAS RIGHT TO FOLLOW YOU YESTERDAY JUST IN CASE.
......
I LET MY GUARD DOWN WHEN I'D CONFIRMED THERE WERE NO SURVEILLANCE CAMERAS......
WERE THERE SENSORS...?
PROB-ABLY.
THOUGH THEY'VE GOTTA BE SIMPLE ONES.
TOGASHI DIDN'T EVEN REALIZE THERE WERE TWO OF US OUTSIDE HIS DOOR.
THE ONLY AREA WHERE YOU CAN INSTALL A SURVEILLANCE CAMERA WITHOUT A PERMIT IS NEAR THE ENTRANCE TO THE OFFICE.
...SO THEY'RE OBEYING THE LAW?
THEY'RE WORRIED ABOUT PROS LIKE ME, NOT CIVILIANS LIKE YOU.
THEY CAN'T AFFORD TO BE RAIDED BY THE COPS FOR SOME STUPID MISTAKE.

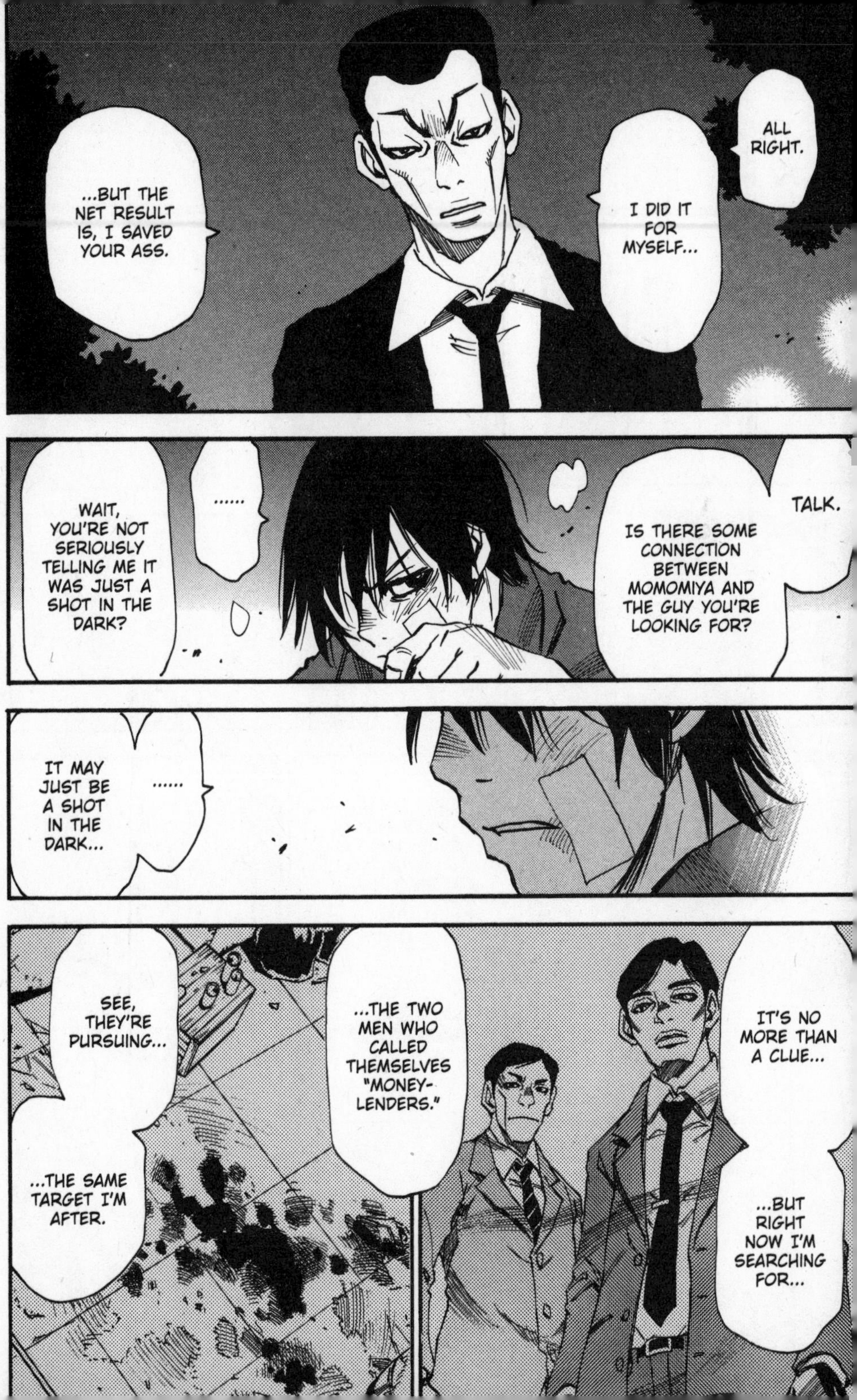
ALL RIGHT.
I DID IT FOR MYSELF...
...BUT THE NET RESULT IS, I SAVED YOUR ASS.
TALK.
IS THERE SOME CONNECTION BETWEEN MOMOMIYA AND THE GUY YOU'RE LOOKING FOR?
......
WAIT, YOU'RE NOT SERIOUSLY TELLING ME IT WAS JUST A SHOT IN THE DARK?
......
IT MAY JUST BE A SHOT IN THE DARK...
IT'S NO MORE THAN A CLUE...
...BUT RIGHT NOW I'M SEARCHING FOR...
...THE TWO MEN WHO CALLED THEMSELVES "MONEY-LENDERS."
SEE, THEY'RE PURSUING...
...THE SAME TARGET I'M AFTER.

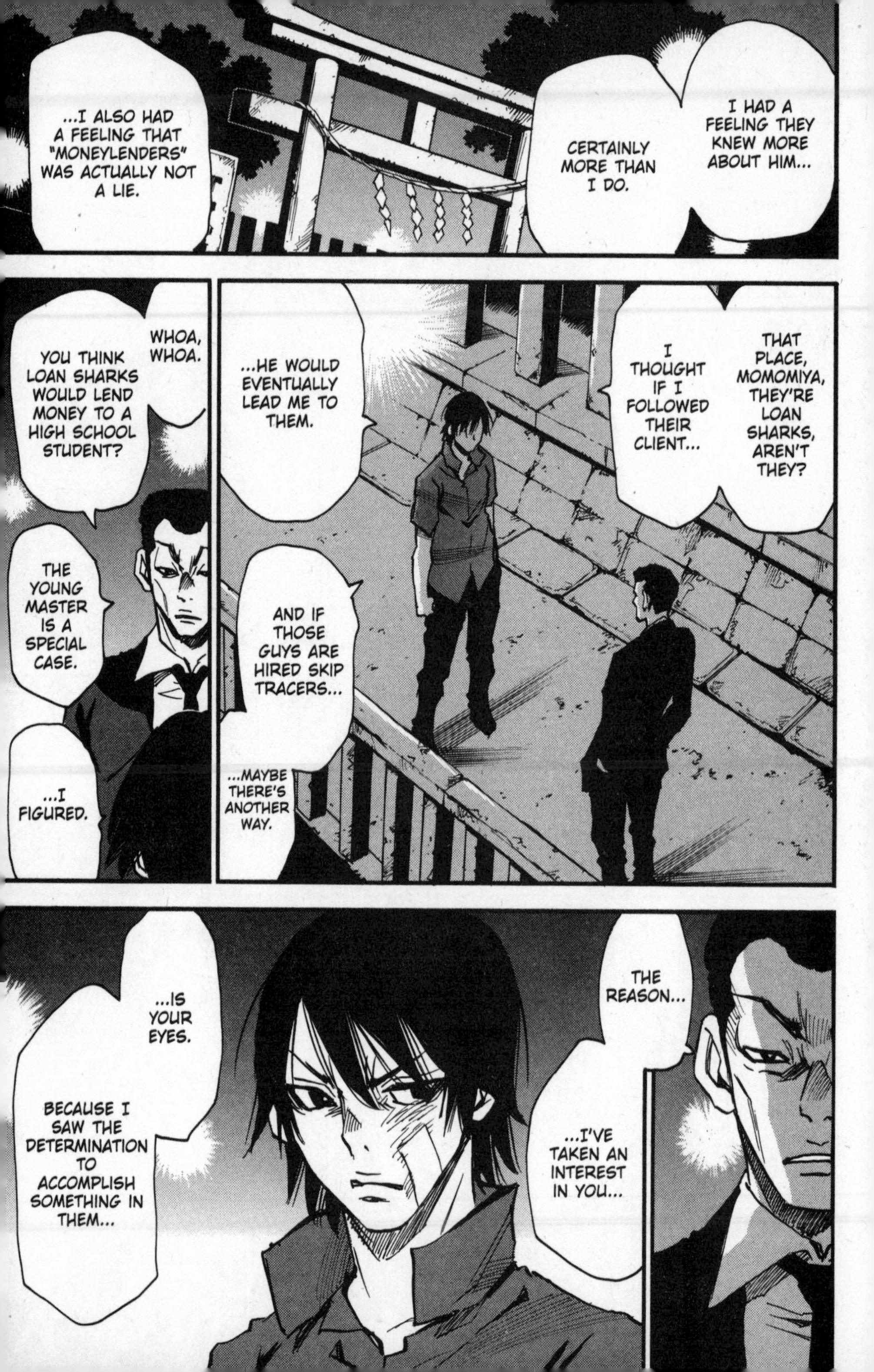
I HAD A FEELING THEY KNEW MORE ABOUT HIM...
CERTAINLY MORE THAN I DO.
...I ALSO HAD A FEELING THAT "MONEYLENDERS" WAS ACTUALLY NOT A LIE.
THAT PLACE, MOMOMIYA, THEY'RE LOAN SHARKS, AREN'T THEY?
I THOUGHT IF I FOLLOWED THEIR CLIENT...
...HE WOULD EVENTUALLY LEAD ME TO THEM.
AND IF THOSE GUYS ARE HIRED SKIP TRACERS...
...MAYBE THERE'S ANOTHER WAY.
WHOA, WHOA.
YOU THINK LOAN SHARKS WOULD LEND MONEY TO A HIGH SCHOOL STUDENT?
THE YOUNG MASTER IS A SPECIAL CASE.
...I FIGURED.
THE REASON...
...I'VE TAKEN AN INTEREST IN YOU...
...IS YOUR EYES.
BECAUSE I SAW THE DETERMINATION TO ACCOMPLISH SOMETHING IN THEM...

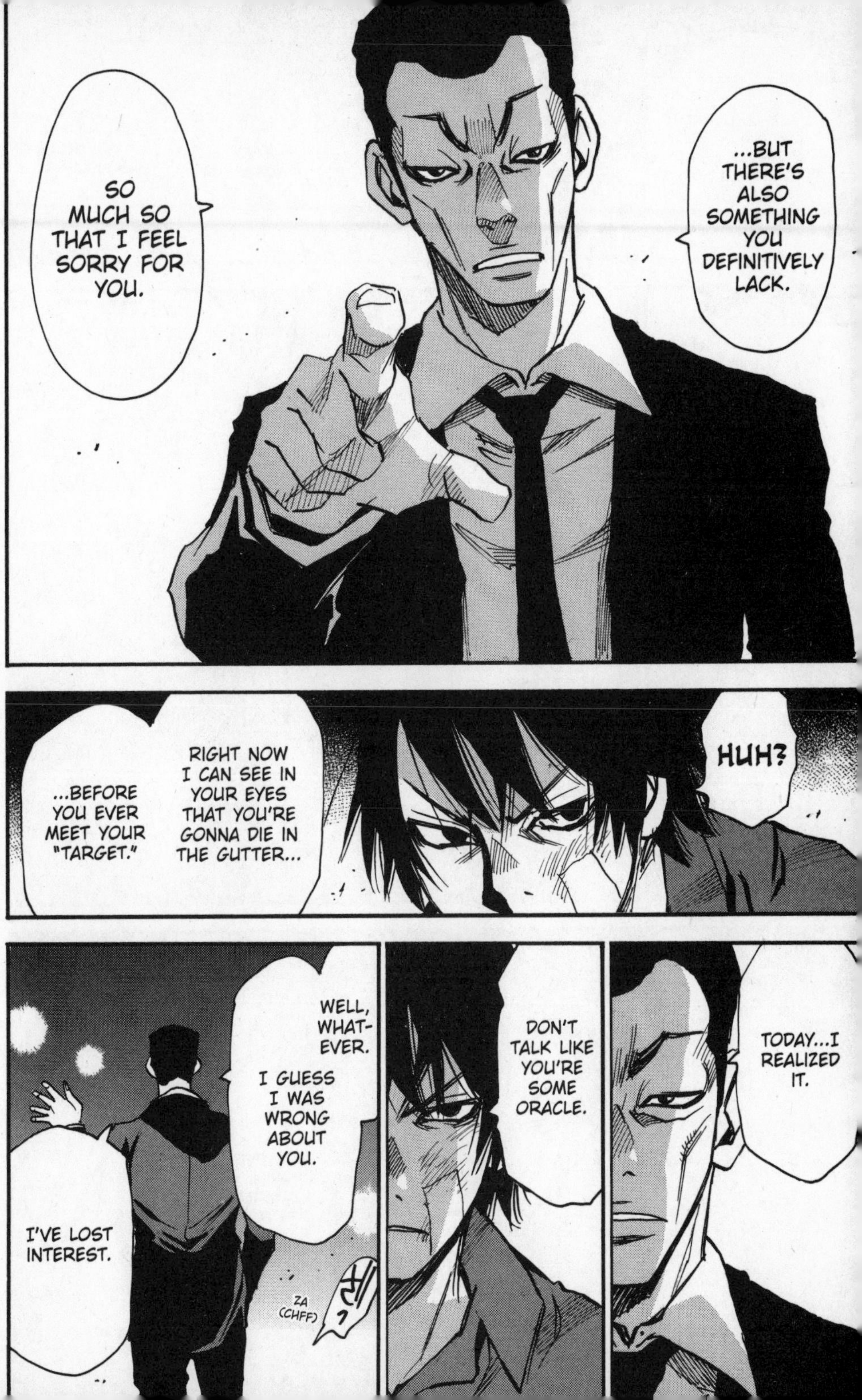
...BUT THERE'S ALSO SOMETHING YOU DEFINITIVELY LACK.
SO MUCH SO THAT I FEEL SORRY FOR YOU.
HUH?
RIGHT NOW I CAN SEE IN YOUR EYES THAT YOU'RE GONNA DIE IN THE GUTTER...
...BEFORE YOU EVER MEET YOUR "TARGET."
TODAY...I REALIZED IT.
DON'T TALK LIKE YOU'RE SOME ORACLE.
WELL, WHAT-EVER.
I GUESS I WAS WRONG ABOUT YOU.
I'VE LOST INTEREST.
ZA (CHFF)

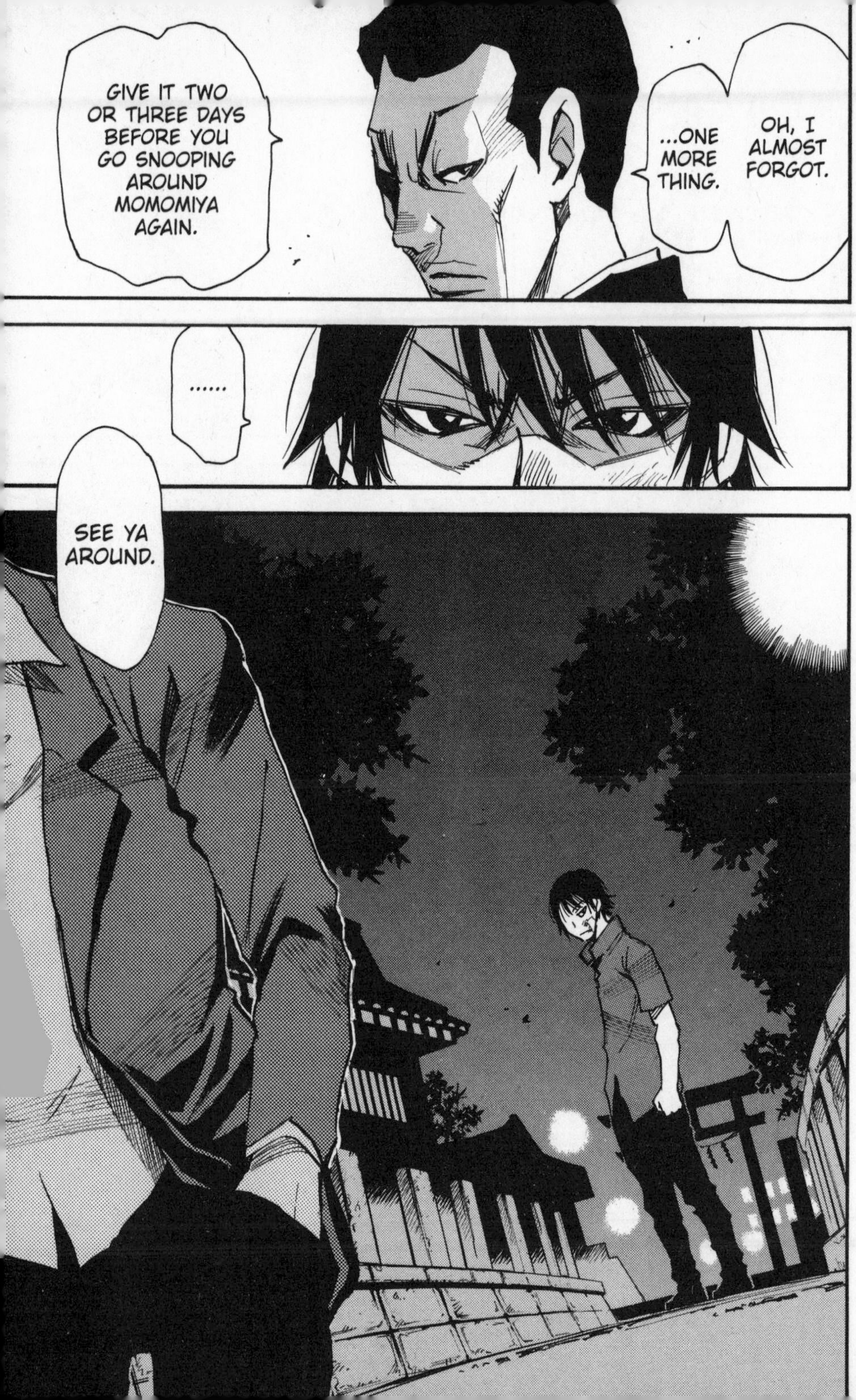
OH, I ALMOST FORGOT.
...ONE MORE THING.
GIVE IT TWO OR THREE DAYS BEFORE YOU GO SNOOPING AROUND MOMOMIYA AGAIN.
......
SEE YA AROUND.

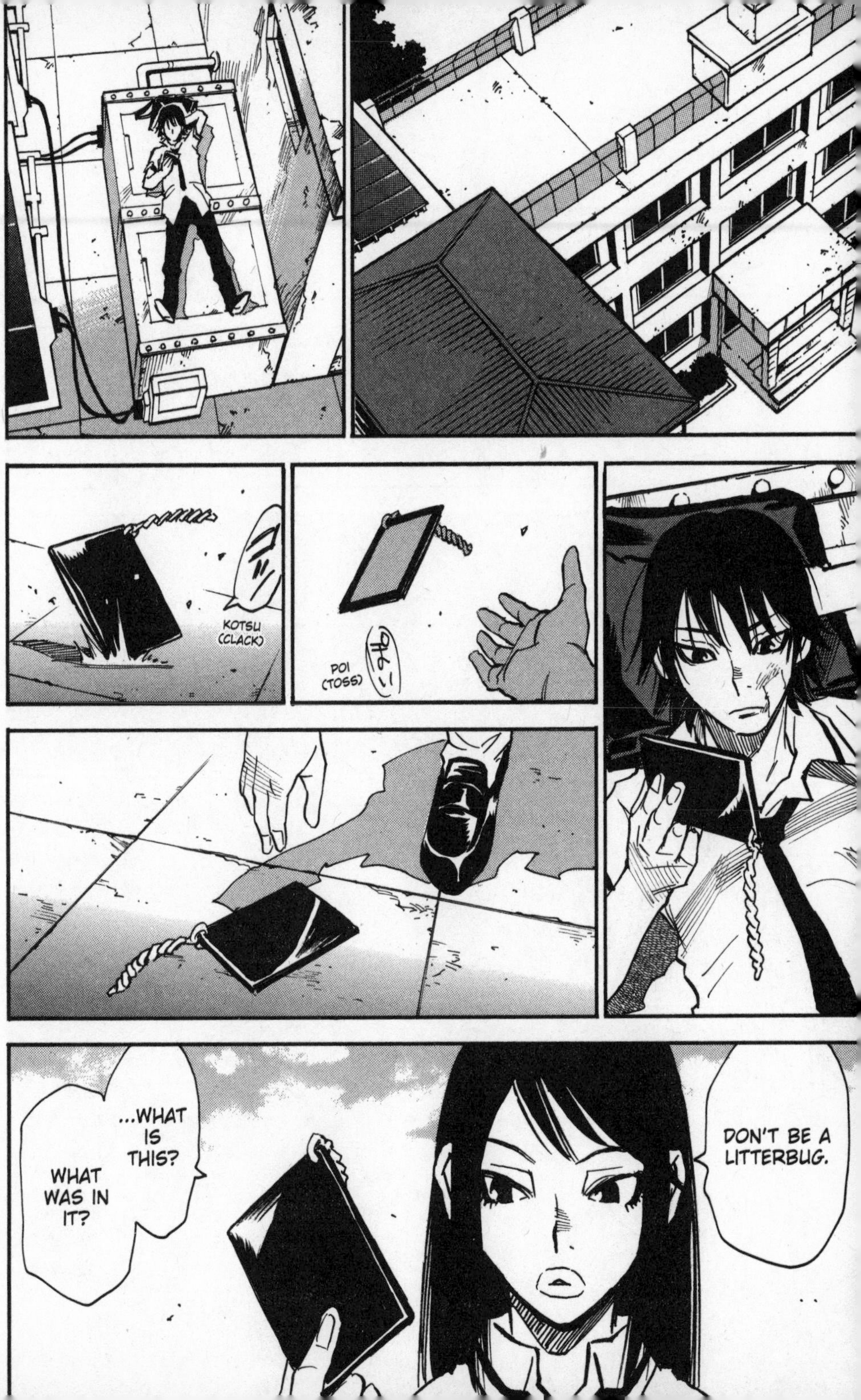
ぽい
POI
(TOSS)
KOTSU
(CLACK)
DON'T BE A LITTERBUG.
...WHAT IS THIS?
WHAT WAS IN IT?

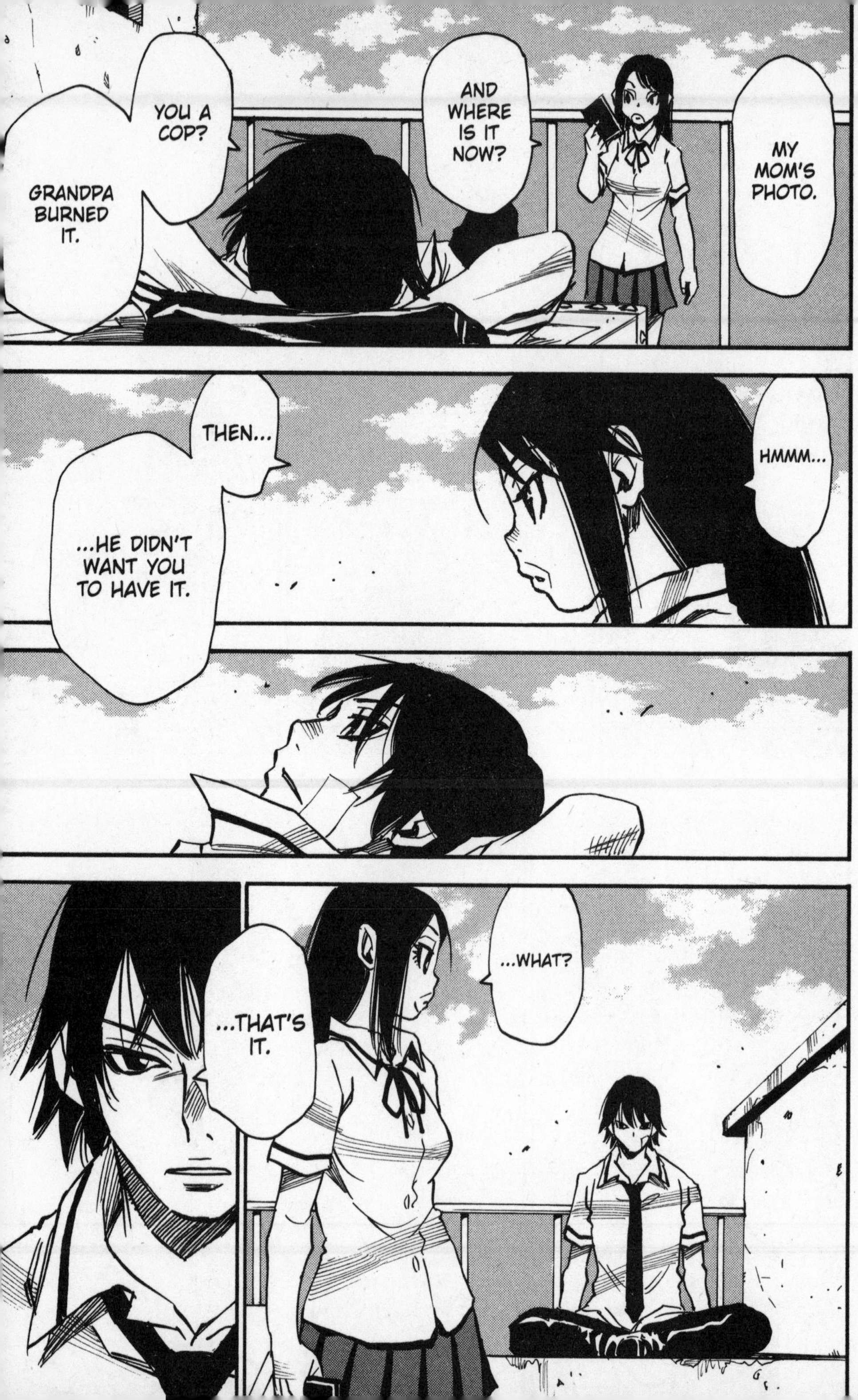
MY MOM'S PHOTO.
AND WHERE IS IT NOW?
YOU A COP?
GRANDPA BURNED IT.
HMMM...
THEN...
...HE DIDN'T WANT YOU TO HAVE IT.
...WHAT?
...THAT'S IT.

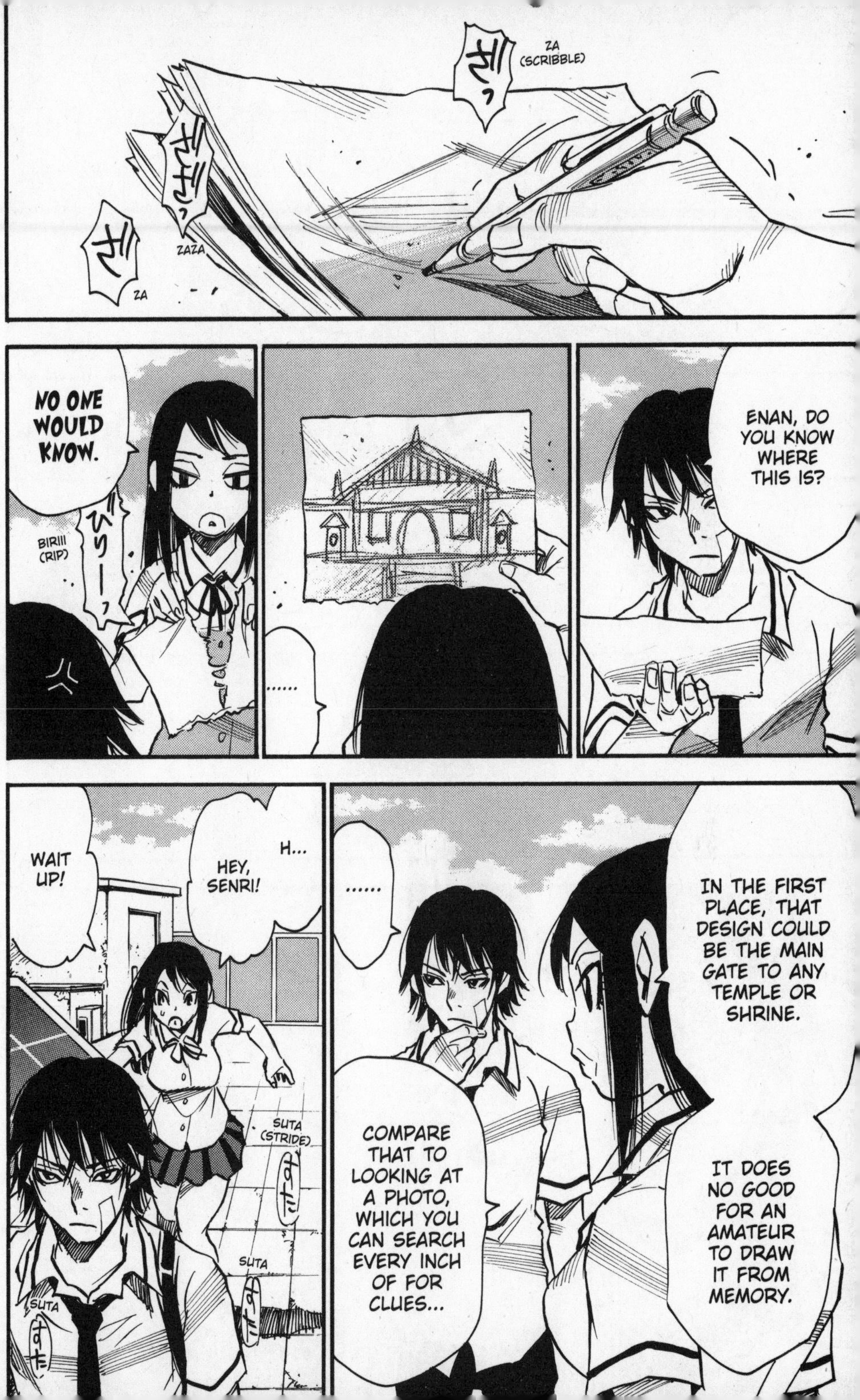
ざっ
ZA (SCRIBBLE)
ざざっ
ZAZA
ざ
ZA
ENAN, DO YOU KNOW WHERE THIS IS?
......
NO ONE WOULD KNOW.
びりーっ
BIRIII (RIP)
IN THE FIRST PLACE, THAT DESIGN COULD BE THE MAIN GATE TO ANY TEMPLE OR SHRINE.
......
IT DOES NO GOOD FOR AN AMATEUR TO DRAW IT FROM MEMORY.
COMPARE THAT TO LOOKING AT A PHOTO, WHICH YOU CAN SEARCH EVERY INCH OF FOR CLUES...
H...
HEY, SENRI!
WAIT UP!
SUTA (STRIDE)
すた
SUTA
すた
SUTA
すた

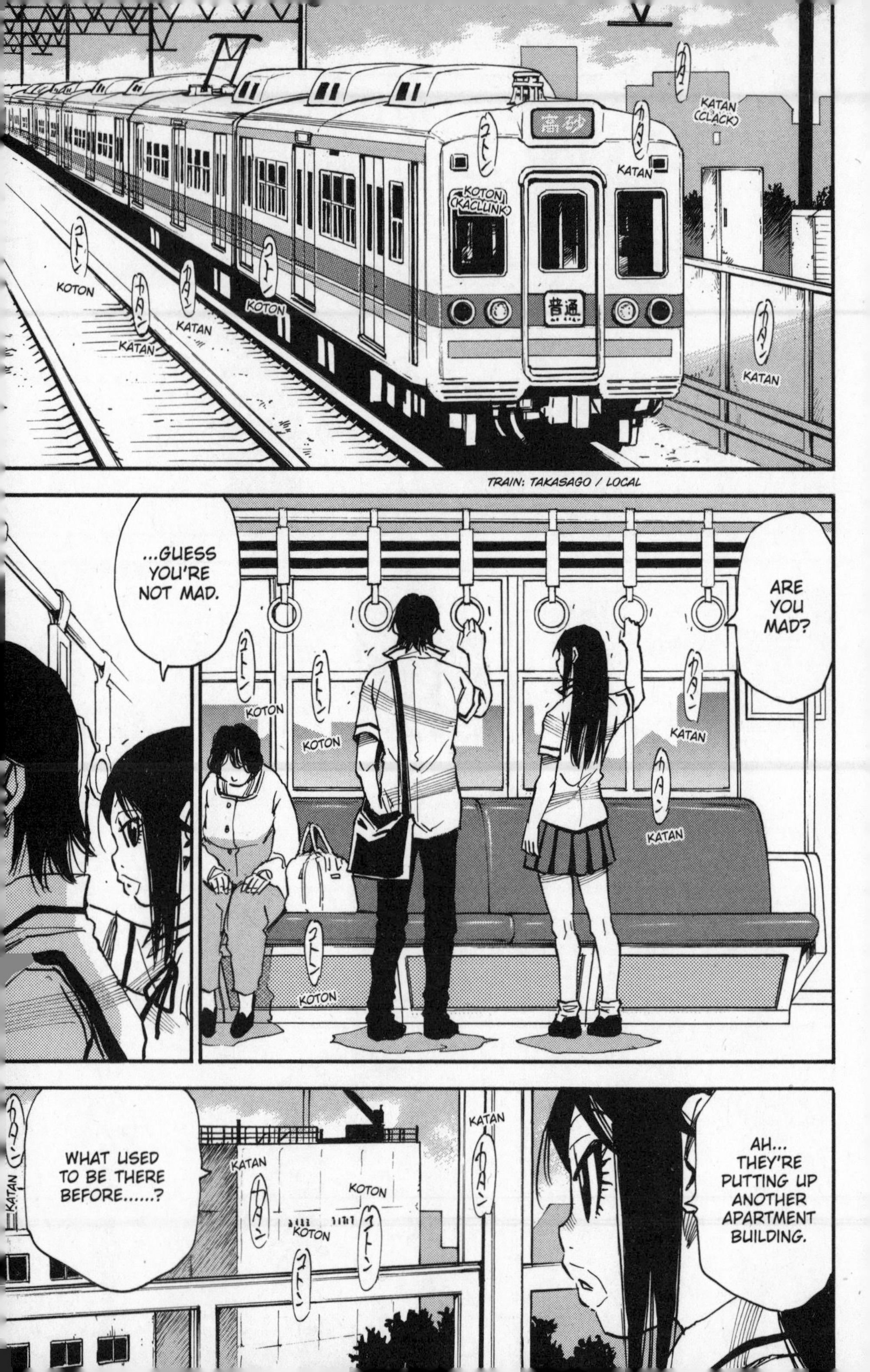

KATAN (CLACK)
KATAN
高砂
普通
KOTON (KACLUNK)
KATAN
KOTON
KATAN
KATAN
KOTON
TRAIN: TAKASAGO / LOCAL
ARE YOU MAD?
KATAN
KATAN
KOTON
KOTON
KOTON
...GUESS YOU'RE NOT MAD.
AH... THEY'RE PUTTING UP ANOTHER APARTMENT BUILDING.
KATAN
KOTON
KOTON
KATAN
WHAT USED TO BE THERE BEFORE......?
KATAN

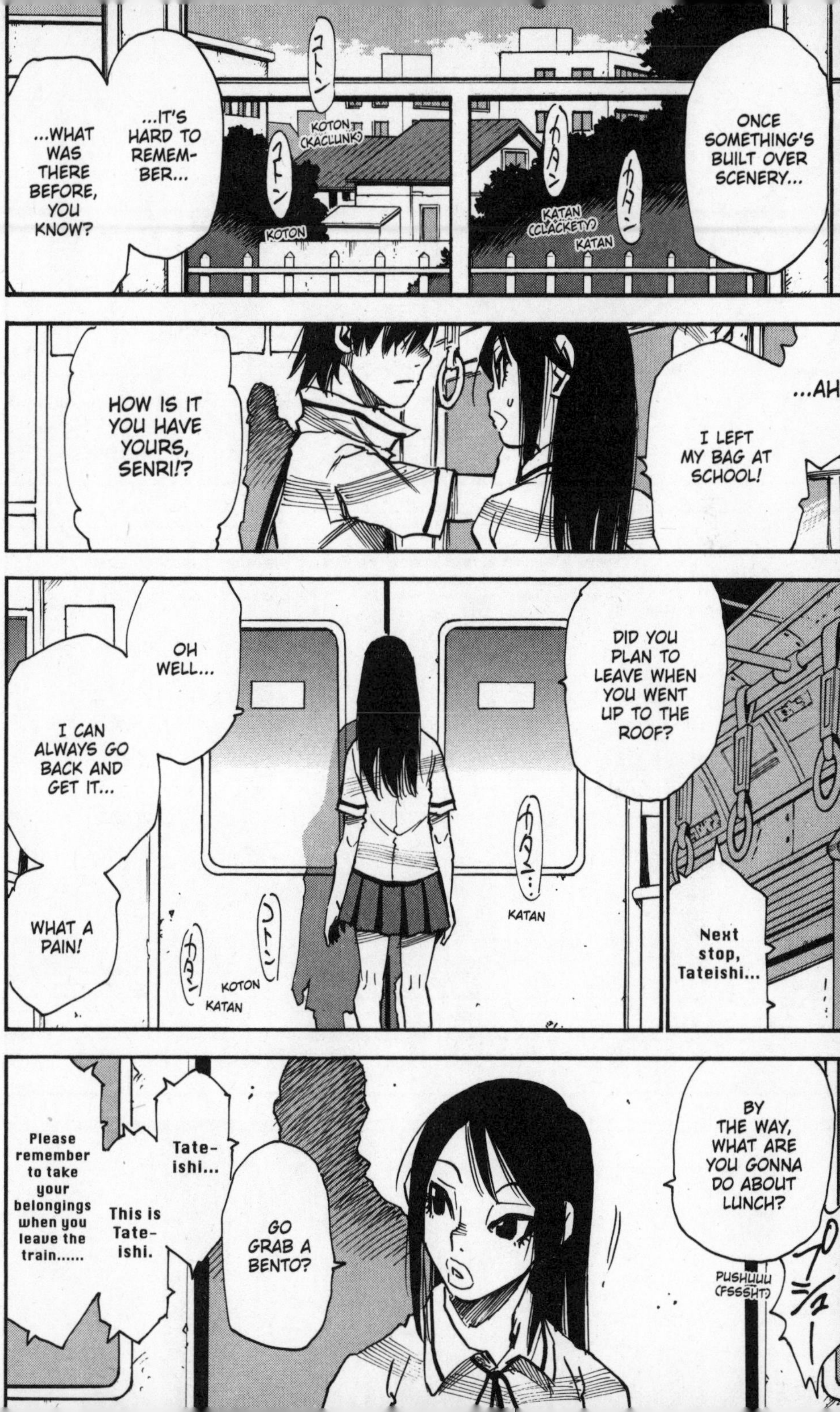
ONCE SOMETHING'S BUILT OVER SCENERY...
KATAN (CLACKETY) KATAN
KOTON (KACLUNK)
KOTON
...IT'S HARD TO REMEMBER...
...WHAT WAS THERE BEFORE, YOU KNOW?
...AH!
I LEFT MY BAG AT SCHOOL!
HOW IS IT YOU HAVE YOURS, SENRI!?
Next stop, Tateishi...
DID YOU PLAN TO LEAVE WHEN YOU WENT UP TO THE ROOF?
KATAN
OH WELL...
I CAN ALWAYS GO BACK AND GET IT...
KOTON
KATAN
WHAT A PAIN!
BY THE WAY, WHAT ARE YOU GONNA DO ABOUT LUNCH?
PUSHUUU (FSSSHT)
GO GRAB A BENTO?
Tateishi...
This is Tateishi.
Please remember to take your belongings when you leave the train......

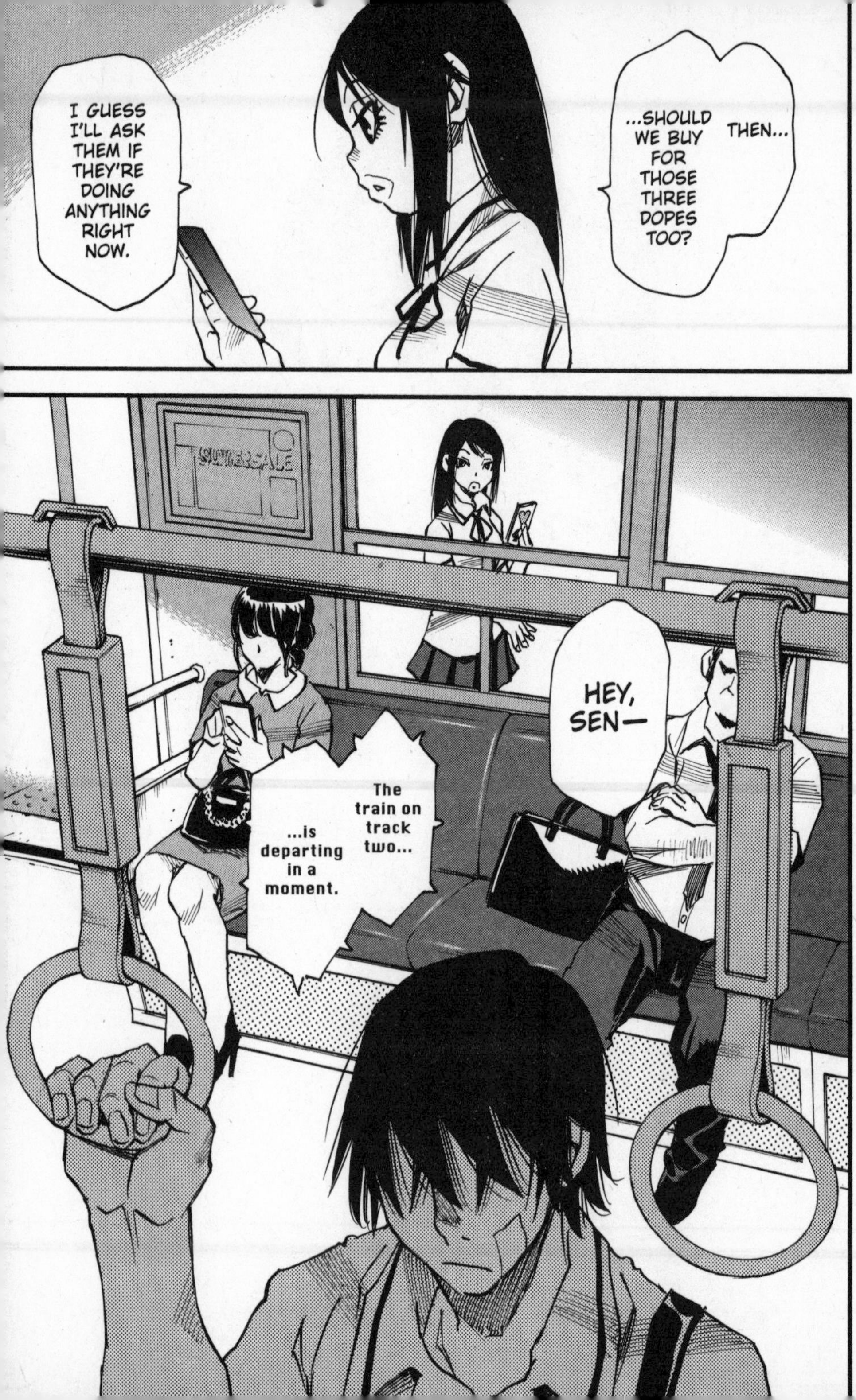
THEN...
...SHOULD WE BUY FOR THOSE THREE DOPES TOO?
I GUESS I'LL ASK THEM IF THEY'RE DOING ANYTHING RIGHT NOW.
HEY, SEN—
The train on track two...
...is departing in a moment.

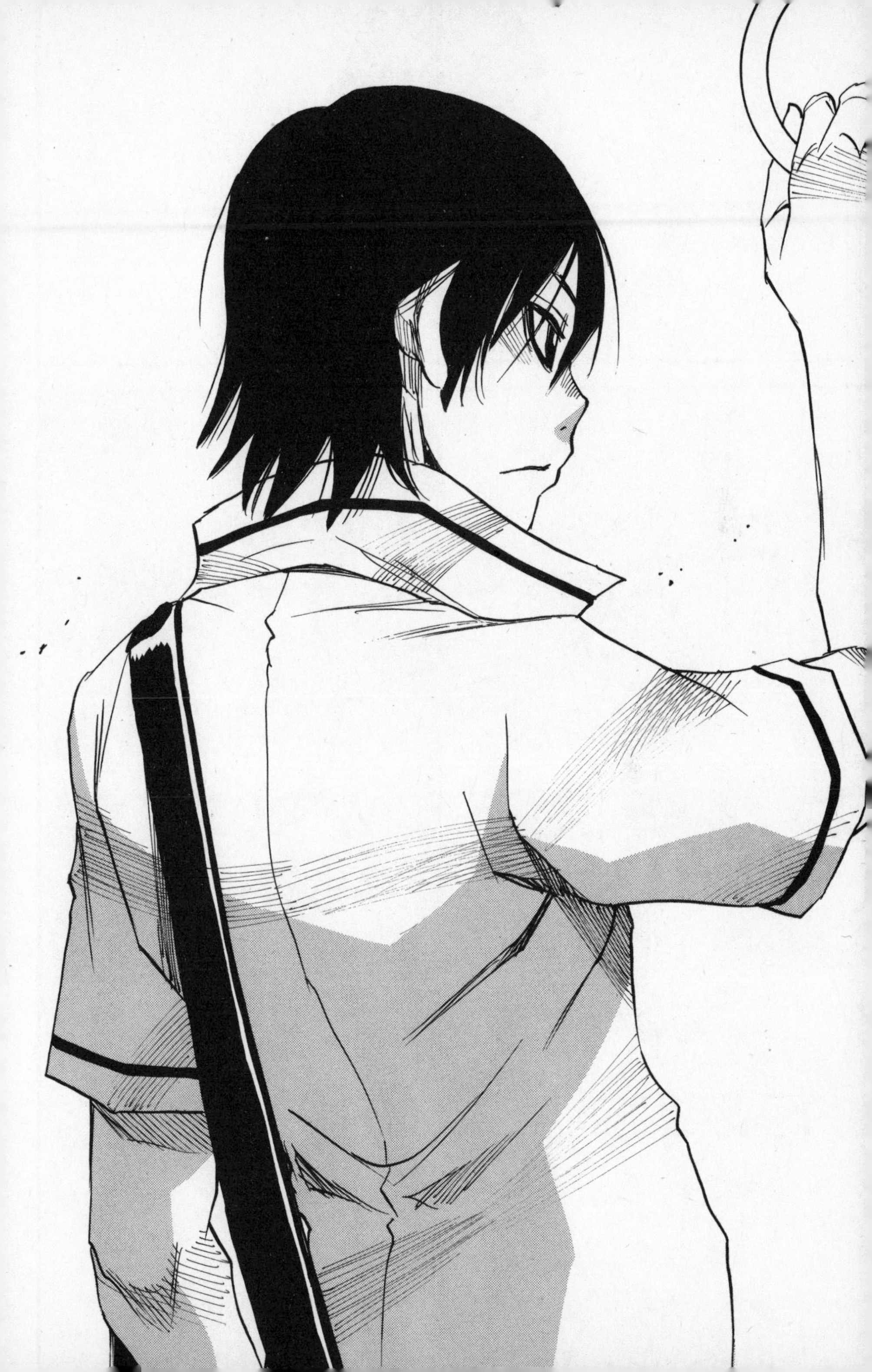

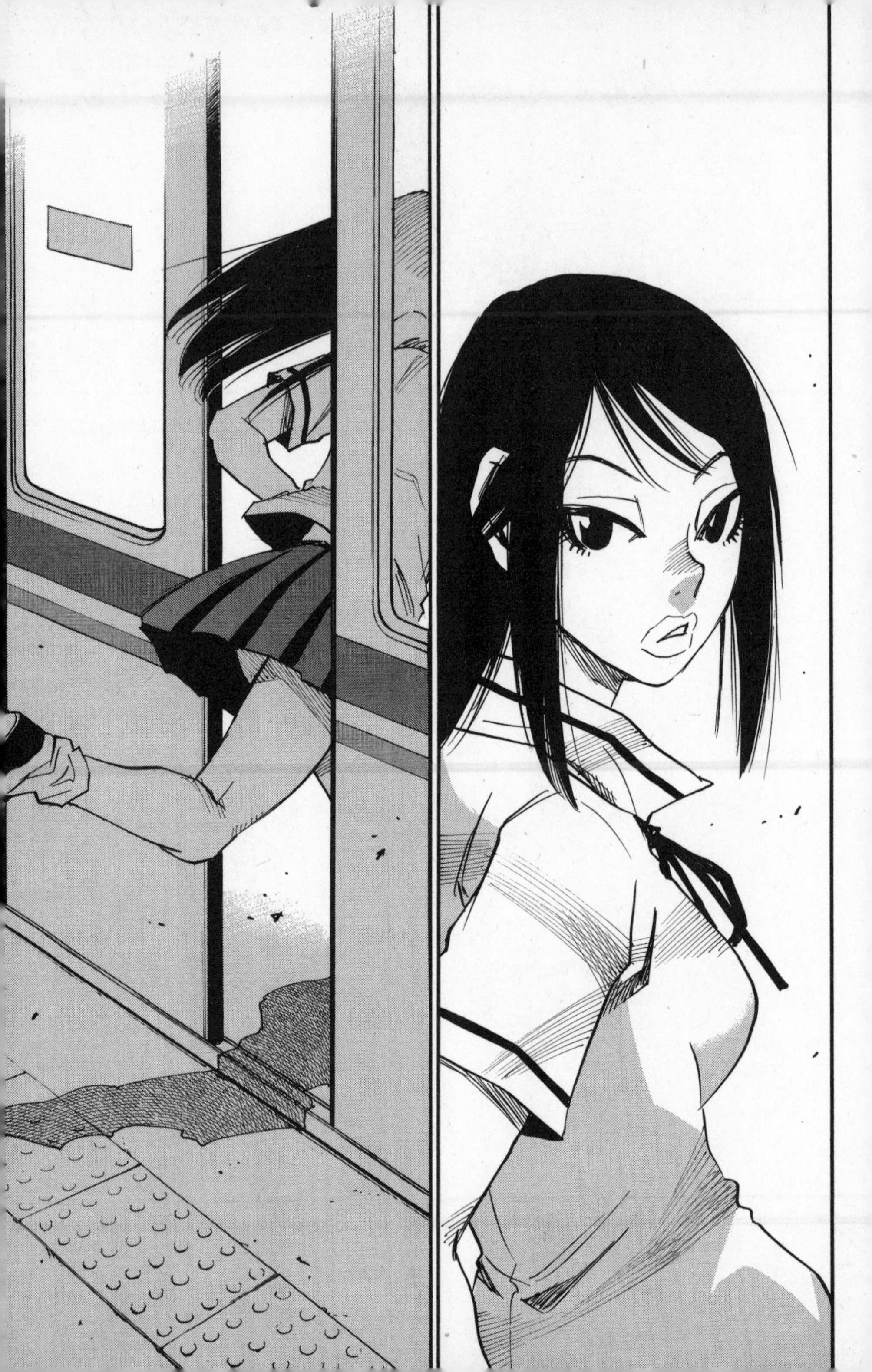

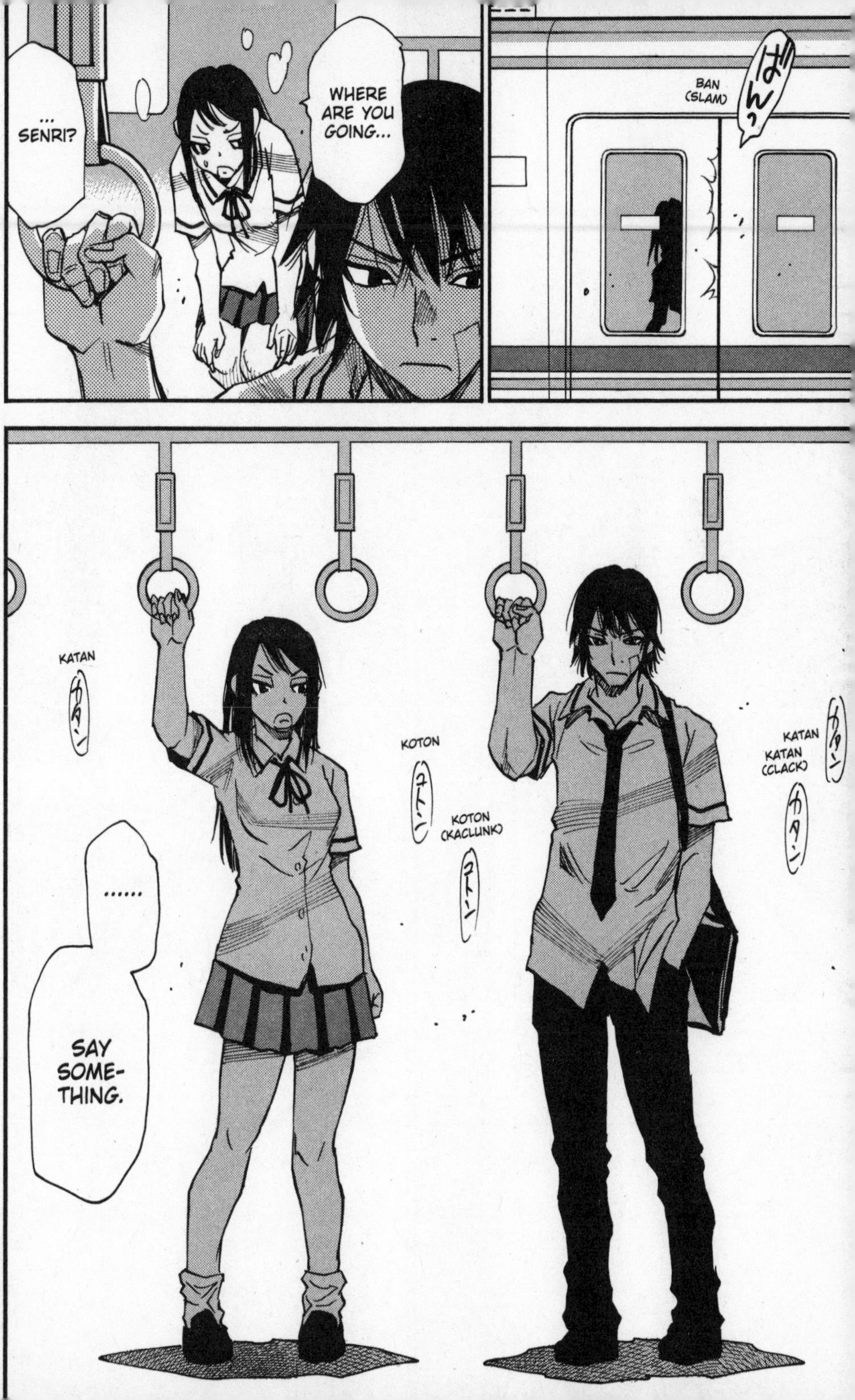
ばんっ
BAN (SLAM)
WHERE ARE YOU GOING...
... SENRI?
カタン カタン
KATAN KATAN (CLACK)
コトン コトン
KOTON KOTON (KACLUNK)
カタン
KATAN
......
SAY SOME-THING.

#9 END

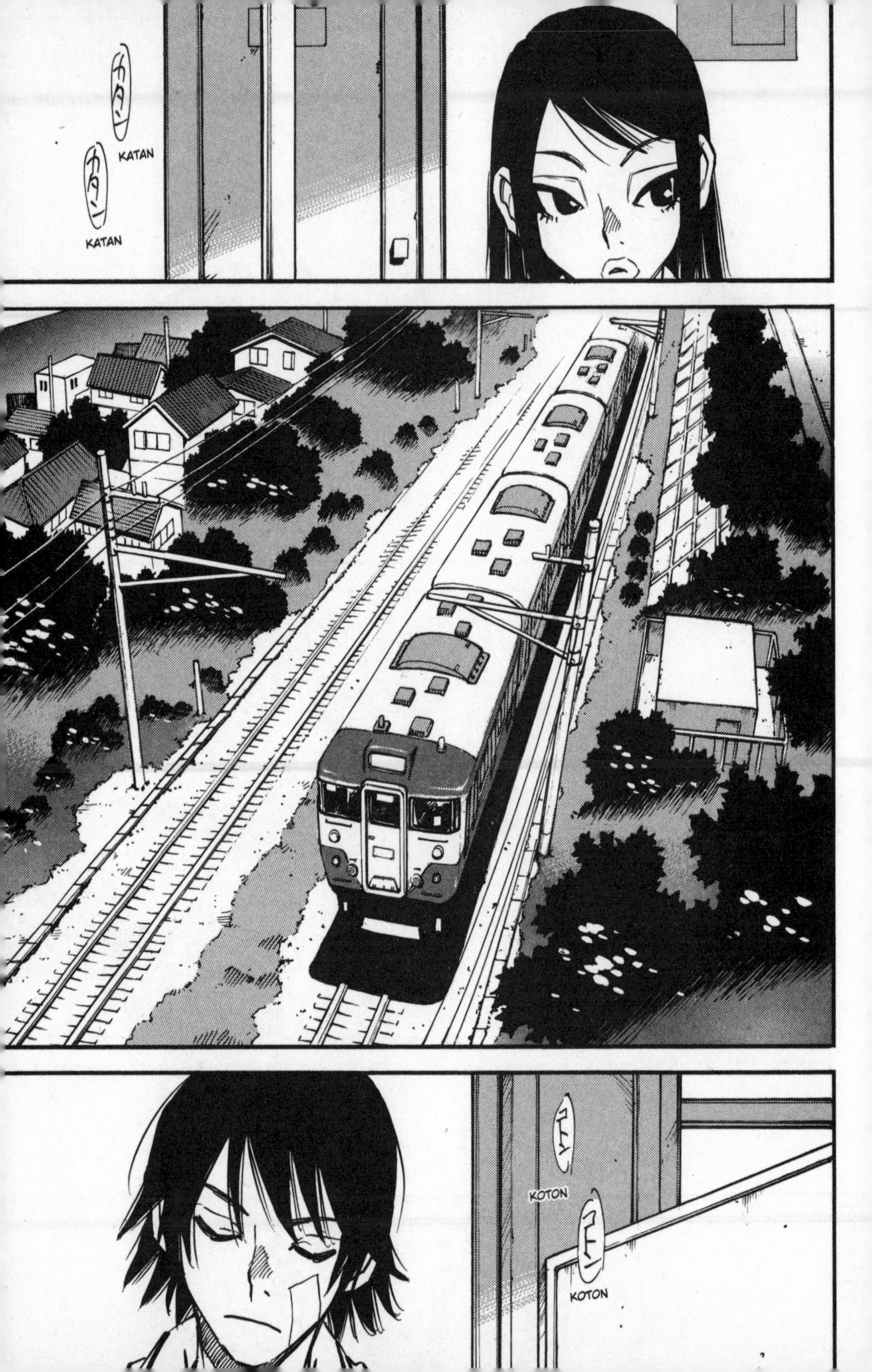
カタン
KATAN
カタン
KATAN
コトン
KOTON
コトン
KOTON

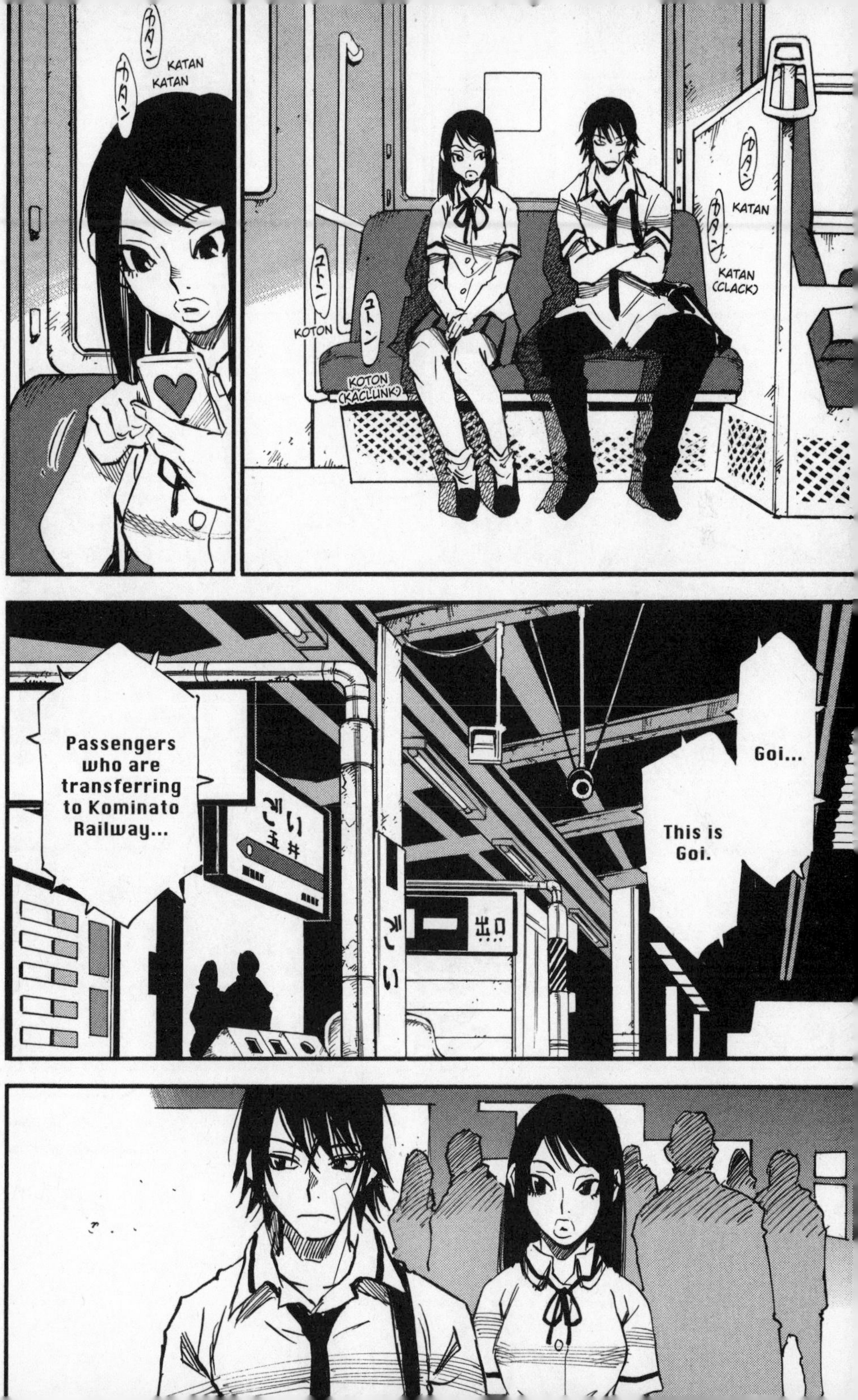

カタン
KATAN
カタン
KATAN (CLACK)
コトン
KOTON
コトン
KOTON (KACLUNK)
カタン
KATAN
カタン
KATAN
Goi...
This is Goi.
Passengers who are transferring to Kominato Railway...
ごい
五井
出口

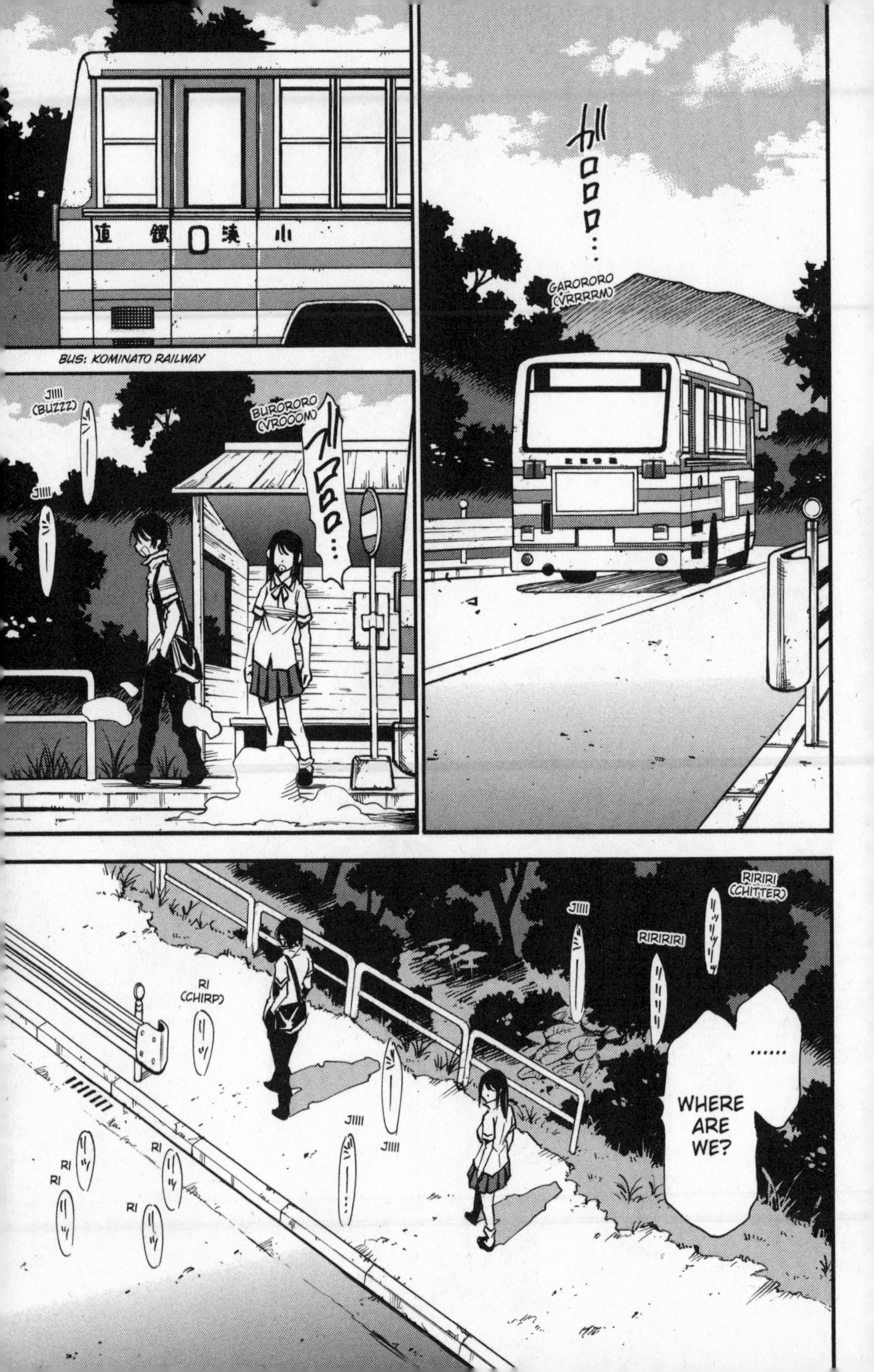
GARORORO (VRRRRM)
BUS: KOMINATO RAILWAY
JIIII (BUZZZ)
BURORORO (VROOOM)
JIIII
RIRIRI (CHITTER)
RIRIRIRI
JIIII
......
WHERE ARE WE?
RI (CHIRP)
JIIII
JIIII
RI
RI
RI
RI

#10 At the Tower

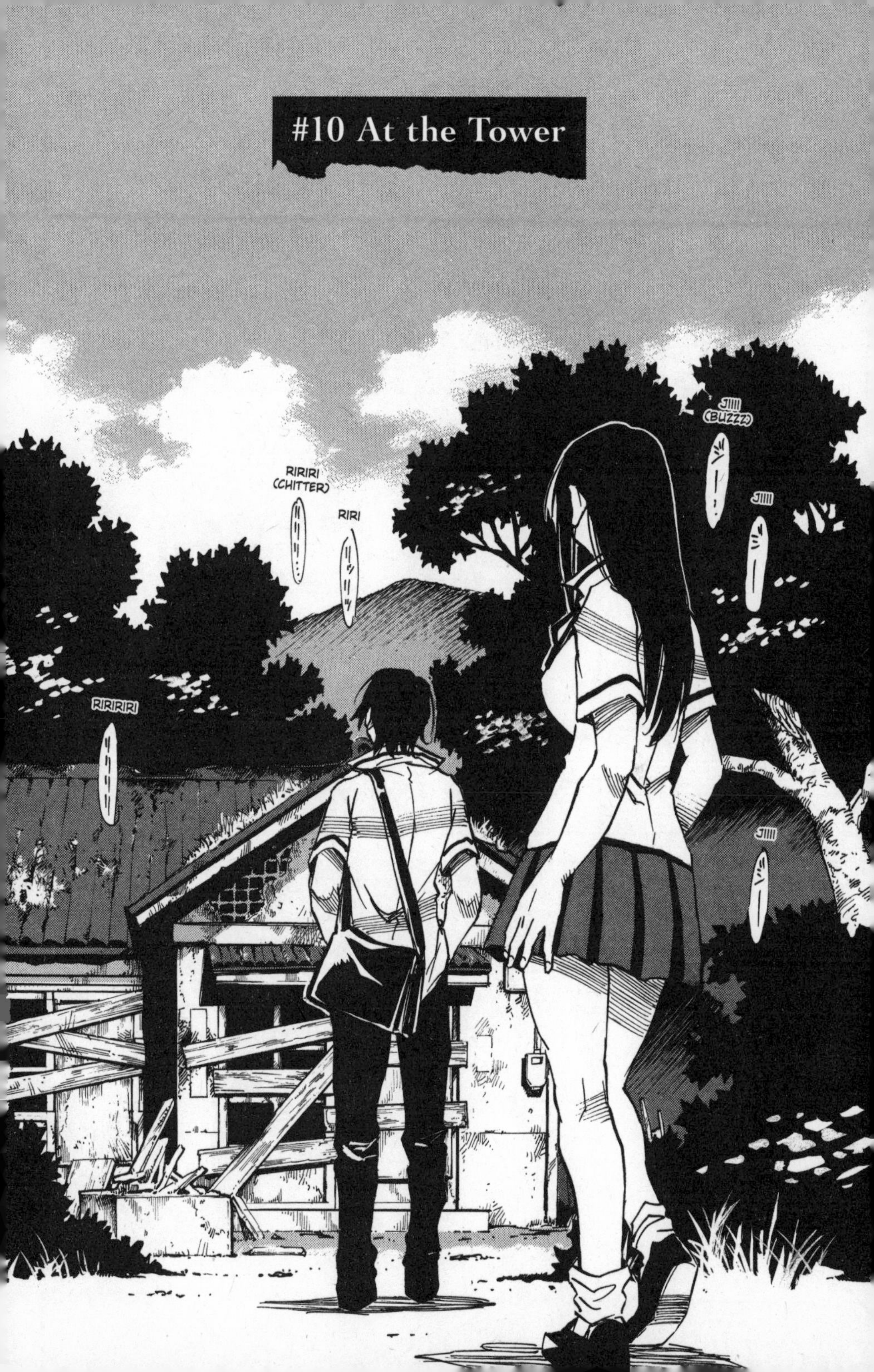
JIIII (BUZZZ)
JIIII
JIIII
RIRI
RIRIRI (CHITTER)
RIRIRIRI

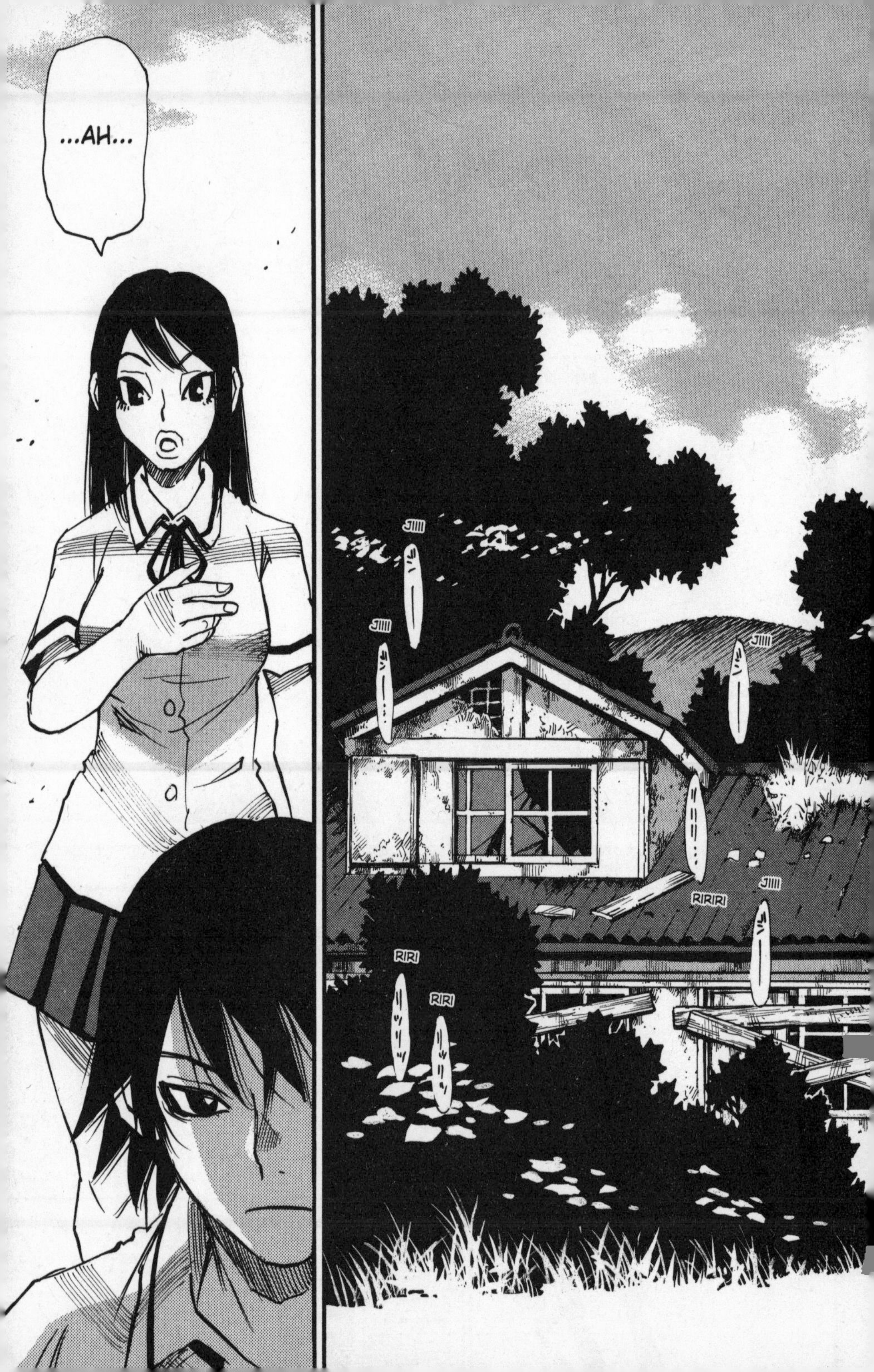
JIIII
JIIII
JIIII
RIRIRI
JIIII
RIRI
RIRI
...AH...

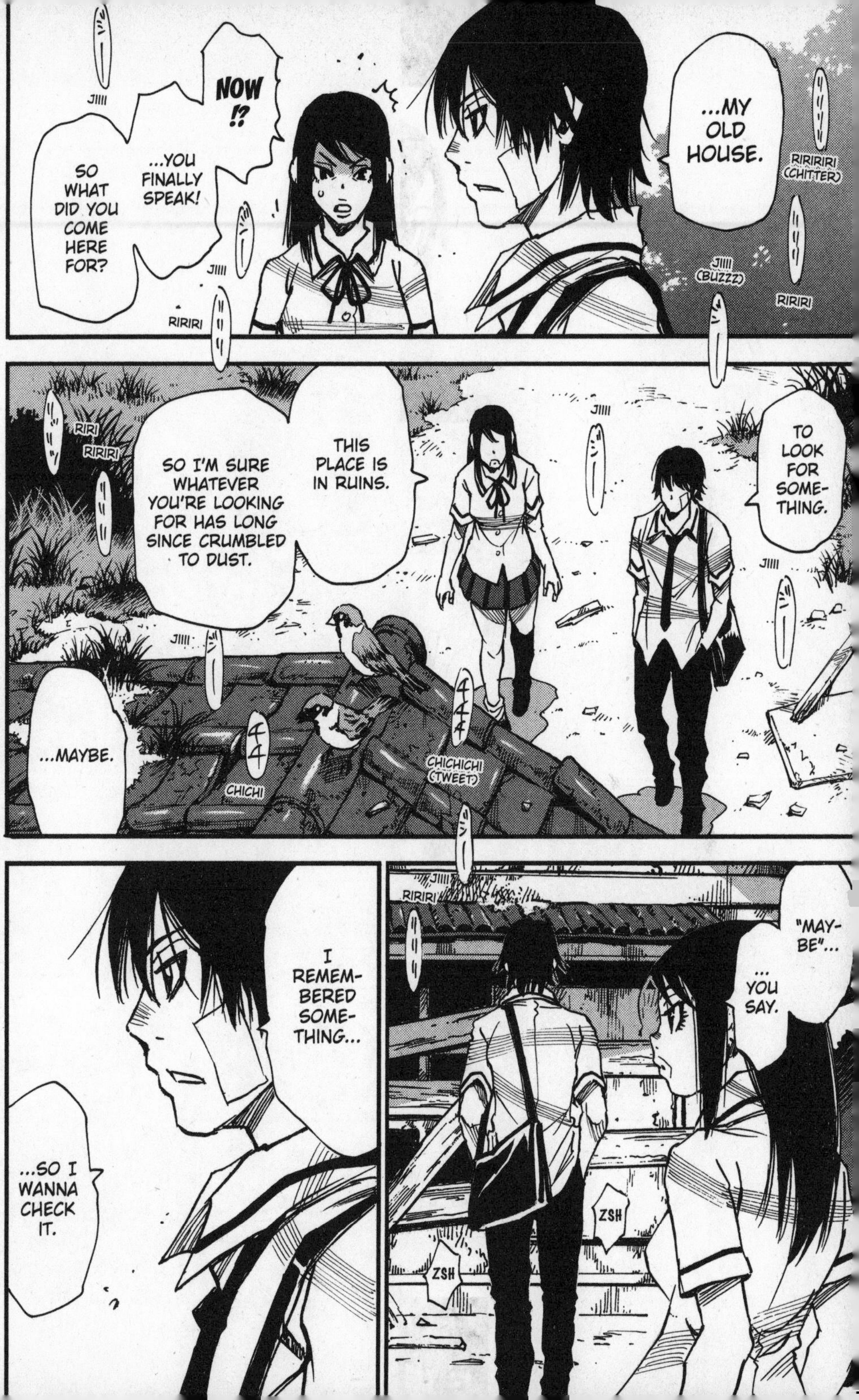
...MY OLD HOUSE.
RIRIRIRI (CHITTER)
JIIII (BUZZZ)
RIRIRI
NOW!?
...YOU FINALLY SPEAK!
SO WHAT DID YOU COME HERE FOR?
JIIII
JIIII
RIRIRI
TO LOOK FOR SOME-THING.
JIIII
JIIII
THIS PLACE IS IN RUINS.
SO I'M SURE WHATEVER YOU'RE LOOKING FOR HAS LONG SINCE CRUMBLED TO DUST.
RIRI
RIRIRI
JIIII
CHICHICHI (TWEET)
CHICHI
...MAYBE.
"MAY-BE"...
... YOU SAY.
JIIII
RIRIRI
ZSH
ZSH
I REMEM-BERED SOME-THING...
...SO I WANNA CHECK IT.

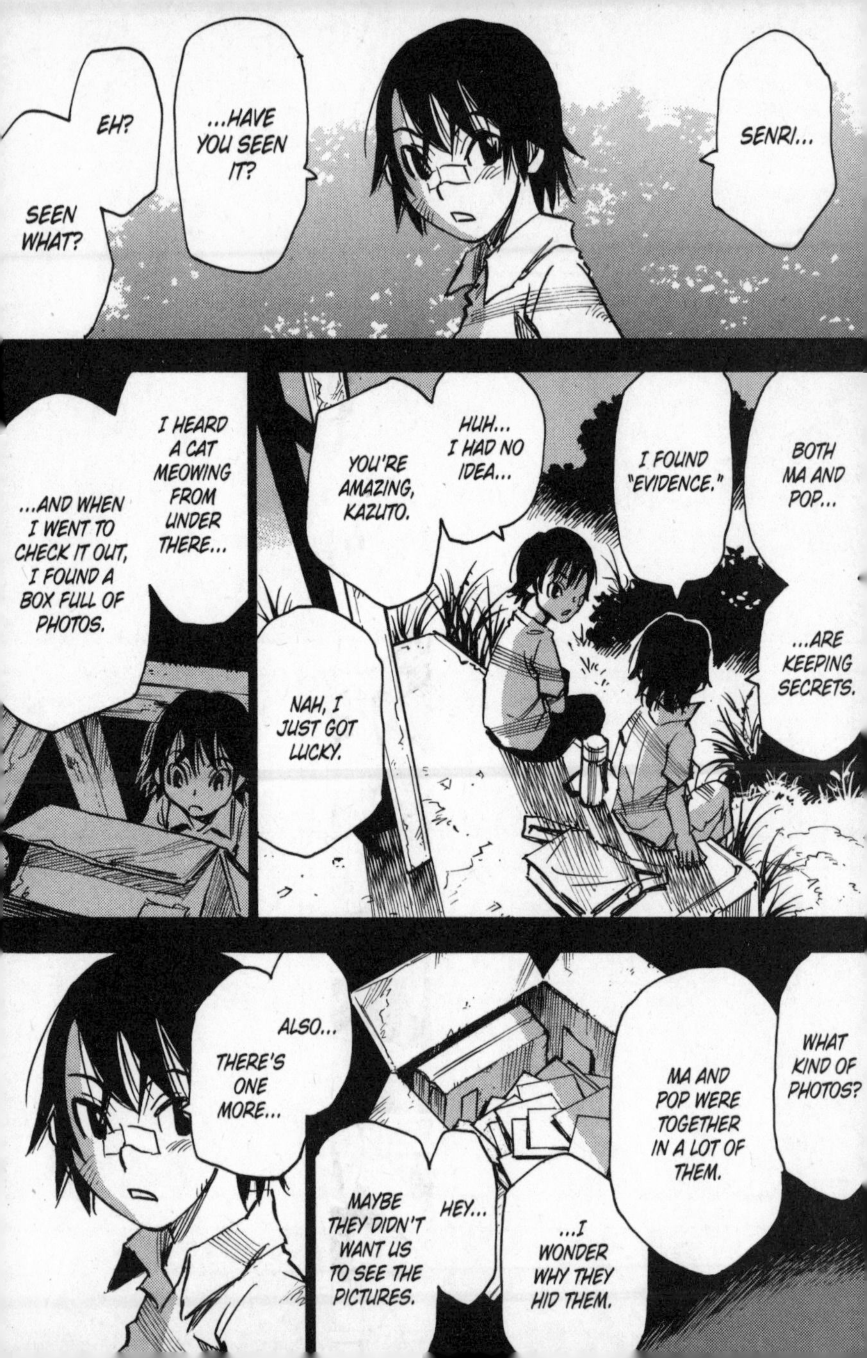
SENRI...
...HAVE YOU SEEN IT?
EH? SEEN WHAT?
BOTH MA AND POP...
...ARE KEEPING SECRETS.
I FOUND "EVIDENCE."
HUH... I HAD NO IDEA...
YOU'RE AMAZING, KAZUTO.
NAH, I JUST GOT LUCKY.
I HEARD A CAT MEOWING FROM UNDER THERE...
...AND WHEN I WENT TO CHECK IT OUT, I FOUND A BOX FULL OF PHOTOS.
WHAT KIND OF PHOTOS?
MA AND POP WERE TOGETHER IN A LOT OF THEM.
...I WONDER WHY THEY HID THEM.
HEY...
MAYBE THEY DIDN'T WANT US TO SEE THE PICTURES.
ALSO...
THERE'S ONE MORE...

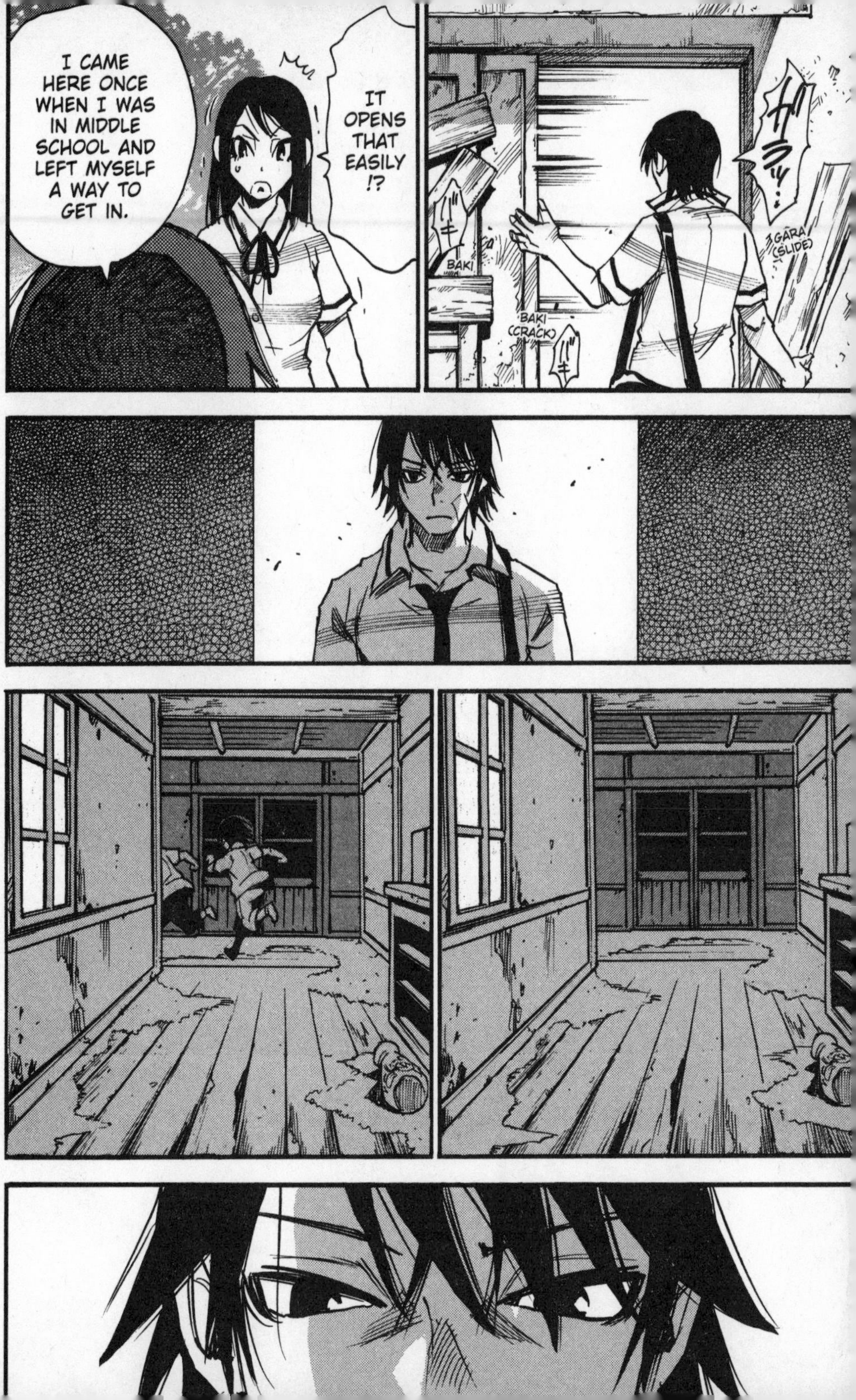
ガラッ
GARA (SLIDE)
バキ
BAKI
BAKI (CRACK)
バキ
IT OPENS THAT EASILY !?
I CAME HERE ONCE WHEN I WAS IN MIDDLE SCHOOL AND LEFT MYSELF A WAY TO GET IN.

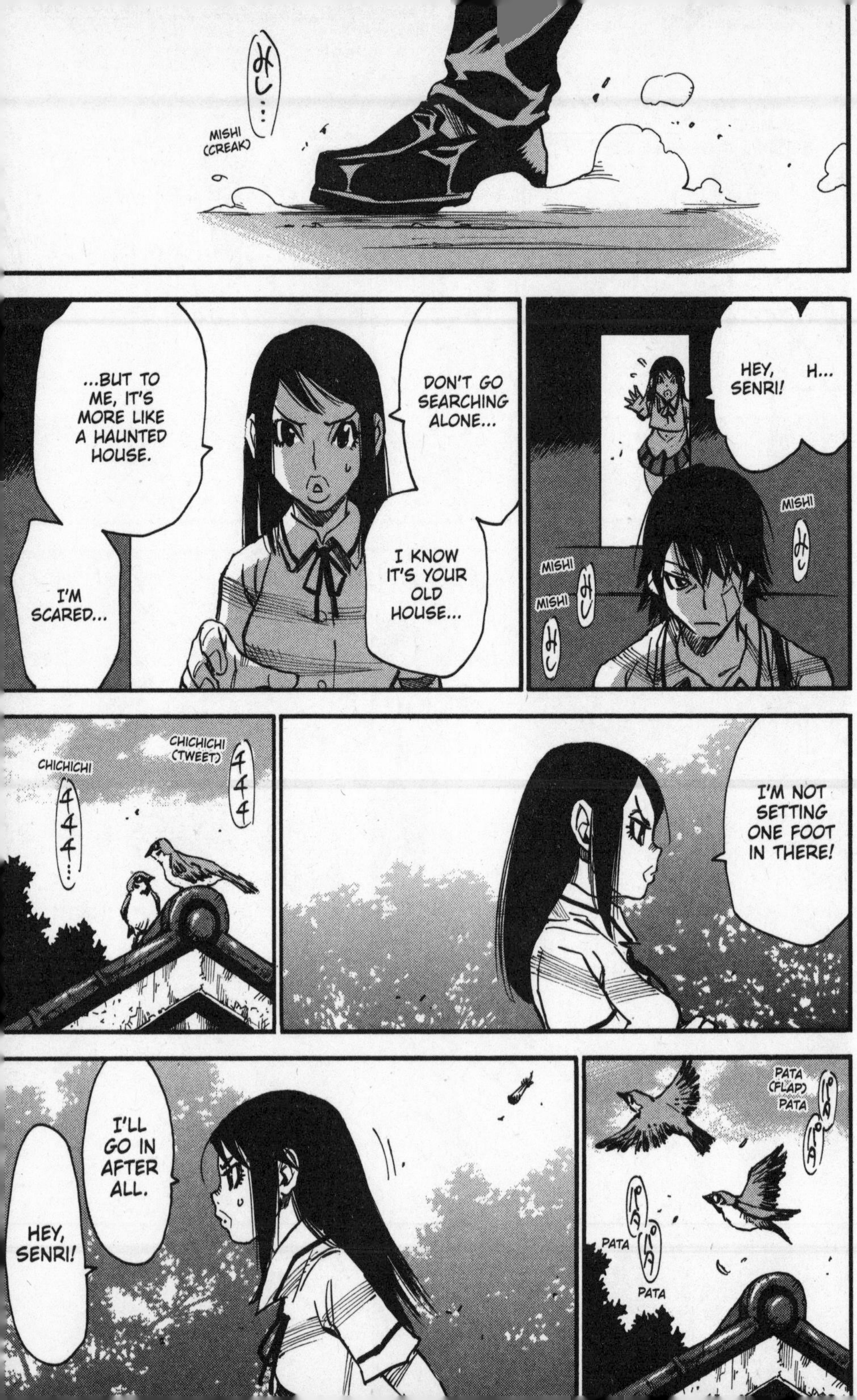
みし…
MISHI (CREAK)
HEY, SENRI!
H...
MISHI
みし
MISHI
みし
MISHI
みし
DON'T GO SEARCHING ALONE...
I KNOW IT'S YOUR OLD HOUSE...
...BUT TO ME, IT'S MORE LIKE A HAUNTED HOUSE.
I'M SCARED...
I'M NOT SETTING ONE FOOT IN THERE!
CHICHICHI (TWEET)
チチチ
CHICHICHI
チチチ…
PATA (FLAP) PATA
ぱたぱた
ぱたぱた
PATA
PATA
I'LL GO IN AFTER ALL.
HEY, SENRI!

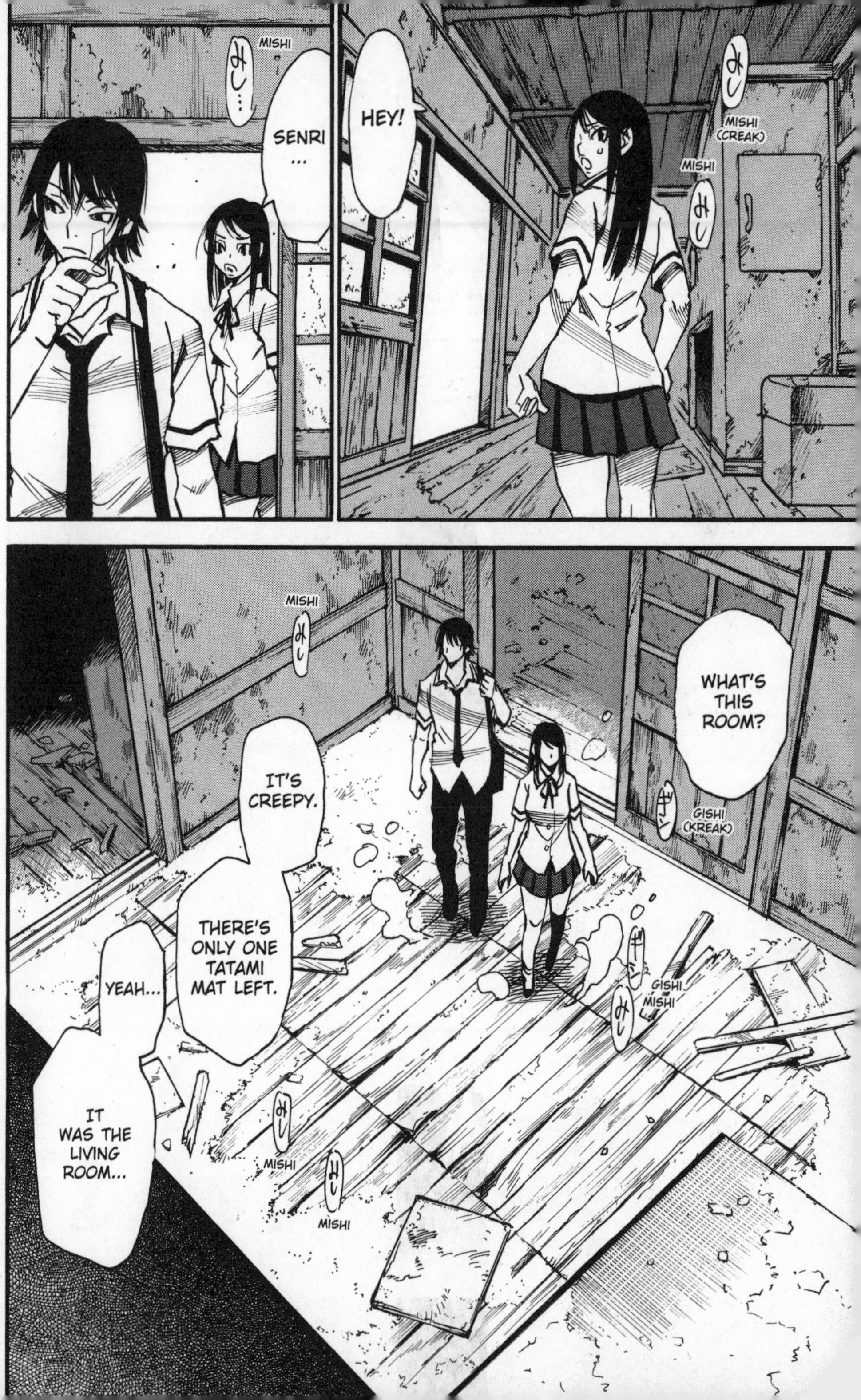
みし
MISHI (CREAK)
HEY!
MISHI
みし
SENRI ...
MISHI
みし…
WHAT'S THIS ROOM?
GISHI (KREAK)
MISHI
みし
GISHI
MISHI
みし
IT'S CREEPY.
THERE'S ONLY ONE TATAMI MAT LEFT.
YEAH...
IT WAS THE LIVING ROOM...
みし
MISHI
みし
MISHI

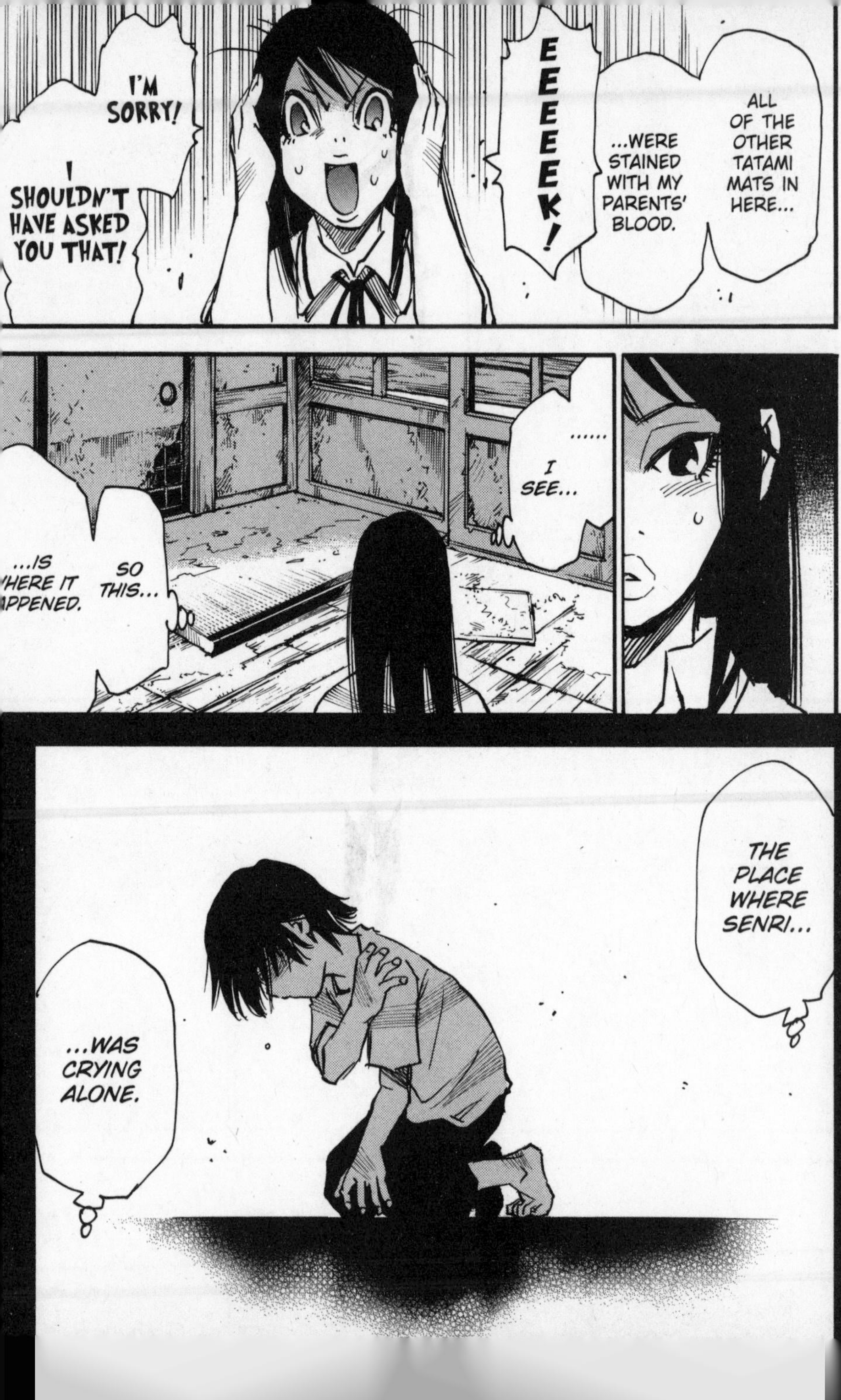
ALL OF THE OTHER TATAMI MATS IN HERE...
...WERE STAINED WITH MY PARENTS' BLOOD.
EEEEEK!
I'M SORRY!
I SHOULDN'T HAVE ASKED YOU THAT!
...... I SEE...
SO THIS...
...IS HERE IT APPENED.
THE PLACE WHERE SENRI...
...WAS CRYING ALONE.

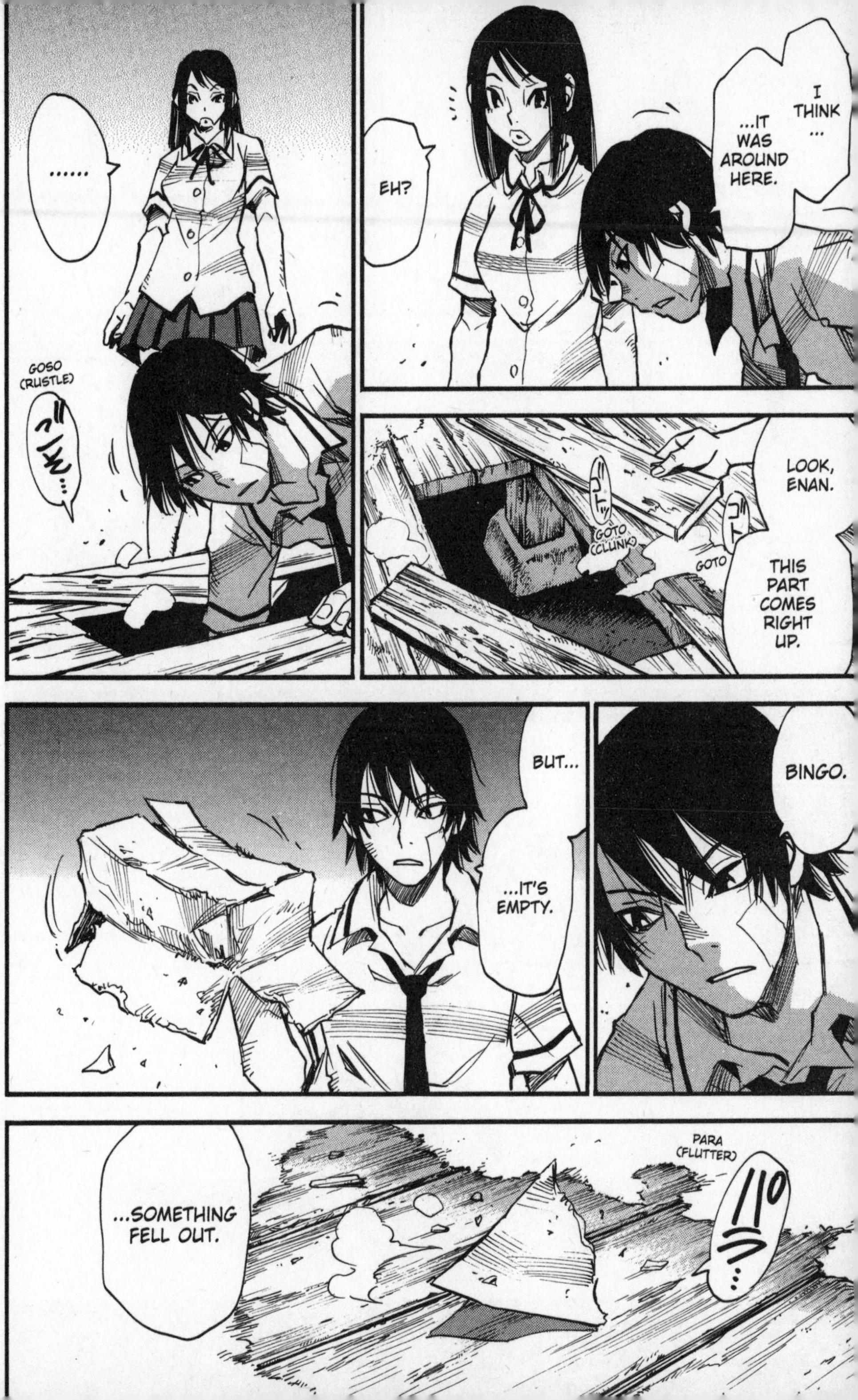
I THINK ...
...IT WAS AROUND HERE.
EH?
LOOK, ENAN.
ゴトッ
GOTO (CLUNK)
ゴト
GOTO
THIS PART COMES RIGHT UP.
......
GOSO (RUSTLE)
ゴソ...
BINGO.
BUT...
...IT'S EMPTY.
PARA (FLUTTER)
パラ...
...SOMETHING FELL OUT.

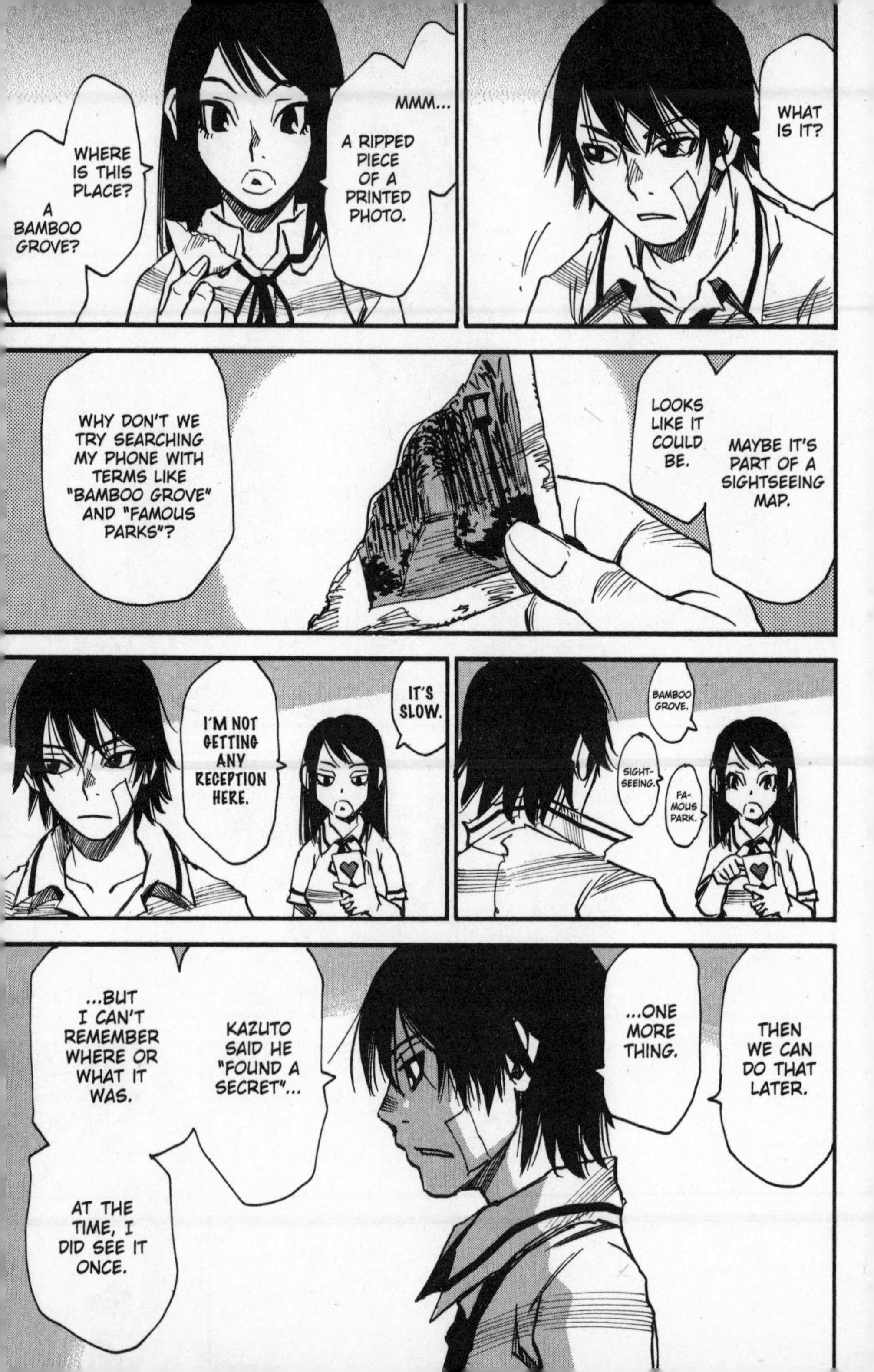
WHAT IS IT?
MMM...
A RIPPED PIECE OF A PRINTED PHOTO.
WHERE IS THIS PLACE?
A BAMBOO GROVE?
MAYBE IT'S PART OF A SIGHTSEEING MAP.
LOOKS LIKE IT COULD BE.
WHY DON'T WE TRY SEARCHING MY PHONE WITH TERMS LIKE "BAMBOO GROVE" AND "FAMOUS PARKS"?
BAMBOO GROVE.
SIGHT-SEEING.
FA-MOUS PARK.
IT'S SLOW.
I'M NOT GETTING ANY RECEPTION HERE.
THEN WE CAN DO THAT LATER.
...ONE MORE THING.
KAZUTO SAID HE "FOUND A SECRET"...
...BUT I CAN'T REMEMBER WHERE OR WHAT IT WAS.
AT THE TIME, I DID SEE IT ONCE.

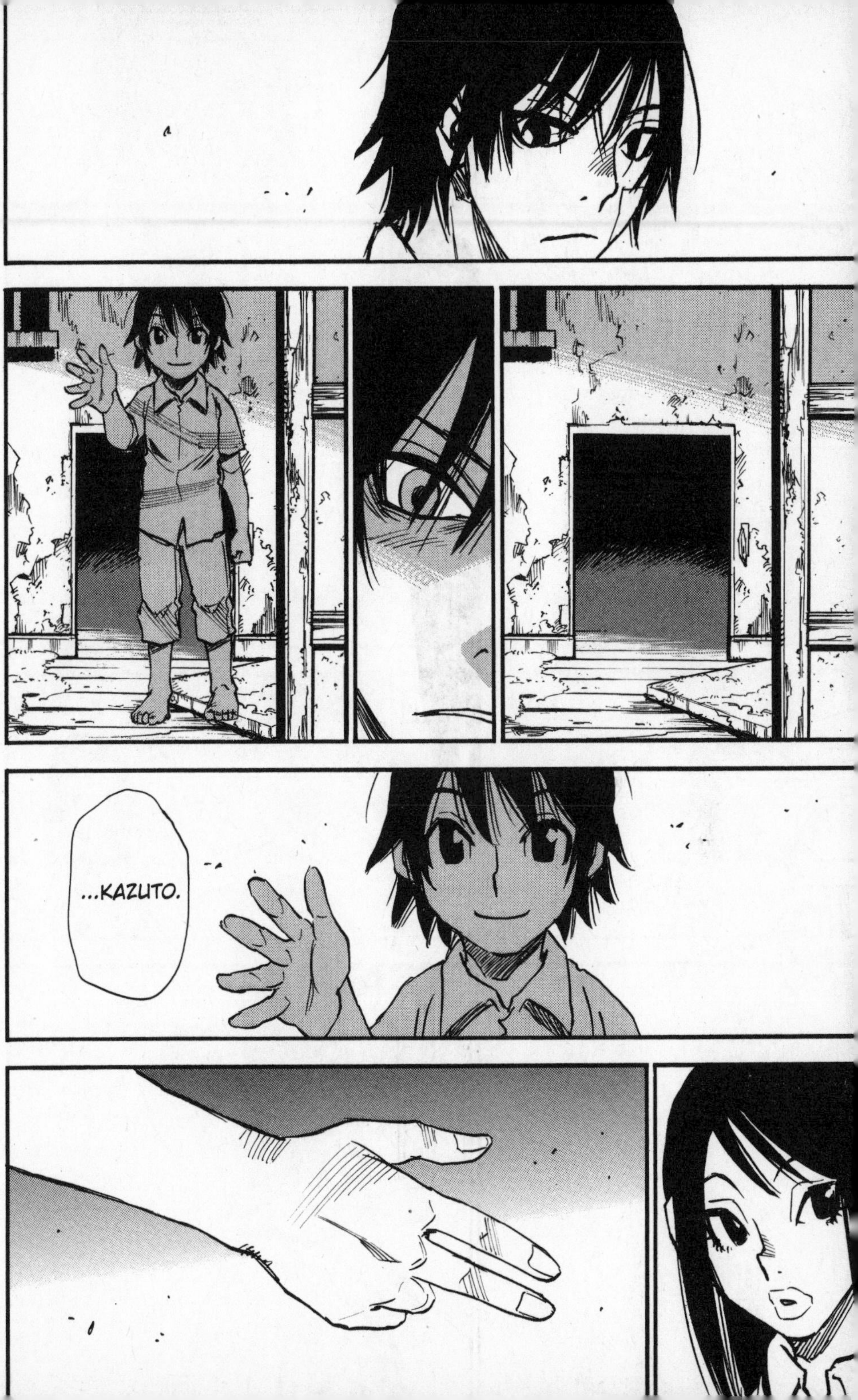
...KAZUTO.

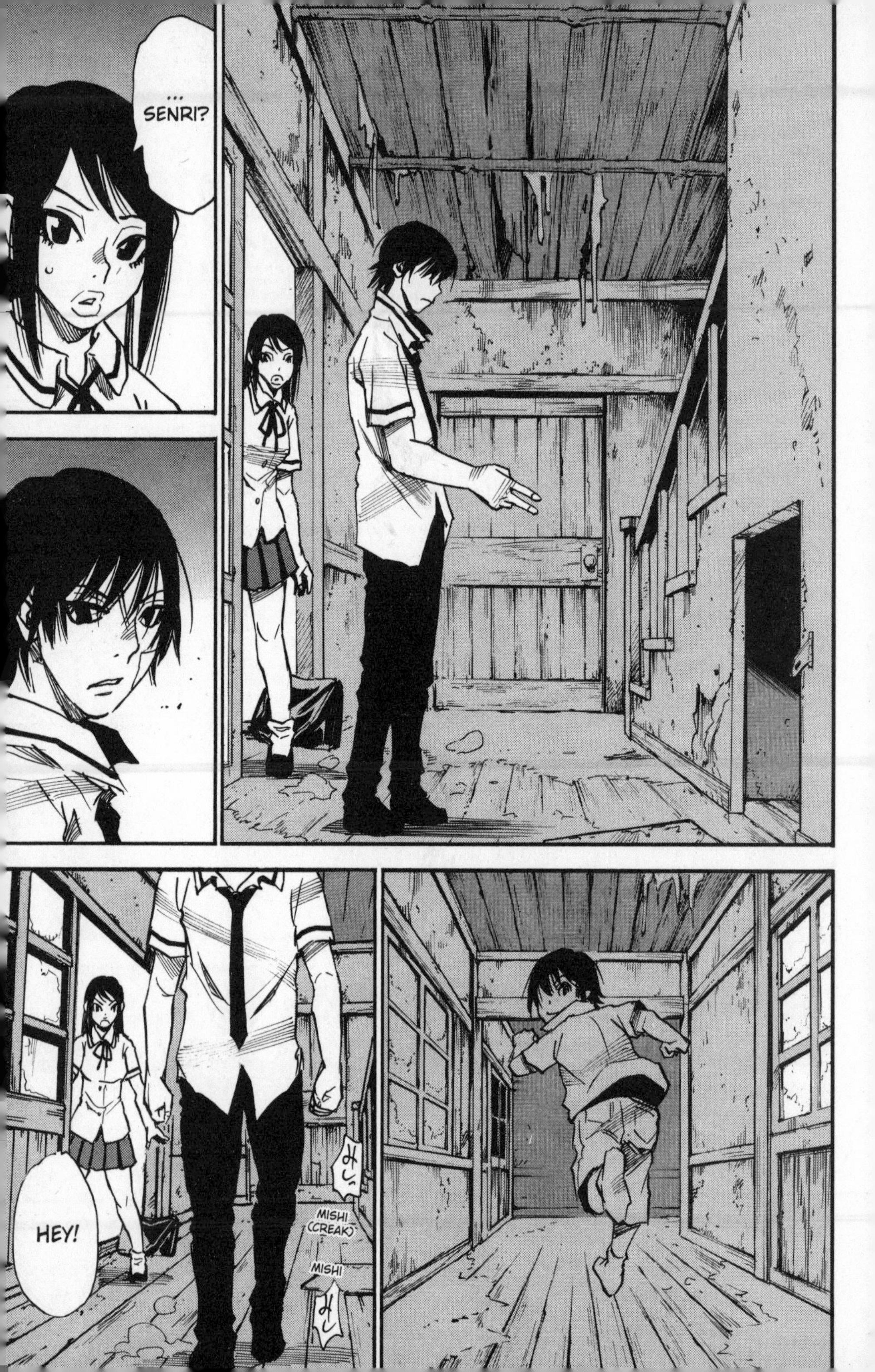
...SENRI?
...
みし
MISHI (CREAK)
HEY!
MISHI
みし

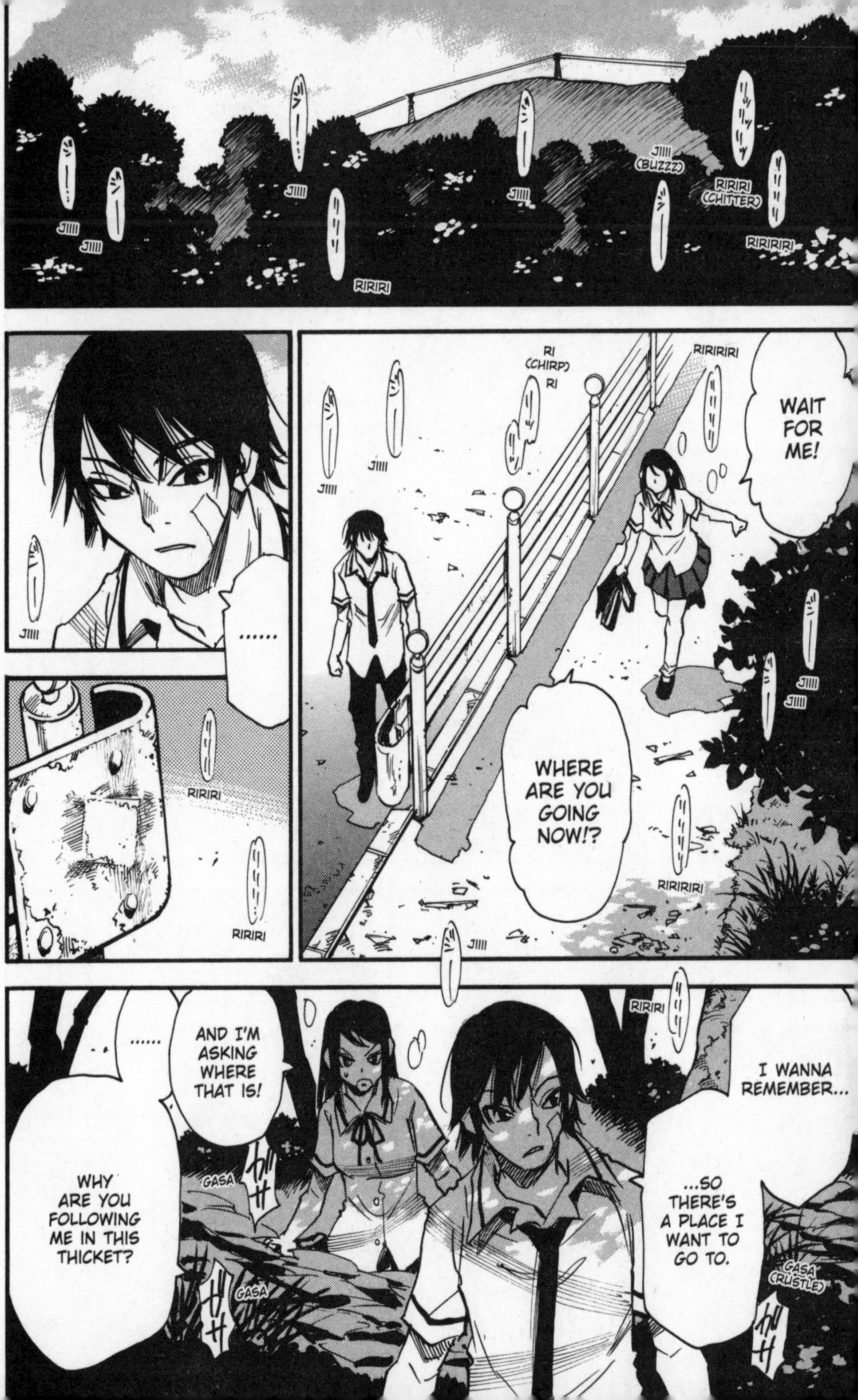
RIRIRI (CHITTER)
RIRIRIRI
JIIII (BUZZZ)
JIIII
RIRIRI
JIIII
JIIII
JIIII
RIRIRIRI
RI (CHIRP) RI
WAIT FOR ME!
JIIII
JIIII
JIIII
WHERE ARE YOU GOING NOW!?
RIRIRIRI
JIIII
JIIII
......
RIRIRI
RIRIRI
RIRIRI
I WANNA REMEMBER...
...SO THERE'S A PLACE I WANT TO GO TO.
GASA (RUSTLE)
AND I'M ASKING WHERE THAT IS!
......
GASA
WHY ARE YOU FOLLOWING ME IN THIS THICKET?
GASA

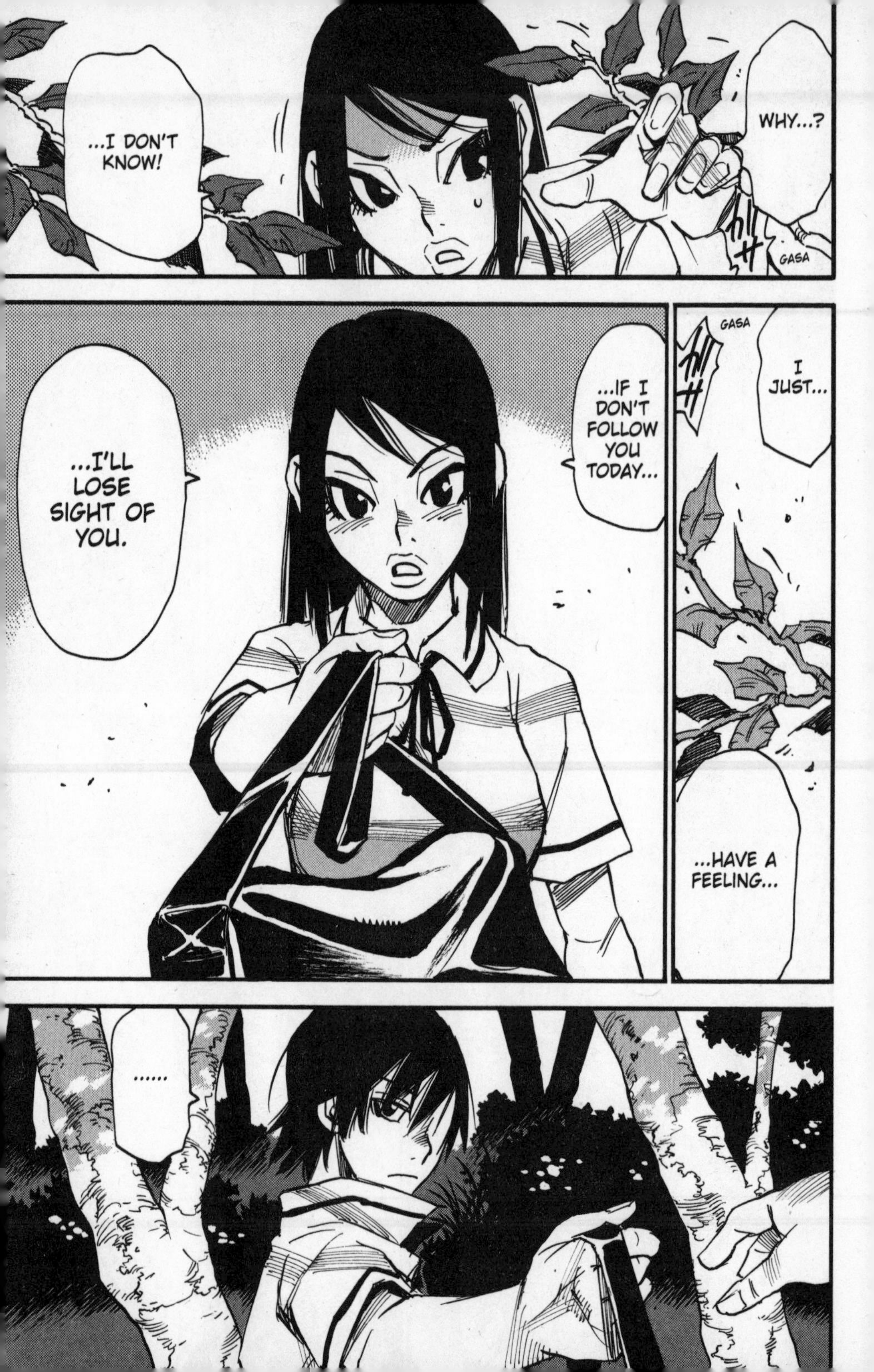
WHY...?
GASA
...I DON'T KNOW!
GASA
I JUST...
...HAVE A FEELING...
...IF I DON'T FOLLOW YOU TODAY...
...I'LL LOSE SIGHT OF YOU.
......

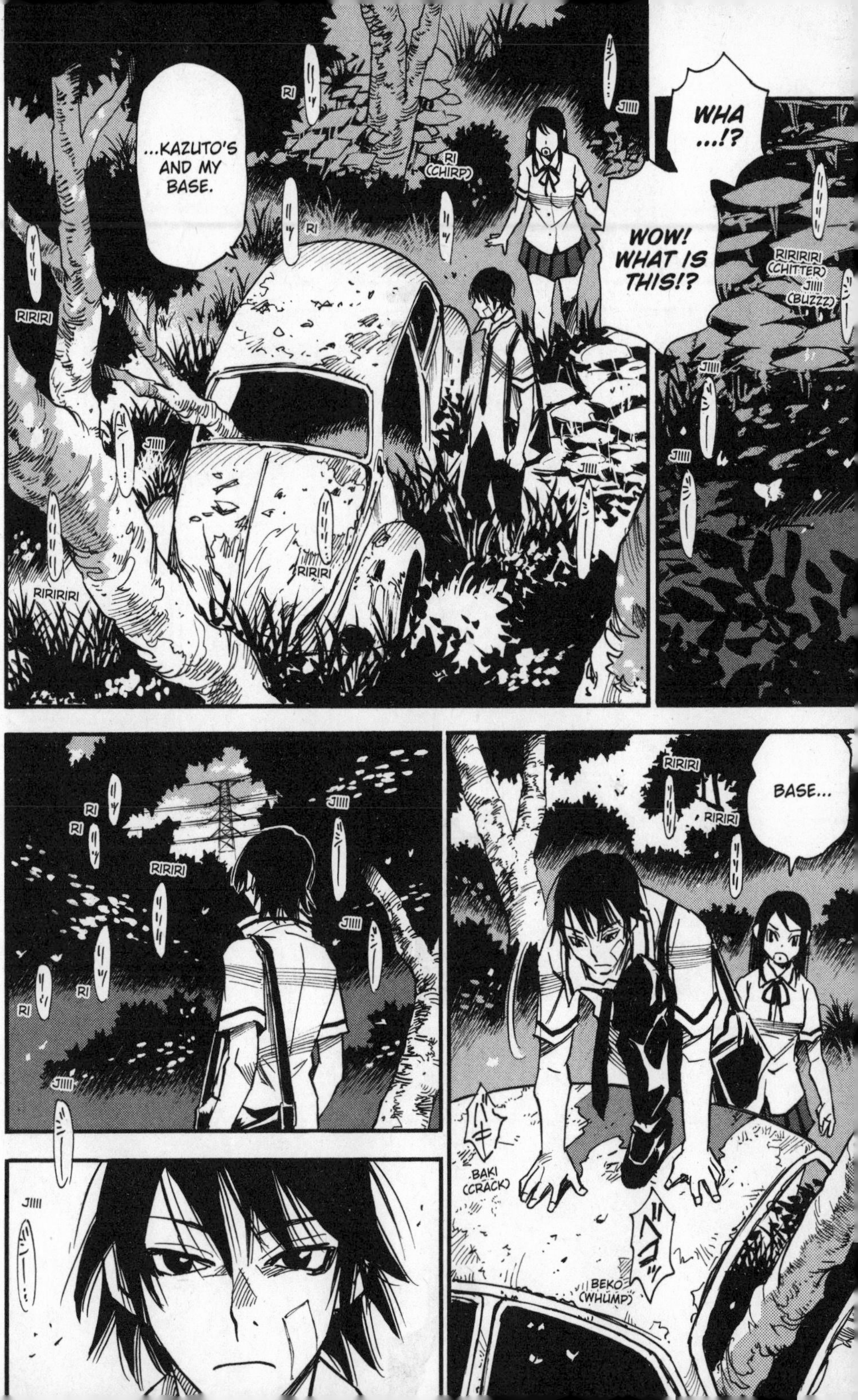
RIRIRIRI (CHITTER)
JIIII (BUZZZ)
JIIII
JIIII
WHA ...!?
WOW! WHAT IS THIS!?
JIIII
RI
...KAZUTO'S AND MY BASE.
RI (CHIRP)
RI
JIIII
RIRIRI
JIIII
RIRIRI
RIRIRIRI
RIRIRI
BASE...
RIRIRI
BAKI (CRACK)
BEKO (WHUMP)
JIIII
RI
RI
RIRIRI
JIIII
RI
RI
JIIII
JIIII

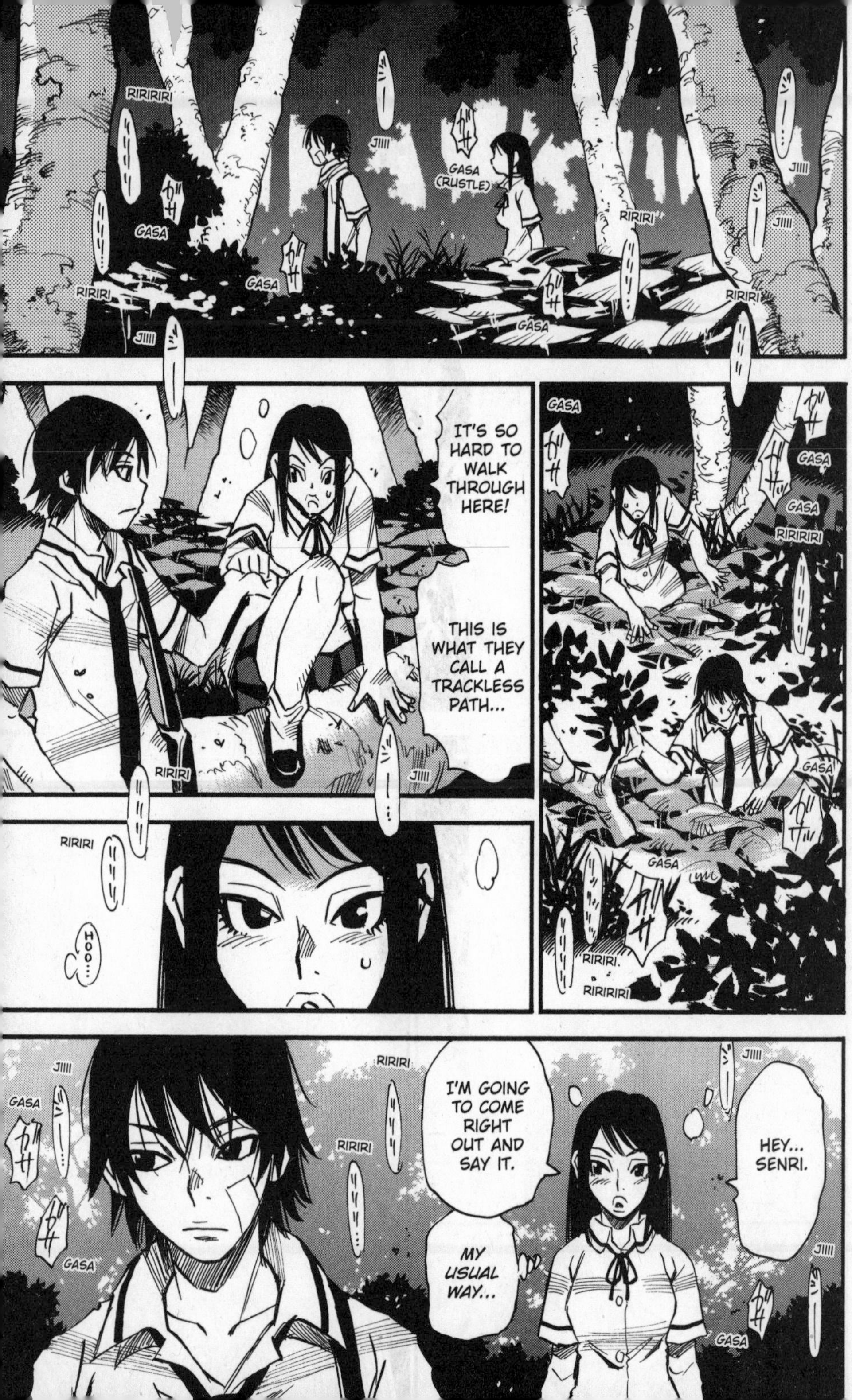
JIIII
RIRIRI
RIRIRI
GASA
GASA
(RUSTLE)
JIIII
RIRIRIRI
GASA
GASA
RIRIRI
JIIII
GASA
GASA
GASA
RIRIRIRI
GASA
GASA
RIRIRI.
RIRIRIRI
IT'S SO HARD TO WALK THROUGH HERE!
THIS IS WHAT THEY CALL A TRACKLESS PATH...
JIIII
RIRIRI
RIRIRI
HOO...
JIIII
HEY... SENRI.
RIRIRI
I'M GOING TO COME RIGHT OUT AND SAY IT.
MY USUAL WAY...
JIIII
GASA
RIRIRI
JIIII
GASA
GASA

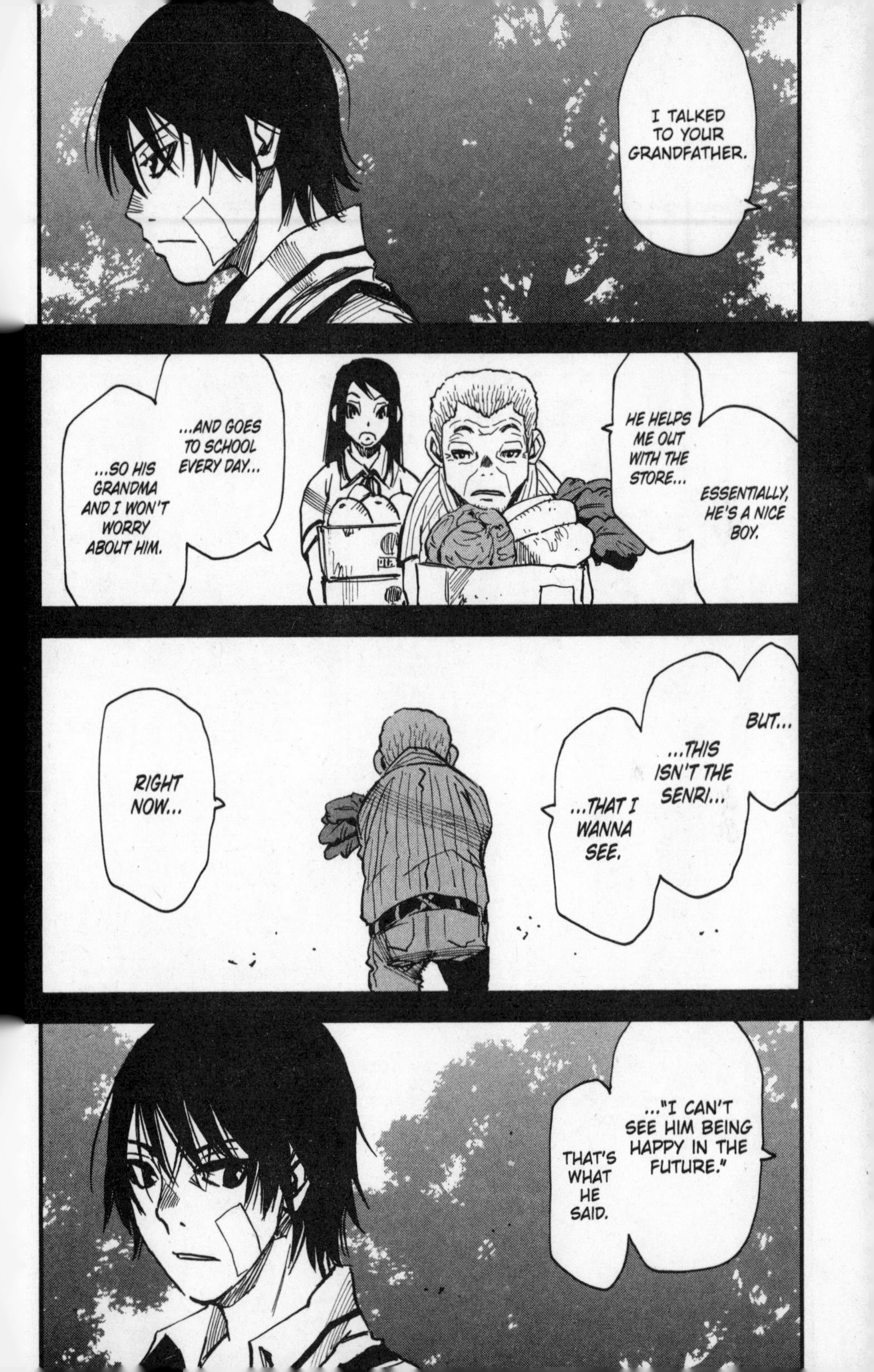
I TALKED TO YOUR GRANDFATHER.
ESSENTIALLY, HE'S A NICE BOY.
HE HELPS ME OUT WITH THE STORE...
...AND GOES TO SCHOOL EVERY DAY...
...SO HIS GRANDMA AND I WON'T WORRY ABOUT HIM.
BUT...
...THIS ISN'T THE SENRI...
...THAT I WANNA SEE.
RIGHT NOW...
..."I CAN'T SEE HIM BEING HAPPY IN THE FUTURE."
THAT'S WHAT HE SAID.

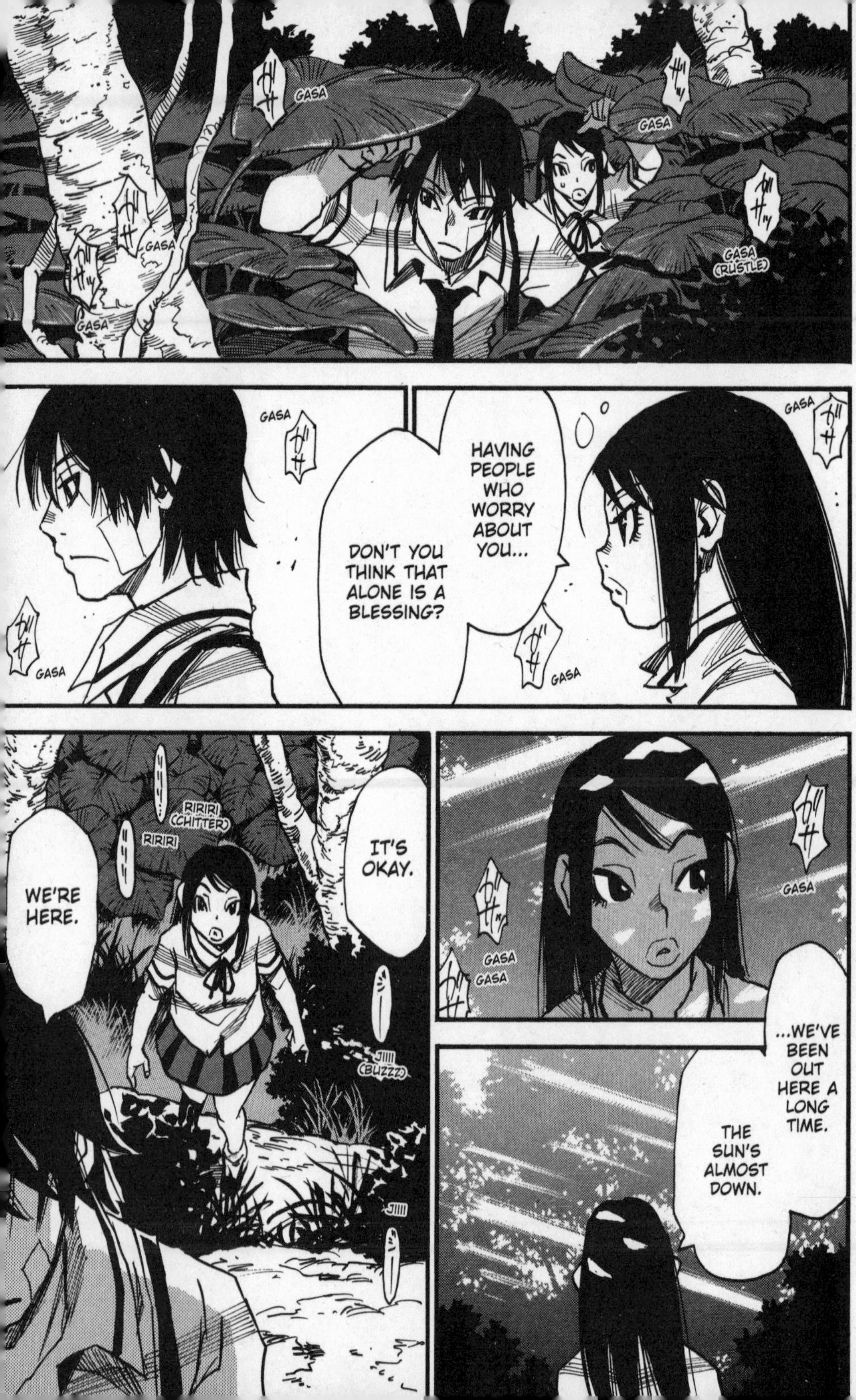
GASA (RUSTLE)
GASA
GASA
GASA
GASA
GASA
HAVING PEOPLE WHO WORRY ABOUT YOU...
DON'T YOU THINK THAT ALONE IS A BLESSING?
GASA
GASA
GASA
GASA
GASA GASA
...WE'VE BEEN OUT HERE A LONG TIME.
THE SUN'S ALMOST DOWN.
IT'S OKAY.
RIRIRI (CHITTER)
RIRIRI
WE'RE HERE.
JIIII (BUZZZ)
JIIII

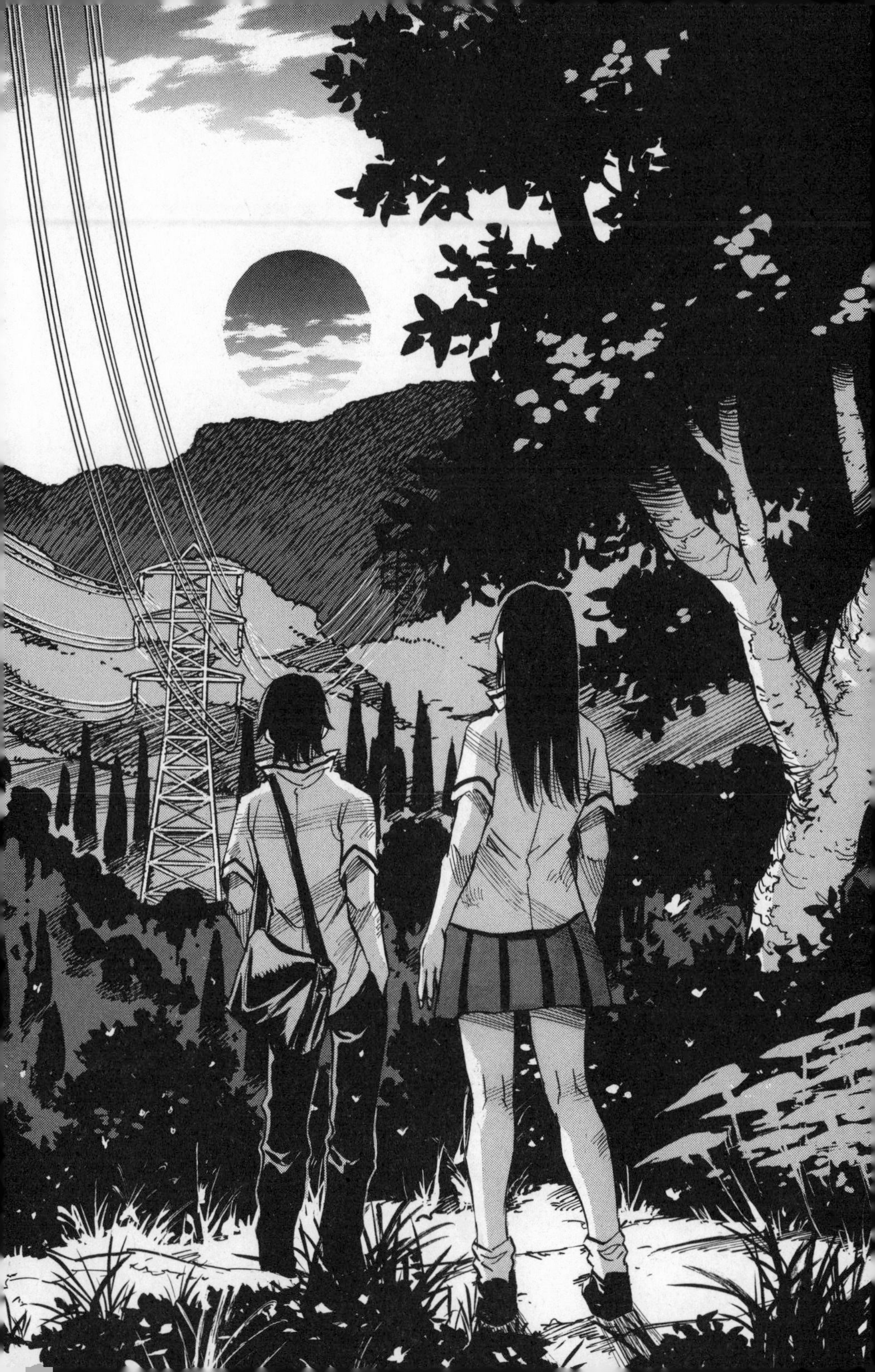

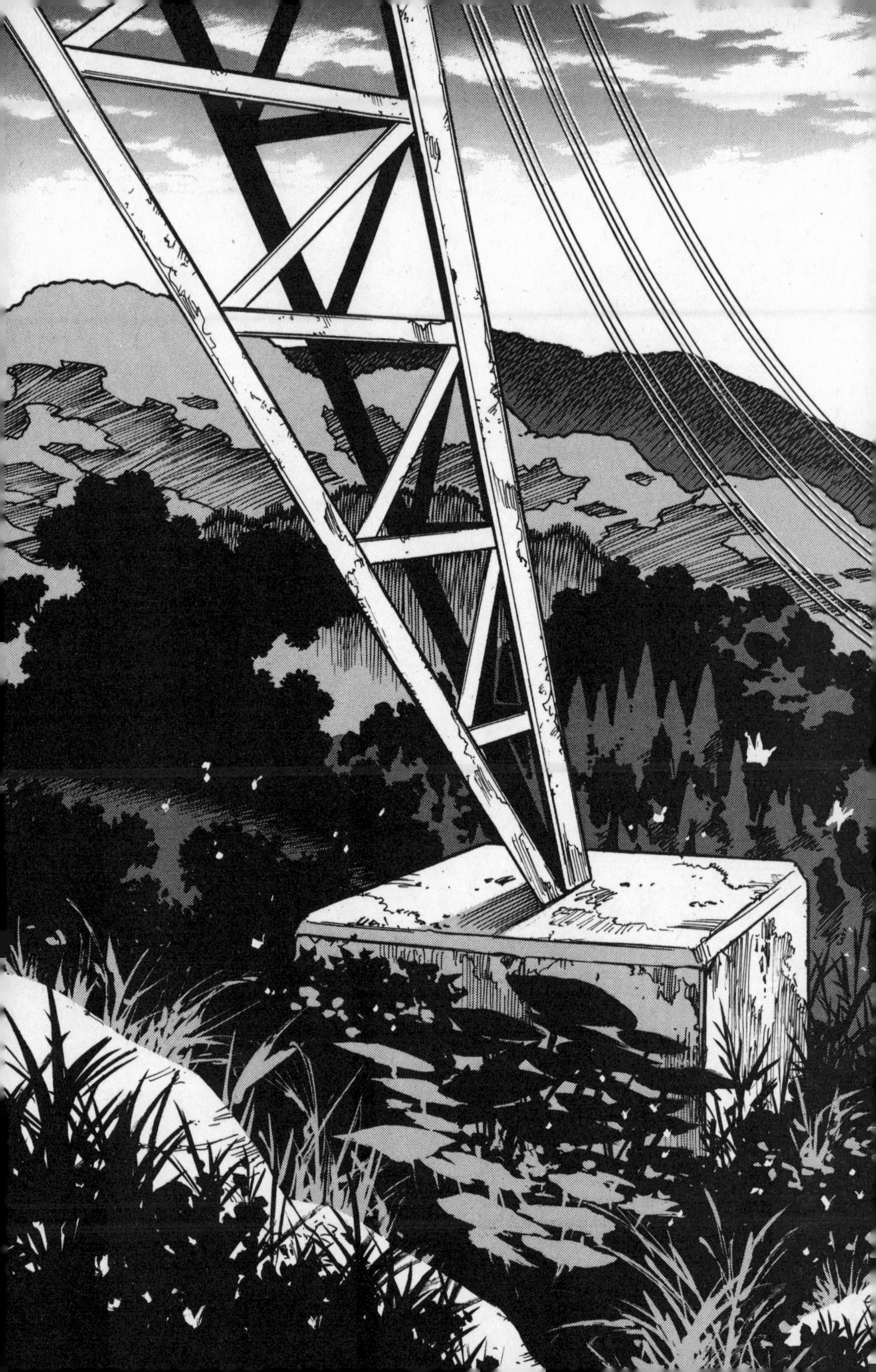

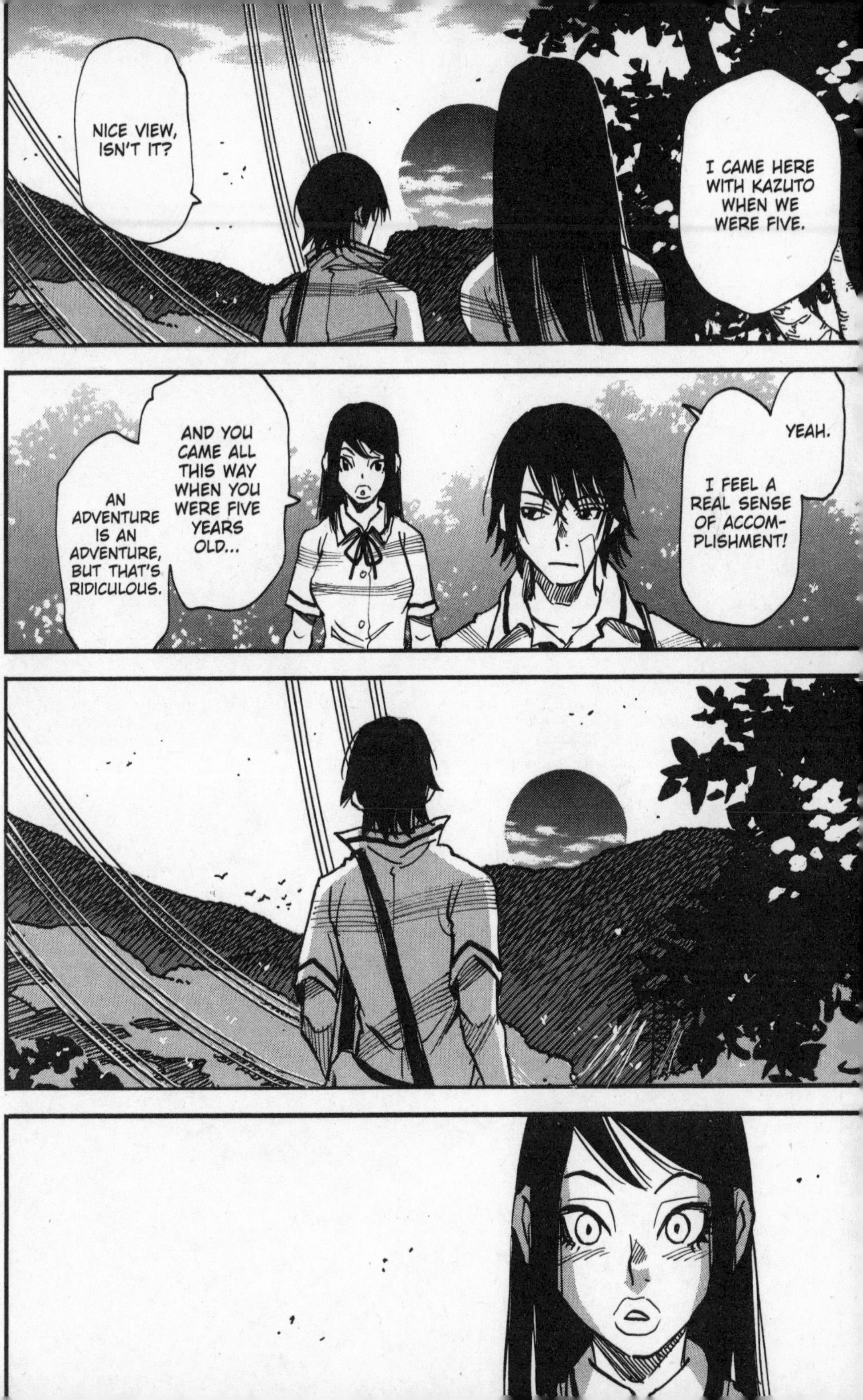
I CAME HERE WITH KAZUTO WHEN WE WERE FIVE.
NICE VIEW, ISN'T IT?
YEAH.
I FEEL A REAL SENSE OF ACCOMPLISHMENT!
AND YOU CAME ALL THIS WAY WHEN YOU WERE FIVE YEARS OLD...
AN ADVENTURE IS AN ADVENTURE, BUT THAT'S RIDICULOUS.

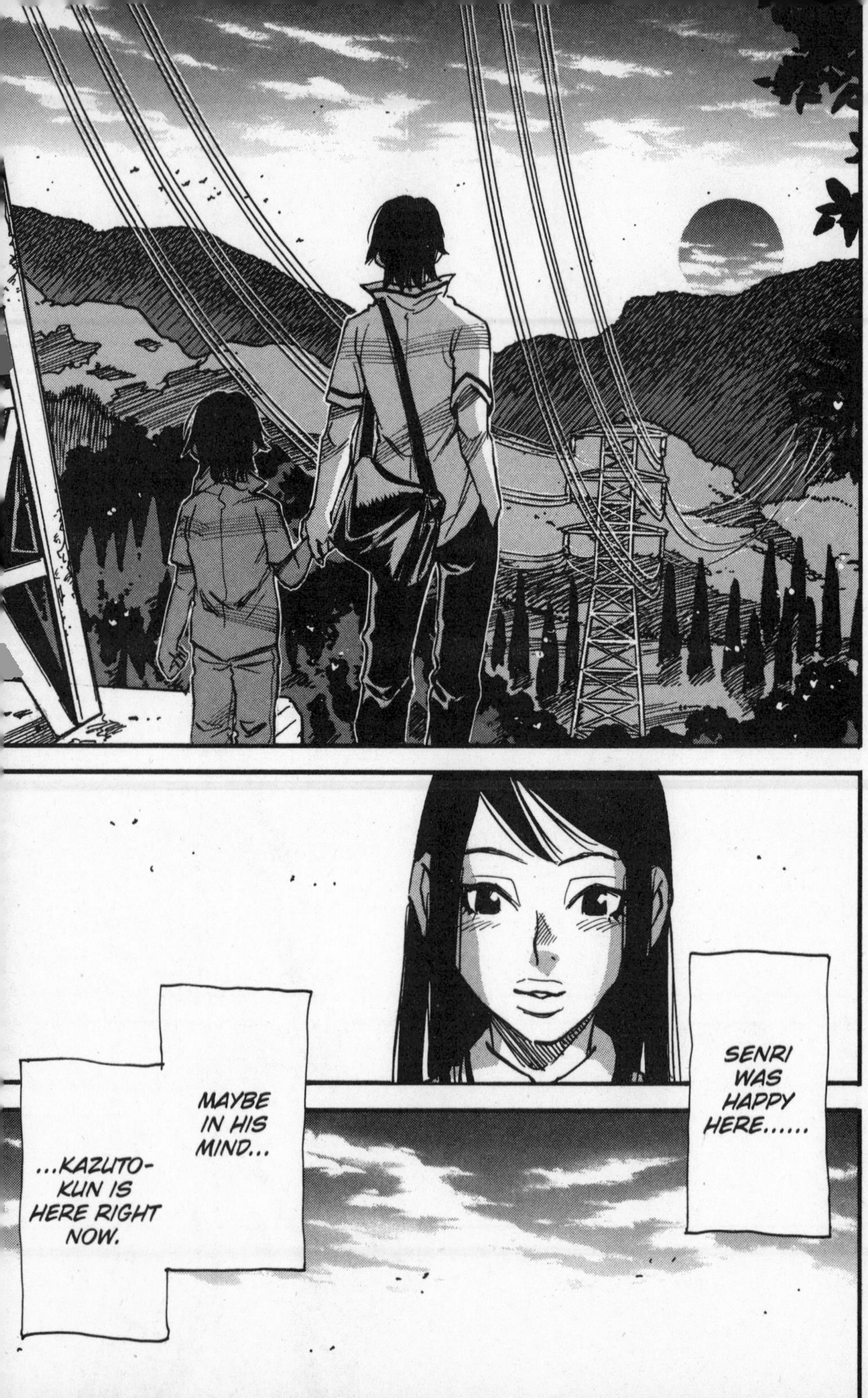
SENRI WAS HAPPY HERE......
MAYBE IN HIS MIND...
...KAZUTO-KUN IS HERE RIGHT NOW.

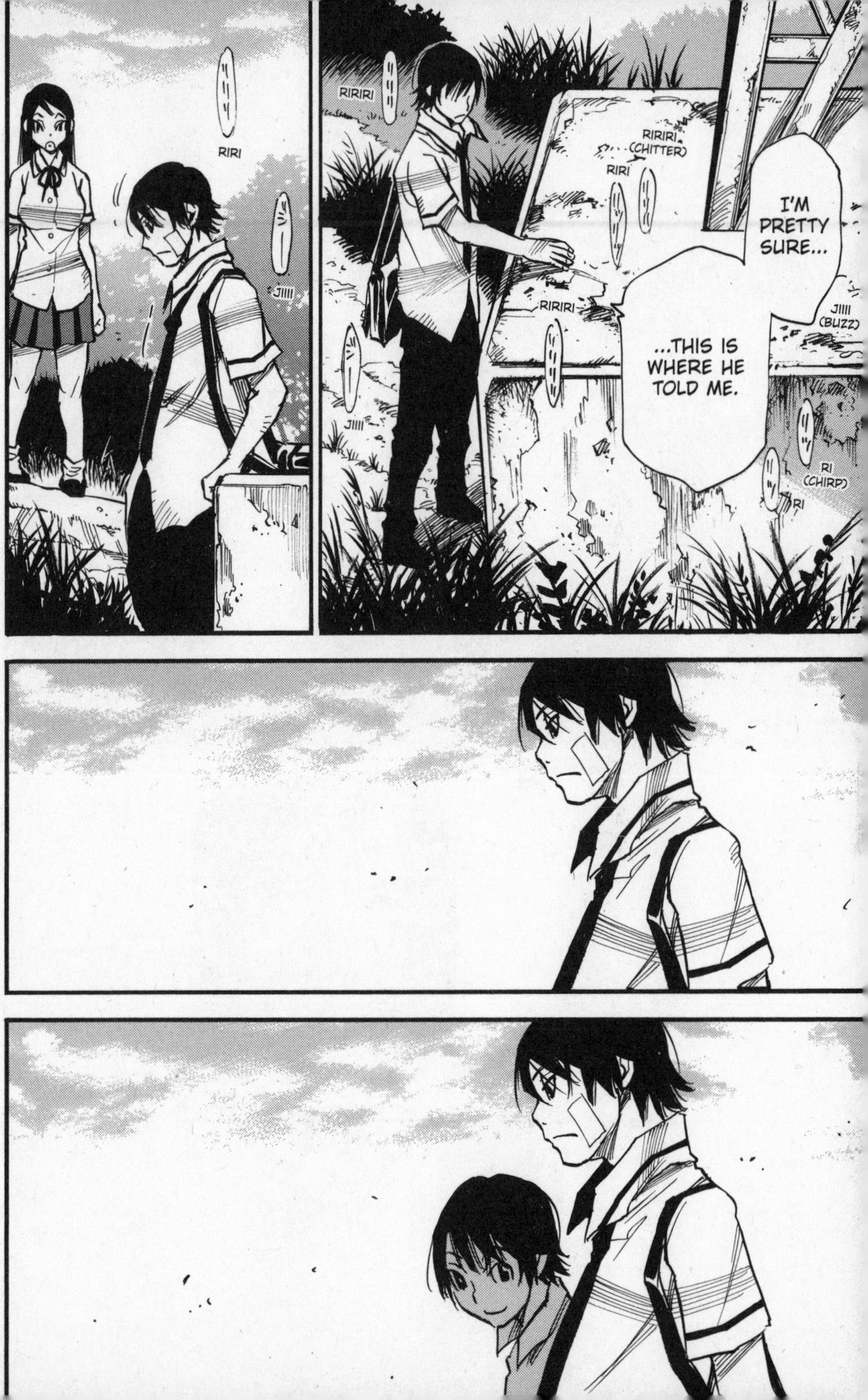
RIRIRI
I'M PRETTY SURE...
RIRIRI (CHITTER)
RIRI
JIIII (BUZZ)
...THIS IS WHERE HE TOLD ME.
RIRIRI
RI (CHIRP)
RI
JIIII
RIRI
JIIII

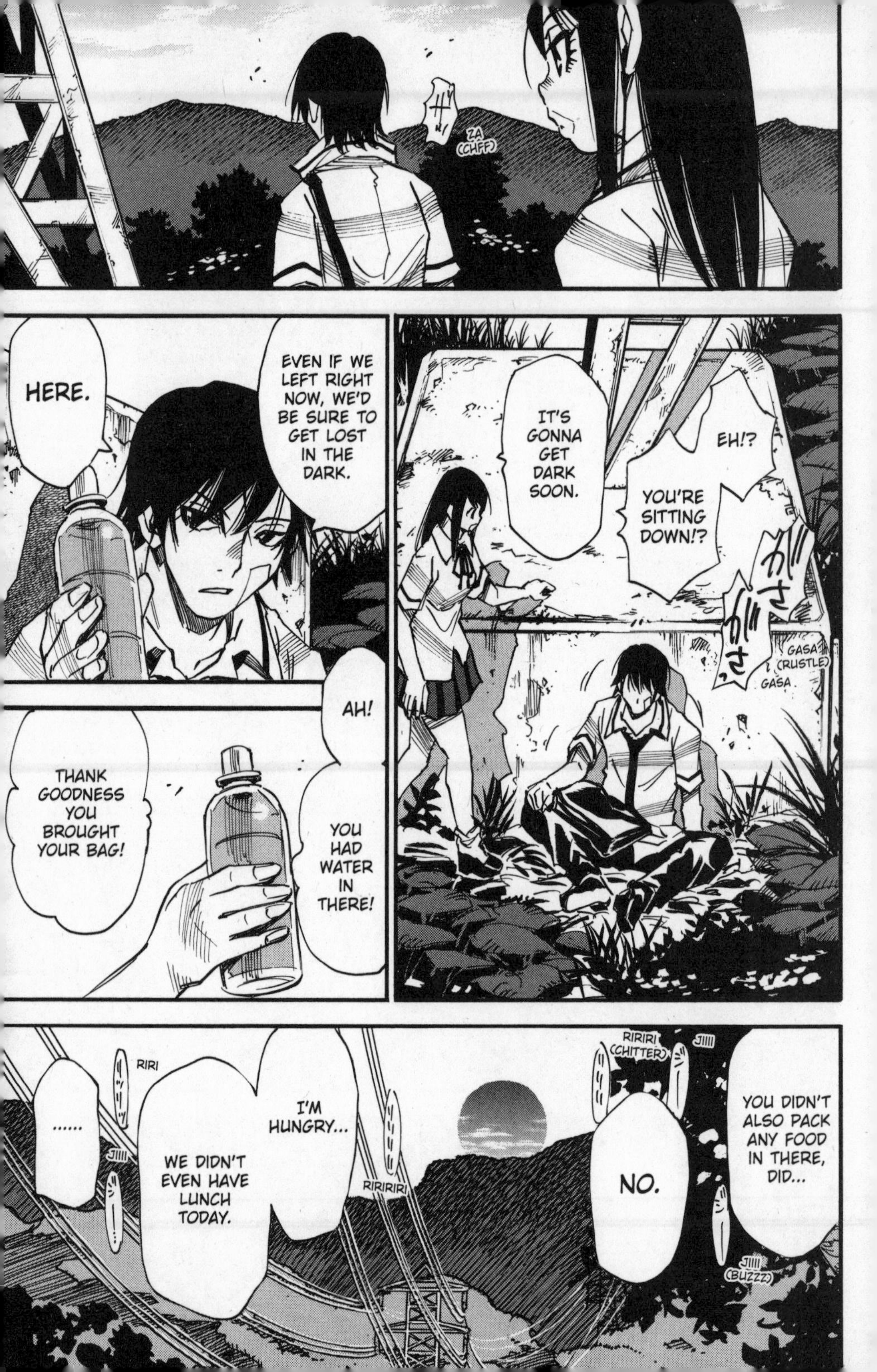
ZA (CHFF)
EH!?
YOU'RE SITTING DOWN!?
IT'S GONNA GET DARK SOON.
GASA (RUSTLE) GASA
EVEN IF WE LEFT RIGHT NOW, WE'D BE SURE TO GET LOST IN THE DARK.
HERE.
AH!
YOU HAD WATER IN THERE!
THANK GOODNESS YOU BROUGHT YOUR BAG!
YOU DIDN'T ALSO PACK ANY FOOD IN THERE, DID...
RIRIRI (CHITTER)
JIIII
NO.
JIIII (BUZZZ)
RIRIRIRI
I'M HUNGRY...
WE DIDN'T EVEN HAVE LUNCH TODAY.
RIRI
JIIII
......

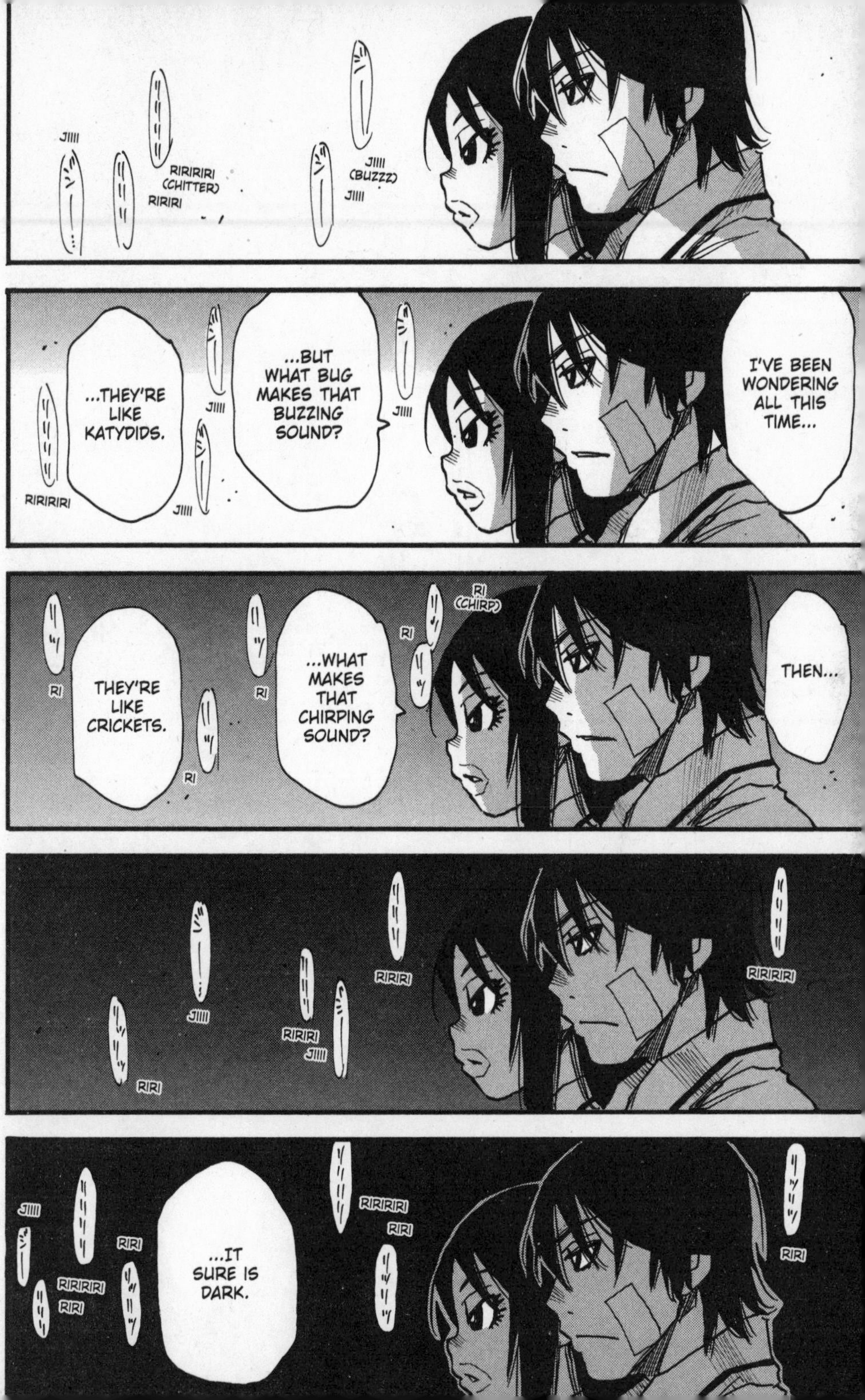
JIIII (BUZZZ)
JIIII
RIRIRIRI (CHITTER)
RIRIRI
JIIII
I'VE BEEN WONDERING ALL THIS TIME...
JIIII
...BUT WHAT BUG MAKES THAT BUZZING SOUND?
JIIII
JIIII
...THEY'RE LIKE KATYDIDS.
RIRIRIRI
THEN...
RI (CHIRP)
RI
...WHAT MAKES THAT CHIRPING SOUND?
RI
THEY'RE LIKE CRICKETS.
RI
RI
RIRIRIRI
RIRIRI
JIIII
RIRIRI
JIIII
RIRI
RIRI
RIRIRIRI
RIRI
...IT SURE IS DARK.
RIRI
RIRIRIRI
RIRI
JIIII

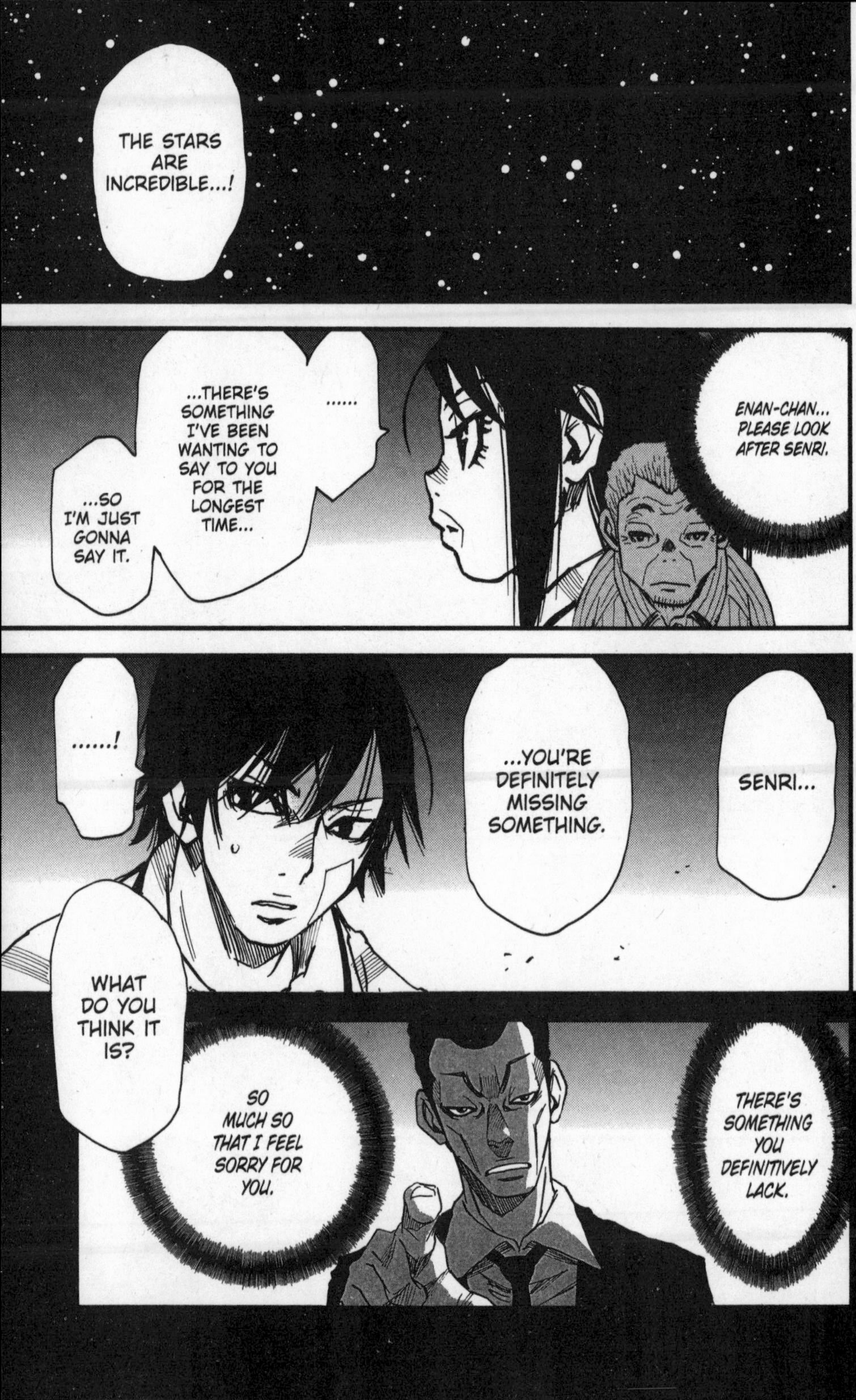
THE STARS ARE INCREDIBLE...!
ENAN-CHAN... PLEASE LOOK AFTER SENRI.
......
...THERE'S SOMETHING I'VE BEEN WANTING TO SAY TO YOU FOR THE LONGEST TIME...
...SO I'M JUST GONNA SAY IT.
SENRI...
...YOU'RE DEFINITELY MISSING SOMETHING.
......!
WHAT DO YOU THINK IT IS?
THERE'S SOMETHING YOU DEFINITIVELY LACK.
SO MUCH SO THAT I FEEL SORRY FOR YOU.

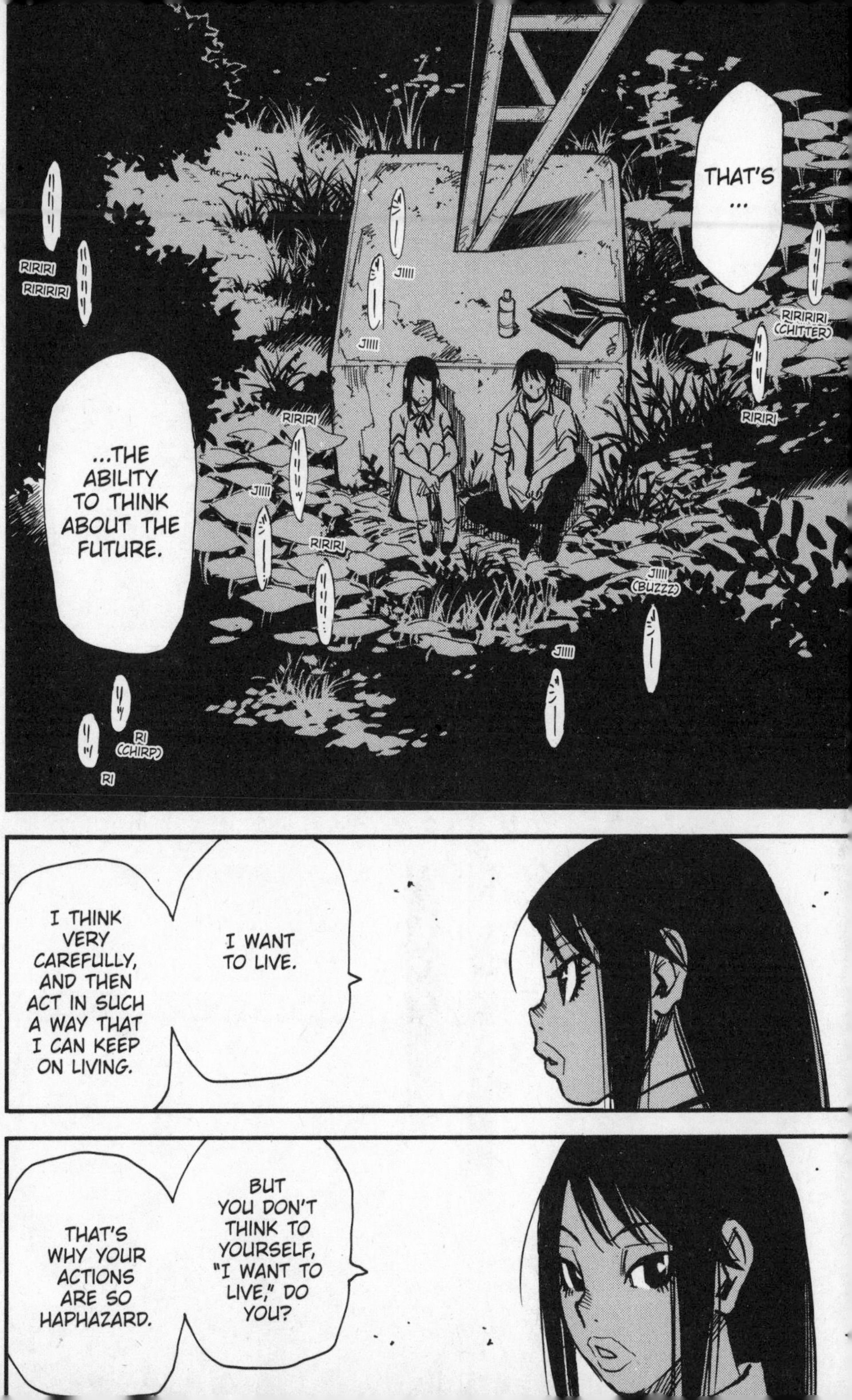
THAT'S ...
RIRIRIRI (CHITTER)
RIRIRI
JIIII
JIIII
RIRIRI
RIRIRIRI
JIIII (BUZZZ)
JIIII
RIRIRI
JIIII
RIRIRI
...THE ABILITY TO THINK ABOUT THE FUTURE.
RI (CHIRP)
RI
I WANT TO LIVE.
I THINK VERY CAREFULLY, AND THEN ACT IN SUCH A WAY THAT I CAN KEEP ON LIVING.
BUT YOU DON'T THINK TO YOURSELF, "I WANT TO LIVE," DO YOU?
THAT'S WHY YOUR ACTIONS ARE SO HAPHAZARD.

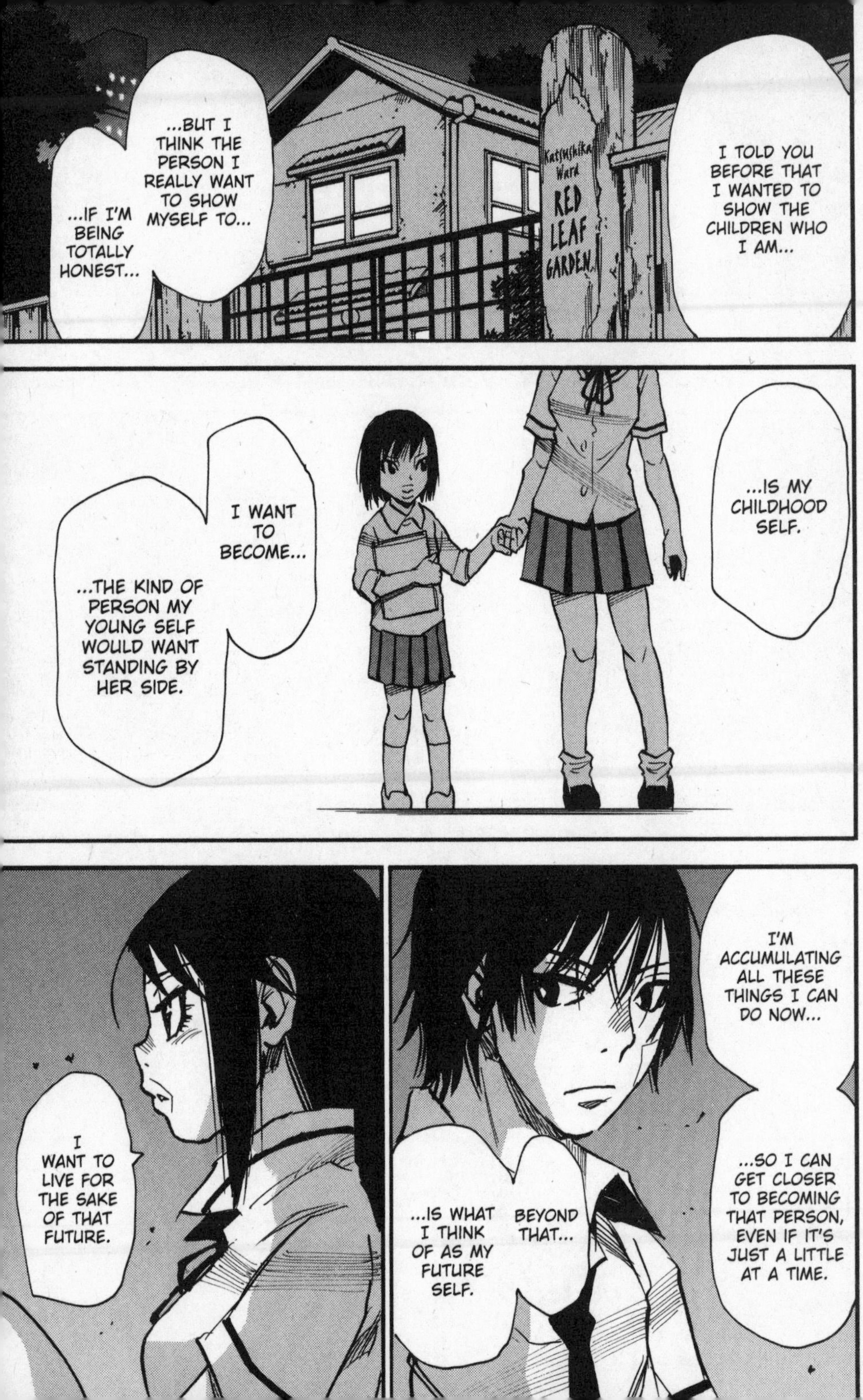
I TOLD YOU BEFORE THAT I WANTED TO SHOW THE CHILDREN WHO I AM...
Katsushika Ward RED LEAF GARDEN
...BUT I THINK THE PERSON I REALLY WANT TO SHOW MYSELF TO...
...IF I'M BEING TOTALLY HONEST...
...IS MY CHILDHOOD SELF.
I WANT TO BECOME...
...THE KIND OF PERSON MY YOUNG SELF WOULD WANT STANDING BY HER SIDE.
I'M ACCUMULATING ALL THESE THINGS I CAN DO NOW...
...SO I CAN GET CLOSER TO BECOMING THAT PERSON, EVEN IF IT'S JUST A LITTLE AT A TIME.
BEYOND THAT...
...IS WHAT I THINK OF AS MY FUTURE SELF.
I WANT TO LIVE FOR THE SAKE OF THAT FUTURE.

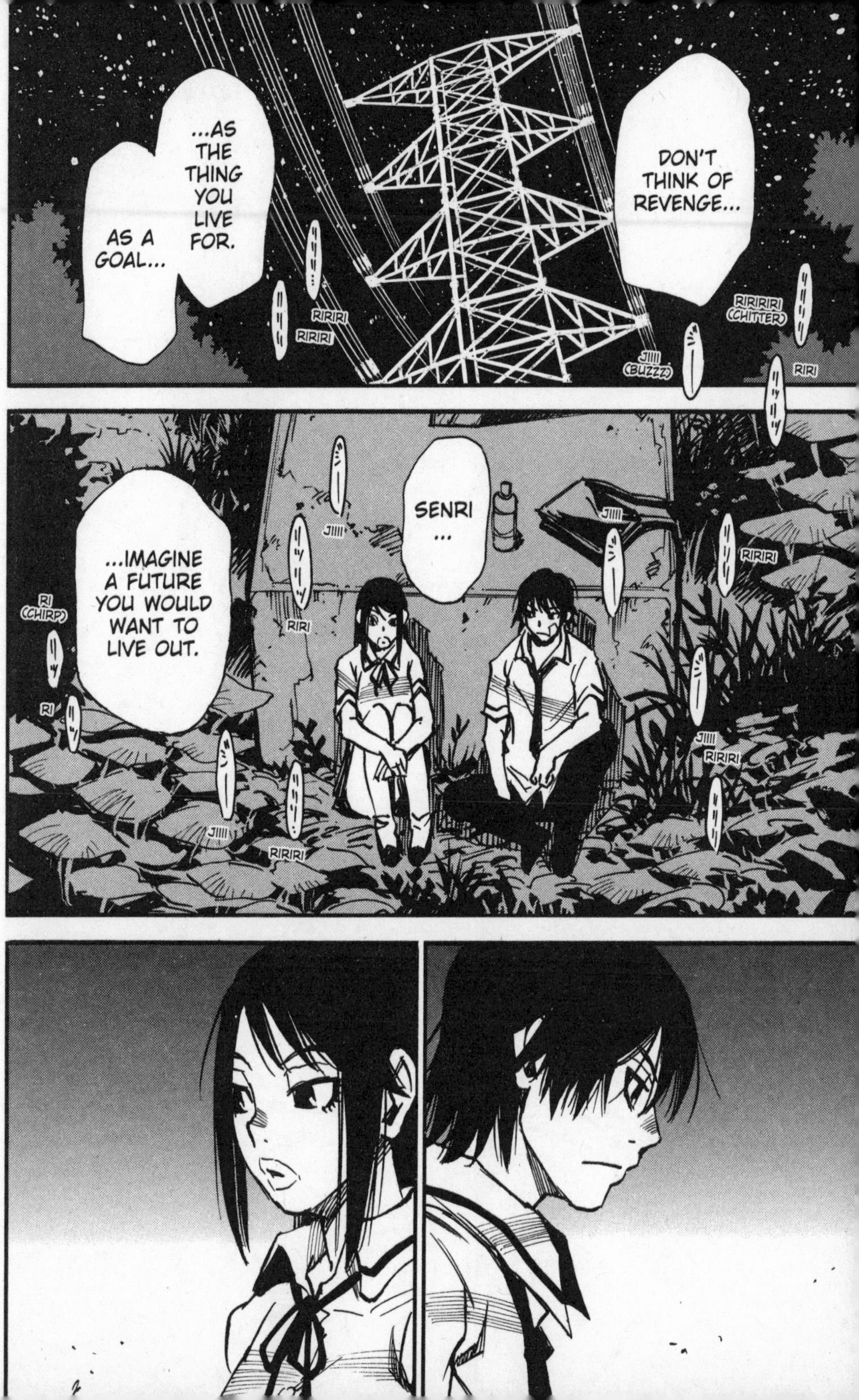
RIRIRI (CHITTER)
RIRI
DON'T THINK OF REVENGE...
JIIII (BUZZZ)
...AS THE THING YOU LIVE FOR.
AS A GOAL...
RIRIRI
RIRIRI
RIRIRI
JIIII
SENRI ...
JIIII
RIRI
...IMAGINE A FUTURE YOU WOULD WANT TO LIVE OUT.
RI (CHIRP)
RI
JIIII
RIRIRI
RIRIRI
JIIII

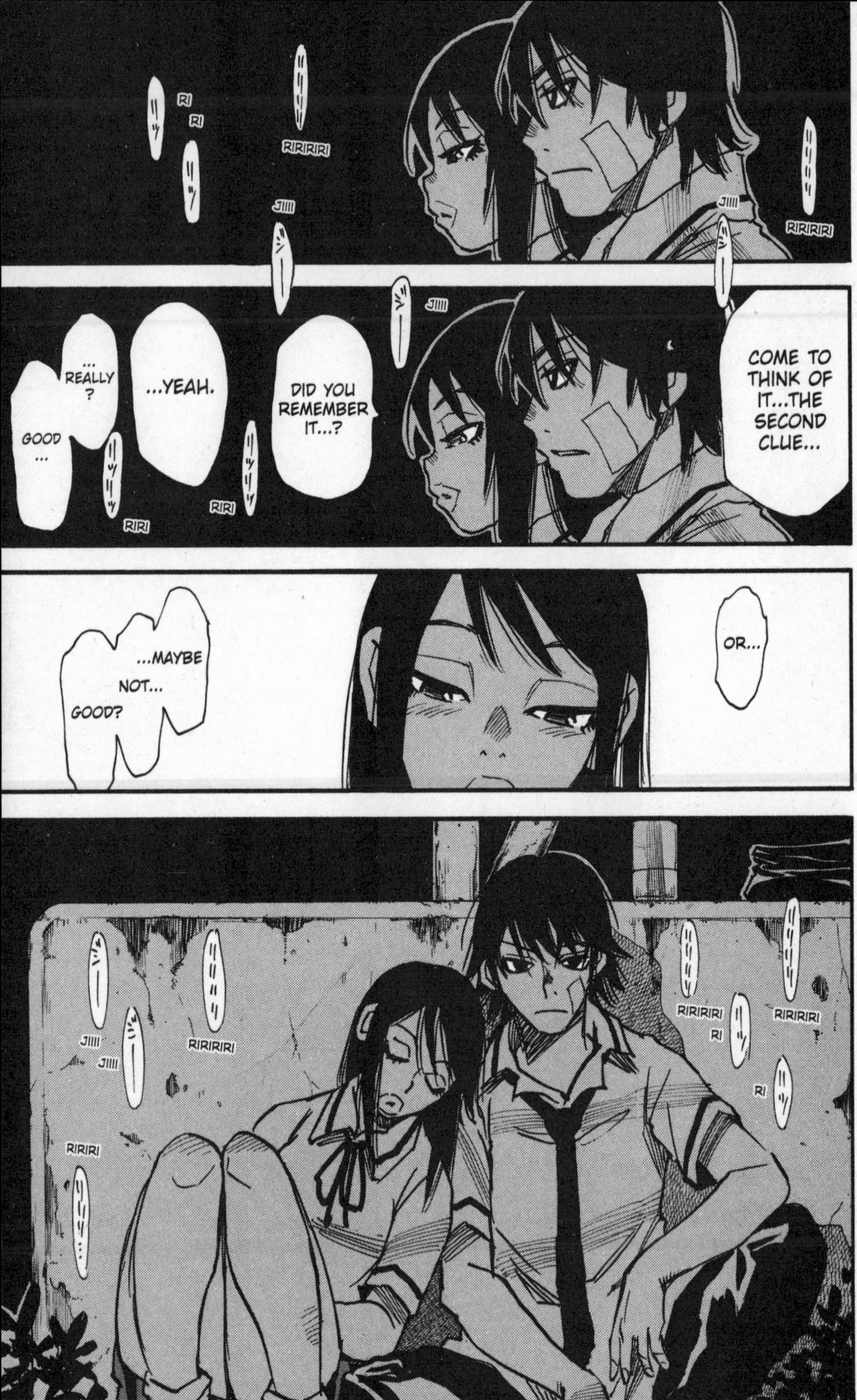
RIRIRIRI
JIIII
RIRIRIRI
JIIII
RI
RI
JIIII
COME TO THINK OF IT...THE SECOND CLUE...
DID YOU REMEMBER IT...?
RIRI
...YEAH.
...REALLY?
GOOD...
RIRI
OR...
...MAYBE NOT... GOOD?
RIRIRIRI
RIRIRIRI
RI
RI
RIRIRIRI
JIIII
JIIII
RIRIRI

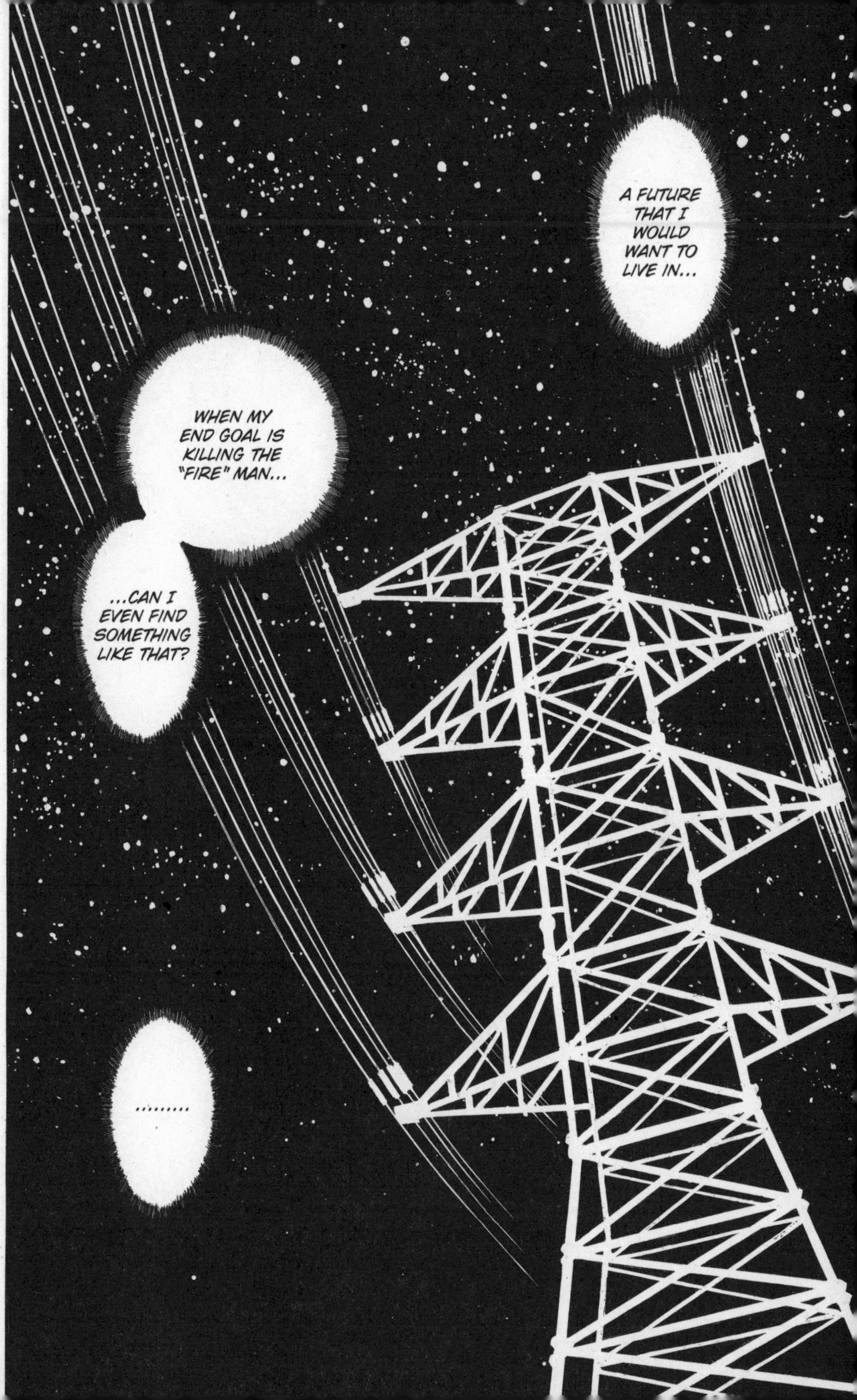
A FUTURE THAT I WOULD WANT TO LIVE IN...
WHEN MY END GOAL IS KILLING THE "FIRE" MAN...
...CAN I EVEN FIND SOMETHING LIKE THAT?
....

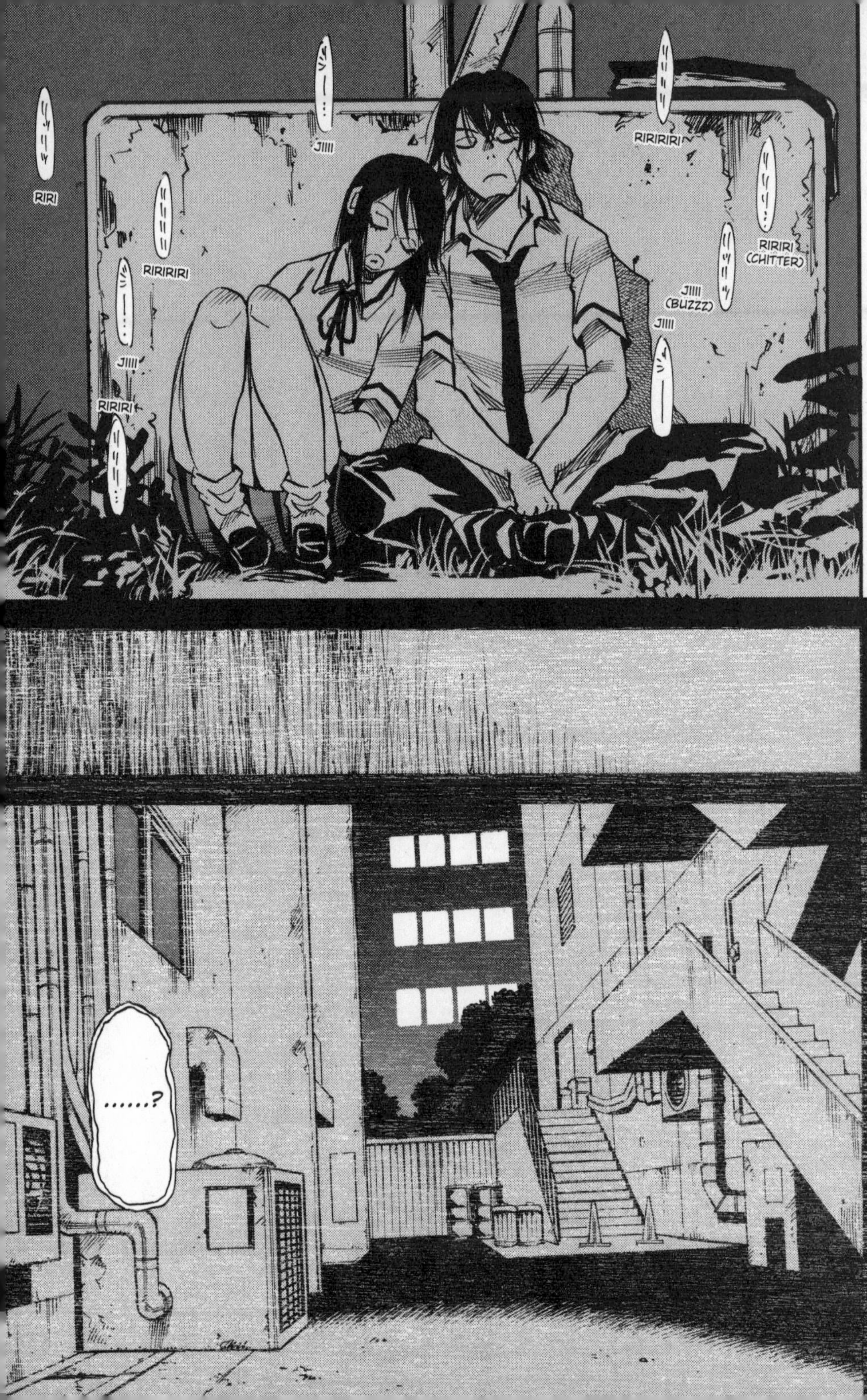

RIRIRIRI
RIRIRI (CHITTER)
JIIII (BUZZZ)
JIIII
JIIII
RIRI
RIRIRIRI
JIIII
RIRIRI
......?

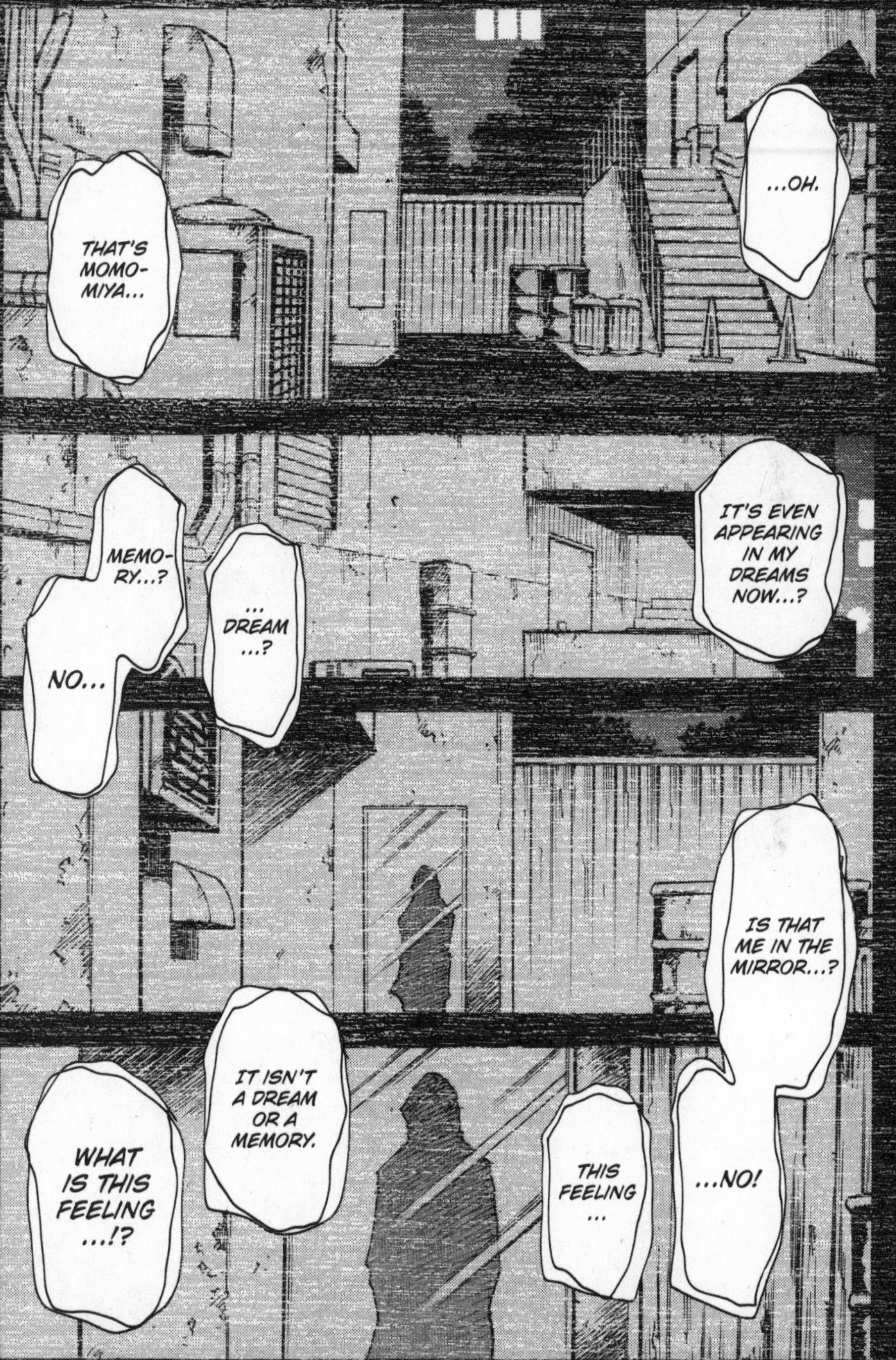
...OH.
THAT'S MOMO-MIYA...
IT'S EVEN APPEARING IN MY DREAMS NOW...?
... DREAM ...?
MEMO-RY...?
NO...
IS THAT ME IN THE MIRROR...?
...NO!
THIS FEELING ...
IT ISN'T A DREAM OR A MEMORY.
WHAT IS THIS FEELING ...!?

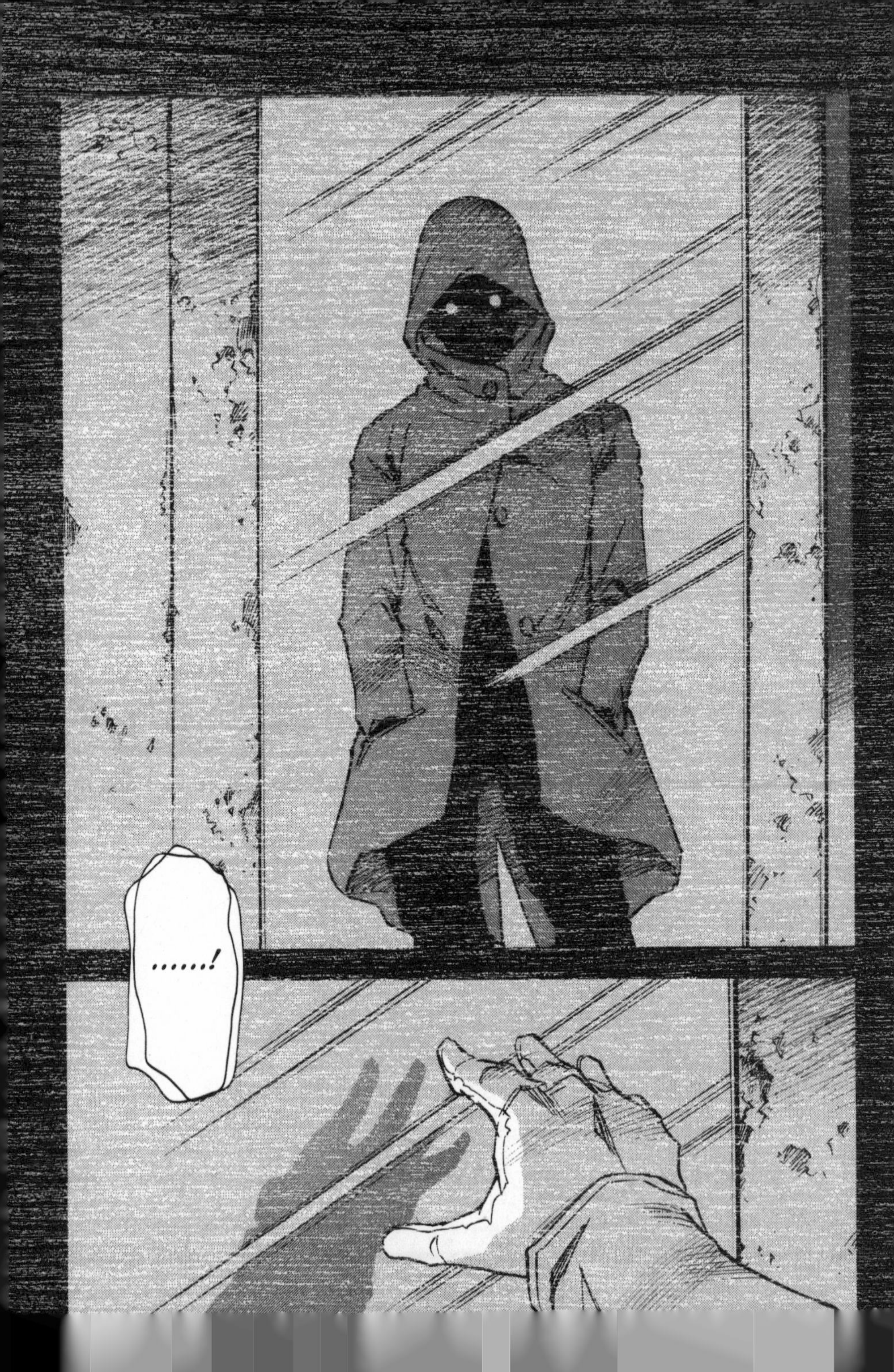
......!

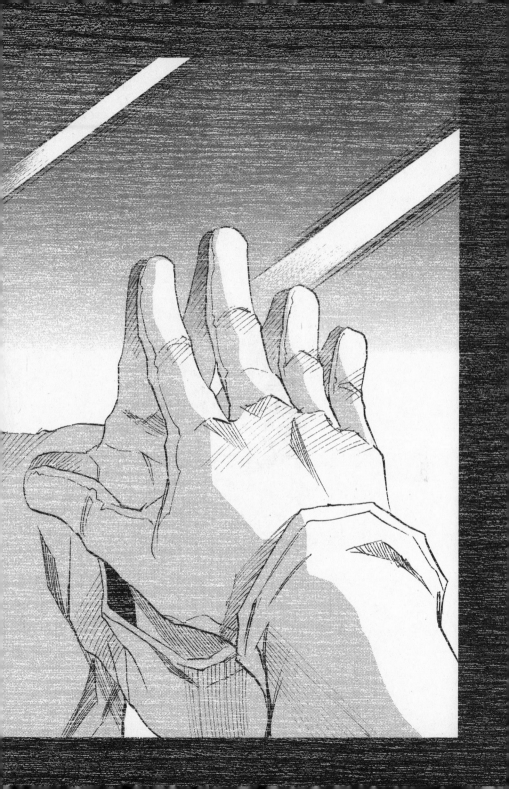

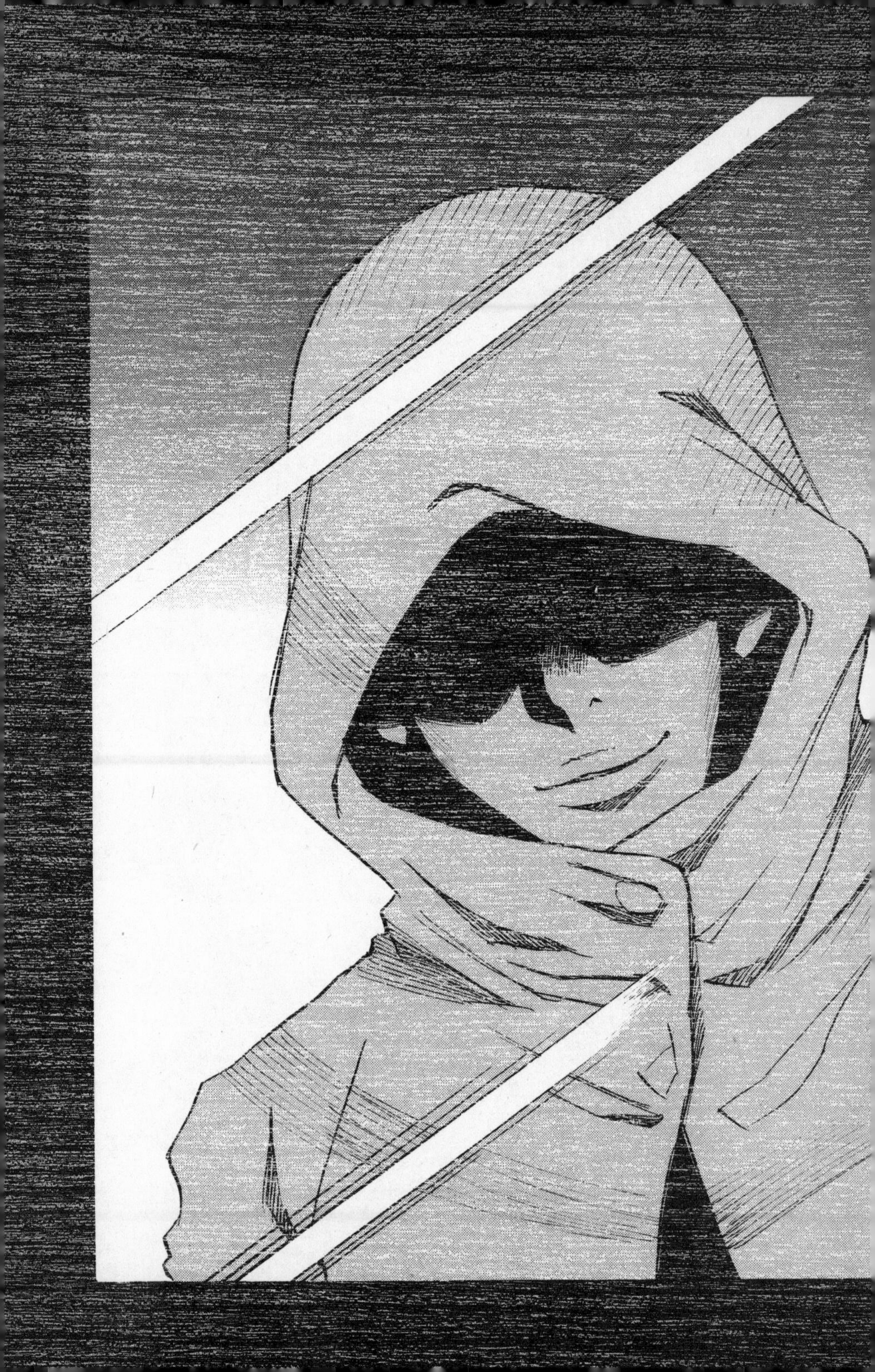

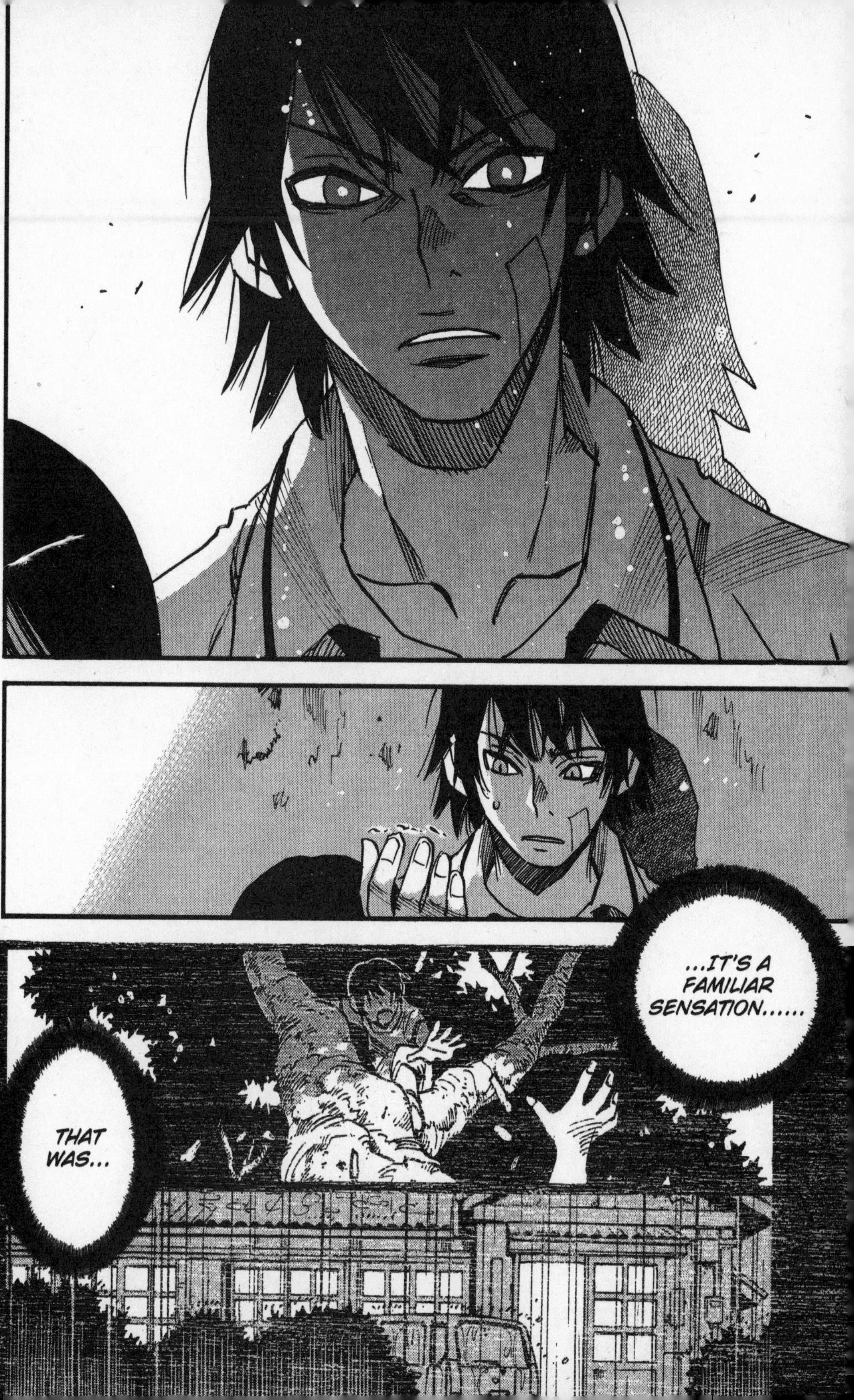
...IT'S A FAMILIAR SENSATION......
THAT WAS...

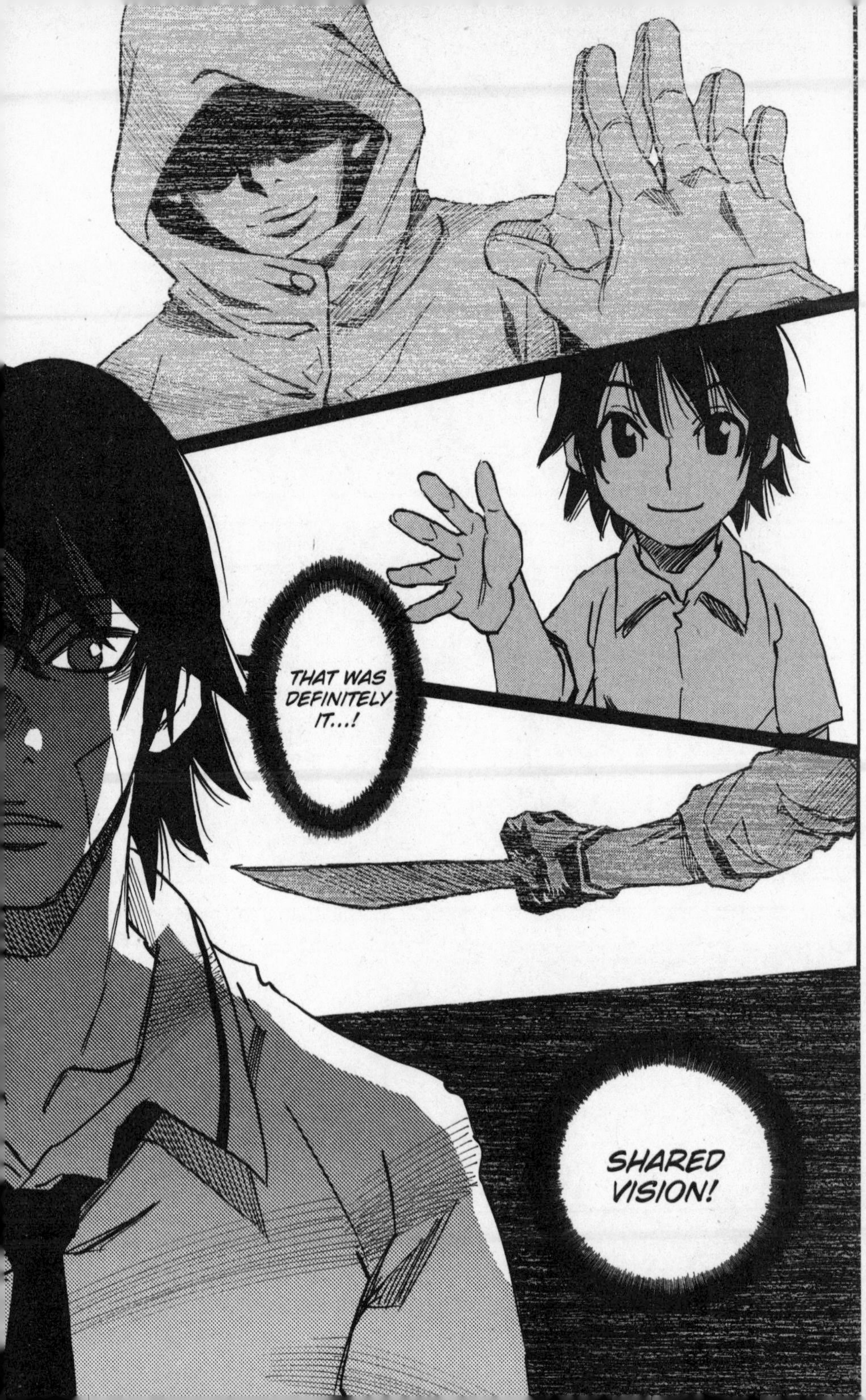
THAT WAS DEFINITELY IT...!
SHARED VISION!

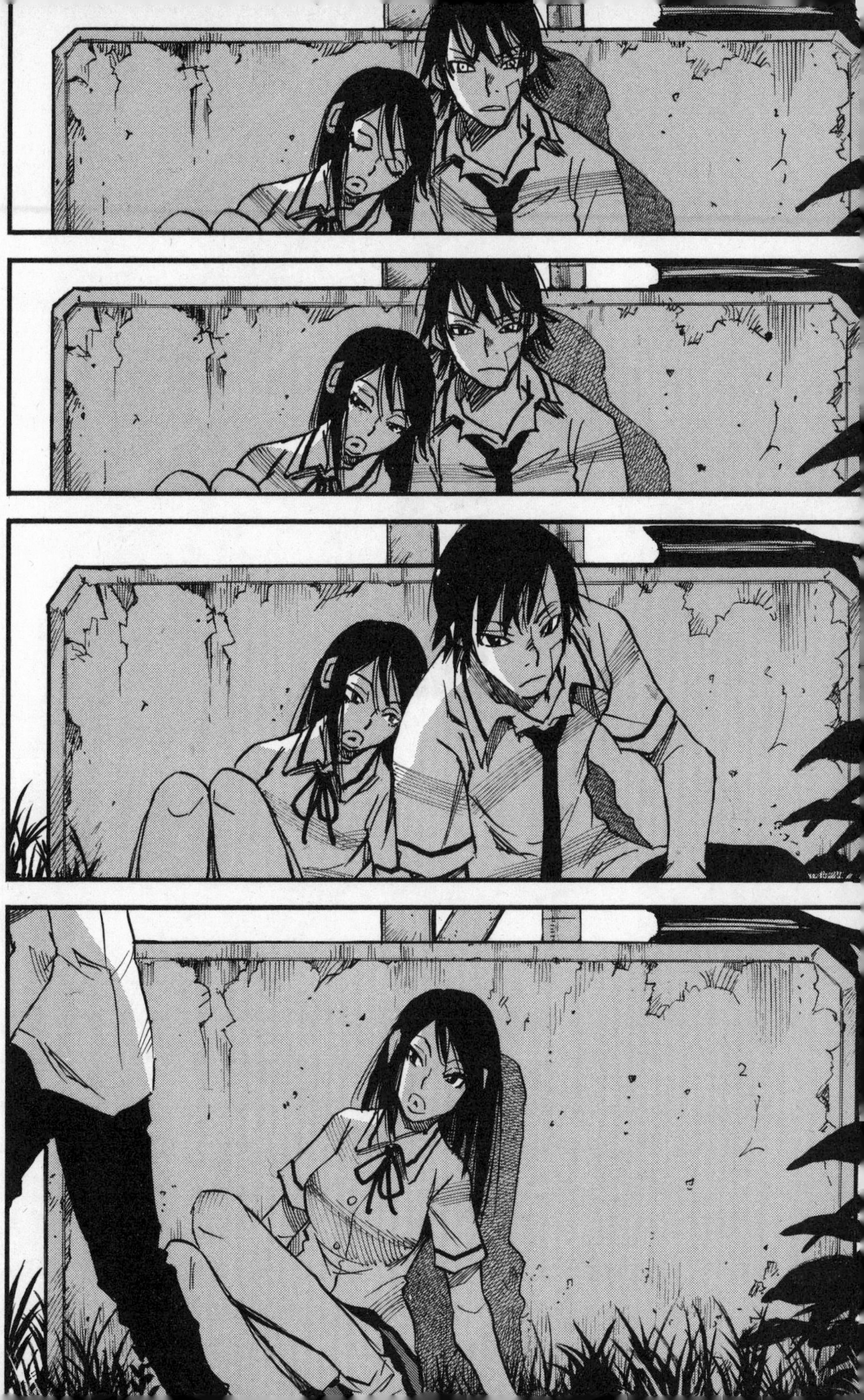

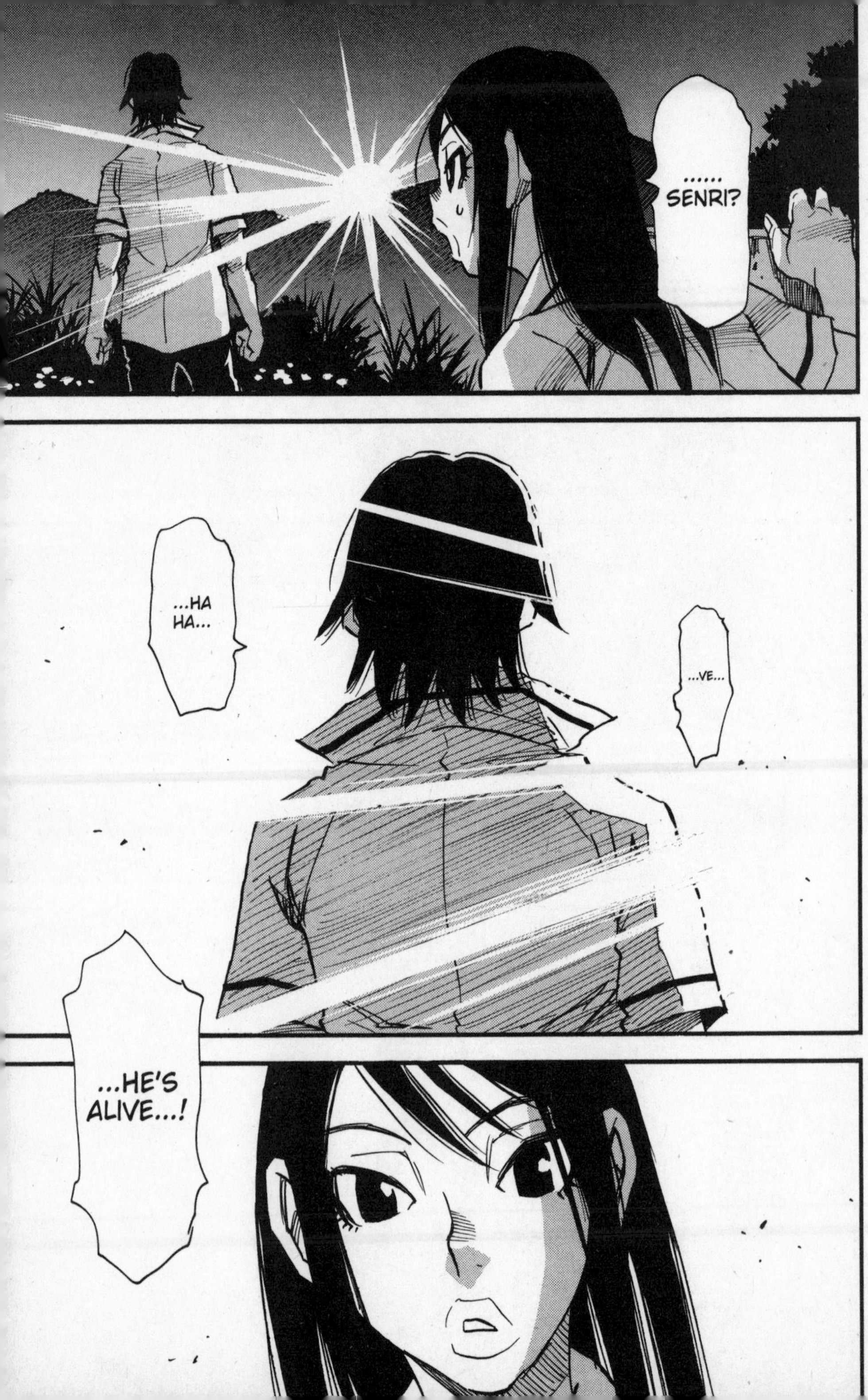
......
SENRI?
...VE...
...HA HA...
...HE'S ALIVE...!

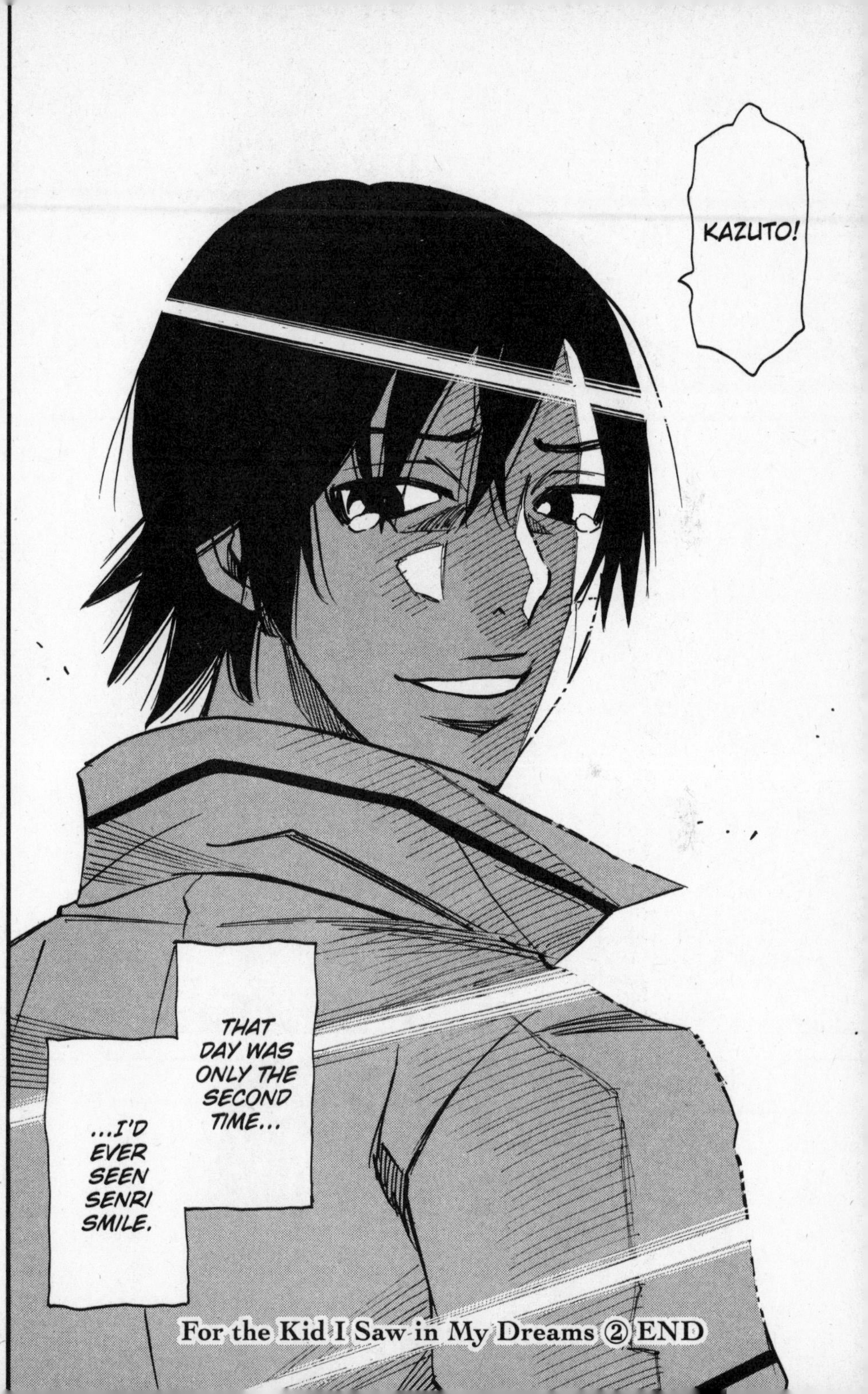
KAZUTO!
THAT DAY WAS ONLY THE SECOND TIME...
...I'D EVER SEEN SENRI SMILE.
For the Kid I Saw in My Dreams ② END

STAFF

Kei Sanbe

Yoichiro Tomita
Manami 18 Sai
Kouji Kikuta

Hidehisa Takagi

Keishi Kanesada

RESEARCH/PHOTOGRAPHY
ASSISTANCE
Houwa Toda

BOOK DESIGN
Yukio Hoshino
VOLARE inc.

EDITOR
Tsunenori Matsumiya

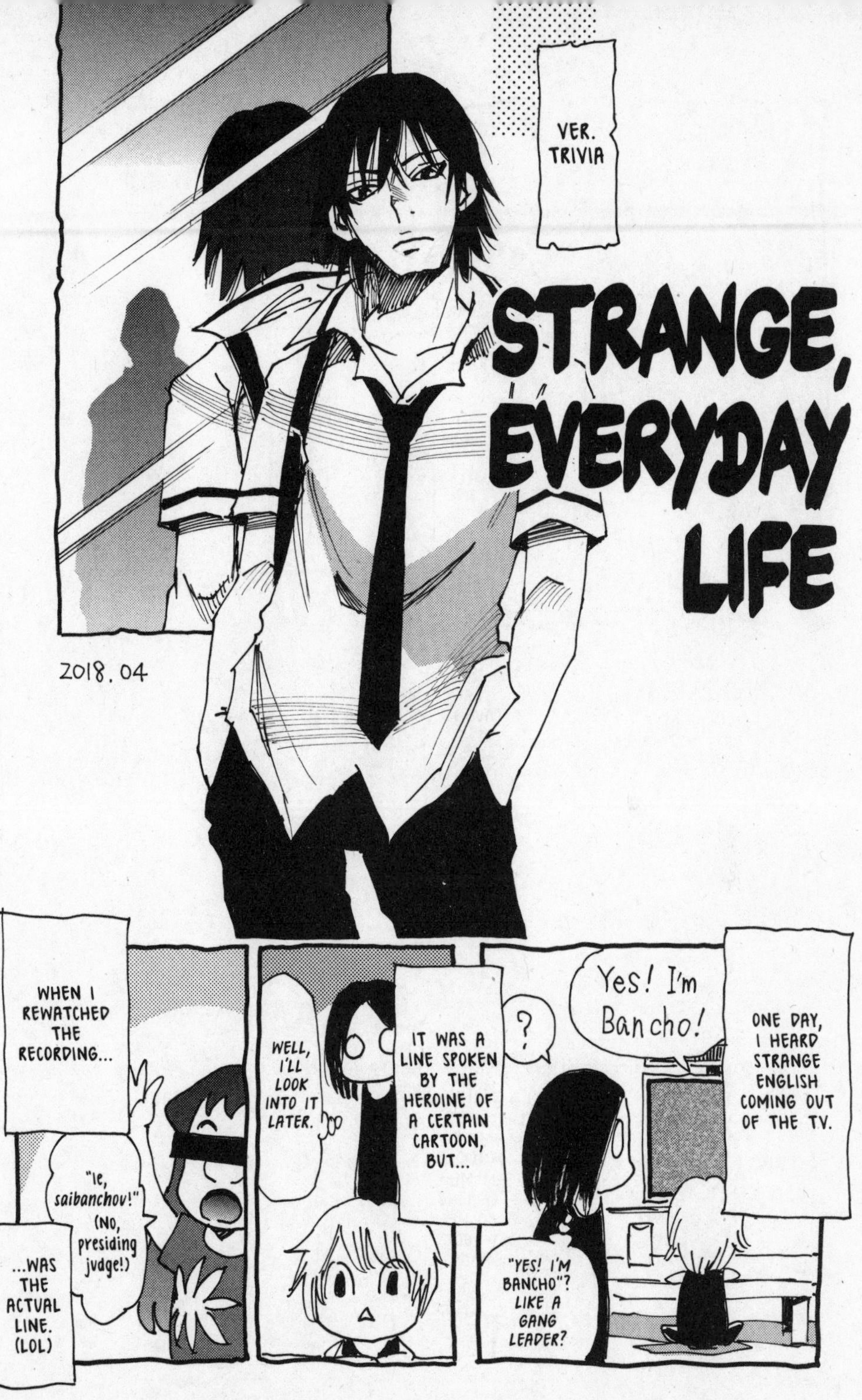
VER. TRIVIA
STRANGE, EVERYDAY LIFE
2018. 04
ONE DAY, I HEARD STRANGE ENGLISH COMING OUT OF THE TV.
Yes! I'm Bancho!
?
"YES! I'M BANCHO"? LIKE A GANG LEADER?
IT WAS A LINE SPOKEN BY THE HEROINE OF A CERTAIN CARTOON, BUT...
WELL, I'LL LOOK INTO IT LATER.
WHEN I REWATCHED THE RECORDING...
"Ie, saibanchou!" (No, presiding judge!)
...WAS THE ACTUAL LINE. (LOL)

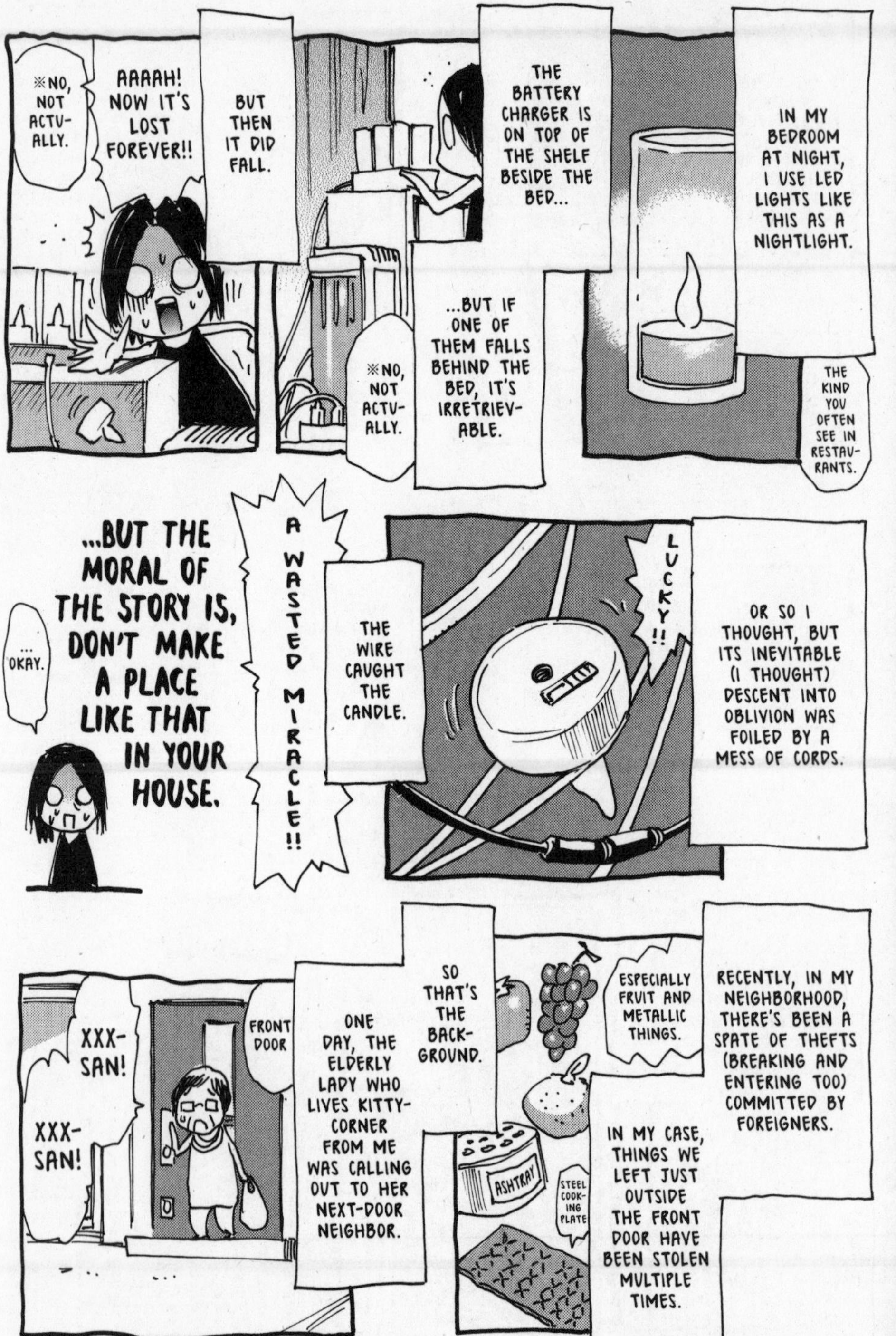
IN MY BEDROOM AT NIGHT, I USE LED LIGHTS LIKE THIS AS A NIGHTLIGHT.
THE KIND YOU OFTEN SEE IN RESTAURANTS.
THE BATTERY CHARGER IS ON TOP OF THE SHELF BESIDE THE BED...
...BUT IF ONE OF THEM FALLS BEHIND THE BED, IT'S IRRETRIEVABLE.
※NO, NOT ACTUALLY.
BUT THEN IT DID FALL.
AAAAH! NOW IT'S LOST FOREVER!!
※NO, NOT ACTUALLY.
OR SO I THOUGHT, BUT ITS INEVITABLE (I THOUGHT) DESCENT INTO OBLIVION WAS FOILED BY A MESS OF CORDS.
LUCKY!!
THE WIRE CAUGHT THE CANDLE.
A WASTED MIRACLE!!
...BUT THE MORAL OF THE STORY IS, DON'T MAKE A PLACE LIKE THAT IN YOUR HOUSE.
...OKAY.
RECENTLY, IN MY NEIGHBORHOOD, THERE'S BEEN A SPATE OF THEFTS (BREAKING AND ENTERING TOO) COMMITTED BY FOREIGNERS.
ESPECIALLY FRUIT AND METALLIC THINGS.
IN MY CASE, THINGS WE LEFT JUST OUTSIDE THE FRONT DOOR HAVE BEEN STOLEN MULTIPLE TIMES.
ASHTRAY
STEEL COOKING PLATE
SO THAT'S THE BACKGROUND.
ONE DAY, THE ELDERLY LADY WHO LIVES KITTY-CORNER FROM ME WAS CALLING OUT TO HER NEXT-DOOR NEIGHBOR.
FRONT DOOR
XXX-SAN!
XXX-SAN!

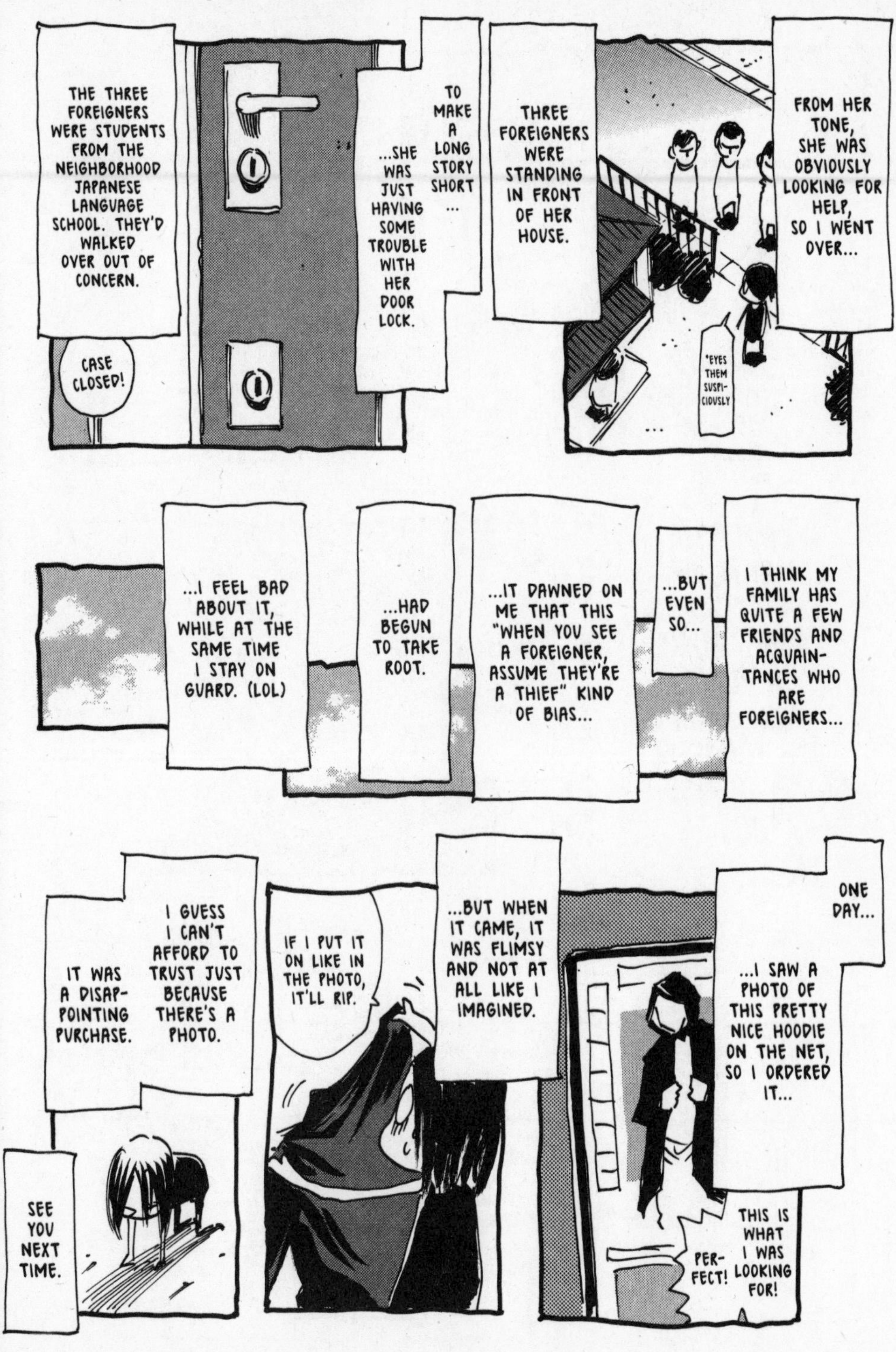
FROM HER TONE, SHE WAS OBVIOUSLY LOOKING FOR HELP, SO I WENT OVER...
THREE FOREIGNERS WERE STANDING IN FRONT OF HER HOUSE.
*EYES THEM SUSPICIOUSLY
...
TO MAKE A LONG STORY SHORT...
...SHE WAS JUST HAVING SOME TROUBLE WITH HER DOOR LOCK.
THE THREE FOREIGNERS WERE STUDENTS FROM THE NEIGHBORHOOD JAPANESE LANGUAGE SCHOOL. THEY'D WALKED OVER OUT OF CONCERN.
CASE CLOSED!
I THINK MY FAMILY HAS QUITE A FEW FRIENDS AND ACQUAINTANCES WHO ARE FOREIGNERS...
...BUT EVEN SO...
...IT DAWNED ON ME THAT THIS "WHEN YOU SEE A FOREIGNER, ASSUME THEY'RE A THIEF" KIND OF BIAS...
...HAD BEGUN TO TAKE ROOT.
...I FEEL BAD ABOUT IT, WHILE AT THE SAME TIME I STAY ON GUARD. (LOL)
ONE DAY...
...I SAW A PHOTO OF THIS PRETTY NICE HOODIE ON THE NET, SO I ORDERED IT...
THIS IS WHAT I WAS LOOKING FOR!
PER-FECT!
...BUT WHEN IT CAME, IT WAS FLIMSY AND NOT AT ALL LIKE I IMAGINED.
IF I PUT IT ON LIKE IN THE PHOTO, IT'LL RIP.
I GUESS I CAN'T AFFORD TO TRUST JUST BECAUSE THERE'S A PHOTO.
IT WAS A DISAP-POINTING PURCHASE.
SEE YOU NEXT TIME.

TRANSLATION NOTES

Common Honorifics
no honorific: Indicates familiarity or closeness; if used without permission or reason, addressing someone in this manner would constitute an insult.
-san: The Japanese equivalent of Mr./Mrs./Miss. If a situation calls for politeness, this is the fail-safe honorific.
-sama: Conveys great respect; may also indicate the social status of the speaker is lower than that of the addressee.
-kun: Used most often when referring to boys, this indicates affection or familiarity. Occasionally used by older men among their peers, but it may also be used by anyone referring to a person of lower standing.
-chan: An affectionate honorific indicating familiarity used mostly in reference to girls; also used in reference to cute persons or animals of either gender.
-sensei: A respectful term for teachers, artists, or high-level professionals.

Currency Conversion
While conversion rates fluctuate daily, an easy estimate for Japanese Yen conversion is ¥100 to 1 USD.

Page 3
Frog sticker: The character pictured is from the long-running Kadokawa Shoten alien invasion comedy series, *Sgt. Frog* (original manga, 1999–present; anime, 2004–2011).

Page 8
Names: The Chinese characters in Kazuto's name literally mean "one climb up/ascend." The Chinese characters in Senri's name mean "one thousand leagues/a long distance."

Page 130
School schedule: Japanese schools often have half days every other Saturday, which is most likely the reason Enan and Senri are able to leave school before lunch.

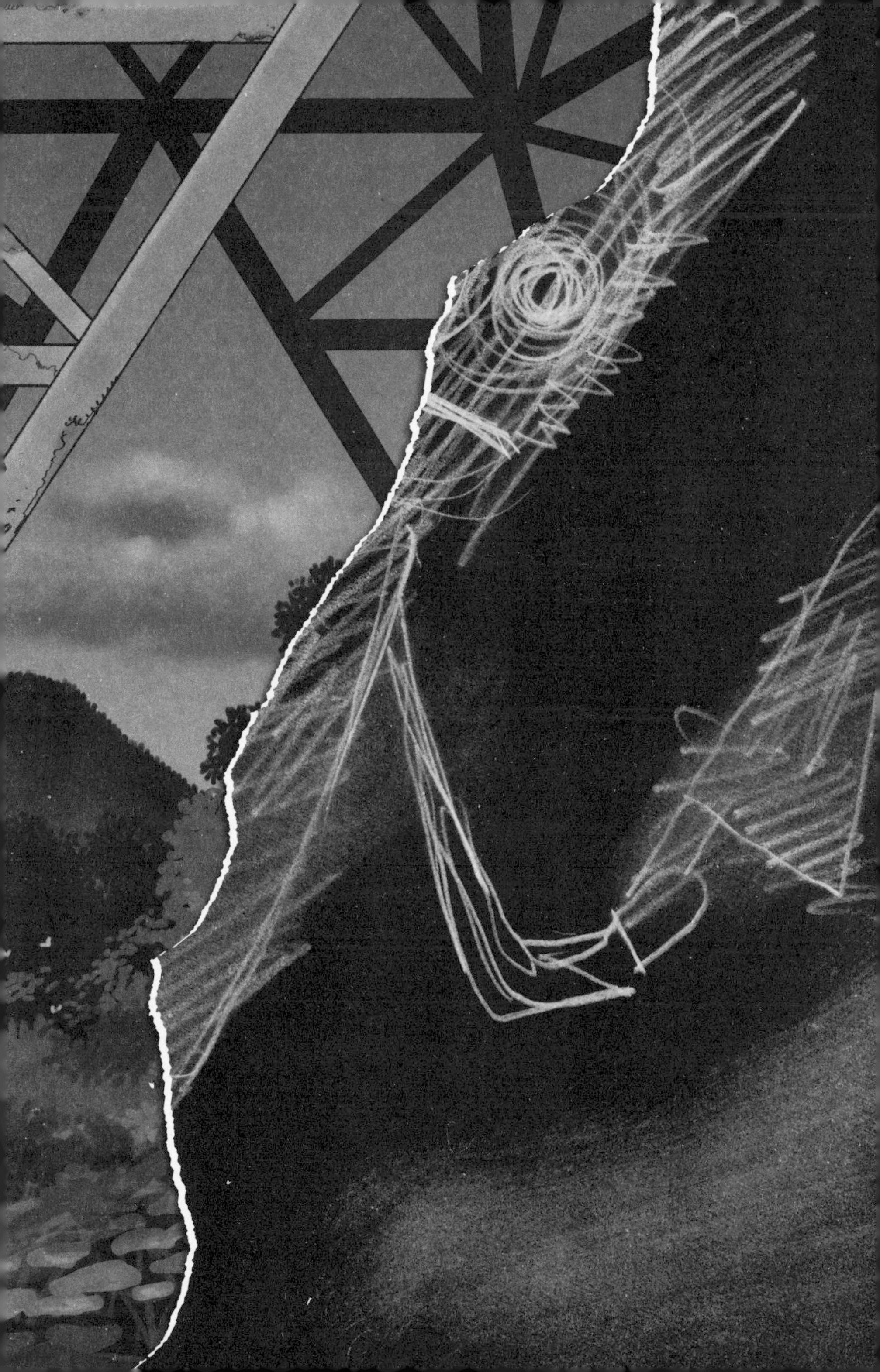